Chibi Vampire

Volume 3

Created by

Yuna Kagesaki

TOKYOPOP®

HAMBURG // LONDON // LOS ANGELES // TOKYO

OUR STORY SO FAR...

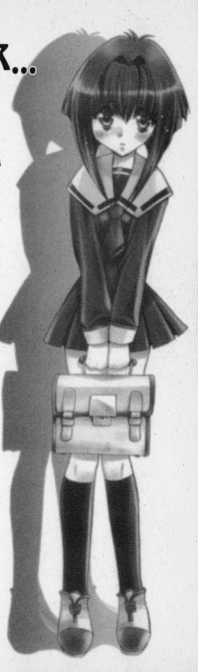

KARIN MAAKA ISN'T LIKE OTHER GIRLS. ONCE A MONTH, SHE EXPERIENCES PAIN, FATIGUE, HUNGER, IRRITABILITY—AND THEN SHE BLEEDS. FROM HER NOSE. KARIN IS A VAMPIRE, FROM A FAMILY OF VAMPIRES, BUT INSTEAD OF NEEDING TO DRINK BLOOD, SHE HAS AN EXCESS OF BLOOD THAT SHE MUST GIVE TO HER VICTIMS. IF DONE RIGHT, GIVING THIS BLOOD TO HER VICTIM CAN BE AN EXTREMELY POSITIVE THING. THE PROBLEM WITH THIS IS THAT KARIN NEVER SEEMS TO DO THINGS RIGHT...

WHEN LAST WE LEFT HER, KARIN WAS HAVING BOY TROUBLE. KENTA USUI—THE HANDSOME NEW STUDENT AT HER SCHOOL AND WORK—IS A NICE ENOUGH GUY, BUT HE EXACERBATES KARIN'S PROBLEM. KARIN, YOU SEE, IS DRAWN TO PEOPLE WHO HAVE SUFFERED MISFORTUNE, AND KENTA HAS SUFFERED PLENTY OF IT. KARIN DISCOVERED THIS WHEN SHE BIT KENTA'S MOTHER, AN INCIDENT THAT WAS UNFORTUNATELY WITNESSED BY KENTA. NOW, KARIN'S CONVINCED THAT SHE CAN KEEP HER NOSEBLEEDS UNDER CONTROL AS LONG AS SHE KEEPS KENTA HAPPY. AND KENTA HAS PROMISED KARIN'S PARENTS THAT HE'D HELP HER OUT DURING THE DAYTIME (SINCE THEY CAN ONLY GO OUTSIDE AT NIGHT). IT COULD BE A RECIPE FOR LOVE OR FOR DISASTER. EITHER WAY, IT SHOULD BE ONE HELLUVA SHOW.

THE MAAKA FAMILY

CALERA MARKER

Karin's overbearing mother. While Calera resents that Karin wasn't born a normal vampire, she does love her daughter in her own obnoxious way. Calera has chosen to keep her European last name.

HENRY MARKER

Karin's father. In general, Henry treats Karin a lot better than she's treated by her mother, but the pants in this particular family are worn by Calera. Henry has also chosen to keep his European last name.

REN MAAKA

Karin's older brother. Ren milks the "sexy creature of the night" thing for all it's worth, and spends his nights in the arms (and beds) of attractive young women.

KARIN MAAKA

Our little heroine. Karin is
vampire living in Japan, bu
instead of sucking blood fro
her victims, she actually GIVE
them some of her blood. She's
vampire in revers

ANJU MAAKA

Karin's little sister. Anju has not
awoken as a full vampire, but she c
control bats and is usually the one w
cleans up after Karin's messes. Rar
seen without her "talking" doll, Boog

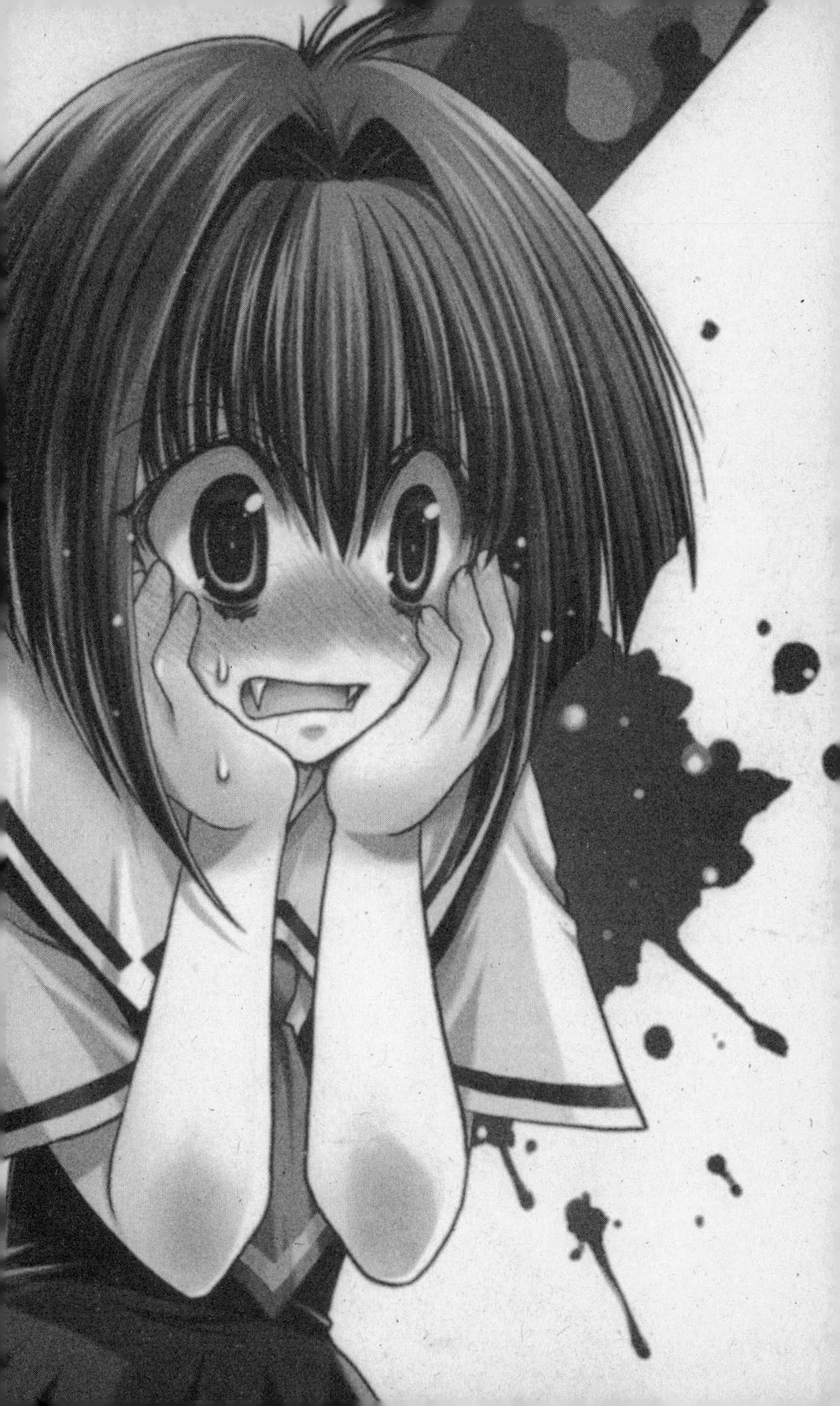

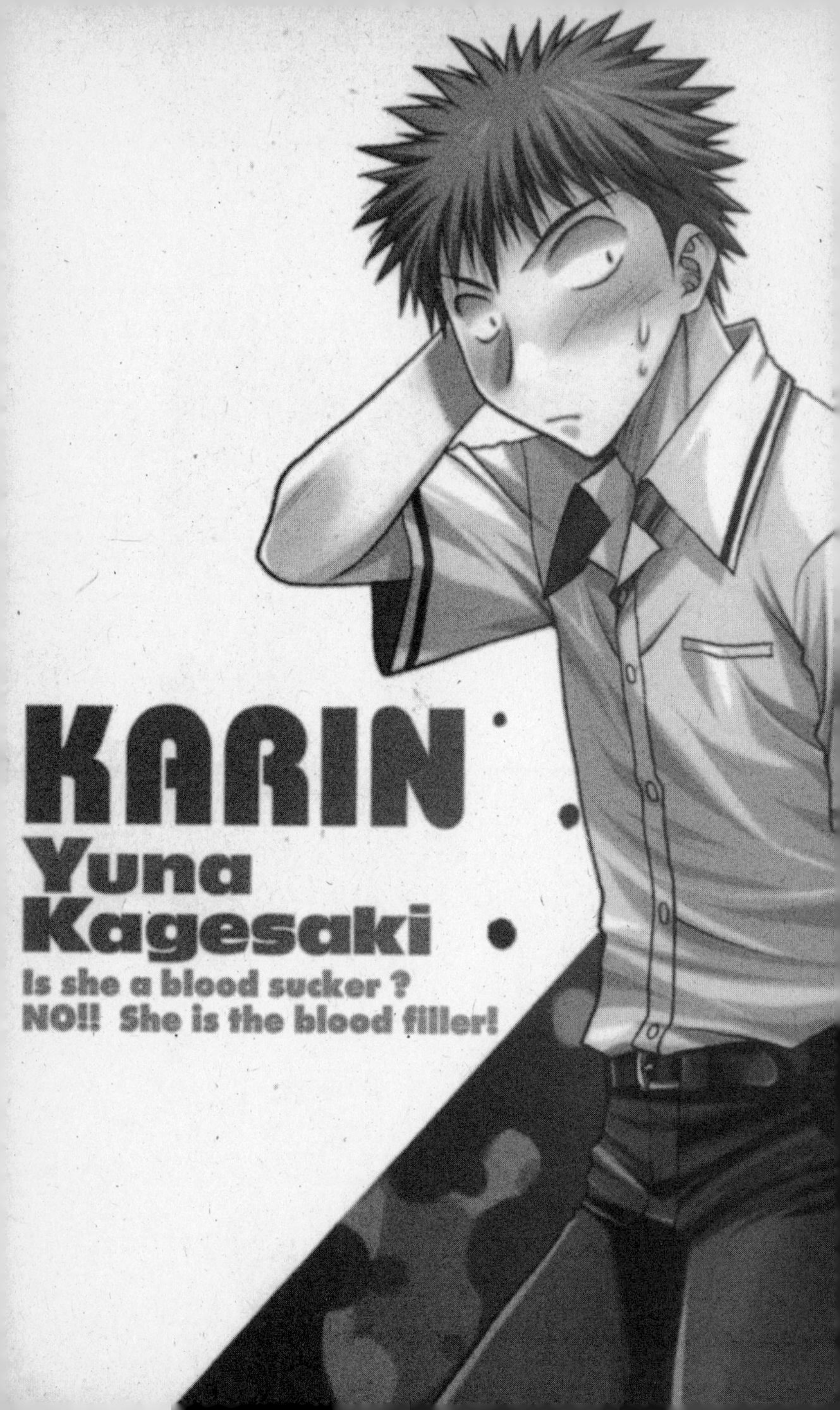
KARIN
Yuna Kagesaki
Is she a blood sucker ?
NO!! She is the blood filler!

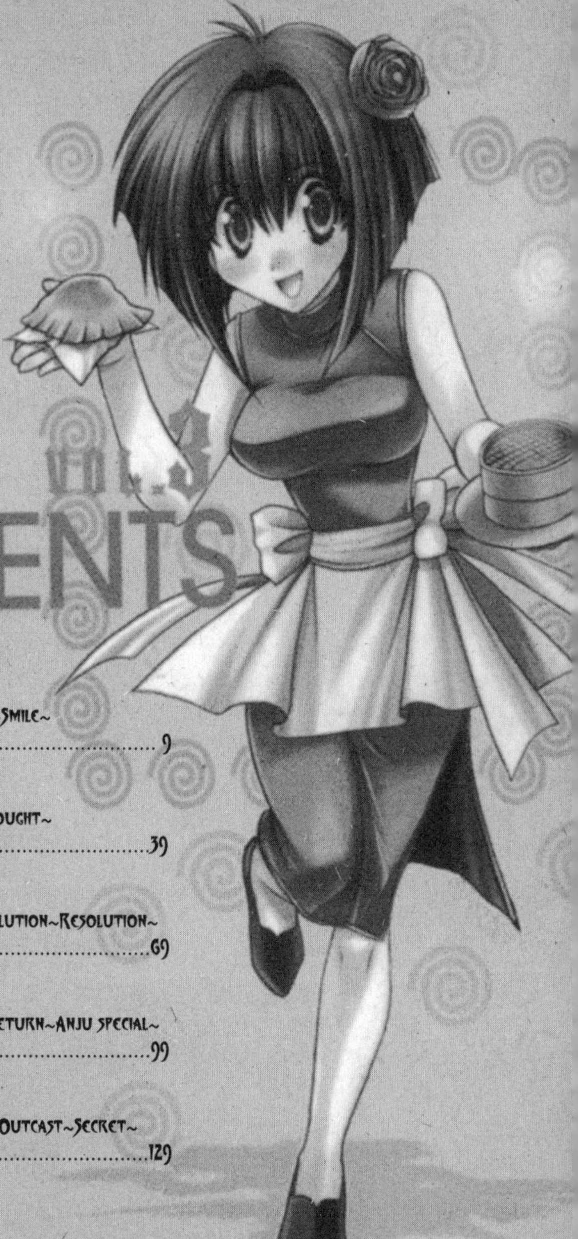

Vol.3 CONTENTS

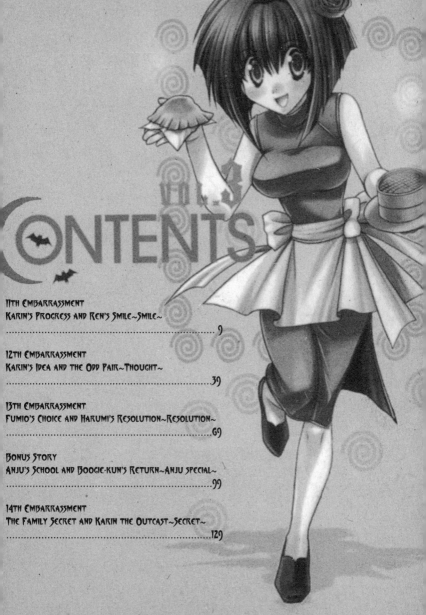

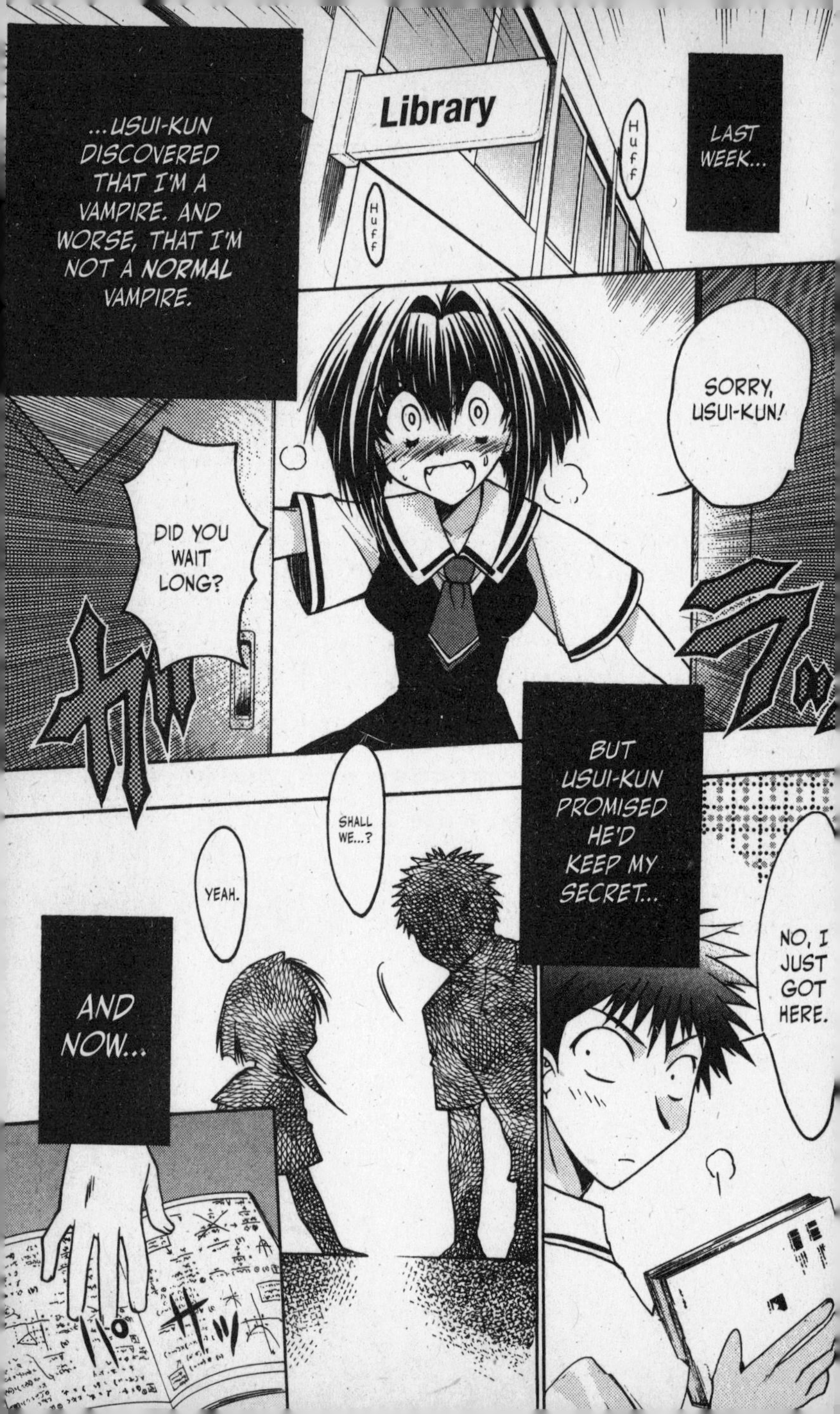
LAST WEEK...
Library
Huff
Huff
...USUI-KUN DISCOVERED THAT I'M A VAMPIRE. AND WORSE, THAT I'M NOT A NORMAL VAMPIRE.
SORRY, USUI-KUN!
DID YOU WAIT LONG?
BUT USUI-KUN PROMISED HE'D KEEP MY SECRET...
NO, I JUST GOT HERE.
SHALL WE...?
YEAH.
AND NOW...

11th Embarrassment—Karin's Progress and Ren's Smile ~Smile~

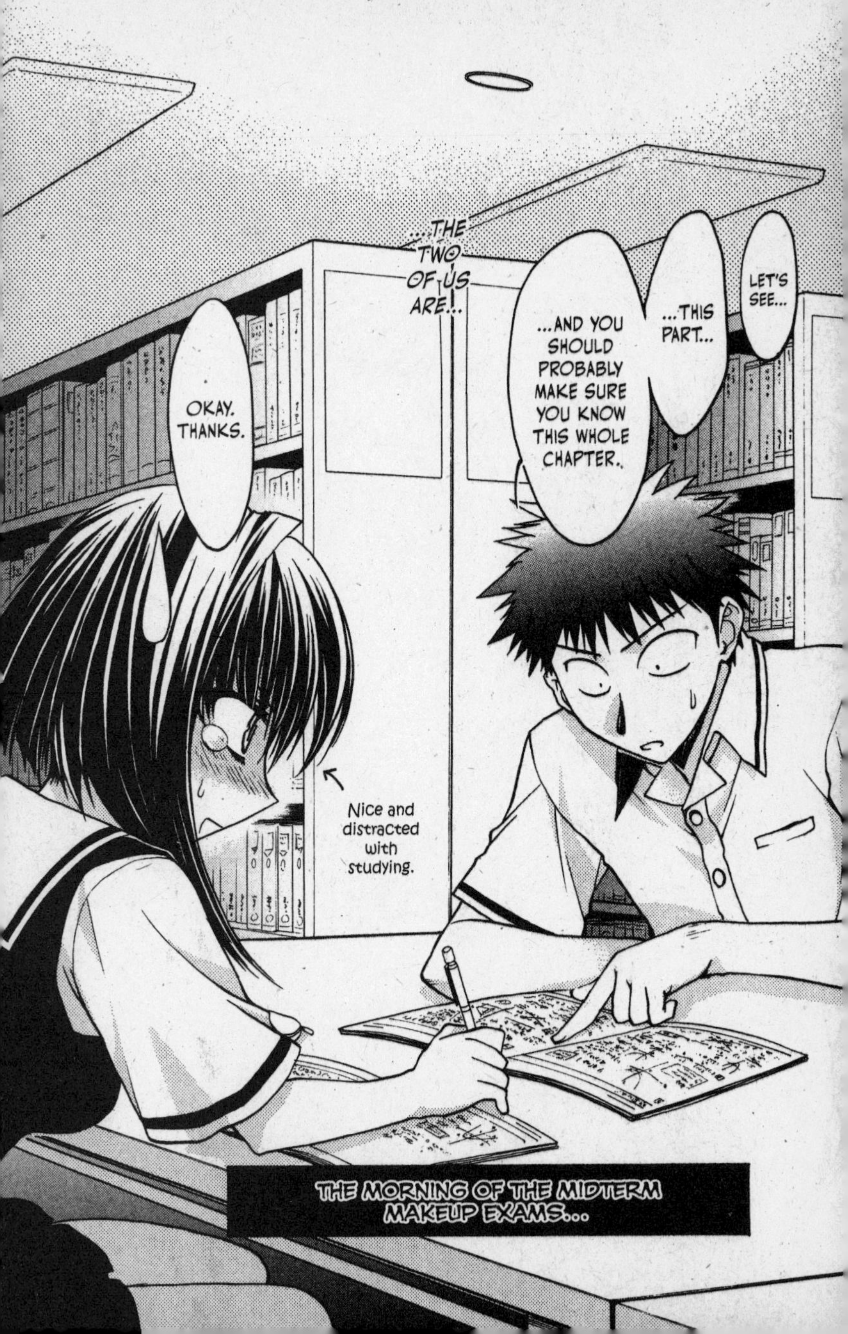
LET'S SEE...
...THIS PART...
...AND YOU SHOULD PROBABLY MAKE SURE YOU KNOW THIS WHOLE CHAPTER.
...THE TWO OF US ARE...
OKAY. THANKS.
Nice and distracted with studying.
THE MORNING OF THE MIDTERM MAKEUP EXAMS...

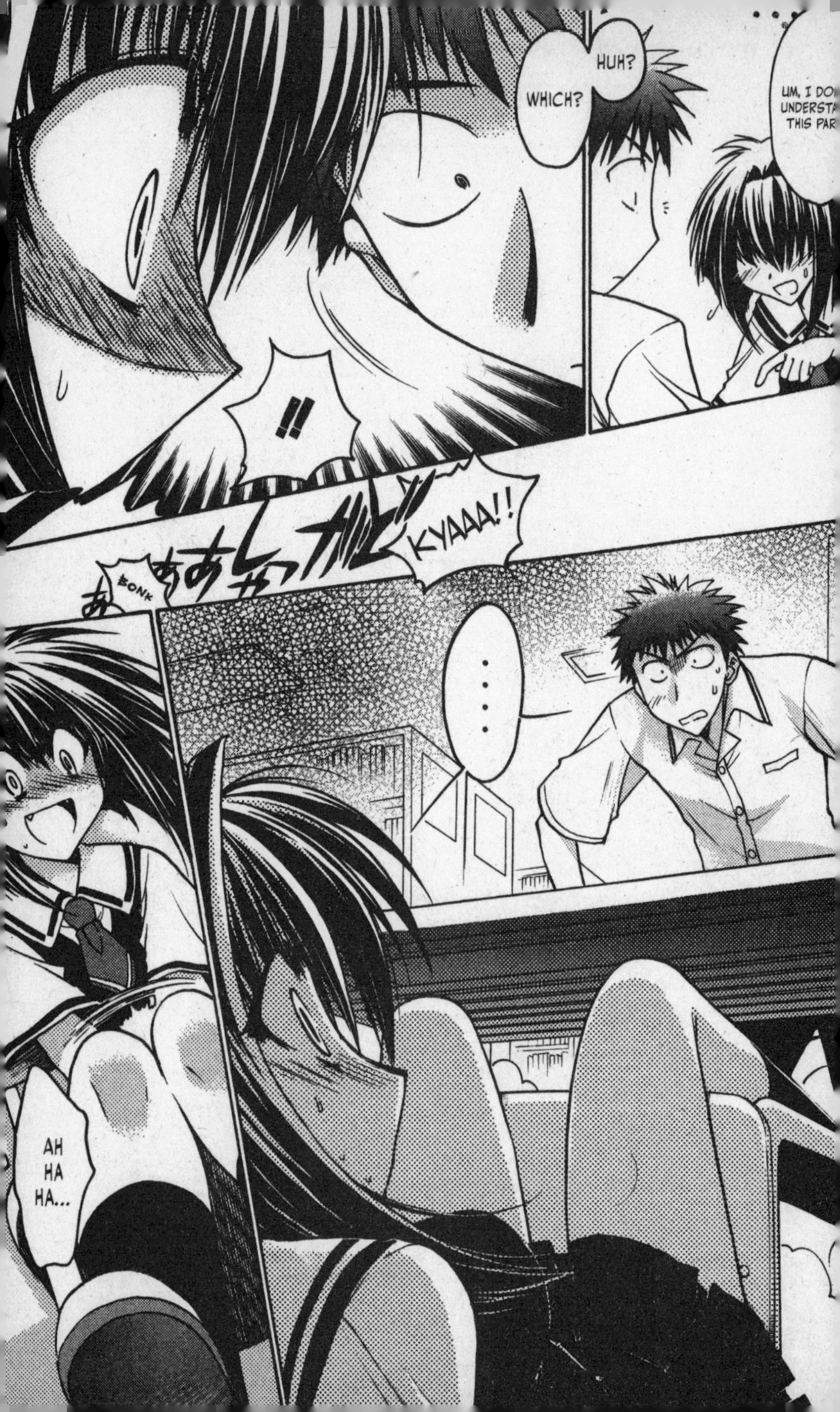
UM, I DO
UNDERSTA
THIS PAR
HUH?
WHICH?
!!
KYAAA!!
BONK
.....
AH HA HA...

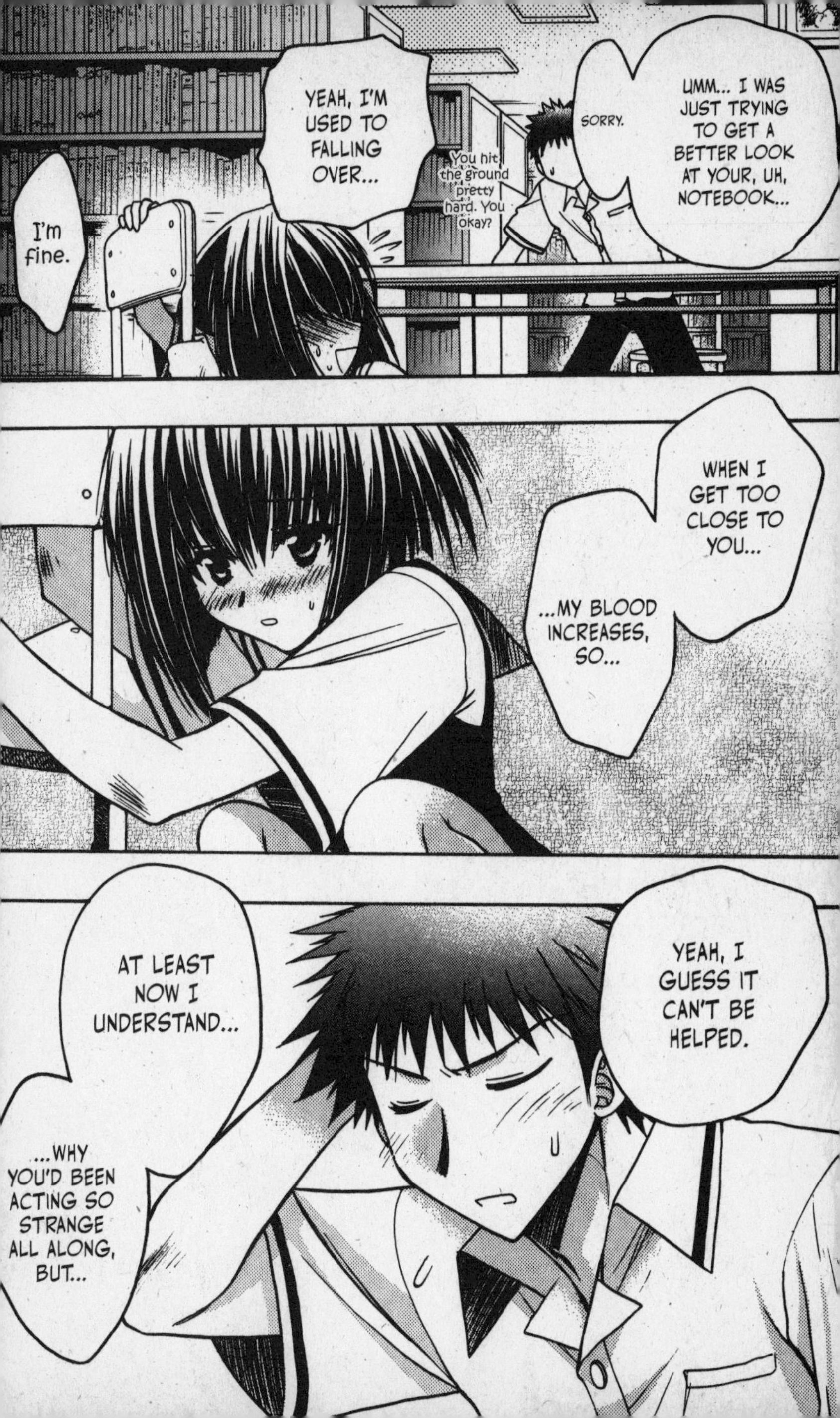
UMM... I WAS JUST TRYING TO GET A BETTER LOOK AT YOUR, UH, NOTEBOOK...
SORRY.
You hit the ground pretty hard. You okay?
YEAH, I'M USED TO FALLING OVER...
I'm fine.
WHEN I GET TOO CLOSE TO YOU...
...MY BLOOD INCREASES, SO...
YEAH, I GUESS IT CAN'T BE HELPED.
AT LEAST NOW I UNDERSTAND...
...WHY YOU'D BEEN ACTING SO STRANGE ALL ALONG, BUT...

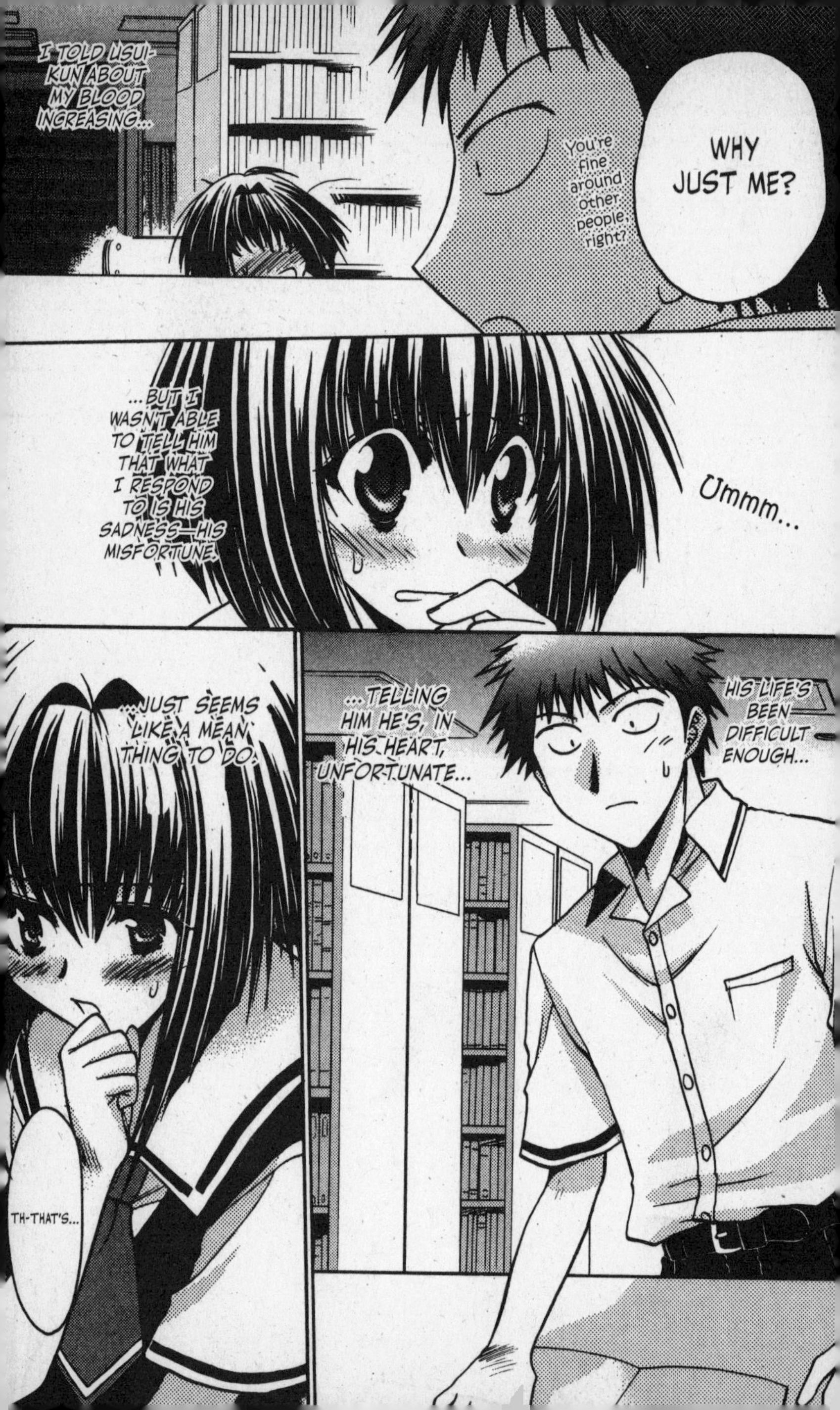
WHY JUST ME?
You're fine around other people, right?
I TOLD USUI-KUN ABOUT MY BLOOD INCREASING...
Ummm...
...BUT I WASN'T ABLE TO TELL HIM THAT WHAT I RESPOND TO IS HIS SADNESS—HIS MISFORTUNE.
HIS LIFE'S BEEN DIFFICULT ENOUGH...
...TELLING HIM HE'S, IN HIS HEART, UNFORTUNATE...
...JUST SEEMS LIKE A MEAN THING TO DO.
TH-THAT'S...

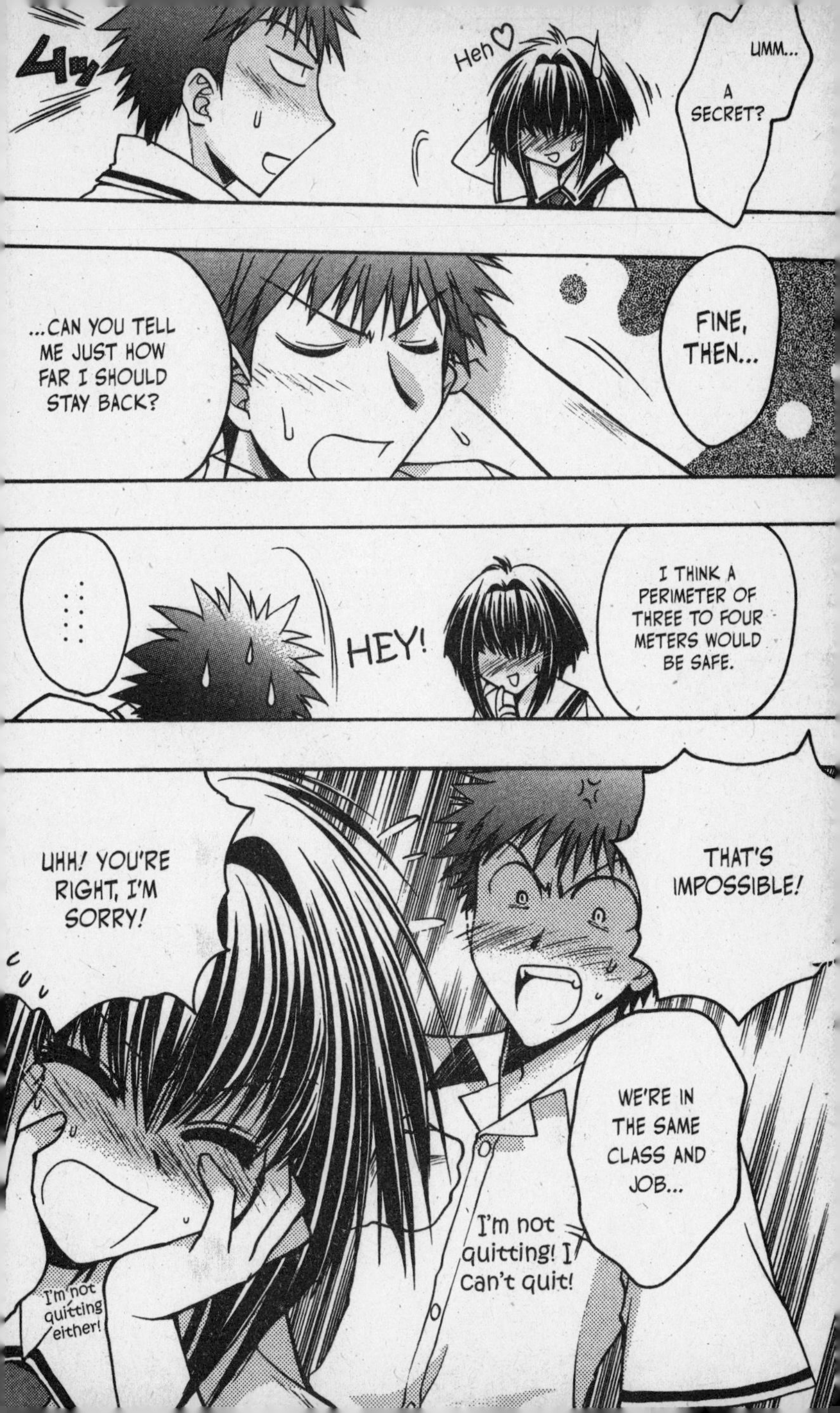
UMM... A SECRET?
Heh♡
FINE, THEN...
...CAN YOU TELL ME JUST HOW FAR I SHOULD STAY BACK?
I THINK A PERIMETER OF THREE TO FOUR METERS WOULD BE SAFE.
HEY!
......
THAT'S IMPOSSIBLE!
WE'RE IN THE SAME CLASS AND JOB...
I'm not quitting! I can't quit!
UHH! YOU'RE RIGHT, I'M SORRY!
I'm not quitting either!

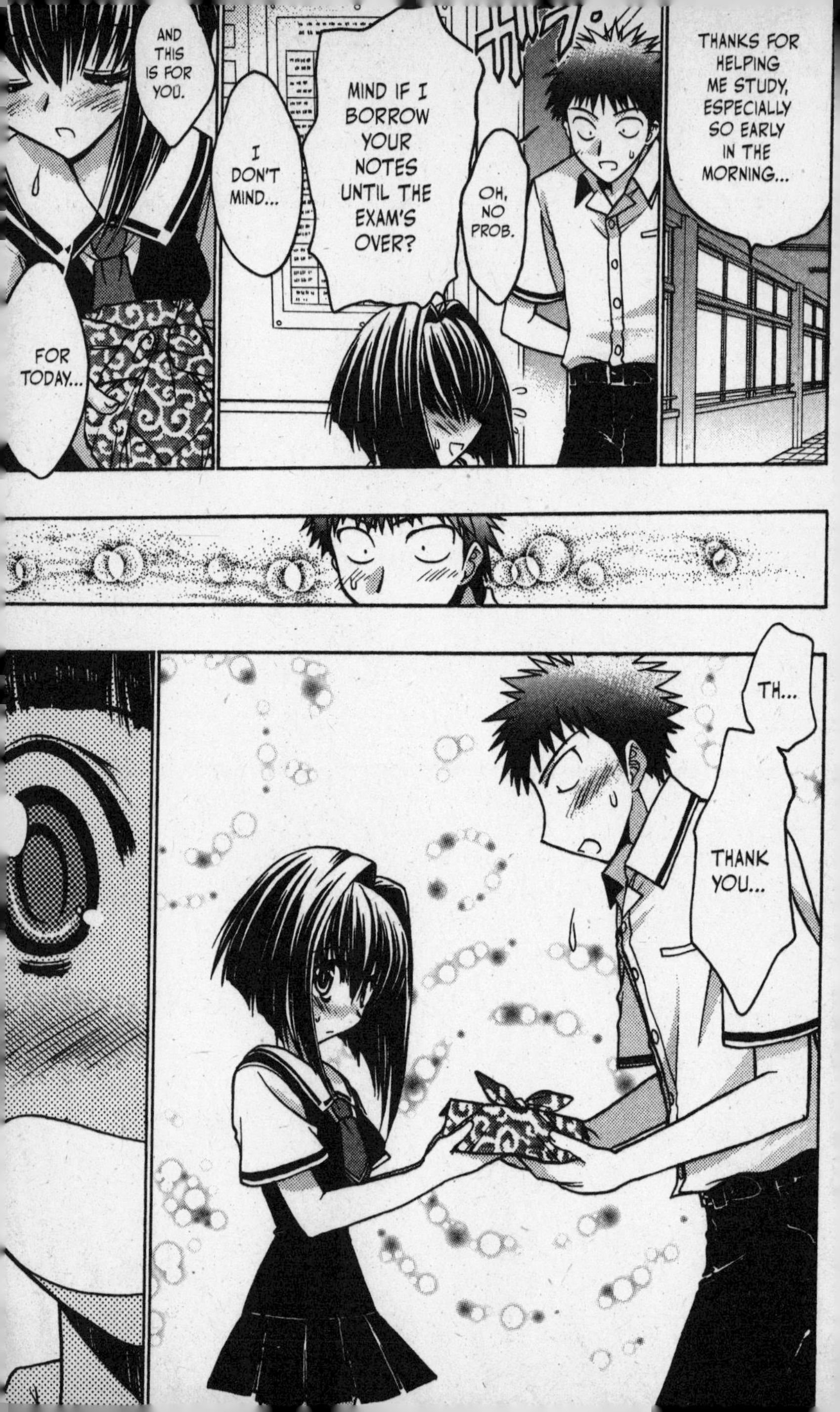
THANKS FOR HELPING ME STUDY, ESPECIALLY SO EARLY IN THE MORNING...
OH, NO PROB.
MIND IF I BORROW YOUR NOTES UNTIL THE EXAM'S OVER?
I DON'T MIND...
AND THIS IS FOR YOU.
FOR TODAY...
TH...
THANK YOU...

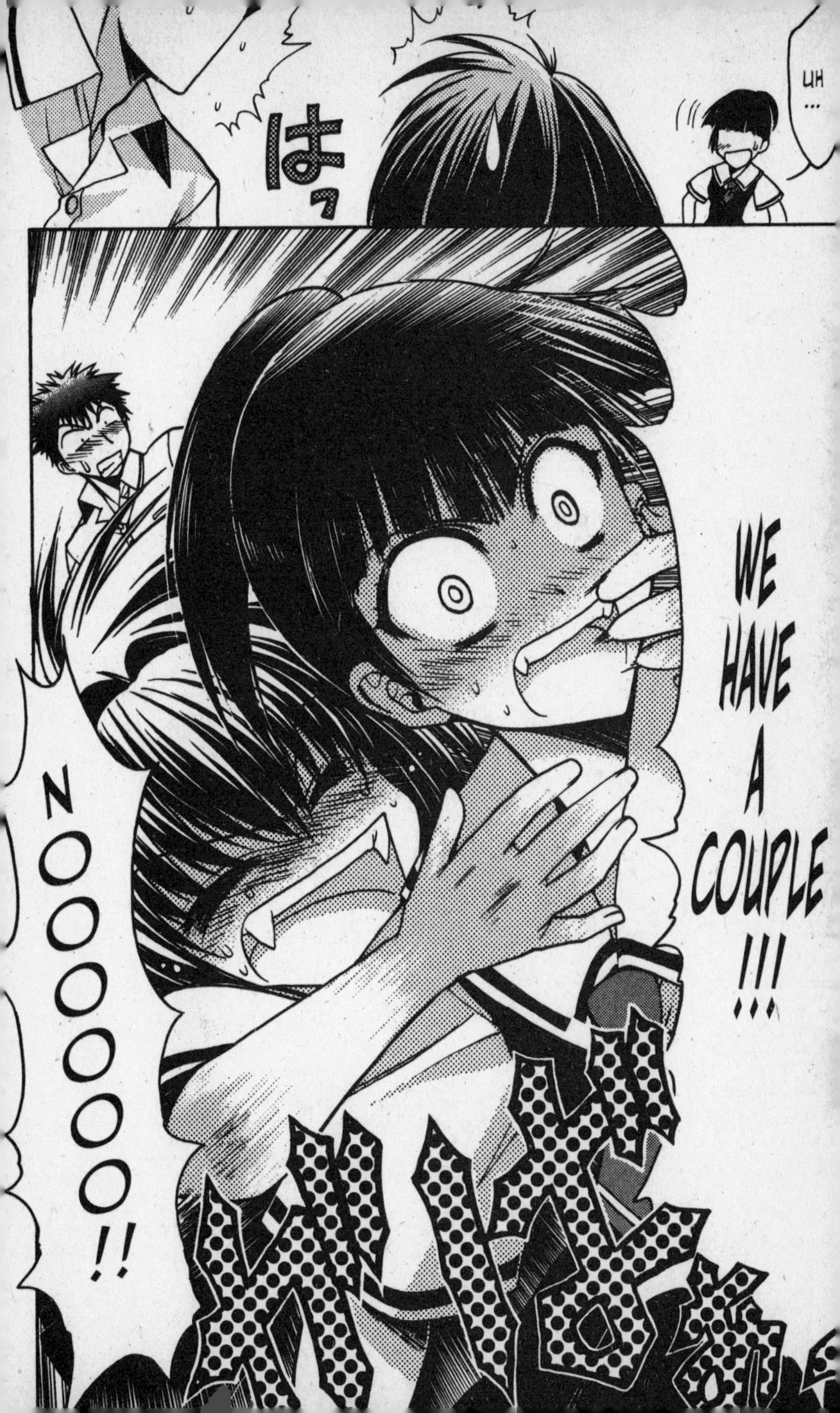
UH ...
はっ
WE HAVE A COUPLE !!!
NOOOOOOO!!

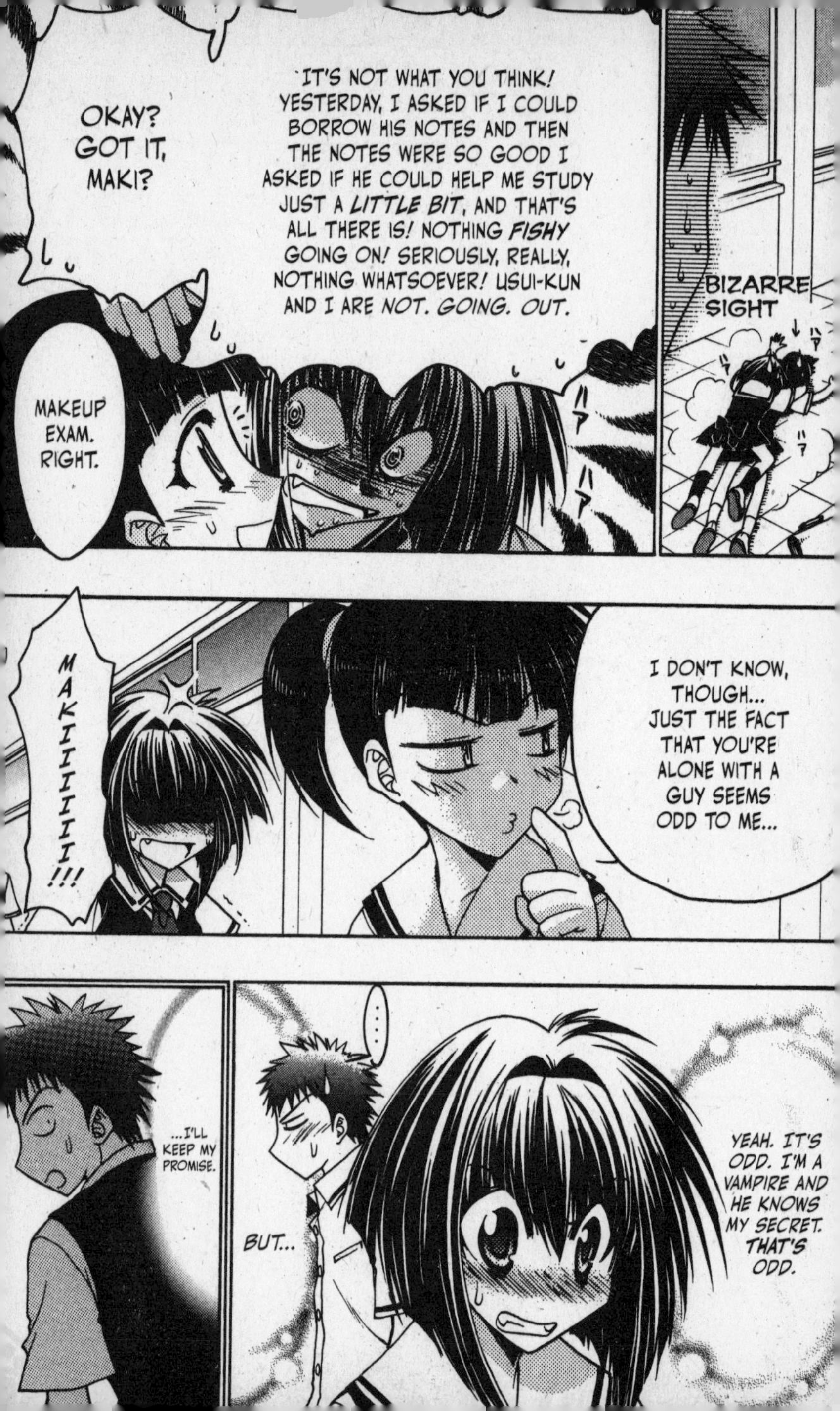
BIZARRE SIGHT
IT'S NOT WHAT YOU THINK! YESTERDAY, I ASKED IF I COULD BORROW HIS NOTES AND THEN THE NOTES WERE SO GOOD I ASKED IF HE COULD HELP ME STUDY JUST A *LITTLE BIT*, AND THAT'S ALL THERE IS! NOTHING *FISHY* GOING ON! SERIOUSLY, REALLY, NOTHING WHATSOEVER! USUI-KUN AND I ARE *NOT. GOING. OUT.*
OKAY? GOT IT, MAKI?
MAKEUP EXAM. RIGHT.
I DON'T KNOW, THOUGH... JUST THE FACT THAT YOU'RE ALONE WITH A GUY SEEMS ODD TO ME...
MAKIIIIIIII!!!
...
YEAH. IT'S ODD. I'M A VAMPIRE AND HE KNOWS MY SECRET. **THAT'S** ODD.
BUT...
...I'LL KEEP MY PROMISE.

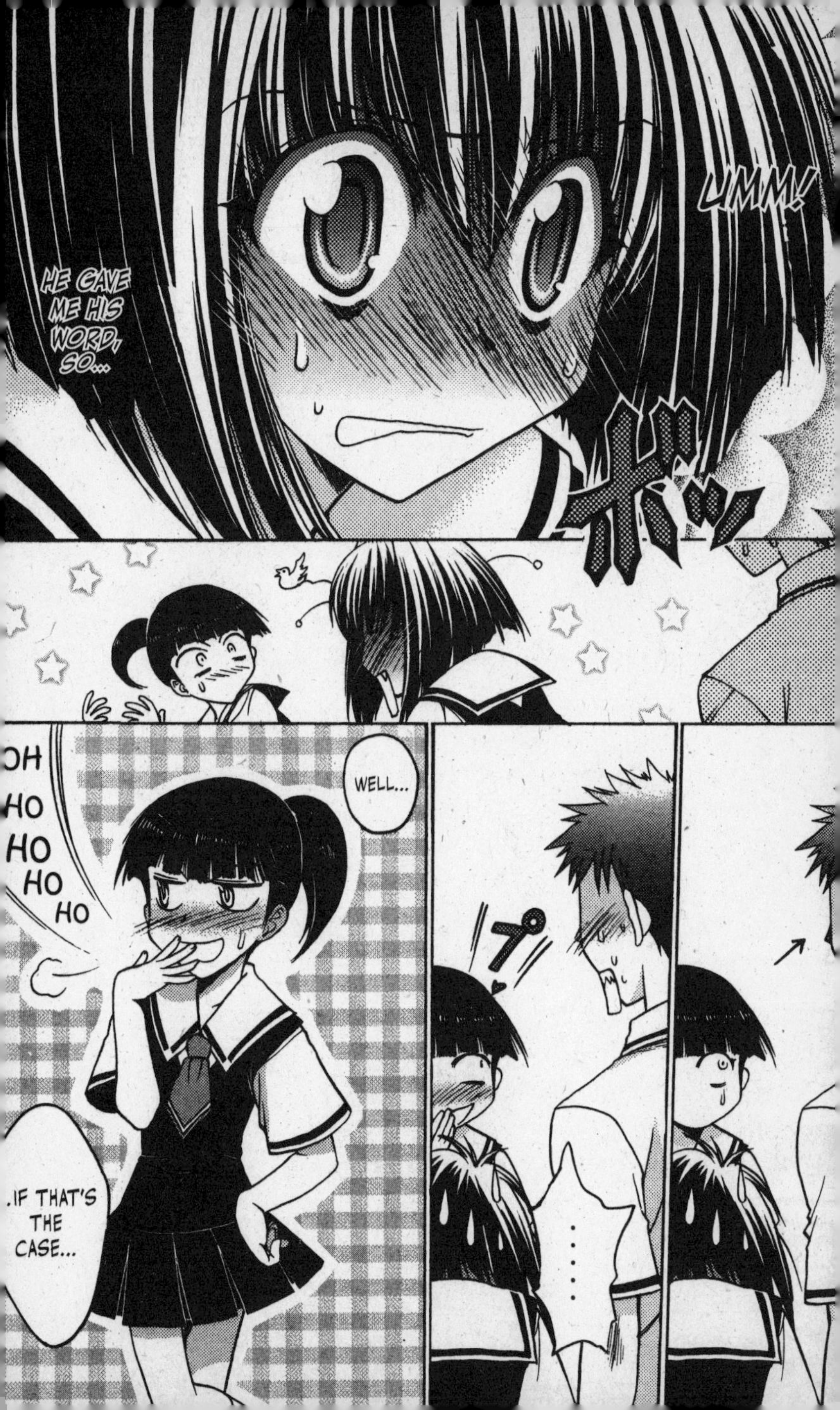
UMM!
HE GAVE ME HIS WORD, SO...
......
WELL...
HO HO HO HO HO
.IF THAT'S THE CASE...

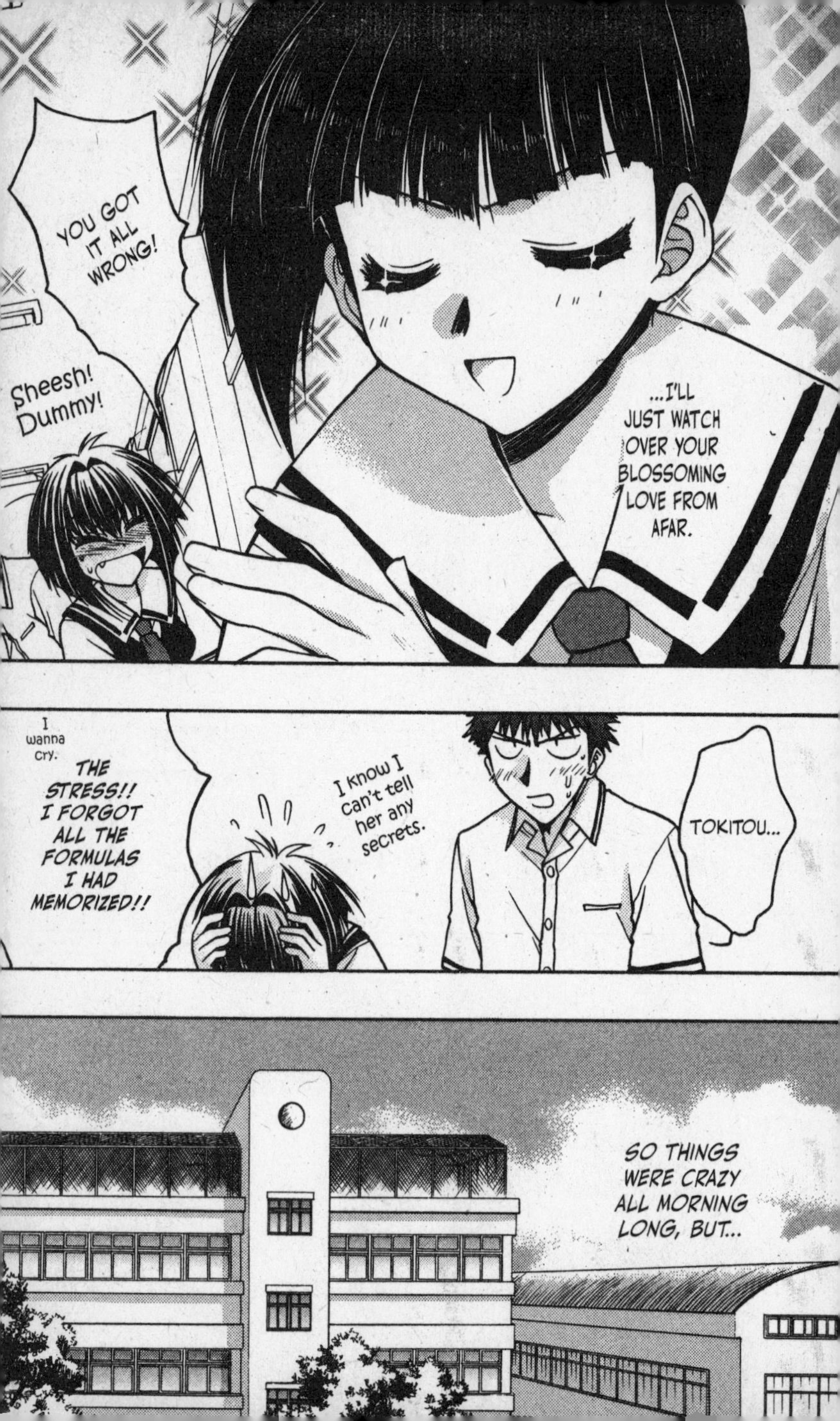
...I'LL JUST WATCH OVER YOUR BLOSSOMING LOVE FROM AFAR.
YOU GOT IT ALL WRONG!
Sheesh! Dummy!
TOKITOU...
I know I can't tell her any secrets.
THE STRESS!! I FORGOT ALL THE FORMULAS I HAD MEMORIZED!!
I wanna cry.
SO THINGS WERE CRAZY ALL MORNING LONG, BUT...

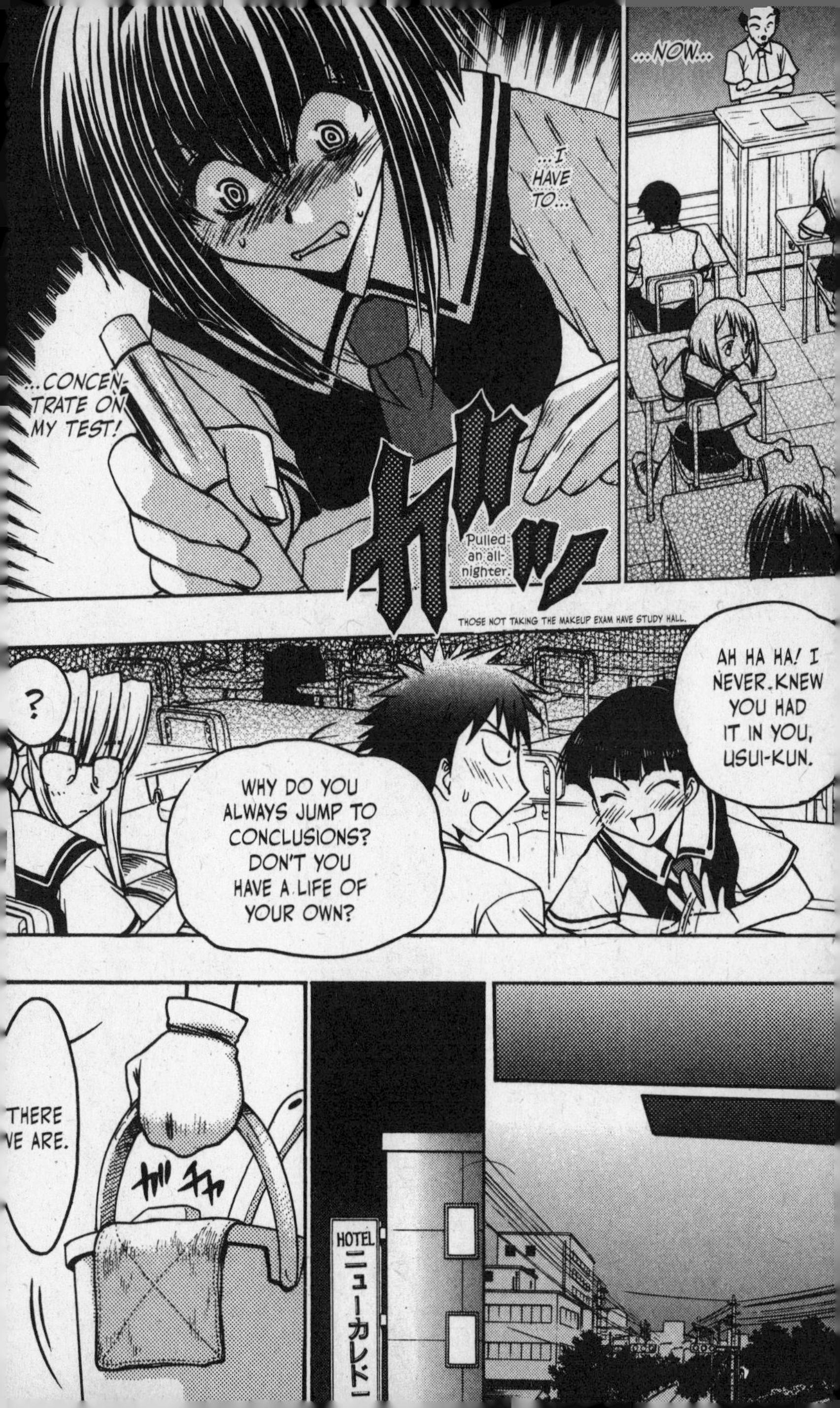
...NOW...
...I HAVE TO...
...CONCEN-TRATE ON MY TEST!
Pulled an all-nighter.
THOSE NOT TAKING THE MAKEUP EXAM HAVE STUDY HALL.
AH HA HA! I NEVER KNEW YOU HAD IT IN YOU, USUI-KUN.
WHY DO YOU ALWAYS JUMP TO CONCLUSIONS? DON'T YOU HAVE A LIFE OF YOUR OWN?
?
HOTEL ニューカレドニ
THERE WE ARE.

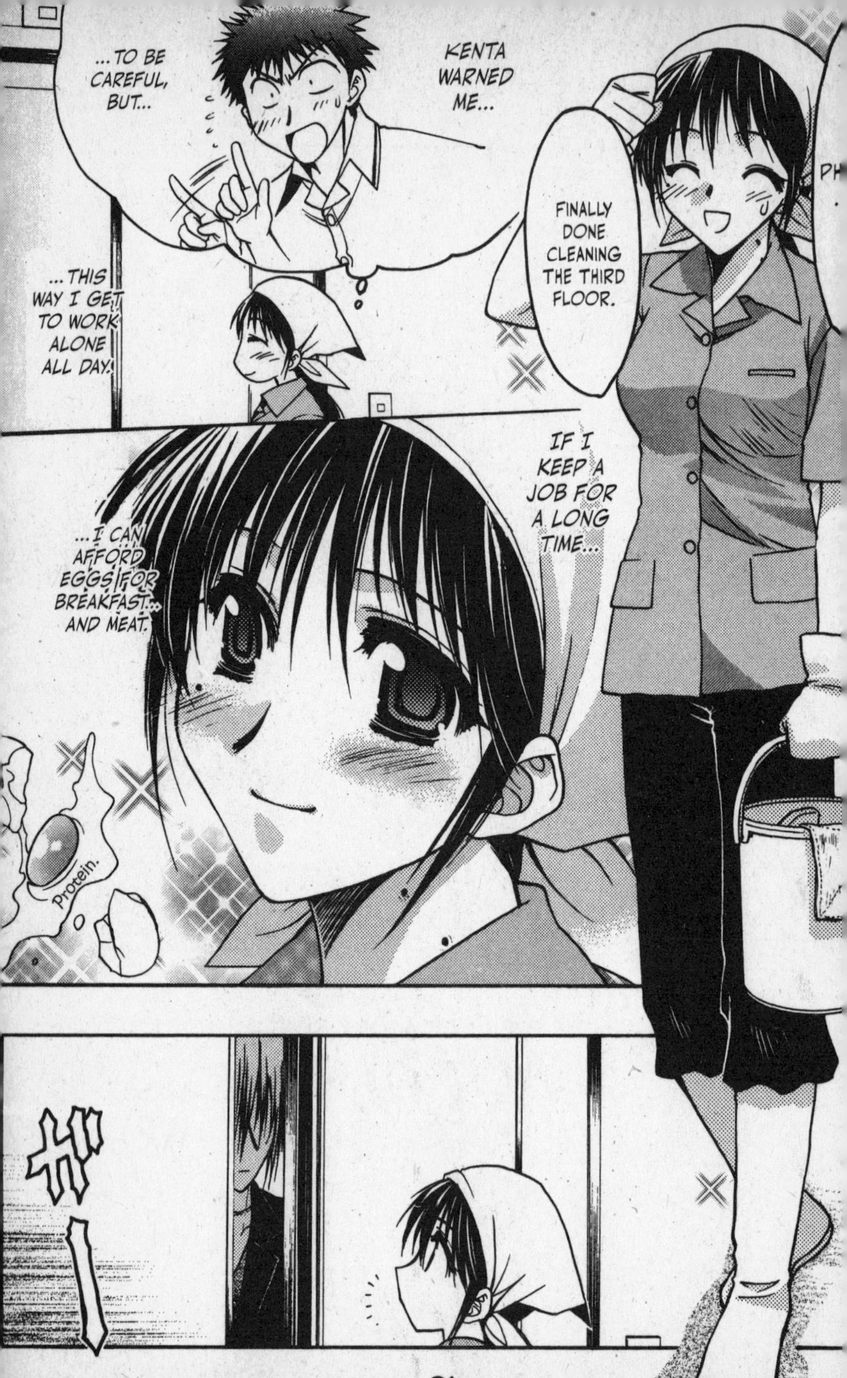

FINALLY DONE CLEANING THE THIRD FLOOR.
PH
KENTA WARNED ME...
...TO BE CAREFUL, BUT...
...THIS WAY I GET TO WORK ALONE ALL DAY.
IF I KEEP A JOB FOR A LONG TIME...
...I CAN AFFORD EGGS FOR BREAKFAST... AND MEAT.
Protein.
ガー

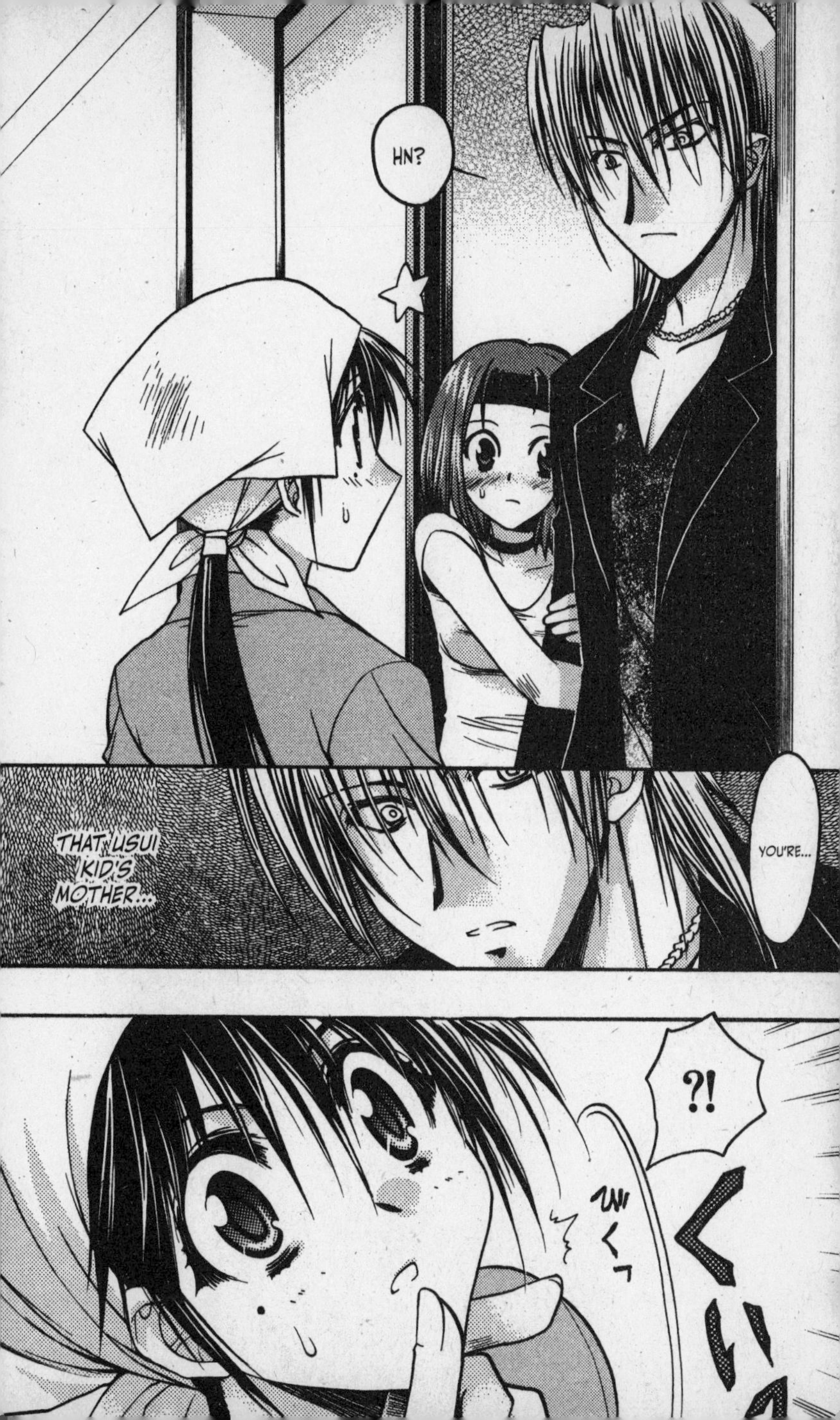
HN?
YOU'RE...
THAT USUI KID'S MOTHER...
?!
びくっ

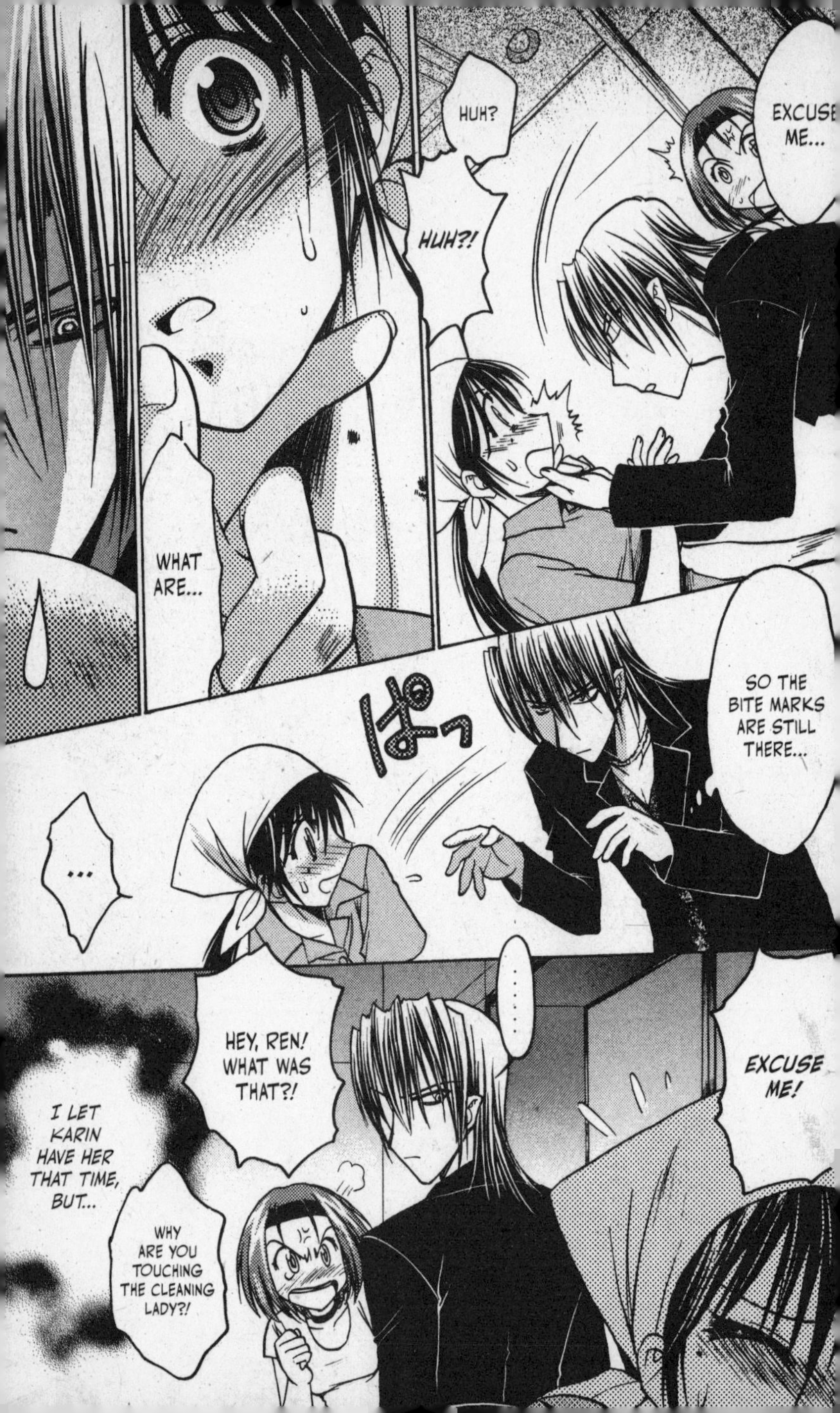
EXCUSE ME...
HUH?
HUH?!
WHAT ARE...
SO THE BITE MARKS ARE STILL THERE...
ぱっ
...
EXCUSE ME!
.....
HEY, REN! WHAT WAS THAT?!
I LET KARIN HAVE HER THAT TIME, BUT...
WHY ARE YOU TOUCHING THE CLEANING LADY?!

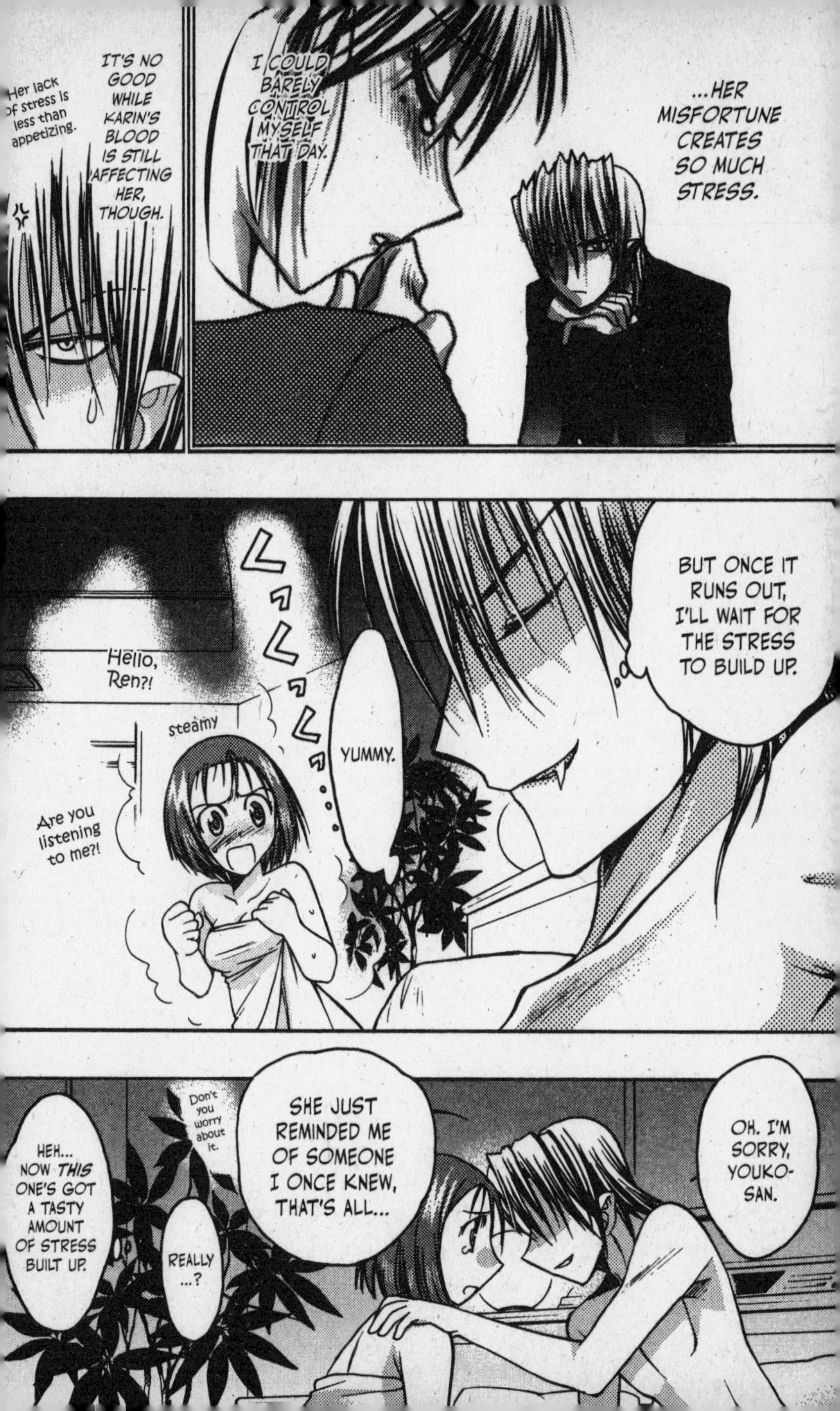
...HER MISFORTUNE CREATES SO MUCH STRESS.
I COULD BARELY CONTROL MYSELF THAT DAY.
IT'S NO GOOD WHILE KARIN'S BLOOD IS STILL AFFECTING HER, THOUGH.
Her lack of stress is less than appetizing.
BUT ONCE IT RUNS OUT, I'LL WAIT FOR THE STRESS TO BUILD UP.
YUMMY.
Hello, Ren?!
steamy
Are you listening to me?!
OH. I'M SORRY, YOUKO-SAN.
SHE JUST REMINDED ME OF SOMEONE I ONCE KNEW, THAT'S ALL...
Don't you worry about it.
REALLY ...?
HEH... NOW *THIS* ONE'S GOT A TASTY AMOUNT OF STRESS BUILT UP.

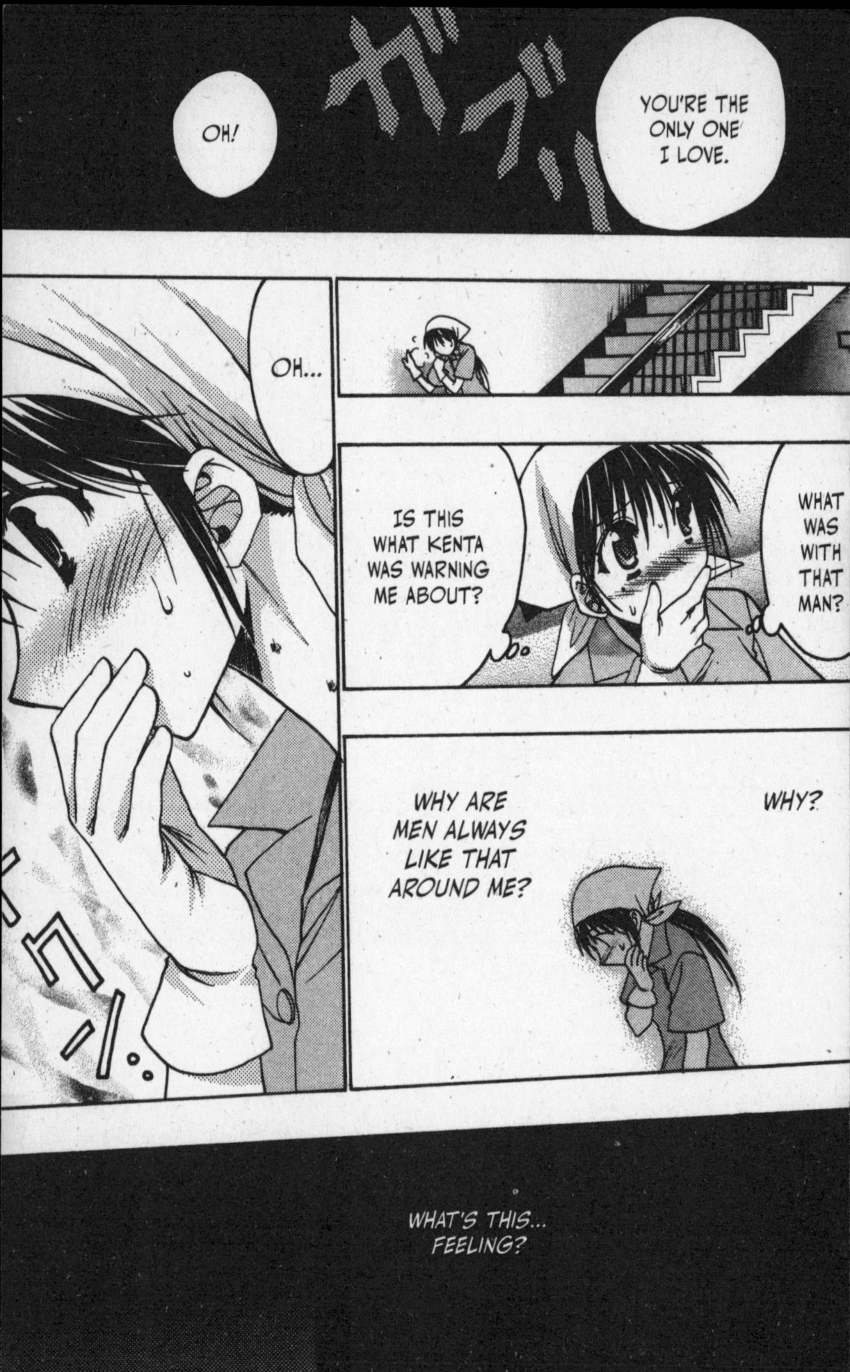
YOU'RE THE ONLY ONE I LOVE.
OH!
WHAT WAS WITH THAT MAN?
IS THIS WHAT KENTA WAS WARNING ME ABOUT?
WHY?
WHY ARE MEN ALWAYS LIKE THAT AROUND ME?
OH...
WHAT'S THIS... FEELING?

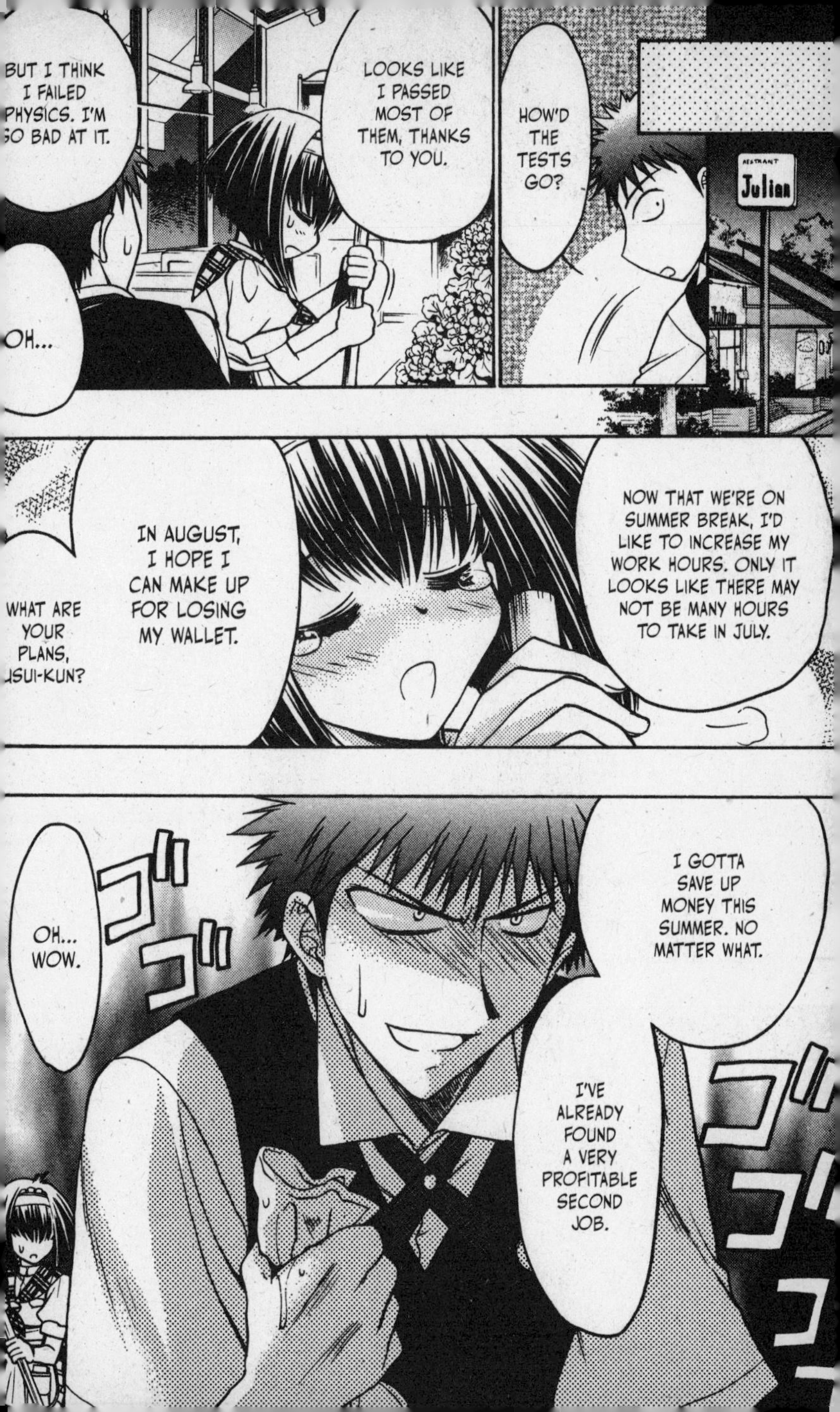
HOW'D THE TESTS GO?
LOOKS LIKE I PASSED MOST OF THEM, THANKS TO YOU.
BUT I THINK I FAILED PHYSICS. I'M SO BAD AT IT.
OH...
NOW THAT WE'RE ON SUMMER BREAK, I'D LIKE TO INCREASE MY WORK HOURS. ONLY IT LOOKS LIKE THERE MAY NOT BE MANY HOURS TO TAKE IN JULY.
IN AUGUST, I HOPE I CAN MAKE UP FOR LOSING MY WALLET.
WHAT ARE YOUR PLANS, USUI-KUN?
I GOTTA SAVE UP MONEY THIS SUMMER. NO MATTER WHAT.
I'VE ALREADY FOUND A VERY PROFITABLE SECOND JOB.
ゴゴ
OH... WOW.
ゴゴ

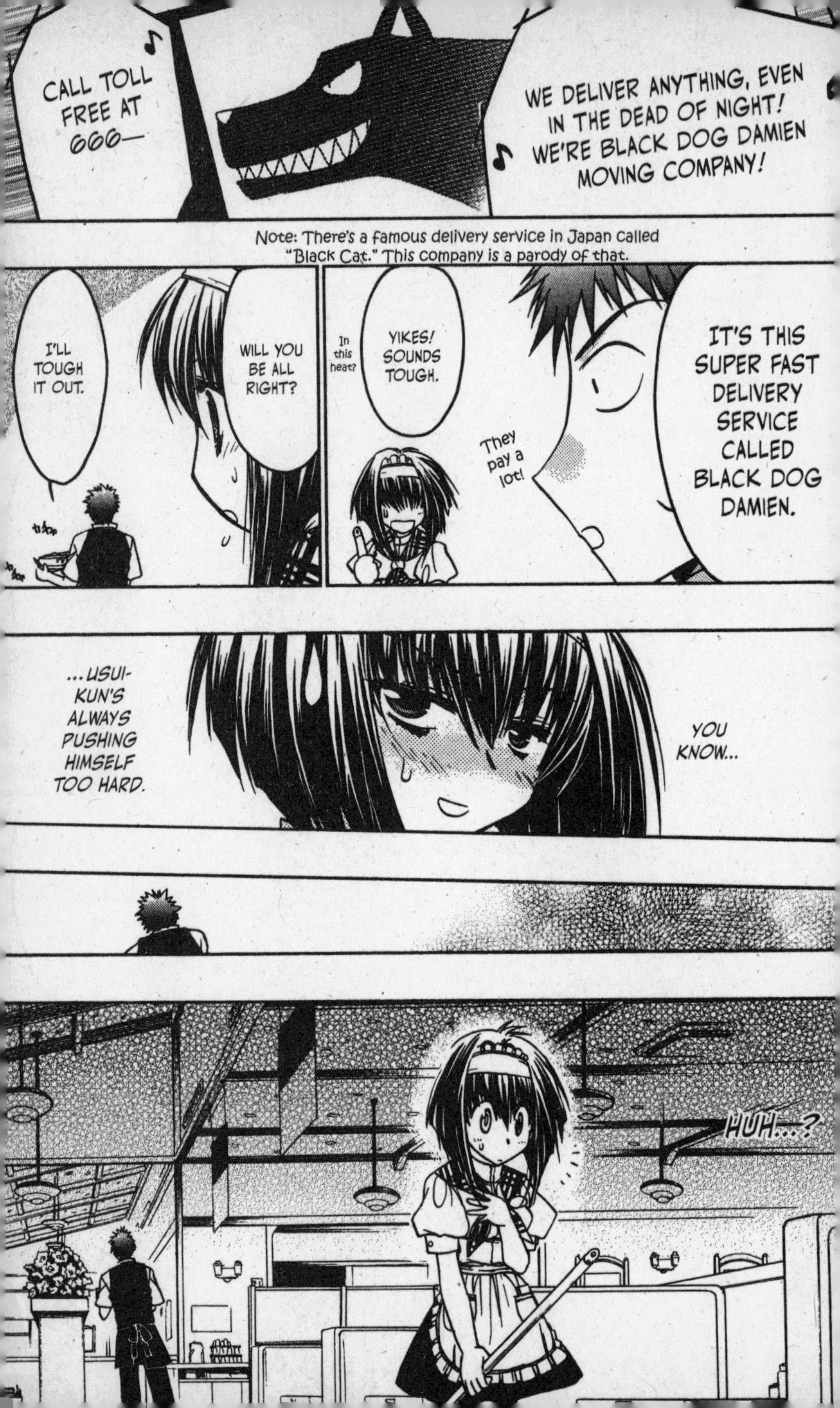
WE DELIVER ANYTHING, EVEN IN THE DEAD OF NIGHT! WE'RE BLACK DOG DAMIEN MOVING COMPANY!
CALL TOLL FREE AT 666—
Note: There's a famous delivery service in Japan called "Black Cat." This company is a parody of that.
IT'S THIS SUPER FAST DELIVERY SERVICE CALLED BLACK DOG DAMIEN.
They pay a lot!
YIKES! SOUNDS TOUGH.
In this heat?
WILL YOU BE ALL RIGHT?
I'LL TOUGH IT OUT.
YOU KNOW...
...USUI-KUN'S ALWAYS PUSHING HIMSELF TOO HARD.
HUH...?

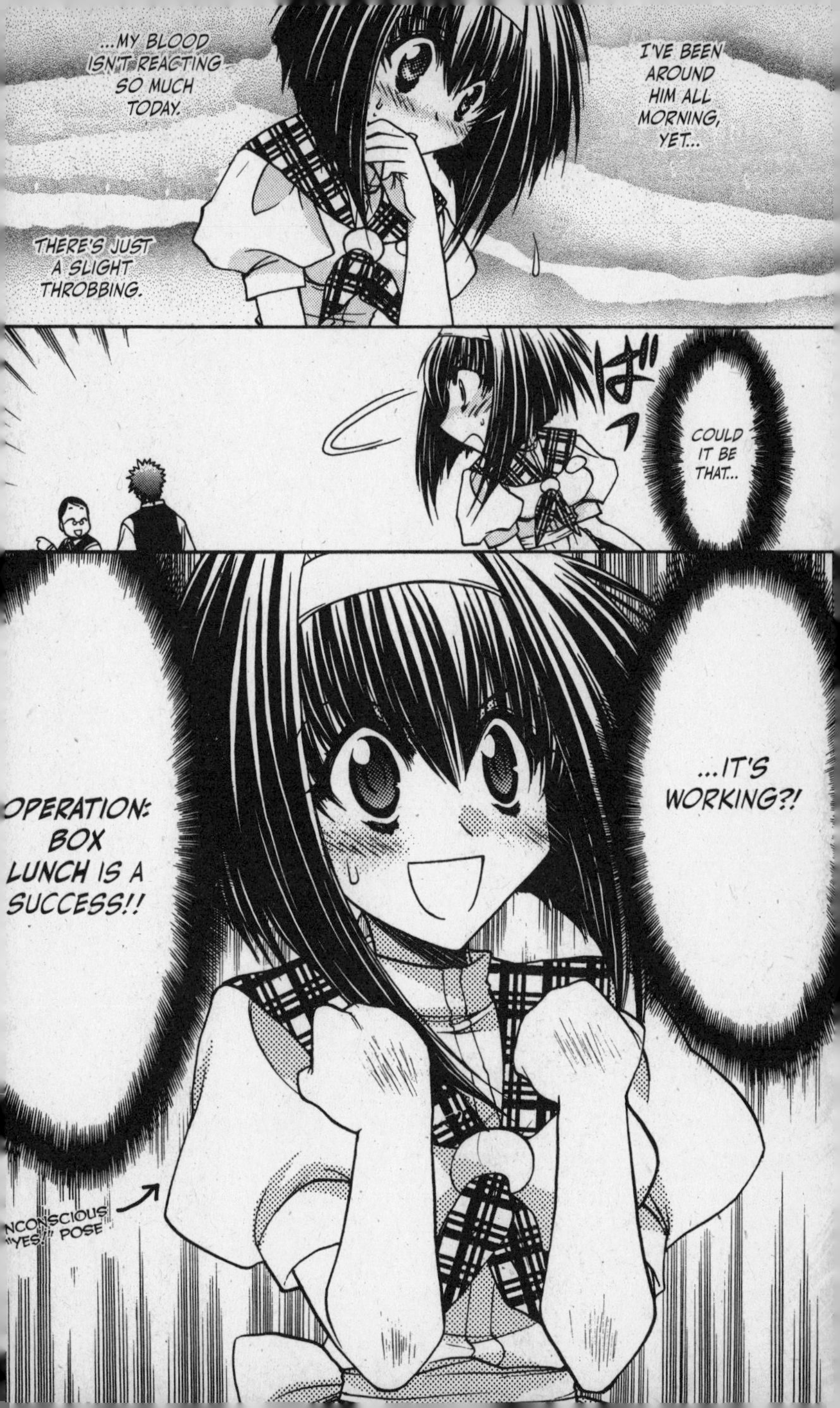
I'VE BEEN AROUND HIM ALL MORNING, YET...
...MY BLOOD ISN'T REACTING SO MUCH TODAY.
THERE'S JUST A SLIGHT THROBBING.
ばっ
COULD IT BE THAT...
...IT'S WORKING?!
OPERATION: BOX LUNCH IS A SUCCESS!!
NCONSCIOUS "YES!" POSE

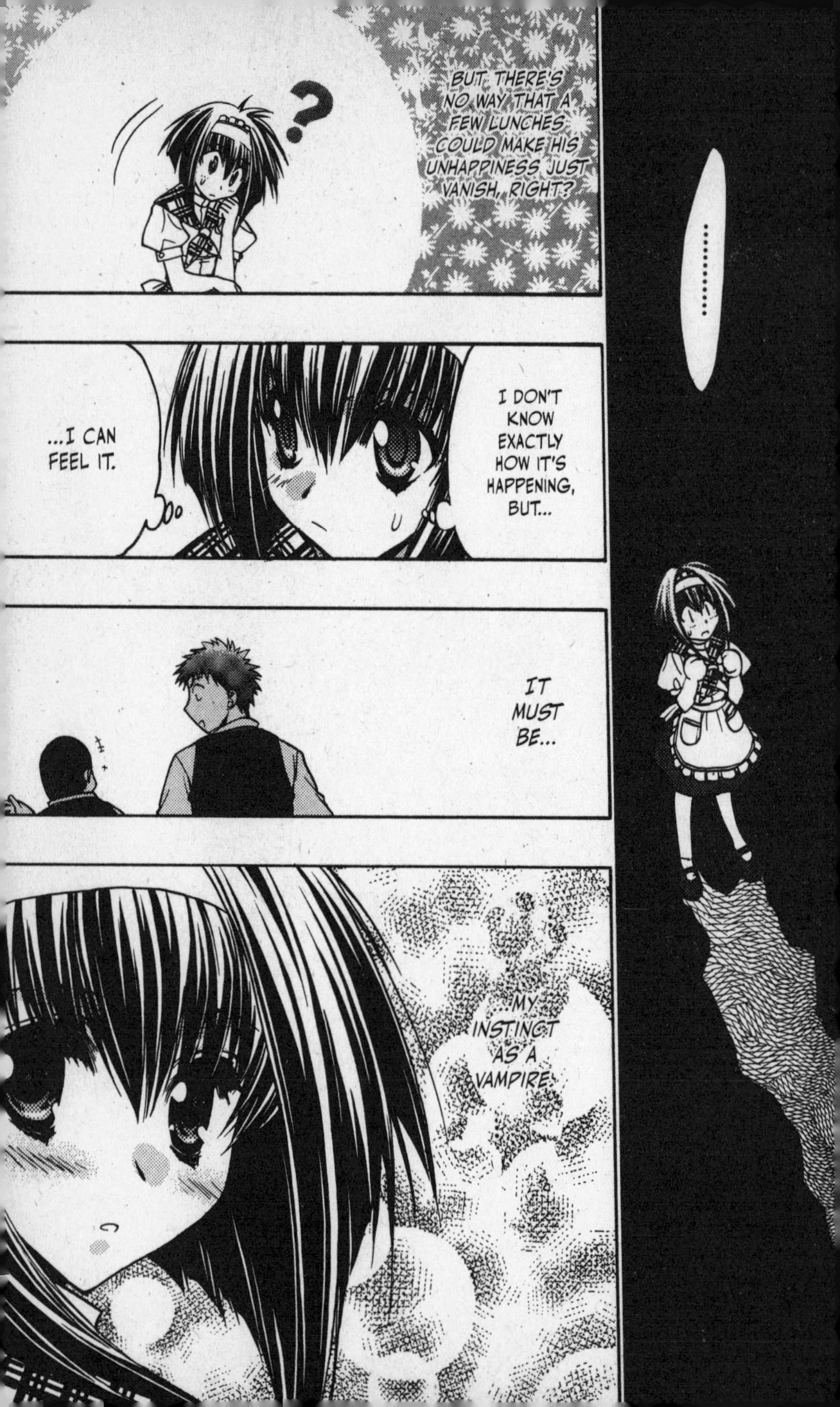
……
BUT THERE'S NO WAY THAT A FEW LUNCHES COULD MAKE HIS UNHAPPINESS JUST VANISH, RIGHT?
I DON'T KNOW EXACTLY HOW IT'S HAPPENING, BUT...
...I CAN FEEL IT.
IT MUST BE...
MY INSTINCT AS A VAMPIRE.

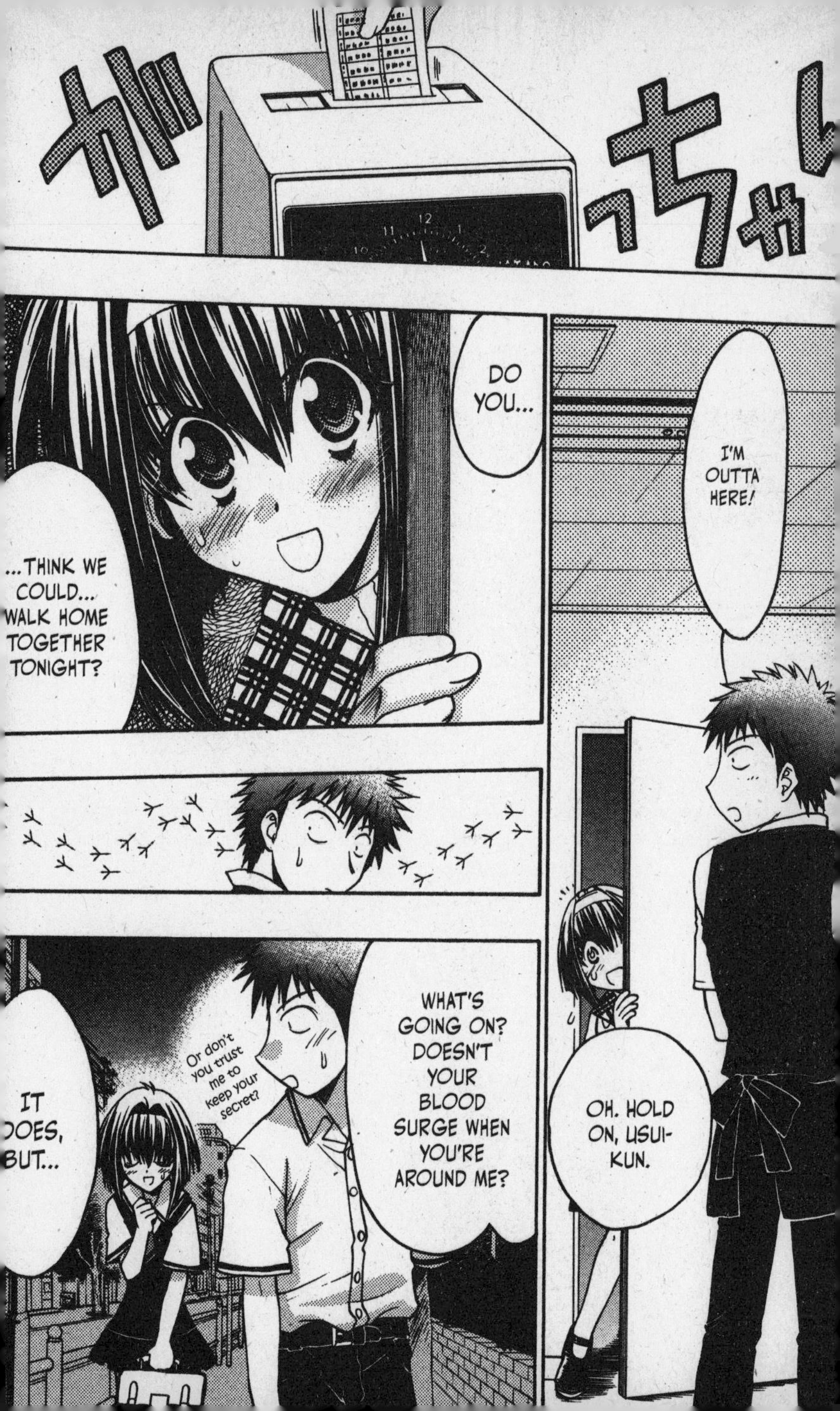
ガっちゃ
I'M OUTTA HERE!
OH. HOLD ON, USUI-KUN.
DO YOU...
...THINK WE COULD... WALK HOME TOGETHER TONIGHT?
WHAT'S GOING ON? DOESN'T YOUR BLOOD SURGE WHEN YOU'RE AROUND ME?
Or don't you trust me to keep your secret?
IT DOES, BUT...

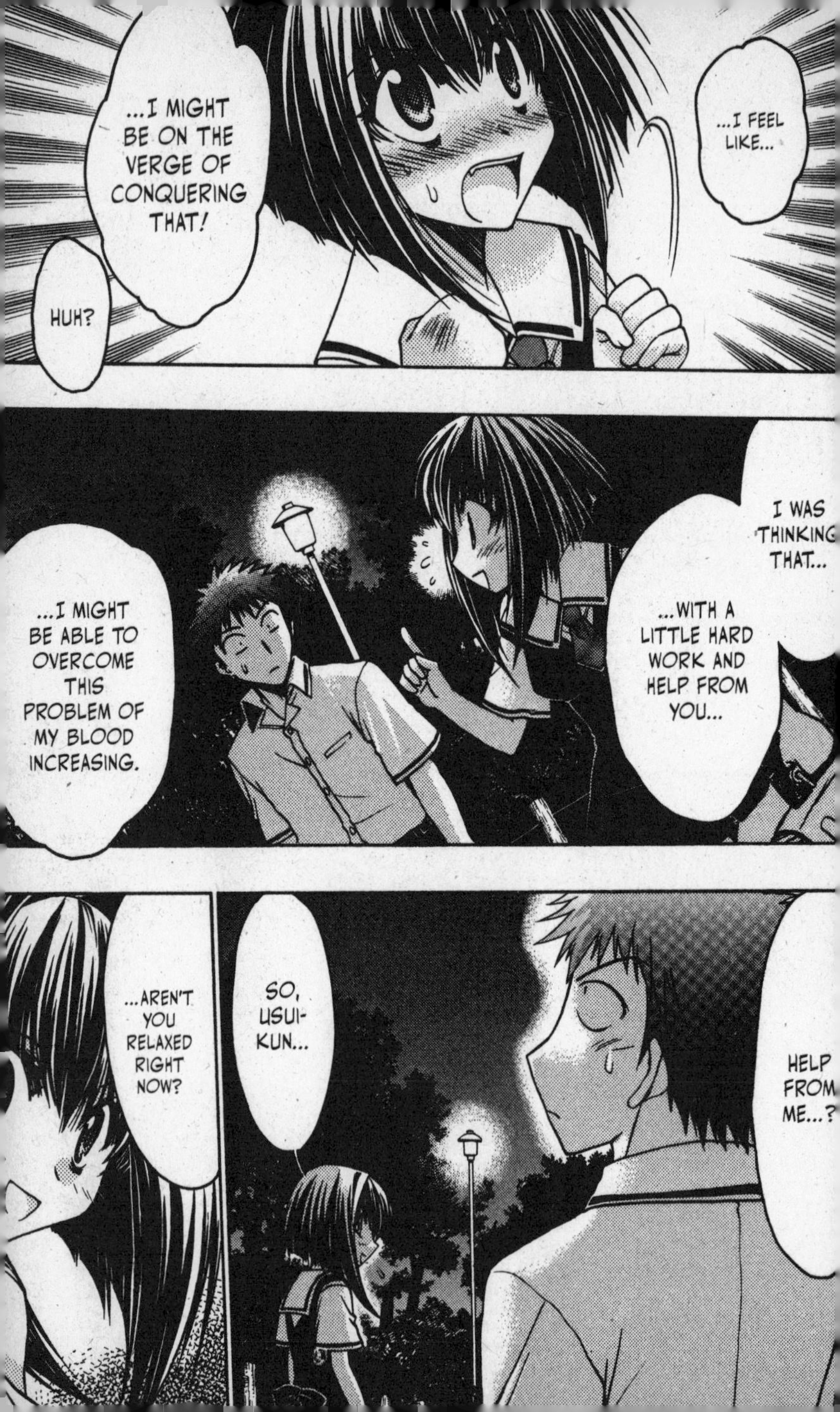
...I FEEL LIKE...
...I MIGHT BE ON THE VERGE OF CONQUERING THAT!
HUH?
I WAS THINKING THAT...
...WITH A LITTLE HARD WORK AND HELP FROM YOU...
...I MIGHT BE ABLE TO OVERCOME THIS PROBLEM OF MY BLOOD INCREASING.
HELP FROM ME...?
SO, USUI-KUN...
...AREN'T YOU RELAXED RIGHT NOW?

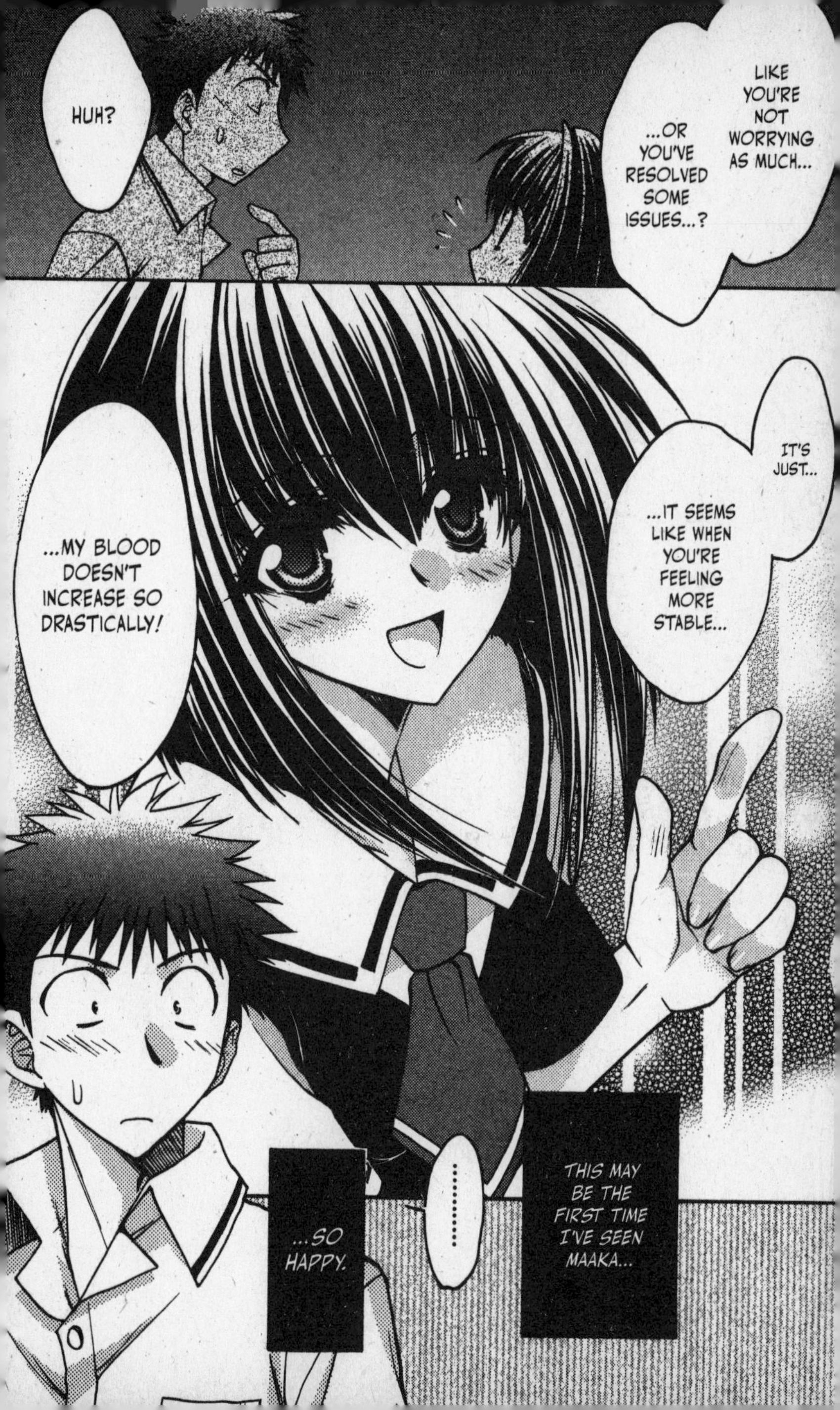
LIKE YOU'RE NOT WORRYING AS MUCH...
...OR YOU'VE RESOLVED SOME ISSUES...?
HUH?
IT'S JUST...
...IT SEEMS LIKE WHEN YOU'RE FEELING MORE STABLE...
...MY BLOOD DOESN'T INCREASE SO DRASTICALLY!
THIS MAY BE THE FIRST TIME I'VE SEEN MAAKA...
......
...SO HAPPY.

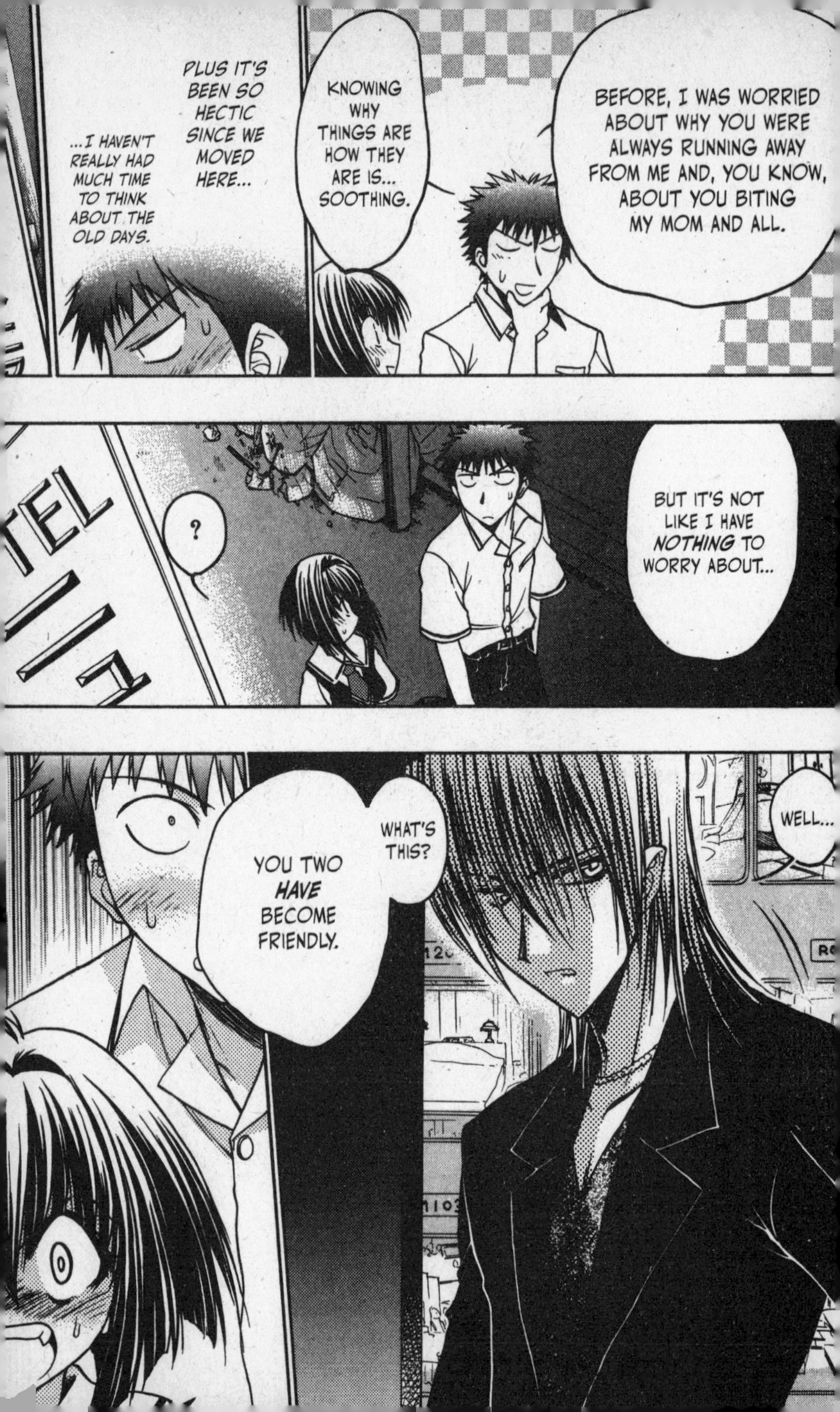
BEFORE, I WAS WORRIED ABOUT WHY YOU WERE ALWAYS RUNNING AWAY FROM ME AND, YOU KNOW, ABOUT YOU BITING MY MOM AND ALL.
KNOWING WHY THINGS ARE HOW THEY ARE IS... SOOTHING.
PLUS IT'S BEEN SO HECTIC SINCE WE MOVED HERE...
...I HAVEN'T REALLY HAD MUCH TIME TO THINK ABOUT THE OLD DAYS.
BUT IT'S NOT LIKE I HAVE *NOTHING* TO WORRY ABOUT...
?
WELL...
WHAT'S THIS?
YOU TWO *HAVE* BECOME FRIENDLY.

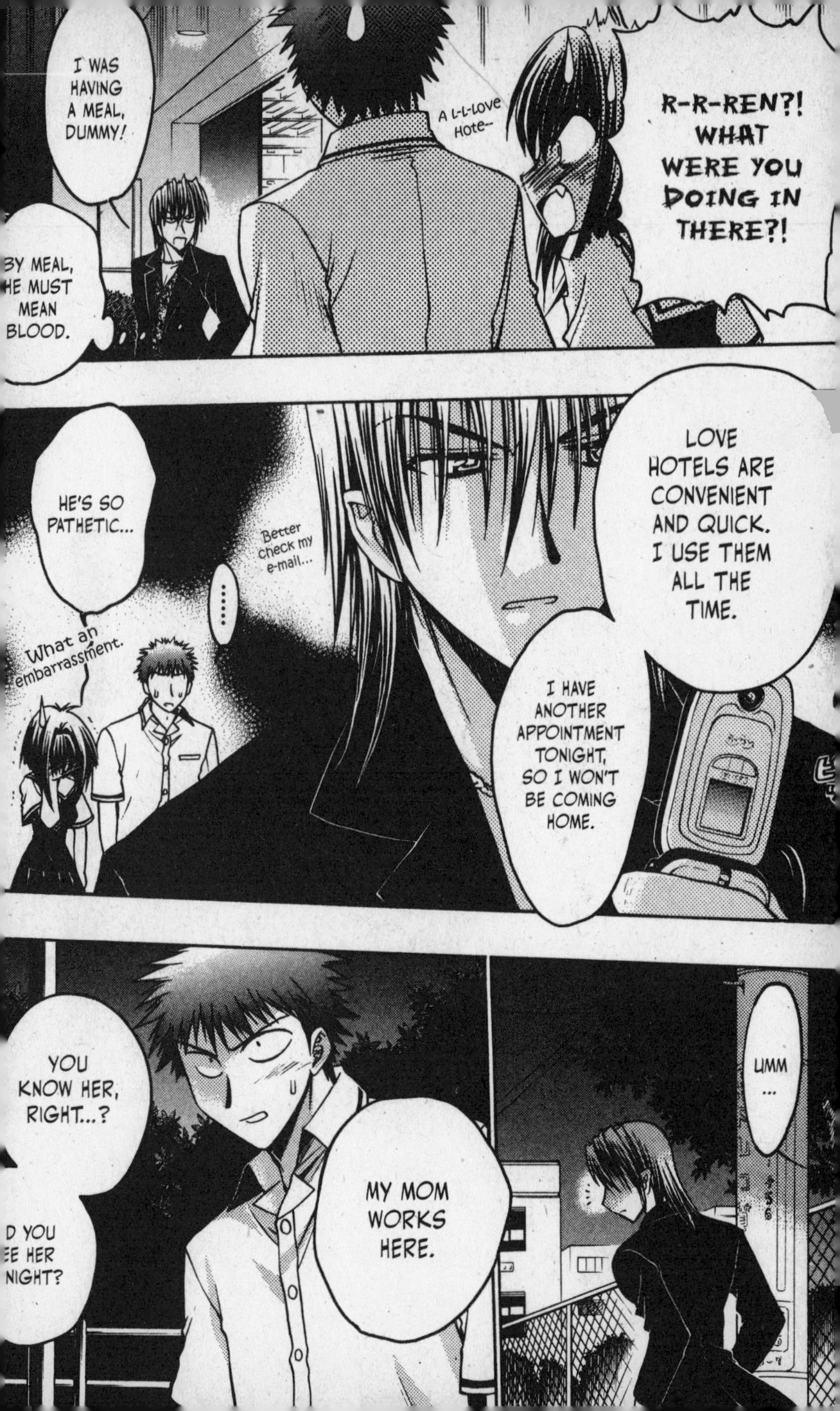

R-R-REN?! WHAT WERE YOU DOING IN THERE?!
A L-L-Love Hote--
I WAS HAVING A MEAL, DUMMY!
BY MEAL, HE MUST MEAN BLOOD.
LOVE HOTELS ARE CONVENIENT AND QUICK. I USE THEM ALL THE TIME.
I HAVE ANOTHER APPOINTMENT TONIGHT, SO I WON'T BE COMING HOME.
Better check my e-mail...
......
HE'S SO PATHETIC...
What an embarrassment.
UMM ...
MY MOM WORKS HERE.
YOU KNOW HER, RIGHT...?
D YOU EE HER NIGHT?

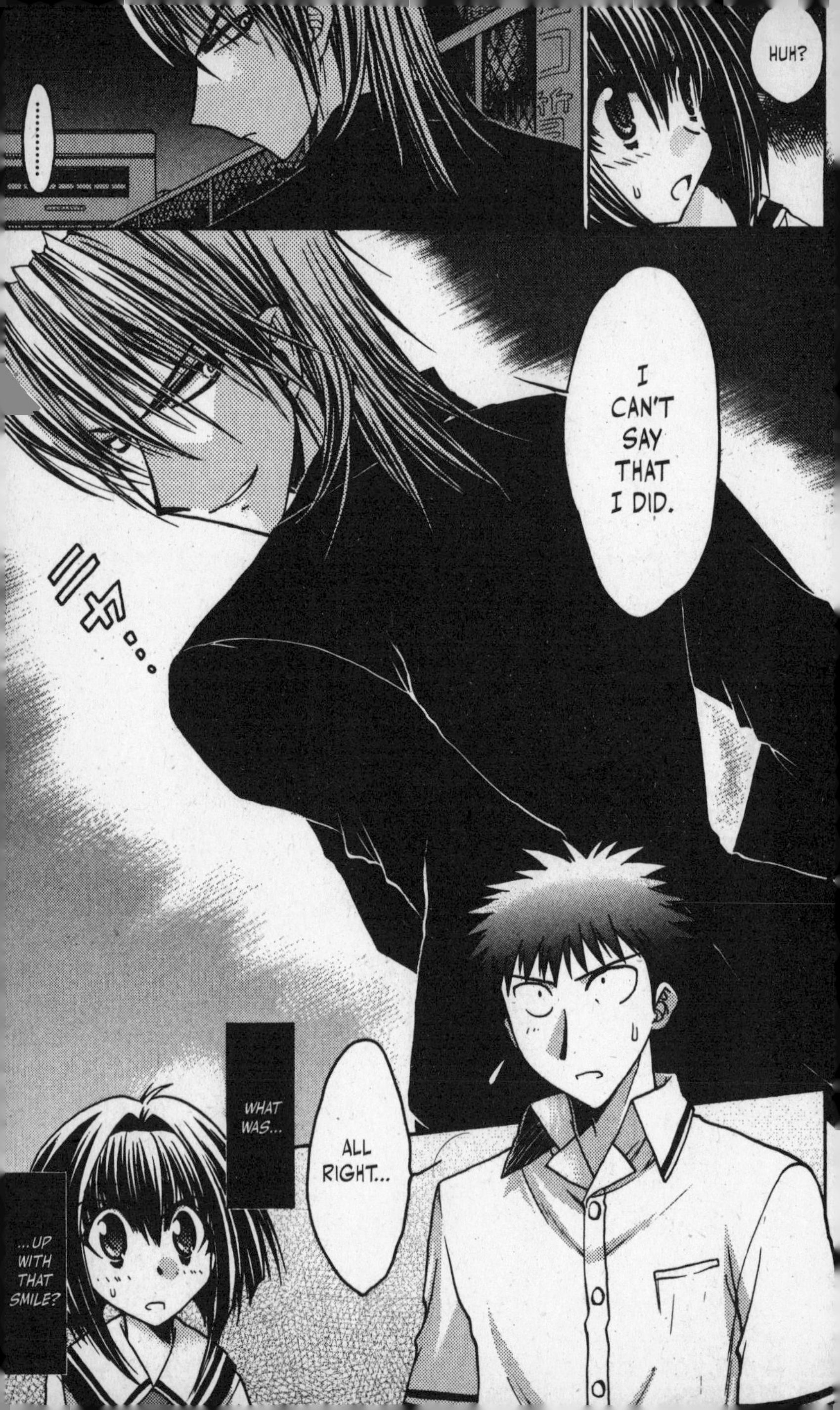
HUH?
......
I CAN'T SAY THAT I DID.
ニヤ...
ALL RIGHT...
WHAT WAS...
...UP WITH THAT SMILE?

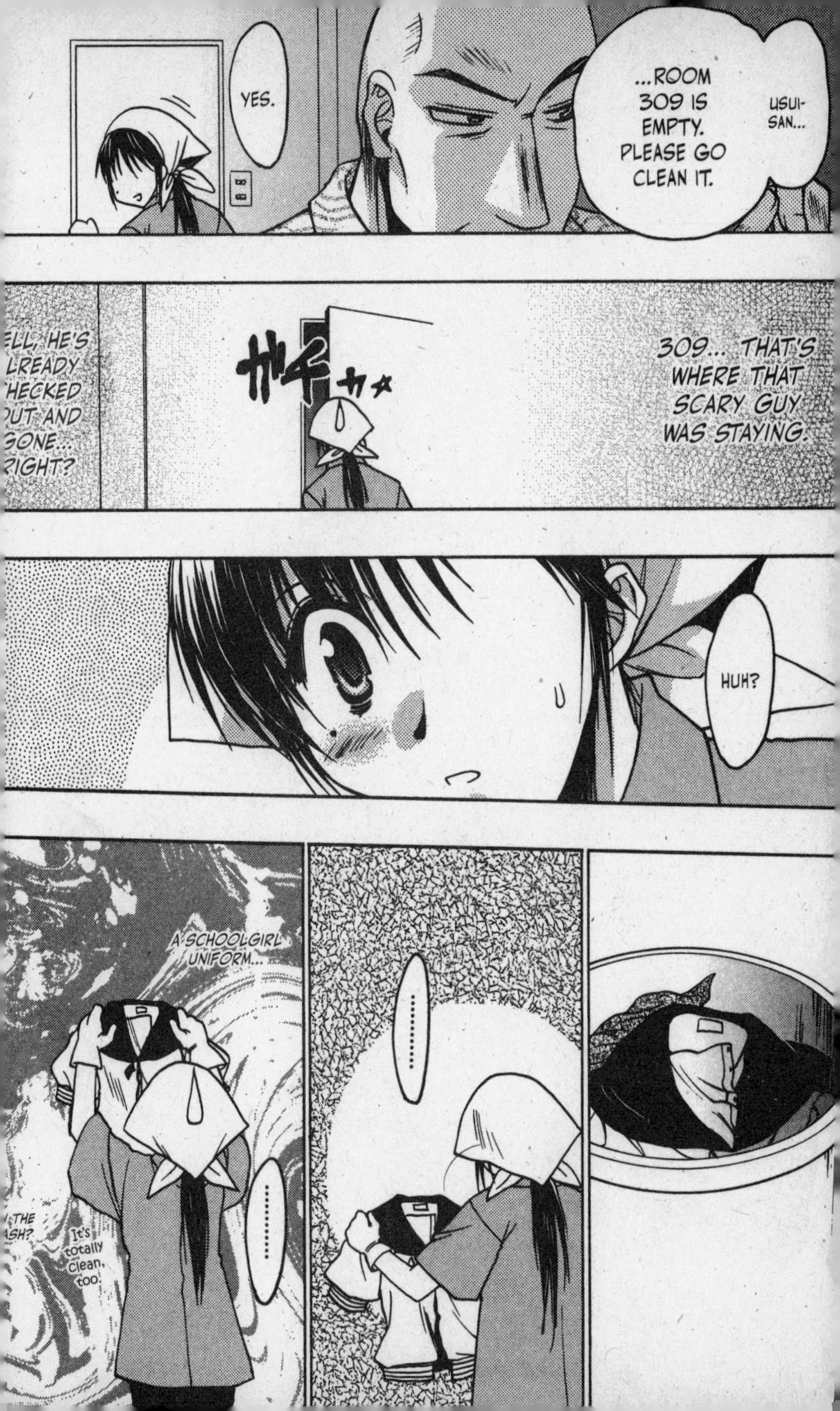
USUI-SAN...
...ROOM 309 IS EMPTY. PLEASE GO CLEAN IT.
YES.
309... THAT'S WHERE THAT SCARY GUY WAS STAYING.
ELL, HE'S LREADY HECKED UT AND GONE... RIGHT?
HUH?
......
A SCHOOLGIRL UNIFORM...
......
THE ASH?
It's totally clean, too.

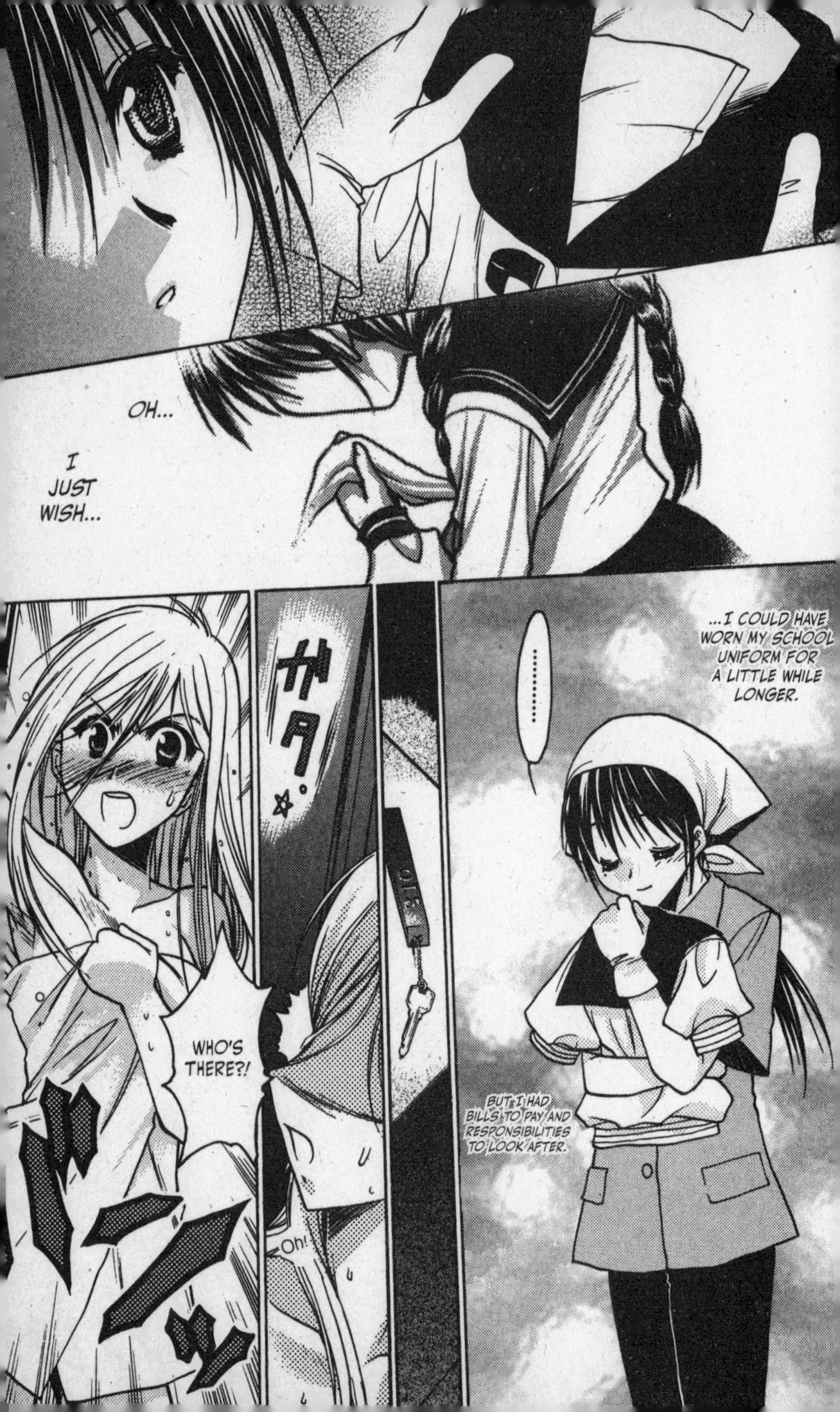
OH...
I JUST WISH...
...I COULD HAVE WORN MY SCHOOL UNIFORM FOR A LITTLE WHILE LONGER.
....
BUT I HAD BILLS TO PAY AND RESPONSIBILITIES TO LOOK AFTER.
カタ。
Oh!
WHO'S THERE?!

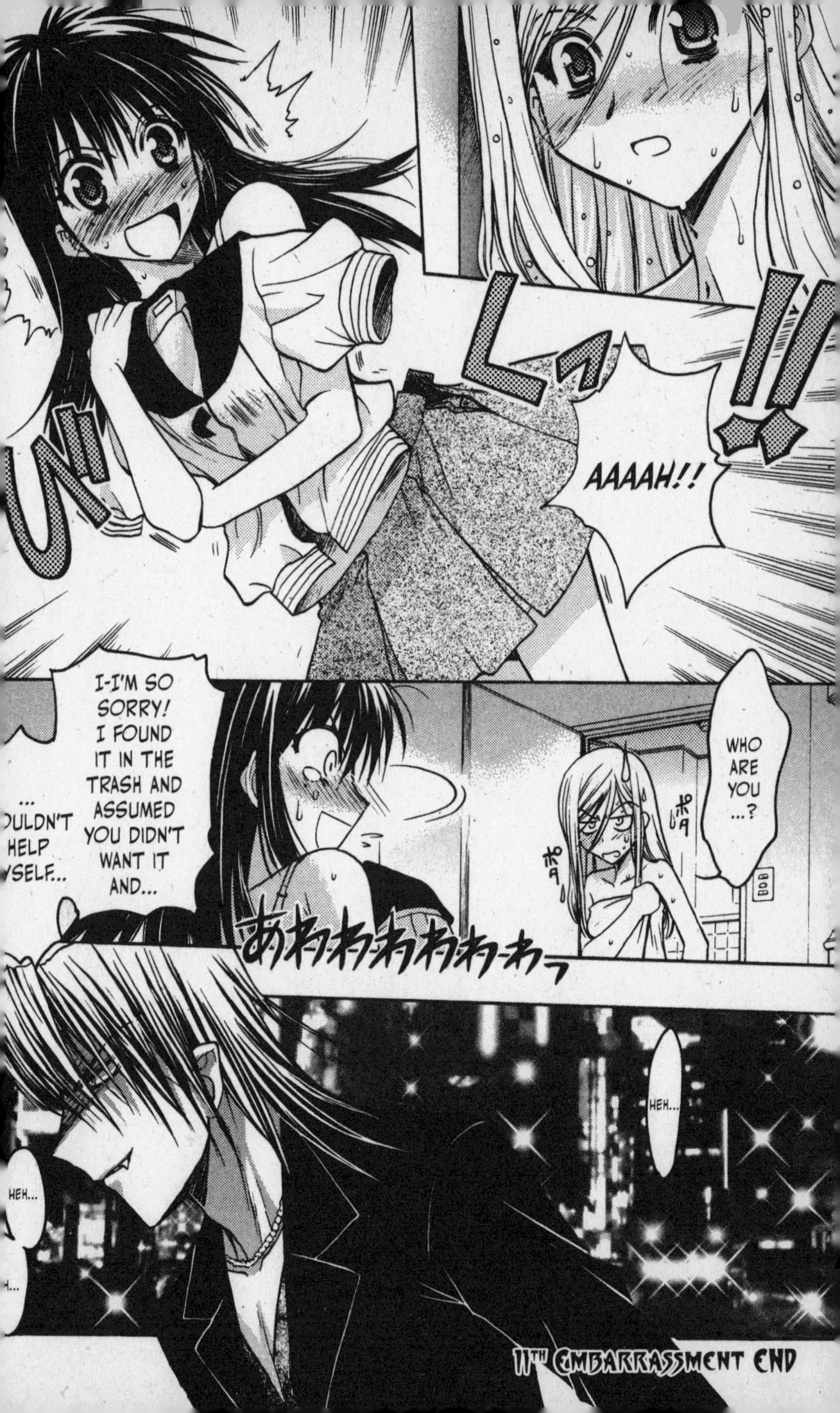
AAAAH!!
WHO ARE YOU ...?
I-I'M SO SORRY! I FOUND IT IN THE TRASH AND ASSUMED YOU DIDN'T WANT IT AND...
... OULDN'T HELP YSELF...
HEH...
HEH...
11TH EMBARRASSMENT END

12TH EMBARRASSMENT) KARIN'S IDEA AND THE ODD PAIR
~THOUGHT~

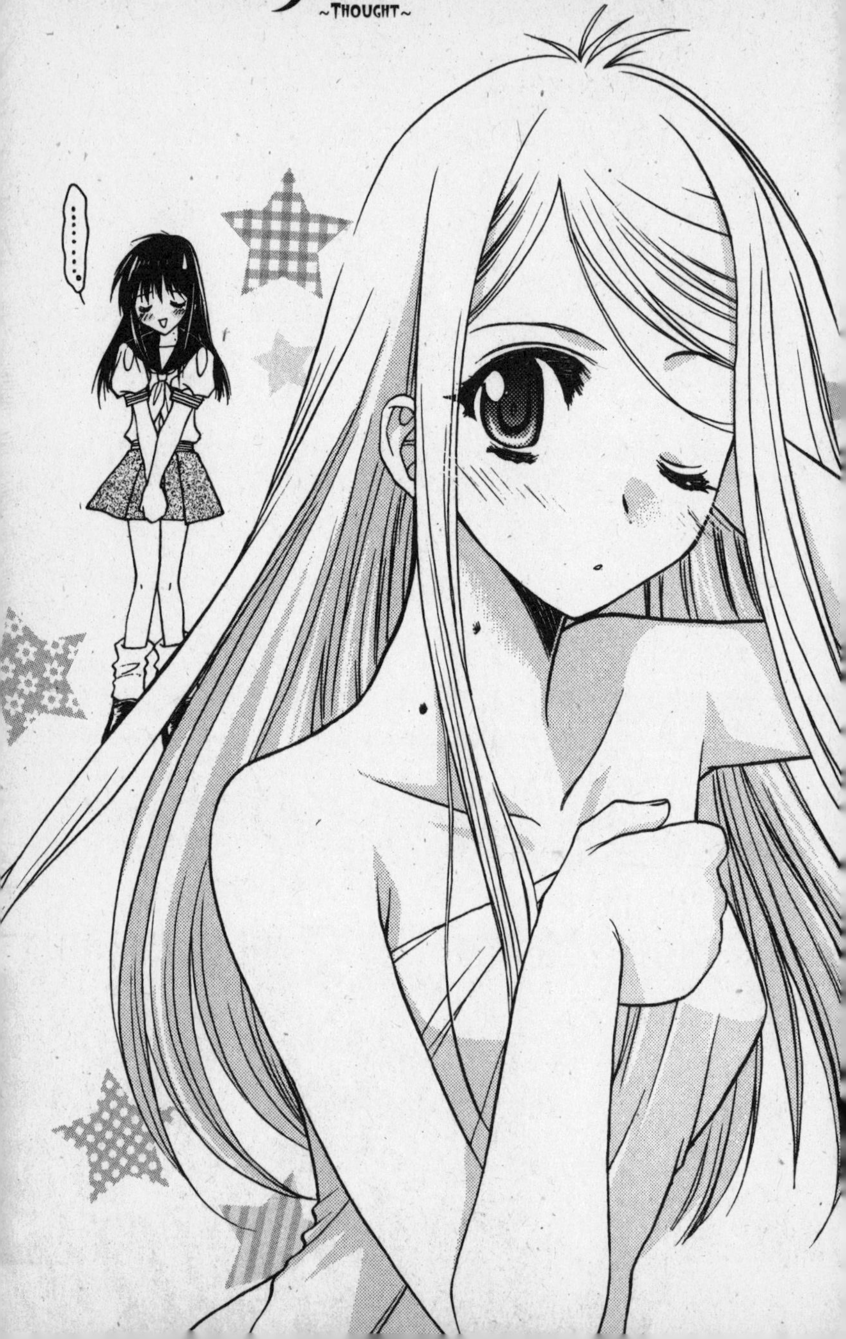
....

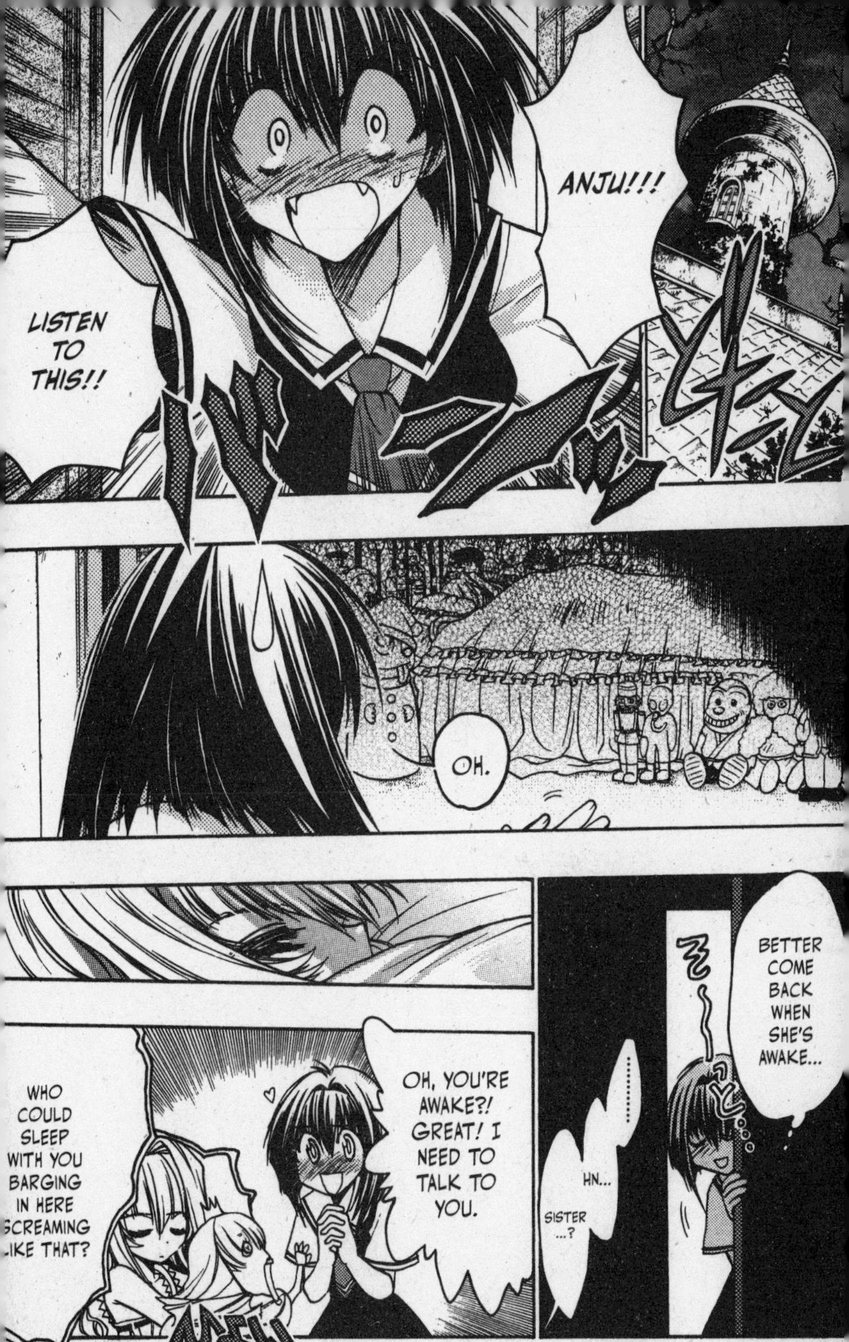
ANJU!!!
LISTEN TO THIS!!
OH.
BETTER COME BACK WHEN SHE'S AWAKE...
......
HN...
SISTER ...?
OH, YOU'RE AWAKE?! GREAT! I NEED TO TALK TO YOU.
WHO COULD SLEEP WITH YOU BARGING IN HERE SCREAMING LIKE THAT?

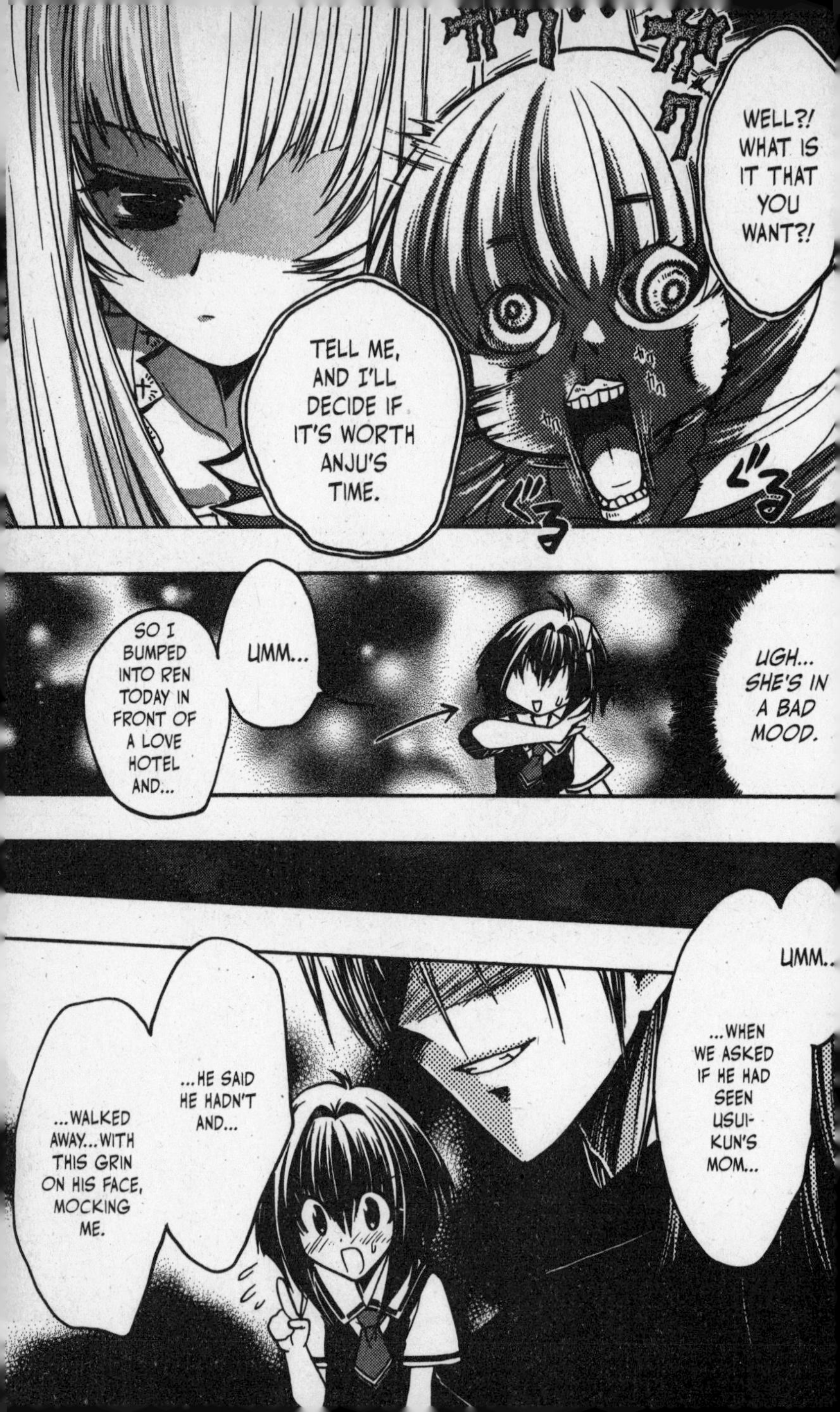
WELL?! WHAT IS IT THAT YOU WANT?!
TELL ME, AND I'LL DECIDE IF IT'S WORTH ANJU'S TIME.
UGH... SHE'S IN A BAD MOOD.
UMM...
SO I BUMPED INTO REN TODAY IN FRONT OF A LOVE HOTEL AND...
UMM...
...WHEN WE ASKED IF HE HAD SEEN USUI-KUN'S MOM...
...HE SAID HE HADN'T AND...
...WALKED AWAY...WITH THIS GRIN ON HIS FACE, MOCKING ME.

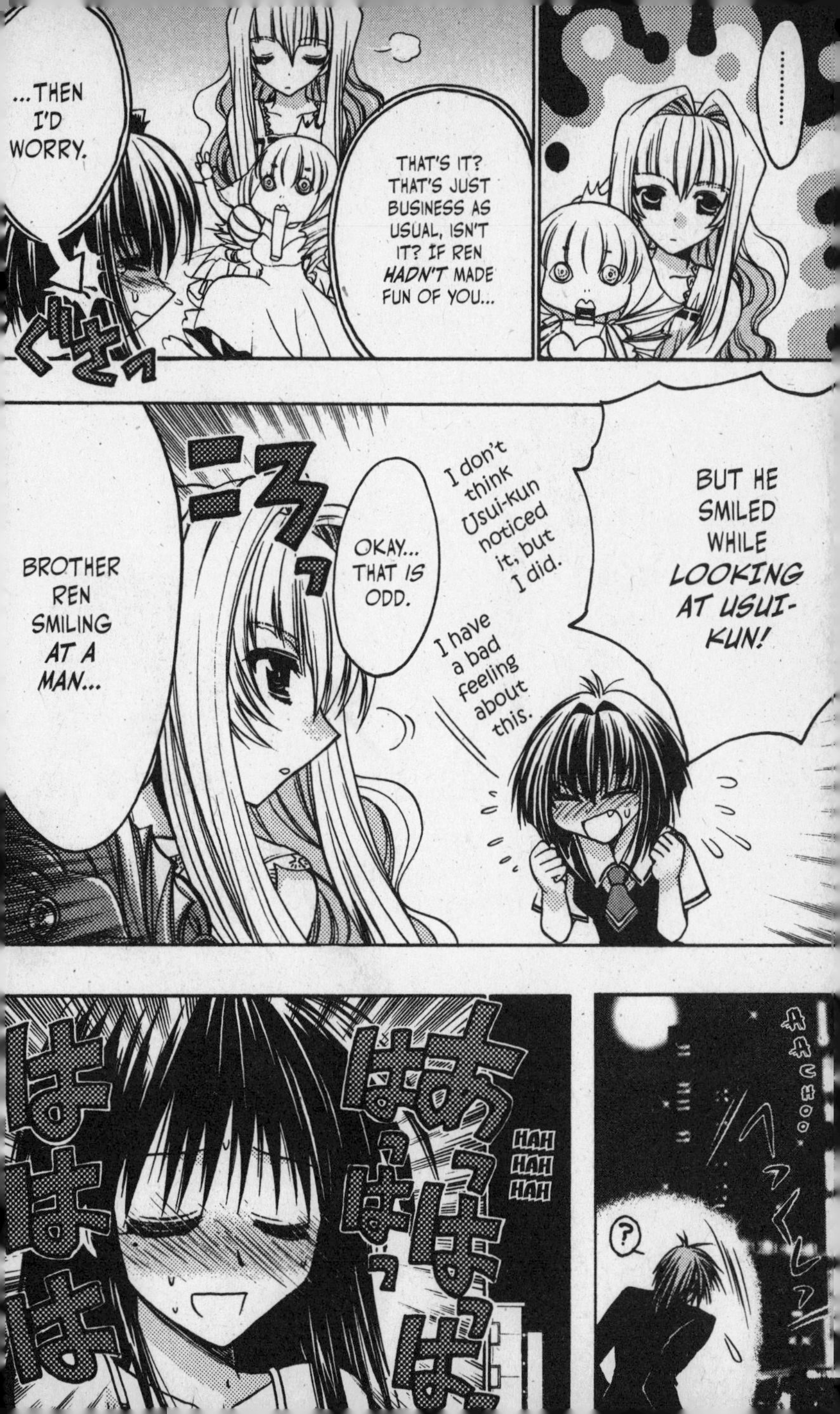

......
THAT'S IT? THAT'S JUST BUSINESS AS USUAL, ISN'T IT? IF REN *HADN'T* MADE FUN OF YOU...
...THEN I'D WORRY.
BUT HE SMILED WHILE *LOOKING AT USUI-KUN!*
I don't think Usui-kun noticed it, but I did.
I have a bad feeling about this.
OKAY... THAT *IS* ODD.
BROTHER REN SMILING *AT A MAN...*
AACHOO...
?
HAH HAH HAH

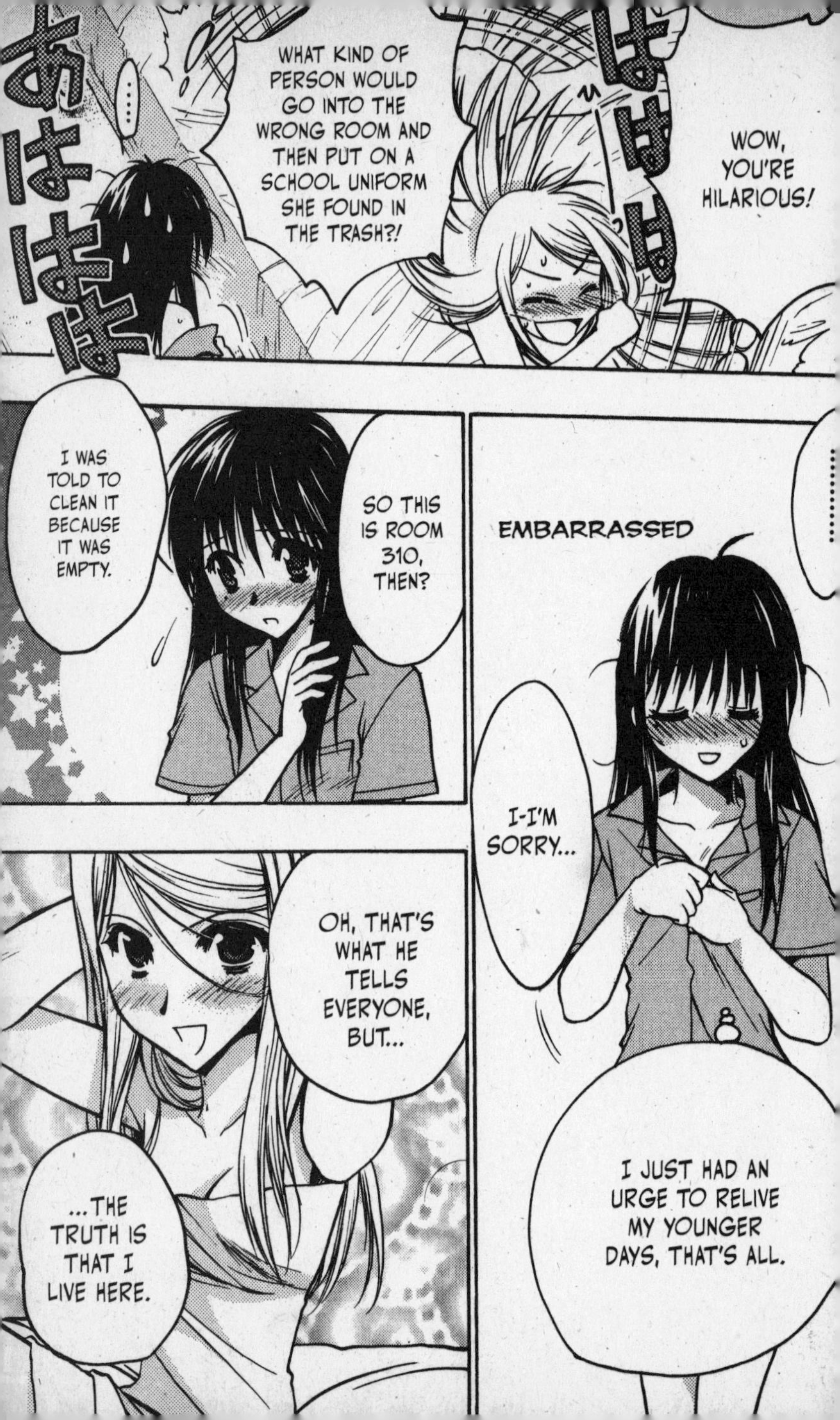

WOW, YOU'RE HILARIOUS!
ははは
WHAT KIND OF PERSON WOULD GO INTO THE WRONG ROOM AND THEN PUT ON A SCHOOL UNIFORM SHE FOUND IN THE TRASH?!
...
あははは
EMBARRASSED
I-I'M SORRY...
I JUST HAD AN URGE TO RELIVE MY YOUNGER DAYS, THAT'S ALL.
SO THIS IS ROOM 310, THEN?
I WAS TOLD TO CLEAN IT BECAUSE IT WAS EMPTY.
OH, THAT'S WHAT HE TELLS EVERYONE, BUT...
...THE TRUTH IS THAT I LIVE HERE.

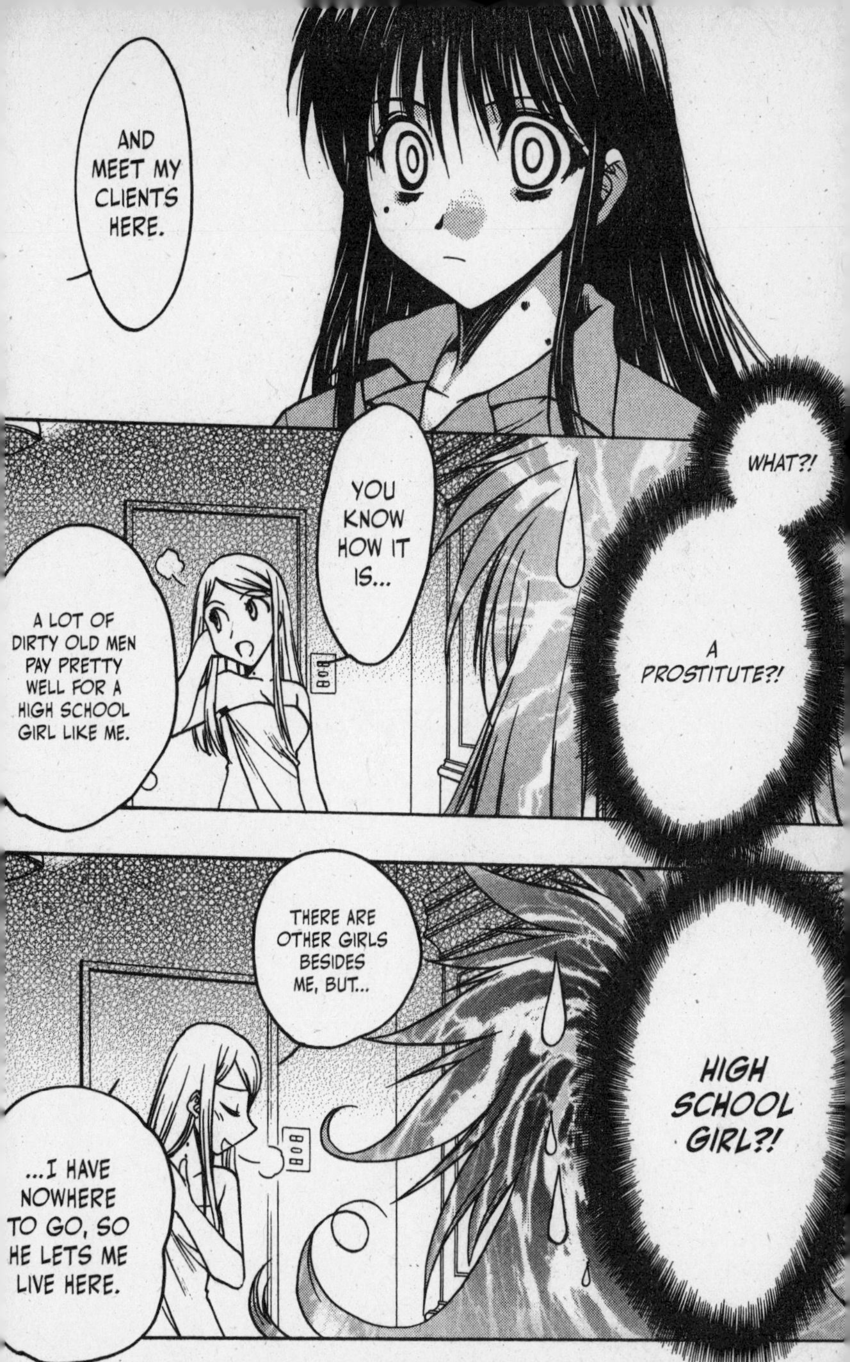
AND MEET MY CLIENTS HERE.
WHAT?!
A PROSTITUTE?!
YOU KNOW HOW IT IS...
A LOT OF DIRTY OLD MEN PAY PRETTY WELL FOR A HIGH SCHOOL GIRL LIKE ME.
HIGH SCHOOL GIRL?!
THERE ARE OTHER GIRLS BESIDES ME, BUT...
...I HAVE NOWHERE TO GO, SO HE LETS ME LIVE HERE.

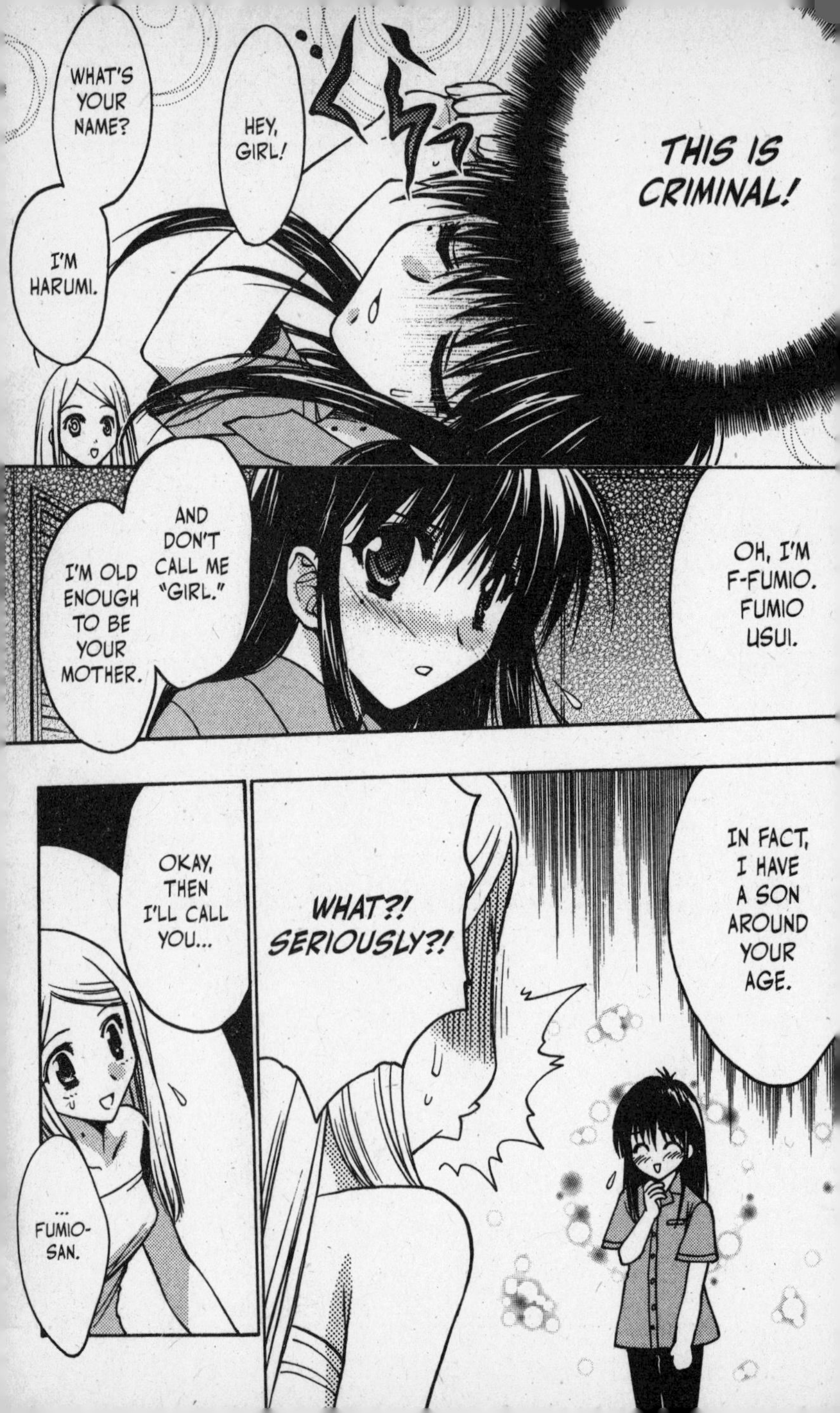
THIS IS CRIMINAL!
HEY, GIRL!
WHAT'S YOUR NAME?
I'M HARUMI.
OH, I'M F-FUMIO. FUMIO USUI.
AND DON'T CALL ME "GIRL."
I'M OLD ENOUGH TO BE YOUR MOTHER.
IN FACT, I HAVE A SON AROUND YOUR AGE.
WHAT?! SERIOUSLY?!
OKAY, THEN I'LL CALL YOU...
... FUMIO-SAN.

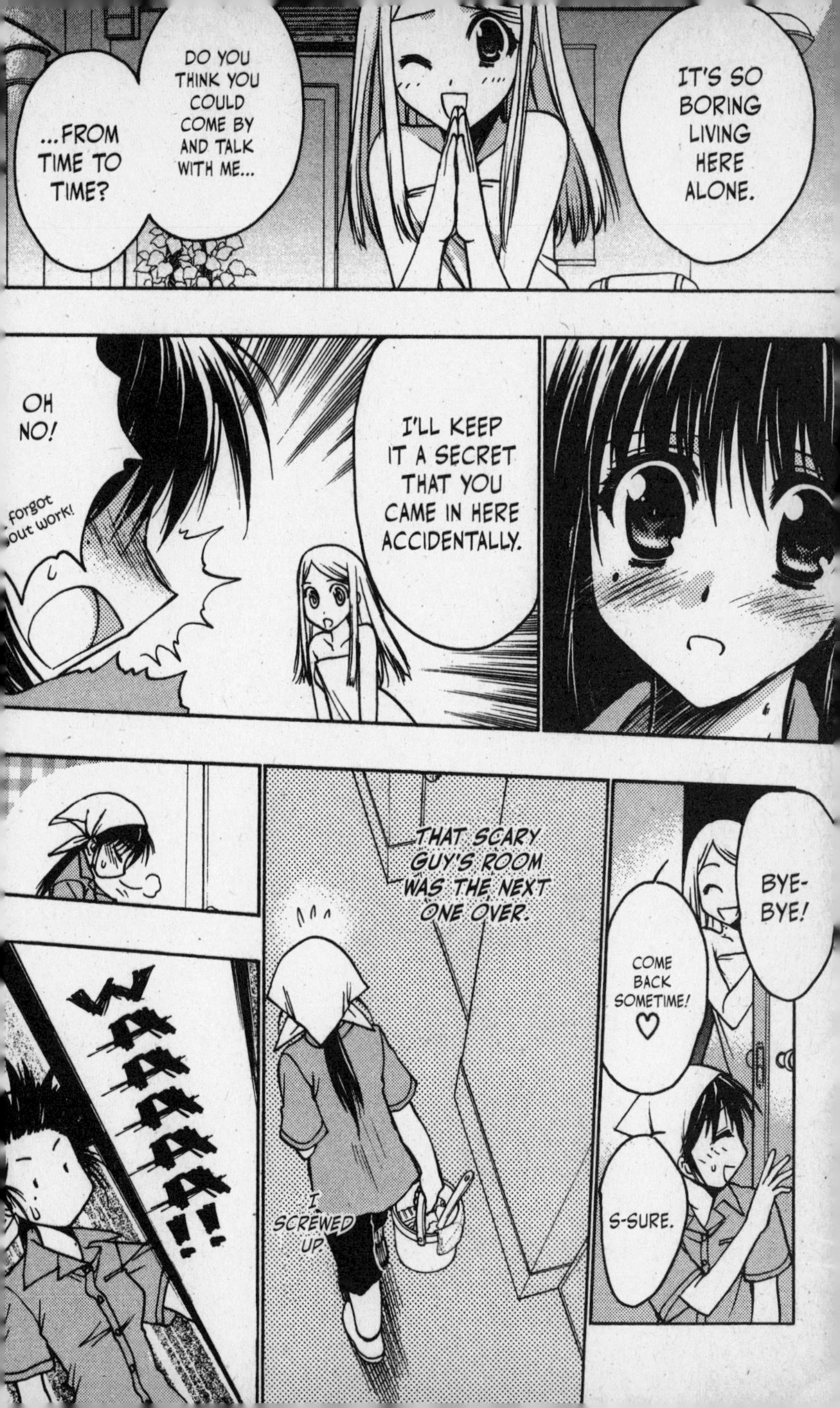
IT'S SO BORING LIVING HERE ALONE.
DO YOU THINK YOU COULD COME BY AND TALK WITH ME...
...FROM TIME TO TIME?
I'LL KEEP IT A SECRET THAT YOU CAME IN HERE ACCIDENTALLY.
OH NO!
forgot
out work!
BYE-BYE!
COME BACK SOMETIME! ♡
S-SURE.
THAT SCARY GUY'S ROOM WAS THE NEXT ONE OVER.
I SCREWED UP.
WAAAAA!!

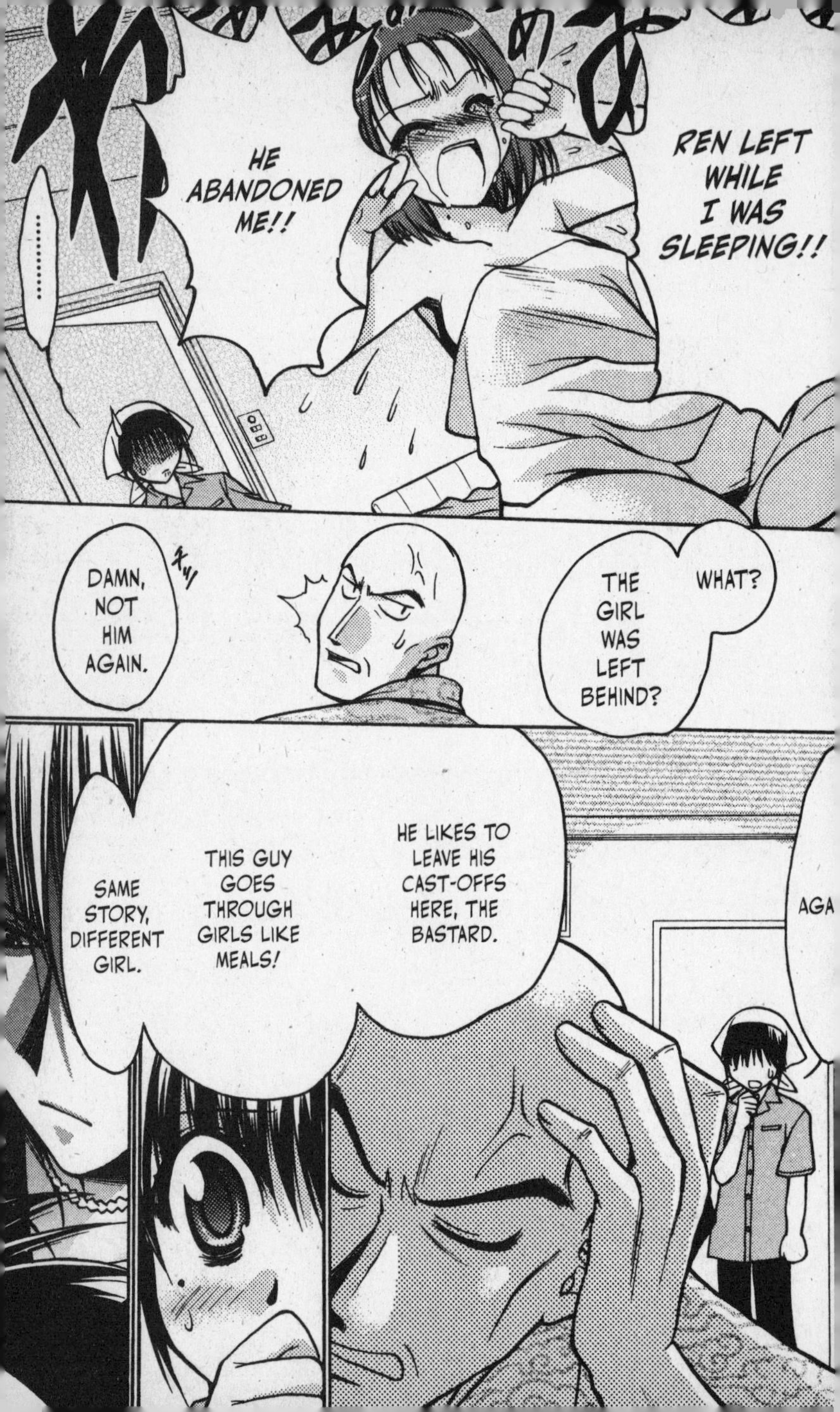
REN LEFT WHILE I WAS SLEEPING!!
HE ABANDONED ME!!
......
WHAT?
THE GIRL WAS LEFT BEHIND?
DAMN, NOT HIM AGAIN.
AGA
HE LIKES TO LEAVE HIS CAST-OFFS HERE, THE BASTARD.
THIS GUY GOES THROUGH GIRLS LIKE MEALS!
SAME STORY, DIFFERENT GIRL.

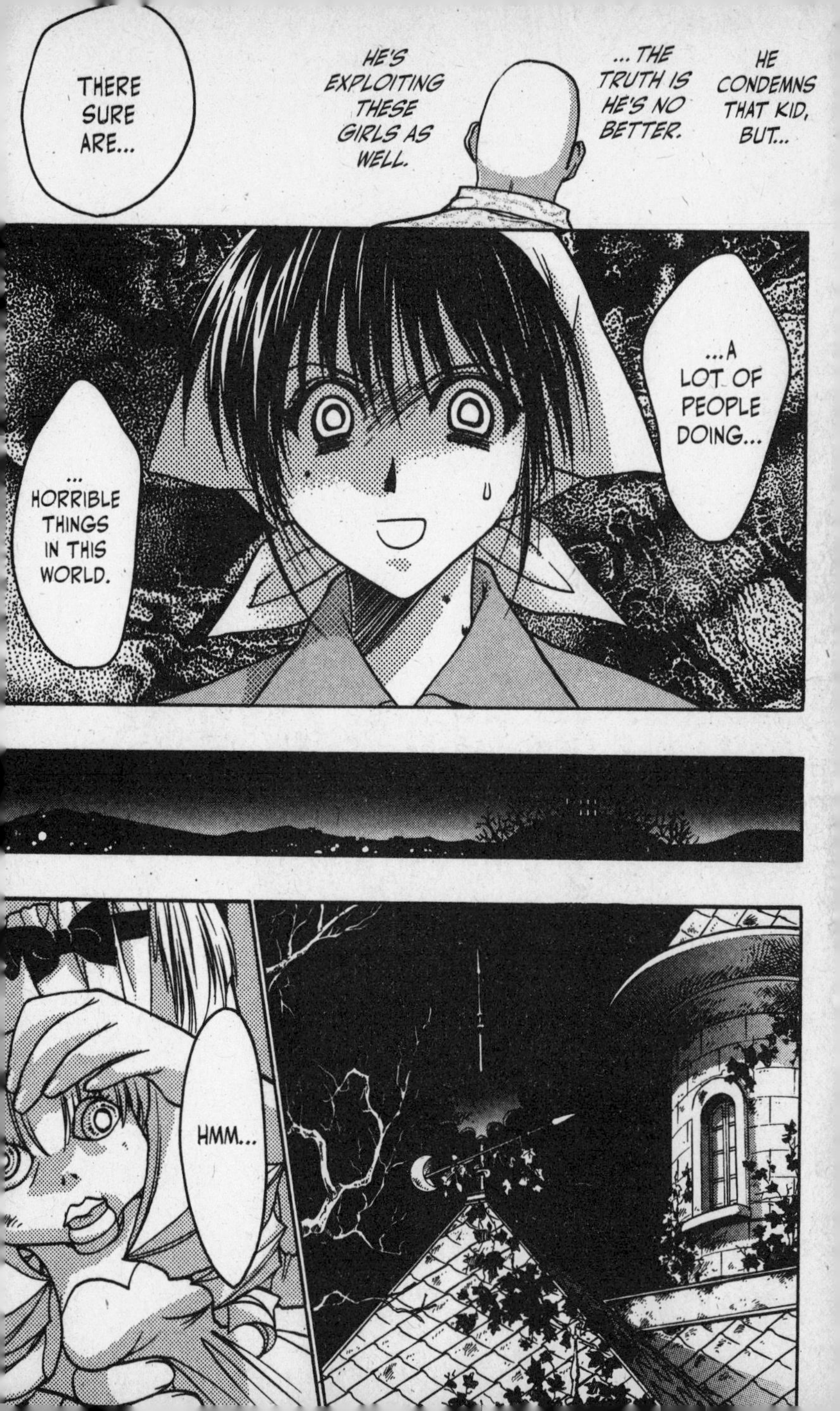
HE CONDEMNS THAT KID, BUT...
...THE TRUTH IS HE'S NO BETTER.
HE'S EXPLOITING THESE GIRLS AS WELL.
THERE SURE ARE...
...A LOT OF PEOPLE DOING...
...HORRIBLE THINGS IN THIS WORLD.
HMM...

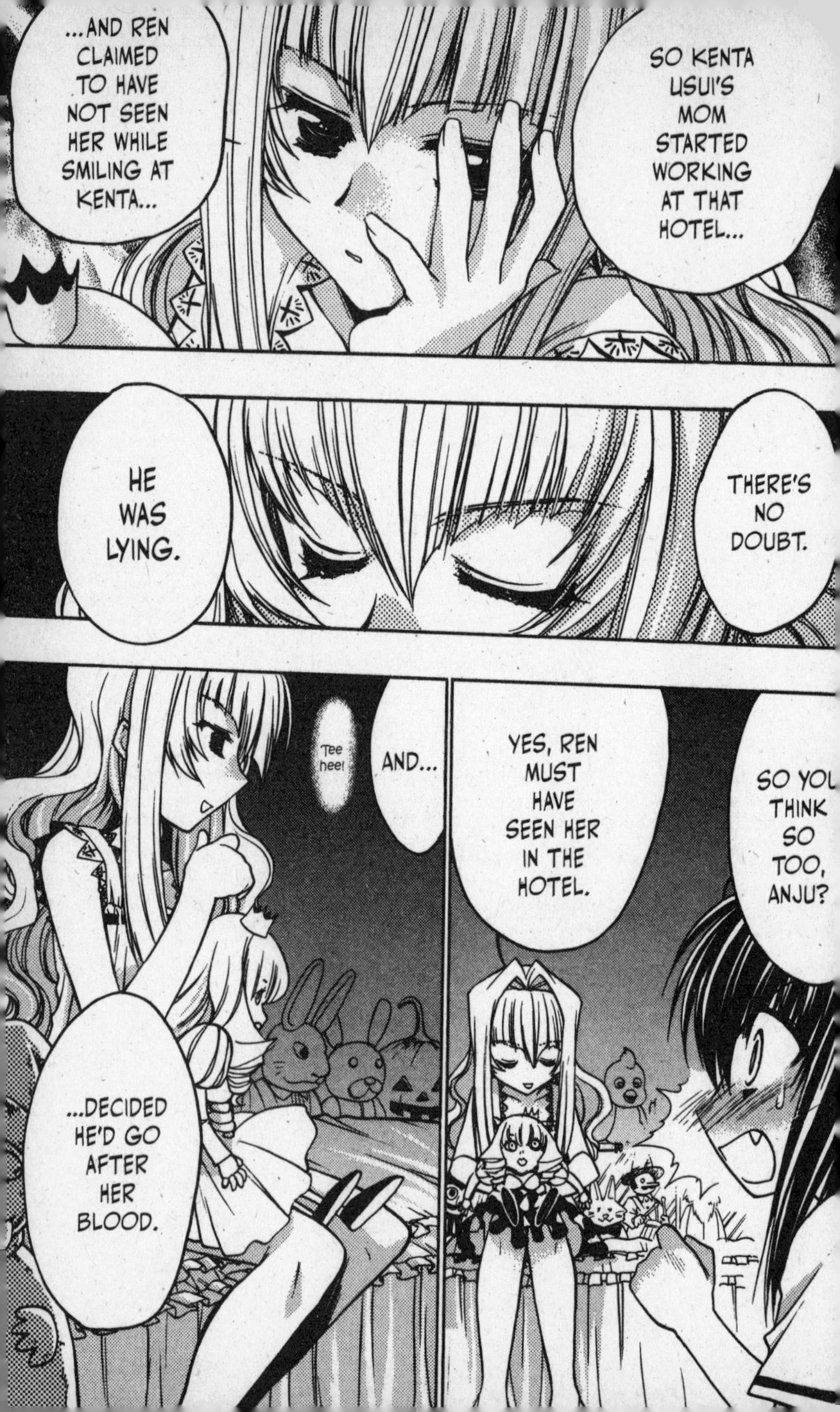

SO KENTA USUI'S MOM STARTED WORKING AT THAT HOTEL...
...AND REN CLAIMED TO HAVE NOT SEEN HER WHILE SMILING AT KENTA...
THERE'S NO DOUBT.
HE WAS LYING.
SO YOU THINK SO TOO, ANJU?
YES, REN MUST HAVE SEEN HER IN THE HOTEL.
AND...
Tee hee!
...DECIDED HE'D GO AFTER HER BLOOD.

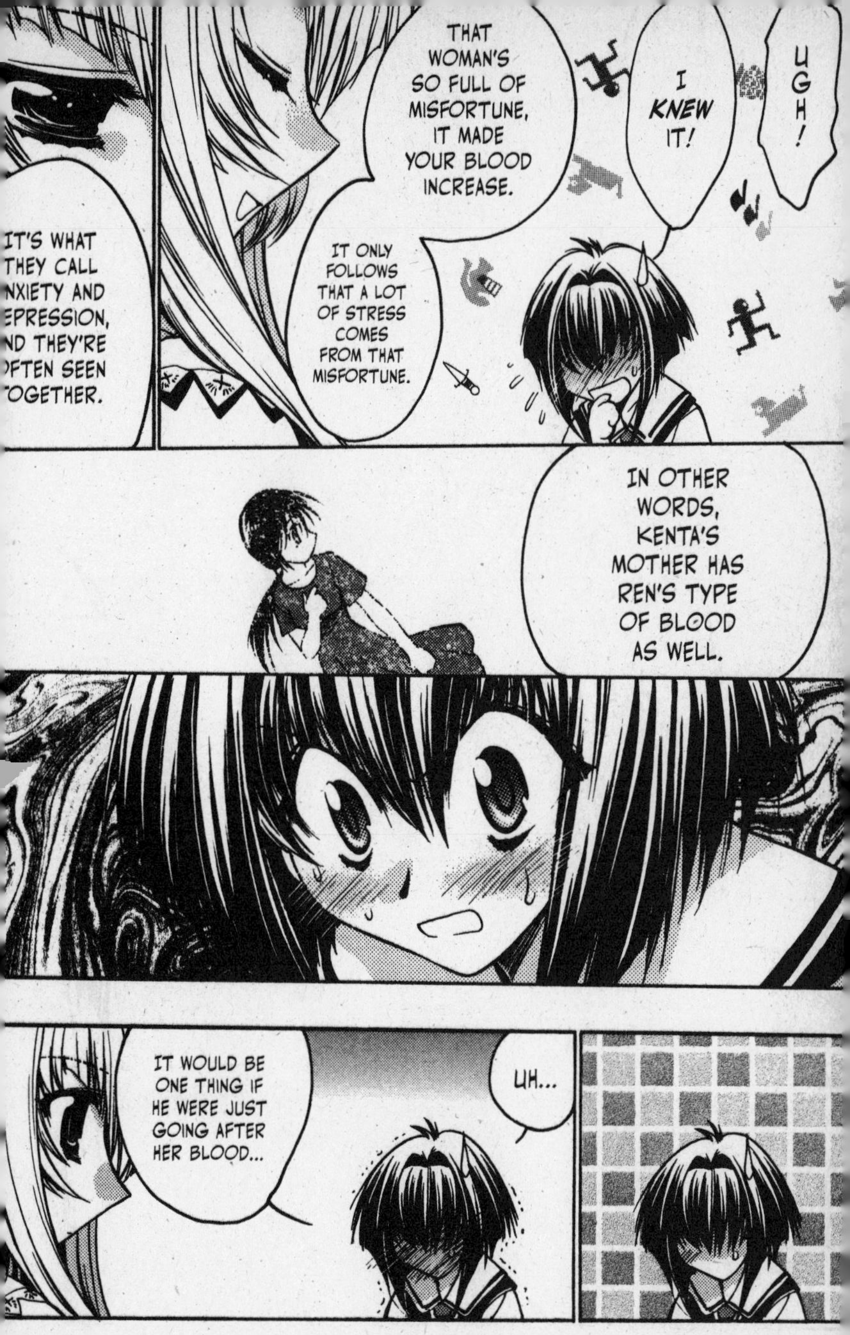
UGH!
I KNEW IT!
THAT WOMAN'S SO FULL OF MISFORTUNE, IT MADE YOUR BLOOD INCREASE.
IT ONLY FOLLOWS THAT A LOT OF STRESS COMES FROM THAT MISFORTUNE.
IT'S WHAT THEY CALL NXIETY AND EPRESSION, ND THEY'RE FTEN SEEN OGETHER.
IN OTHER WORDS, KENTA'S MOTHER HAS REN'S TYPE OF BLOOD AS WELL.
UH...
IT WOULD BE ONE THING IF HE WERE JUST GOING AFTER HER BLOOD...

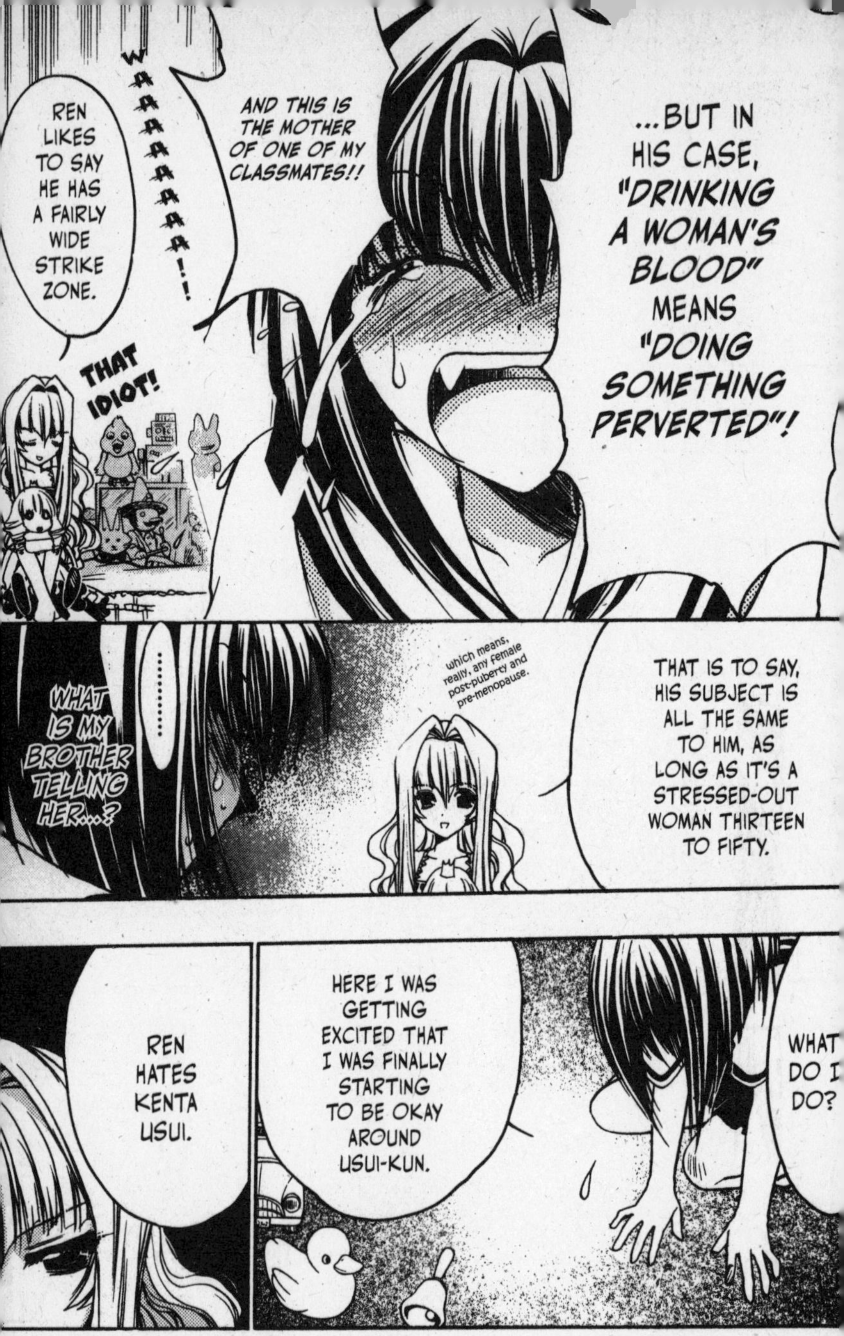
...BUT IN HIS CASE, "DRINKING A WOMAN'S BLOOD" MEANS "DOING SOMETHING PERVERTED"!
AND THIS IS THE MOTHER OF ONE OF MY CLASSMATES!!
WAAAAAAAA!!
REN LIKES TO SAY HE HAS A FAIRLY WIDE STRIKE ZONE.
THAT IDIOT!
THAT IS TO SAY, HIS SUBJECT IS ALL THE SAME TO HIM, AS LONG AS IT'S A STRESSED-OUT WOMAN THIRTEEN TO FIFTY.
which means, really, any female post-puberty and pre-menopause.
......
WHAT IS MY BROTHER TELLING HER...?
WHAT DO I DO?
HERE I WAS GETTING EXCITED THAT I WAS FINALLY STARTING TO BE OKAY AROUND USUI-KUN.
REN HATES KENTA USUI.

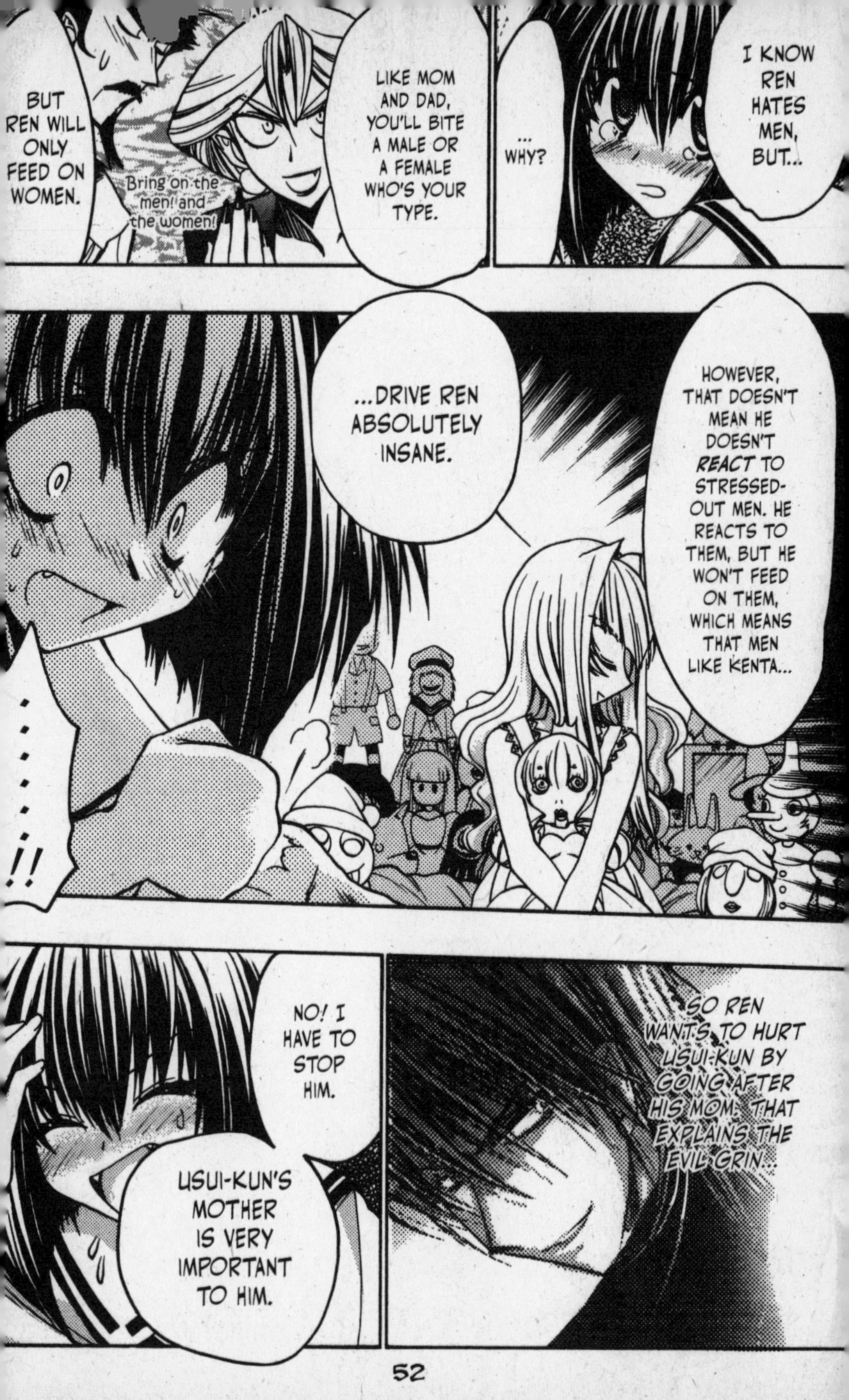
I KNOW REN HATES MEN, BUT...
... WHY?
LIKE MOM AND DAD, YOU'LL BITE A MALE OR A FEMALE WHO'S YOUR TYPE.
BUT REN WILL ONLY FEED ON WOMEN.
Bring on the men! and the women!
HOWEVER, THAT DOESN'T MEAN HE DOESN'T *REACT* TO STRESSED-OUT MEN. HE REACTS TO THEM, BUT HE WON'T FEED ON THEM, WHICH MEANS THAT MEN LIKE KENTA...
...DRIVE REN ABSOLUTELY INSANE.
.......!!
SO REN WANTS TO HURT USUI-KUN BY GOING AFTER HIS MOM. THAT EXPLAINS THE EVIL GRIN...
NO! I HAVE TO STOP HIM.
USUI-KUN'S MOTHER IS VERY IMPORTANT TO HIM.

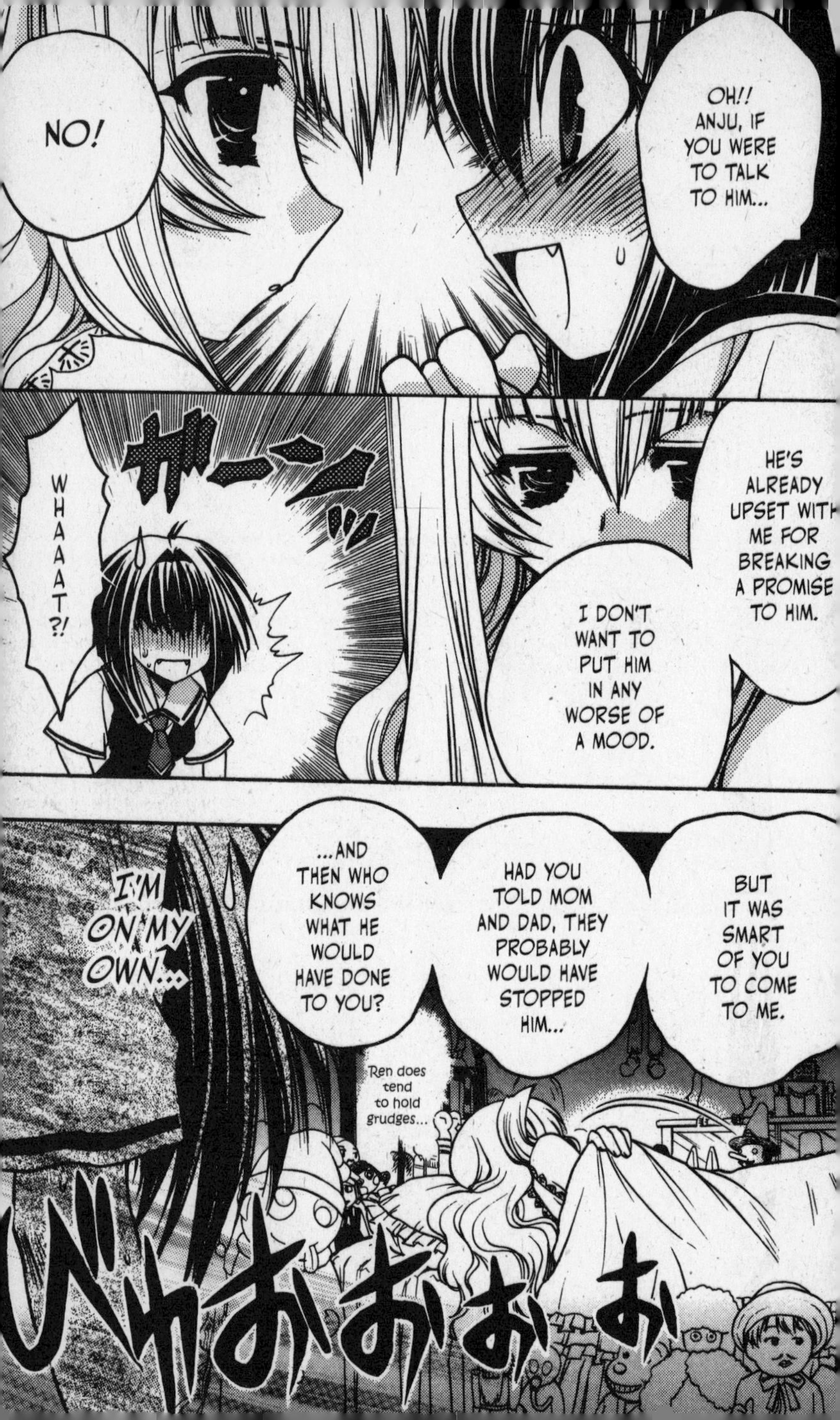
OH!! ANJU, IF YOU WERE TO TALK TO HIM...
NO!
HE'S ALREADY UPSET WITH ME FOR BREAKING A PROMISE TO HIM.
I DON'T WANT TO PUT HIM IN ANY WORSE OF A MOOD.
WHAAAAT?!
BUT IT WAS SMART OF YOU TO COME TO ME.
HAD YOU TOLD MOM AND DAD, THEY PROBABLY WOULD HAVE STOPPED HIM...
...AND THEN WHO KNOWS WHAT HE WOULD HAVE DONE TO YOU?
I'M ON MY OWN...
Ren does tend to hold grudges...

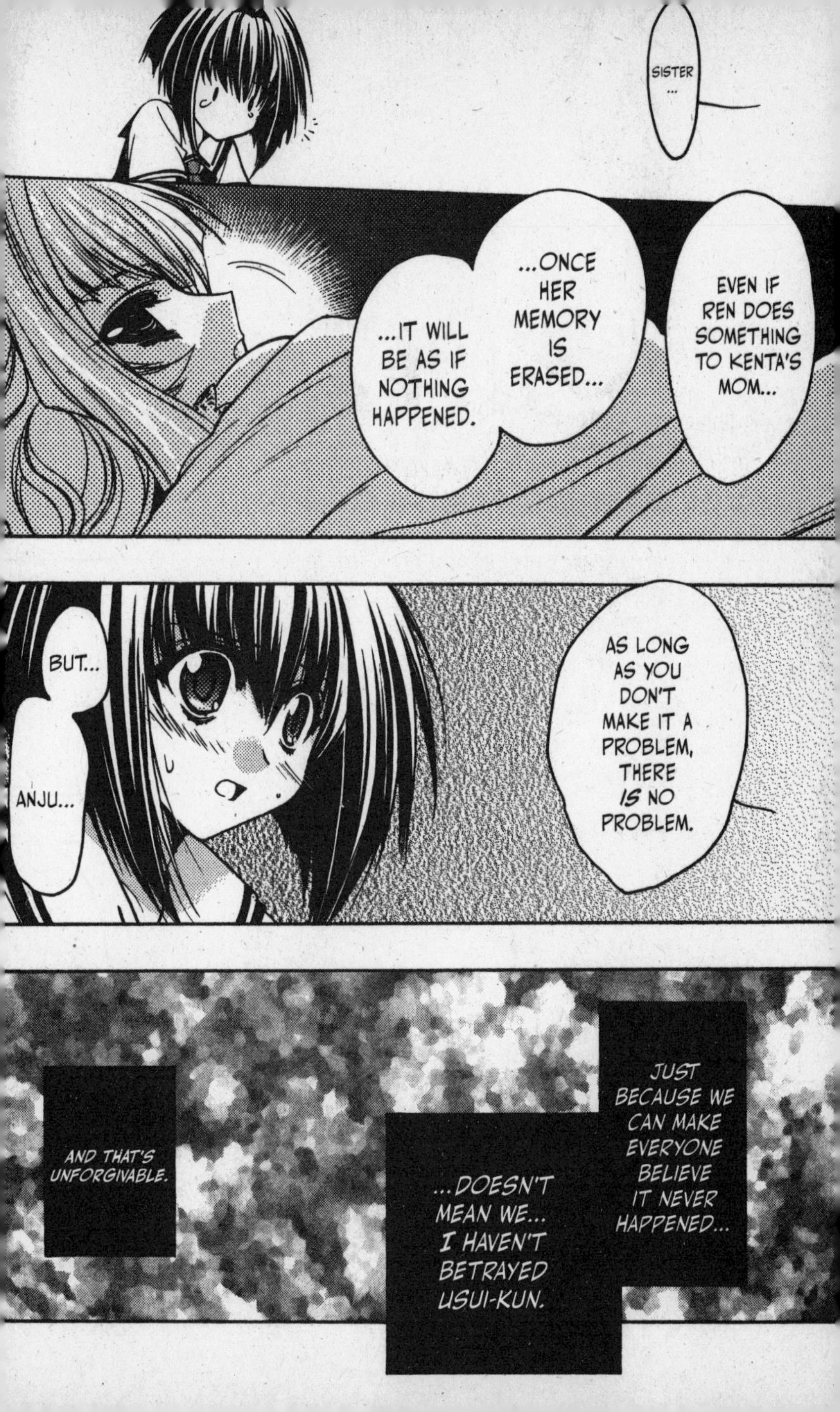
SISTER...
EVEN IF REN DOES SOMETHING TO KENTA'S MOM...
...ONCE HER MEMORY IS ERASED...
...IT WILL BE AS IF NOTHING HAPPENED.
AS LONG AS YOU DON'T MAKE IT A PROBLEM, THERE *IS* NO PROBLEM.
BUT...
ANJU...
JUST BECAUSE WE CAN MAKE EVERYONE BELIEVE IT NEVER HAPPENED...
...DOESN'T MEAN WE... I HAVEN'T BETRAYED USUI-KUN.
AND THAT'S UNFORGIVABLE.

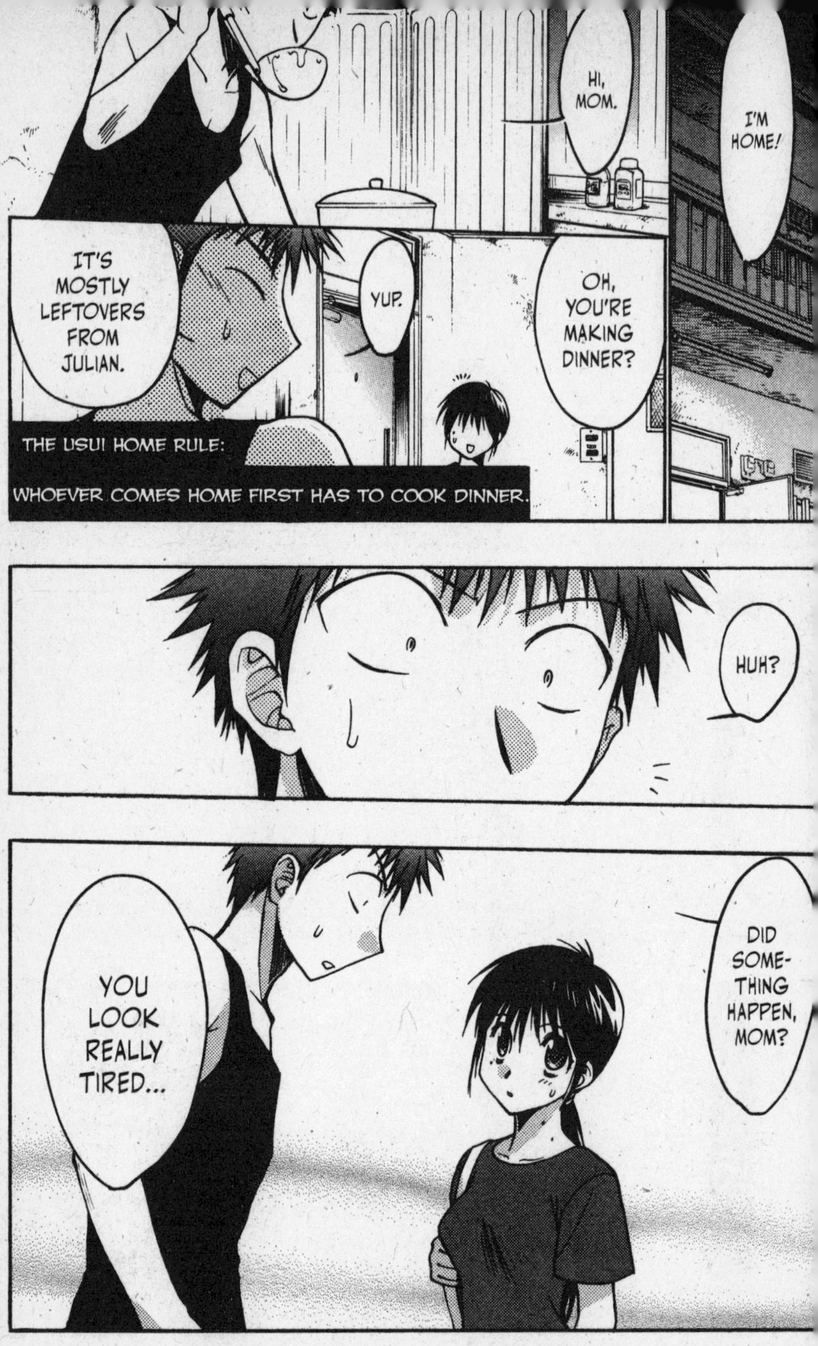
I'M HOME!
HI, MOM.
OH, YOU'RE MAKING DINNER?
YUP.
IT'S MOSTLY LEFTOVERS FROM JULIAN.
THE USUI HOME RULE:
WHOEVER COMES HOME FIRST HAS TO COOK DINNER.
HUH?
DID SOMETHING HAPPEN, MOM?
YOU LOOK REALLY TIRED...

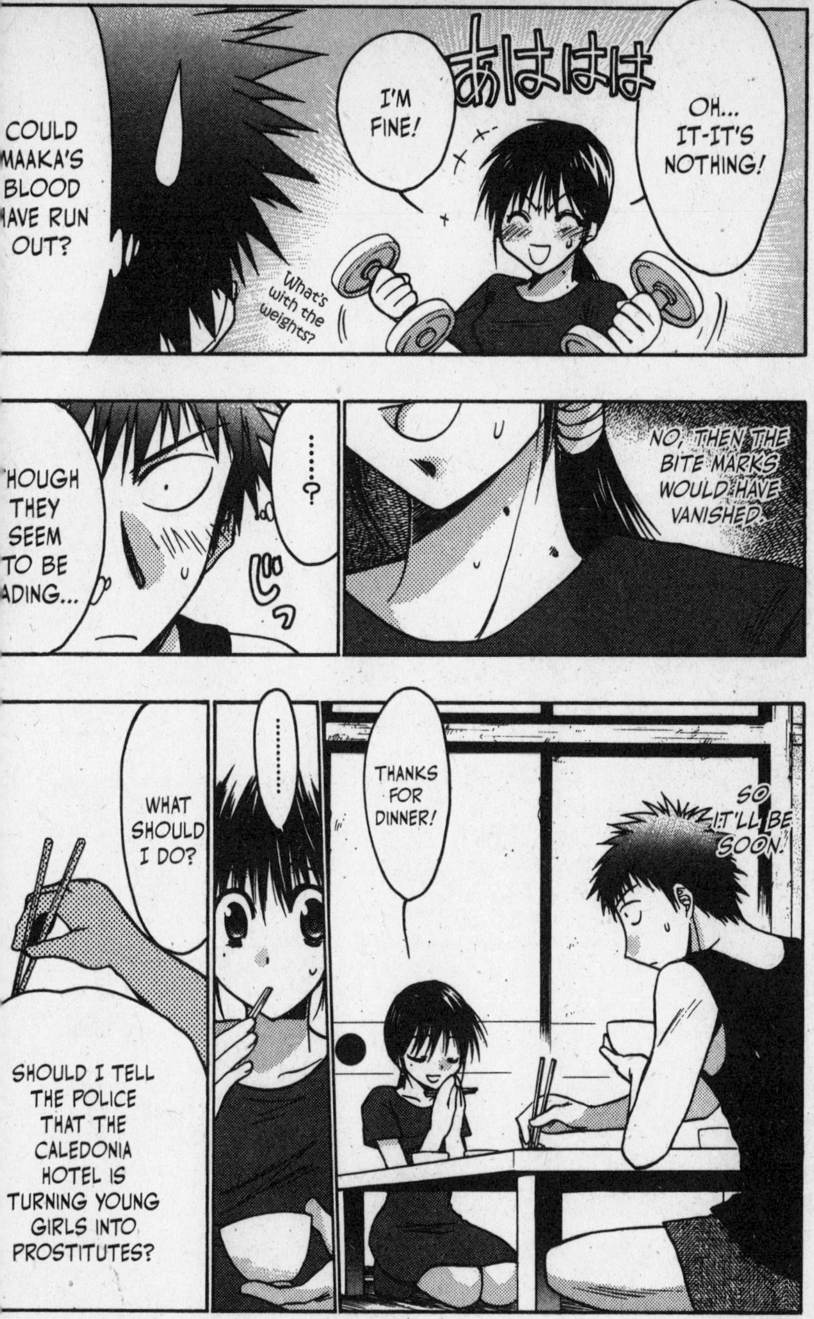

OH... IT-IT'S NOTHING!
あははは
I'M FINE!
What's with the weights?
COULD MAAKA'S BLOOD HAVE RUN OUT?
NO, THEN THE BITE MARKS WOULD HAVE VANISHED.
......?
じっ
THOUGH THEY SEEM TO BE FADING...
SO IT'LL BE SOON.
THANKS FOR DINNER!
....
WHAT SHOULD I DO?
SHOULD I TELL THE POLICE THAT THE CALEDONIA HOTEL IS TURNING YOUNG GIRLS INTO PROSTITUTES?

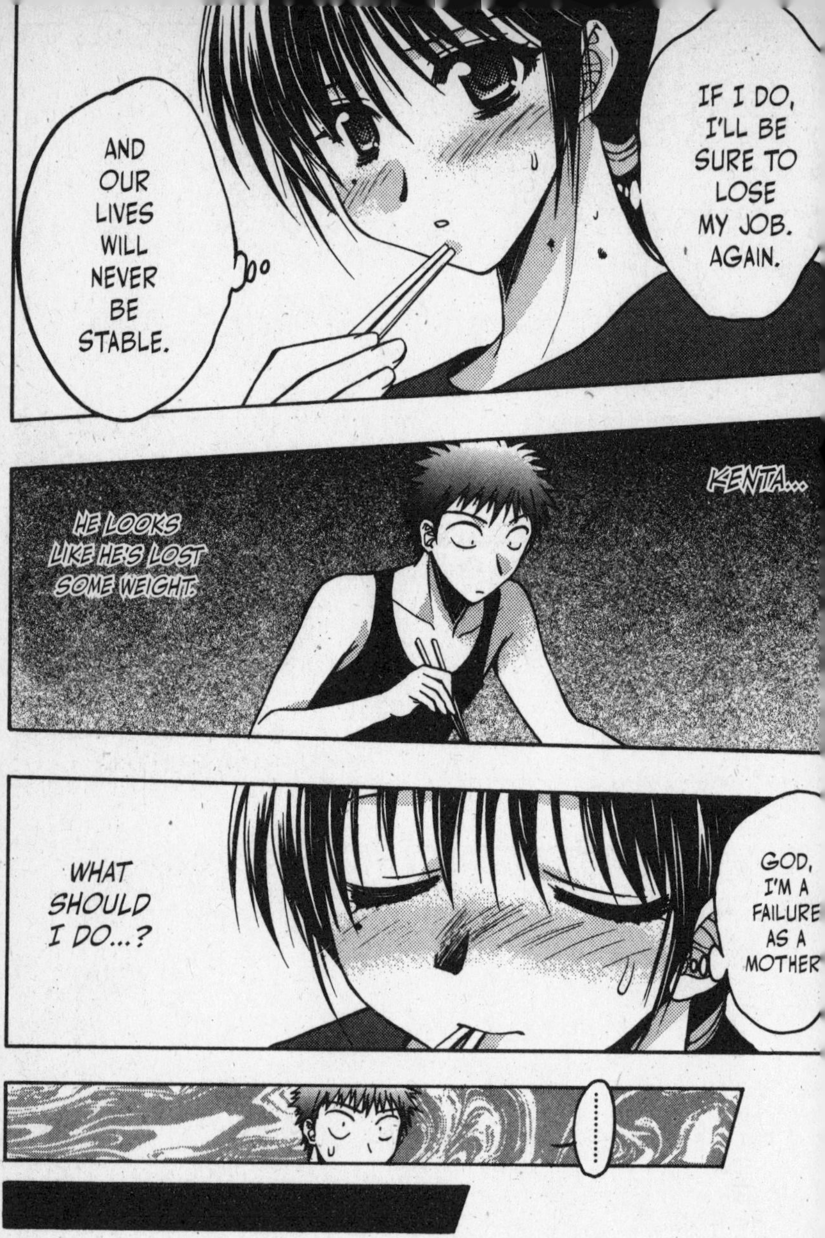
IF I DO, I'LL BE SURE TO LOSE MY JOB. AGAIN.
AND OUR LIVES WILL NEVER BE STABLE.
KENTA...
HE LOOKS LIKE HE'S LOST SOME WEIGHT.
GOD, I'M A FAILURE AS A MOTHER
WHAT SHOULD I DO...?
......

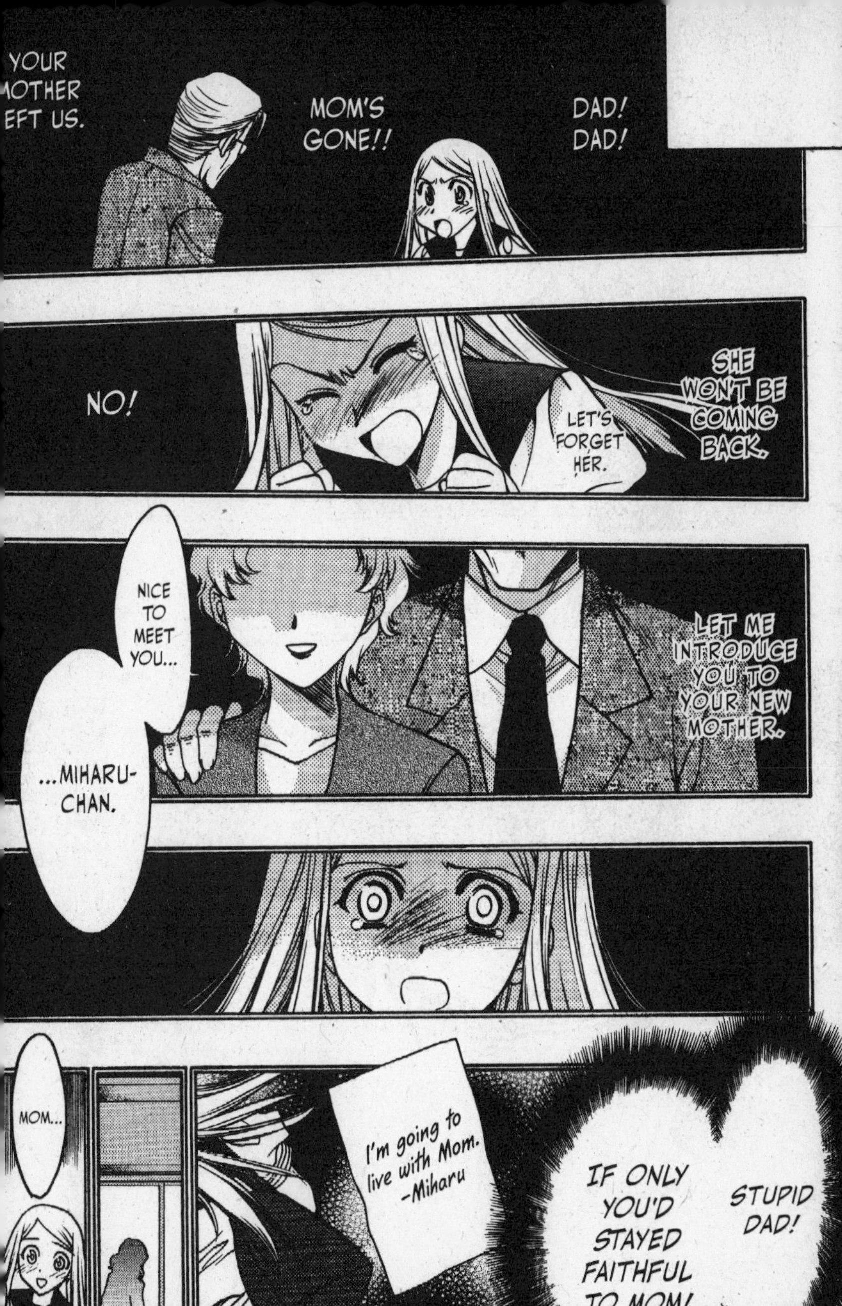
DAD! DAD!
MOM'S GONE!!
YOUR OTHER EFT US.
SHE WON'T BE COMING BACK.
LET'S FORGET HER.
NO!
LET ME INTRODUCE YOU TO YOUR NEW MOTHER.
NICE TO MEET YOU...
...MIHARU-CHAN.
STUPID DAD!
IF ONLY YOU'D STAYED FAITHFUL TO MOM!
I'm going to live with Mom. -Miharu
MOM...

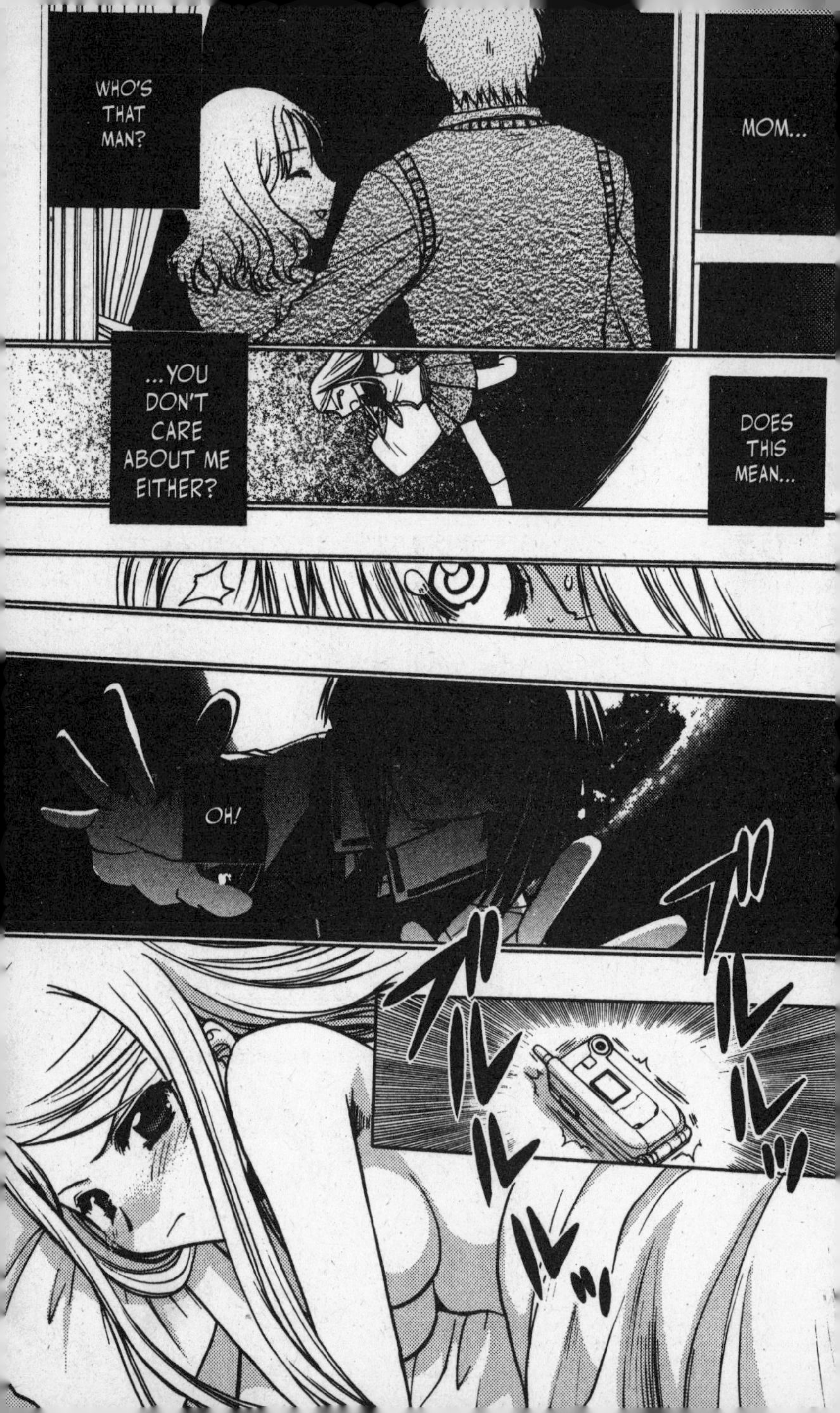
MOM...
WHO'S THAT MAN?
DOES THIS MEAN...
...YOU DON'T CARE ABOUT ME EITHER?
OH!

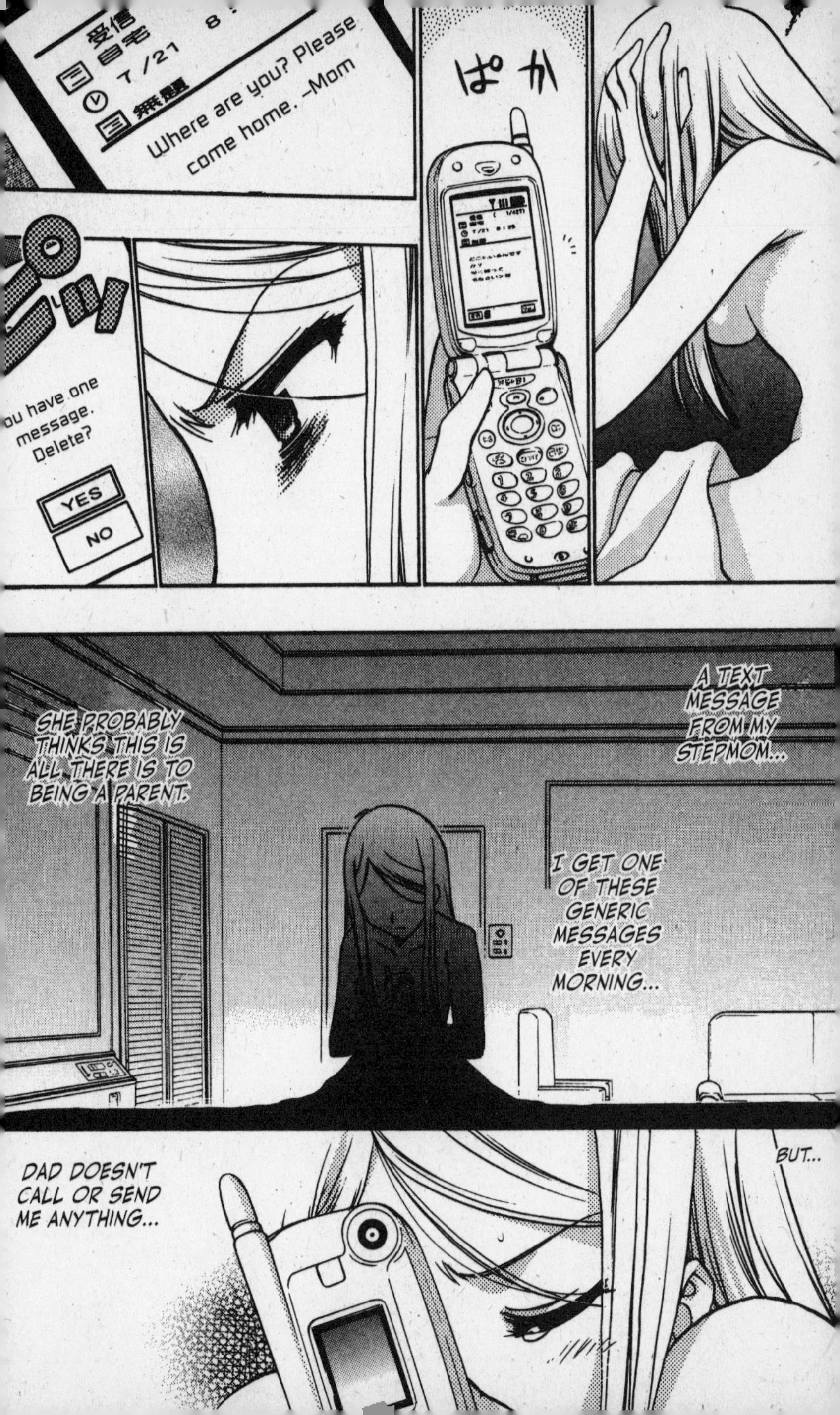
ぱか
受信
自宅
7/21 8:
無題
Where are you? Please come home. -Mom
ou have one message. Delete?
YES
NO
A TEXT MESSAGE FROM MY STEPMOM...
I GET ONE OF THESE GENERIC MESSAGES EVERY MORNING...
SHE PROBABLY THINKS THIS IS ALL THERE IS TO BEING A PARENT.
BUT...
DAD DOESN'T CALL OR SEND ME ANYTHING...

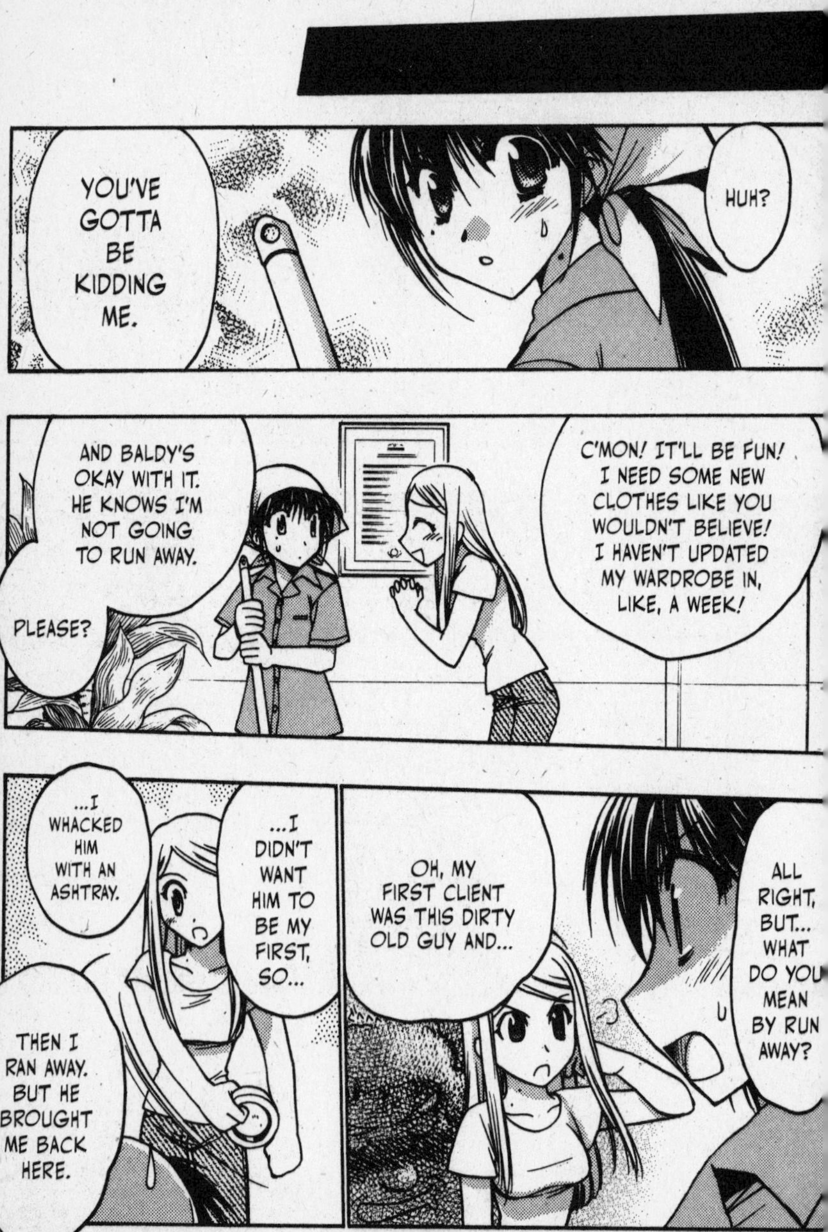
HUH?
YOU'VE GOTTA BE KIDDING ME.
C'MON! IT'LL BE FUN! I NEED SOME NEW CLOTHES LIKE YOU WOULDN'T BELIEVE! I HAVEN'T UPDATED MY WARDROBE IN, LIKE, A WEEK!
AND BALDY'S OKAY WITH IT. HE KNOWS I'M NOT GOING TO RUN AWAY.
PLEASE?
ALL RIGHT, BUT... WHAT DO YOU MEAN BY RUN AWAY?
OH, MY FIRST CLIENT WAS THIS DIRTY OLD GUY AND...
...I DIDN'T WANT HIM TO BE MY FIRST, SO...
...I WHACKED HIM WITH AN ASHTRAY.
THEN I RAN AWAY. BUT HE BROUGHT ME BACK HERE.

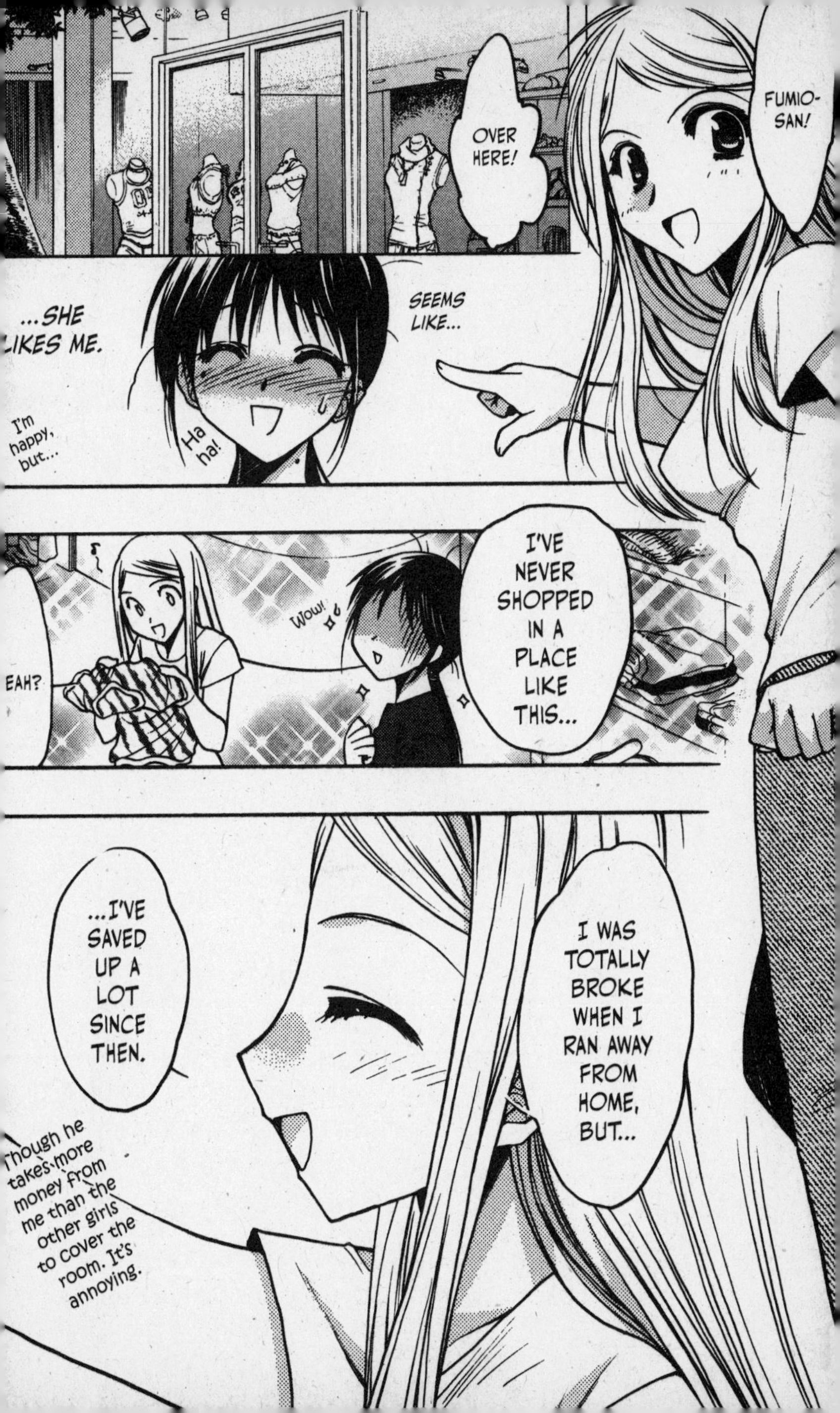
FUMIO-SAN!
OVER HERE!
SEEMS LIKE...
...SHE LIKES ME.
Ha ha!
I'm happy, but...
I'VE NEVER SHOPPED IN A PLACE LIKE THIS...
Wow!
EAH?
I WAS TOTALLY BROKE WHEN I RAN AWAY FROM HOME, BUT...
...I'VE SAVED UP A LOT SINCE THEN.
Though he takes more money from me than the other girls to cover the room. It's annoying.

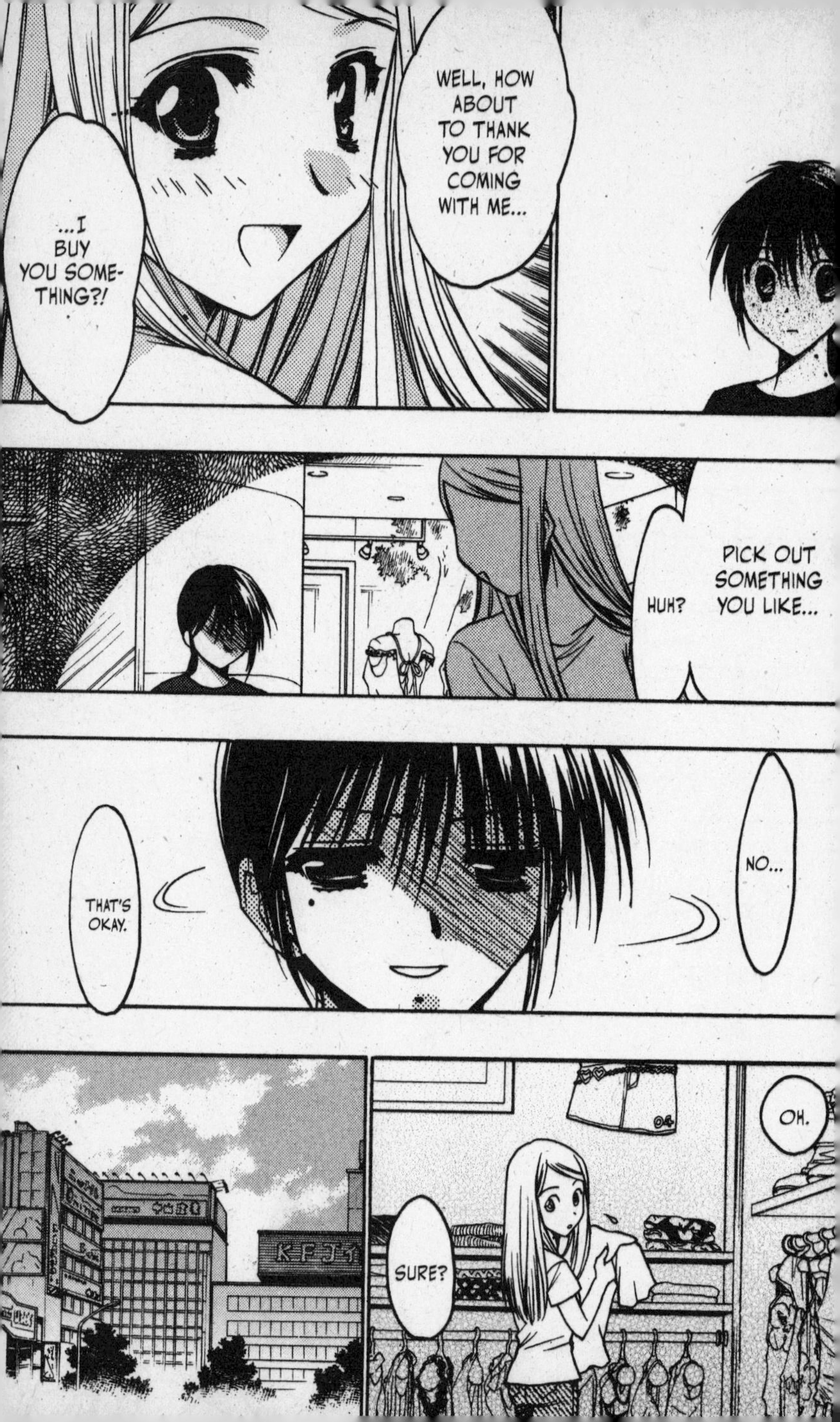
WELL, HOW ABOUT TO THANK YOU FOR COMING WITH ME...
...I BUY YOU SOME-THING?!
PICK OUT SOMETHING YOU LIKE...
HUH?
NO...
THAT'S OKAY.
OH.
SURE?

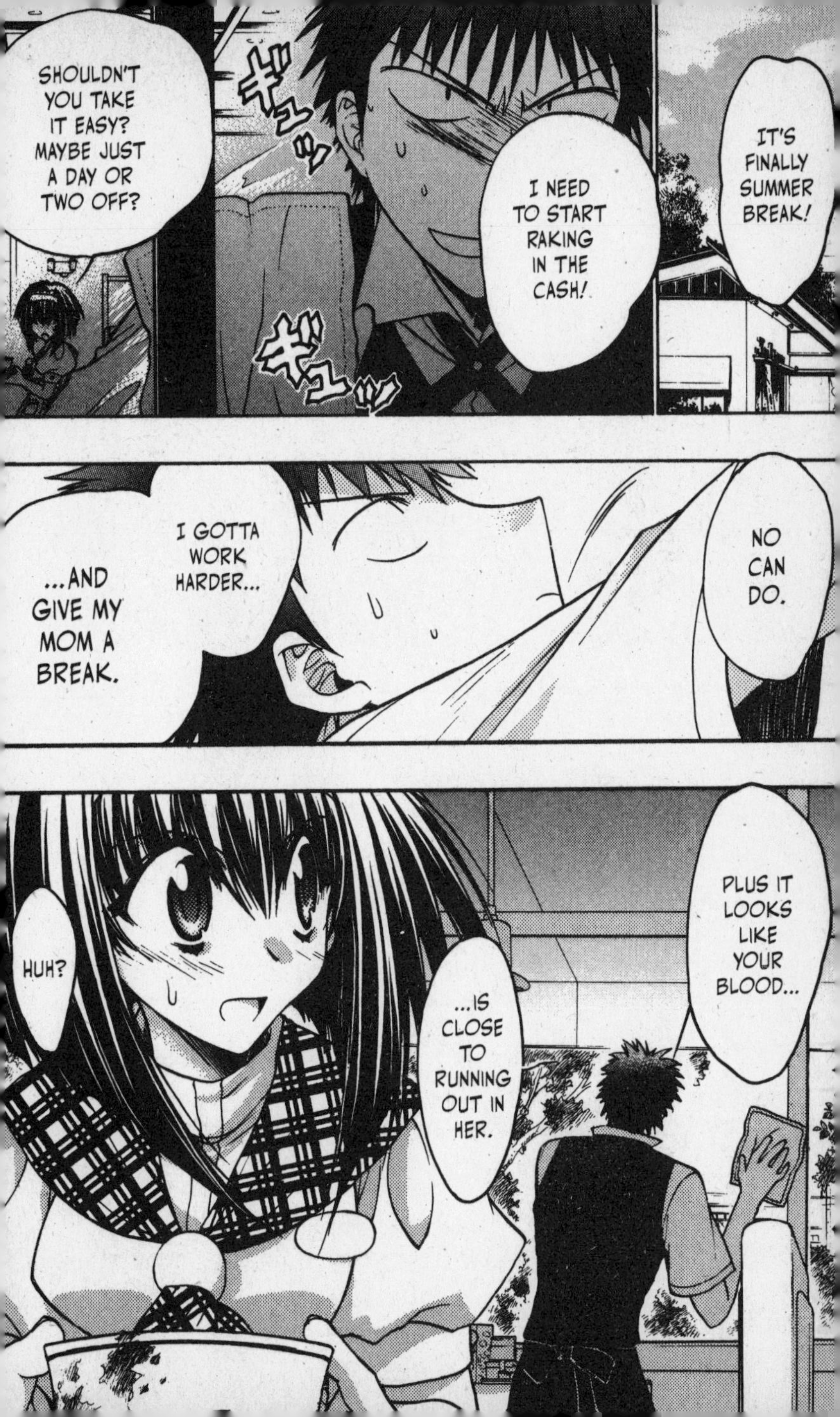
IT'S FINALLY SUMMER BREAK!
I NEED TO START RAKING IN THE CASH!
ギュッ
ギュッ
SHOULDN'T YOU TAKE IT EASY? MAYBE JUST A DAY OR TWO OFF?
NO CAN DO.
I GOTTA WORK HARDER...
...AND GIVE MY MOM A BREAK.
PLUS IT LOOKS LIKE YOUR BLOOD...
...IS CLOSE TO RUNNING OUT IN HER.
HUH?

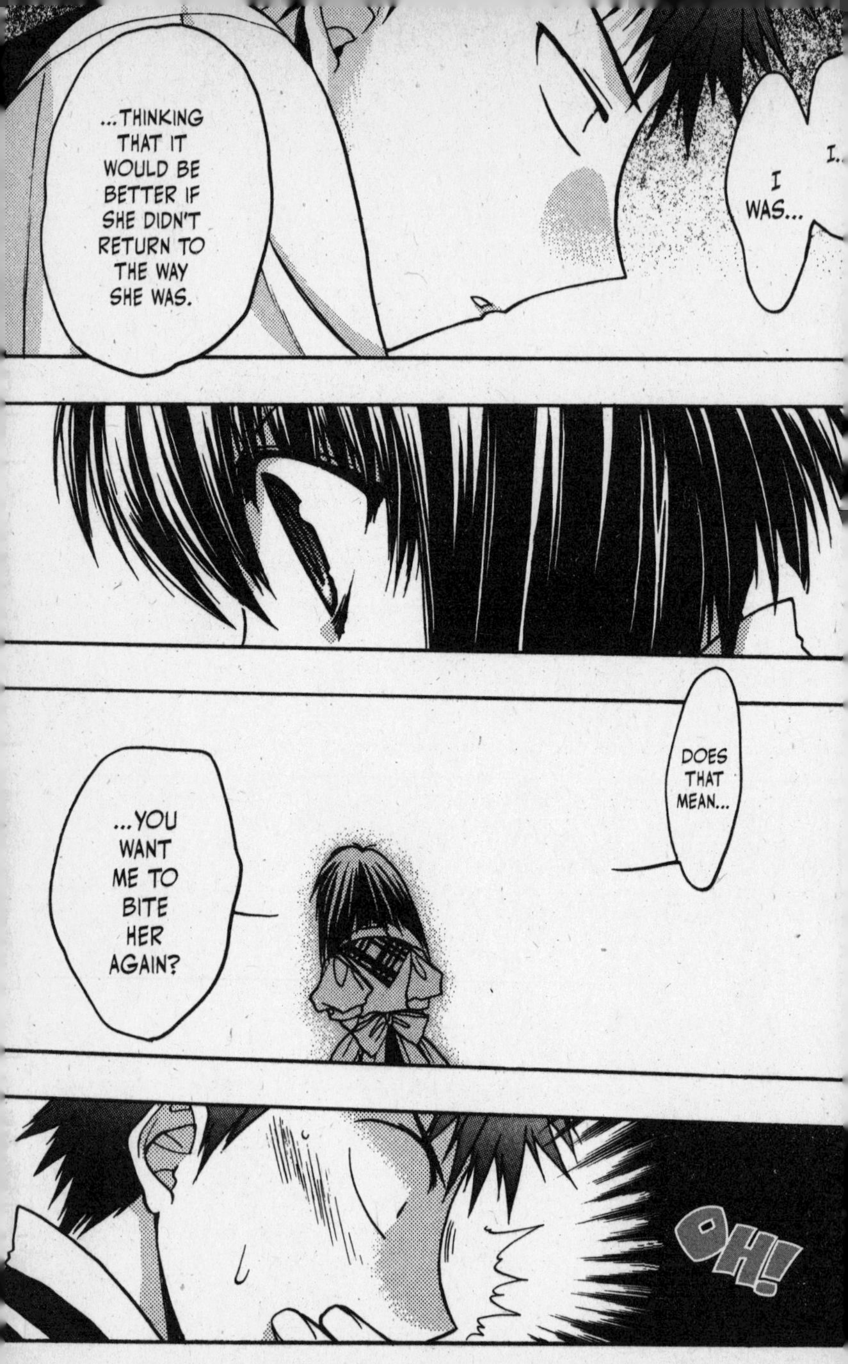
I... I WAS...
...THINKING THAT IT WOULD BE BETTER IF SHE DIDN'T RETURN TO THE WAY SHE WAS.
DOES THAT MEAN...
...YOU WANT ME TO BITE HER AGAIN?
OH!

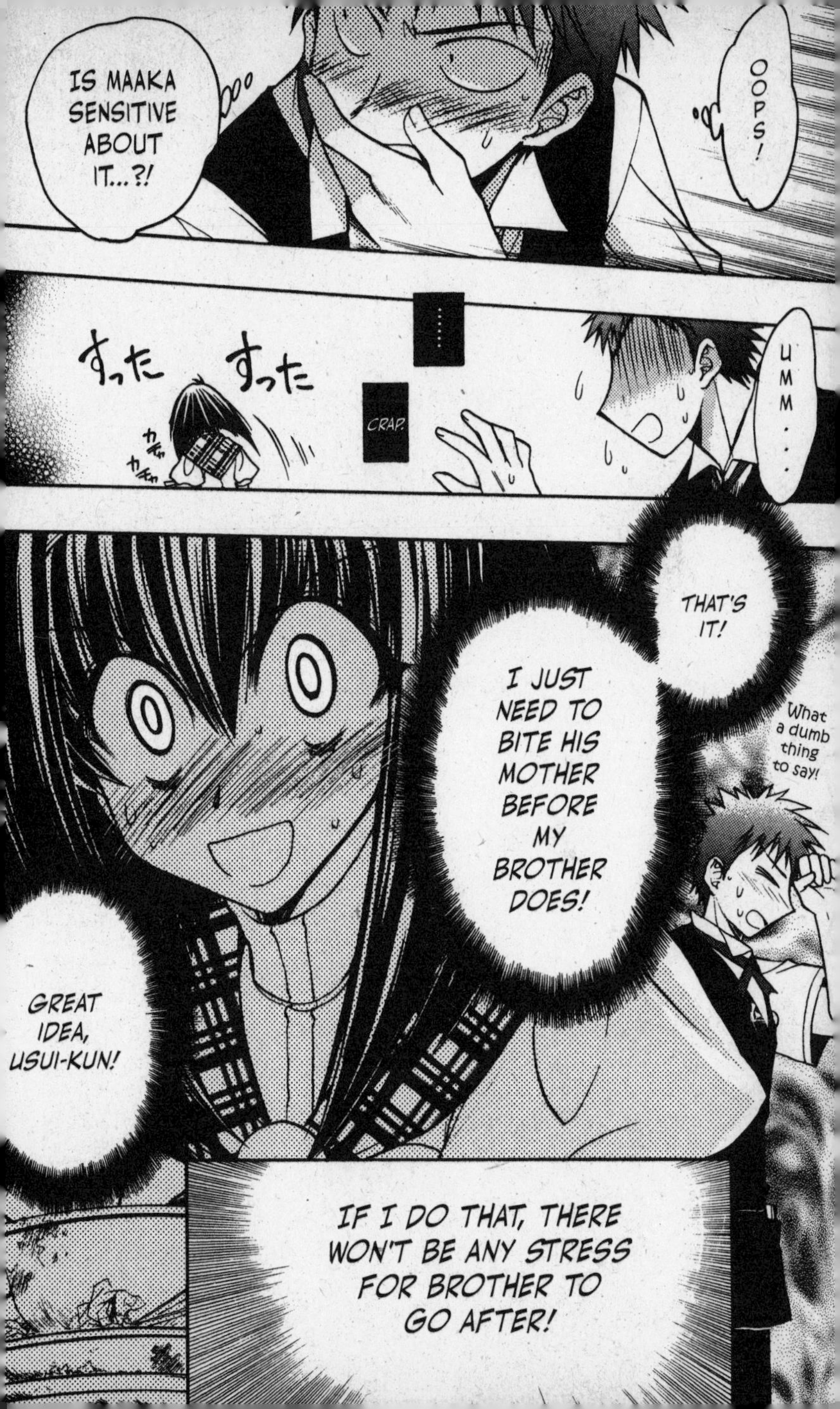
OOPS!
IS MAAKA SENSITIVE ABOUT IT...?!
UMM...
......
CRAP.
すった すった
THAT'S IT!
I JUST NEED TO BITE HIS MOTHER BEFORE MY BROTHER DOES!
What a dumb thing to say!
GREAT IDEA, USUI-KUN!
IF I DO THAT, THERE WON'T BE ANY STRESS FOR BROTHER TO GO AFTER!

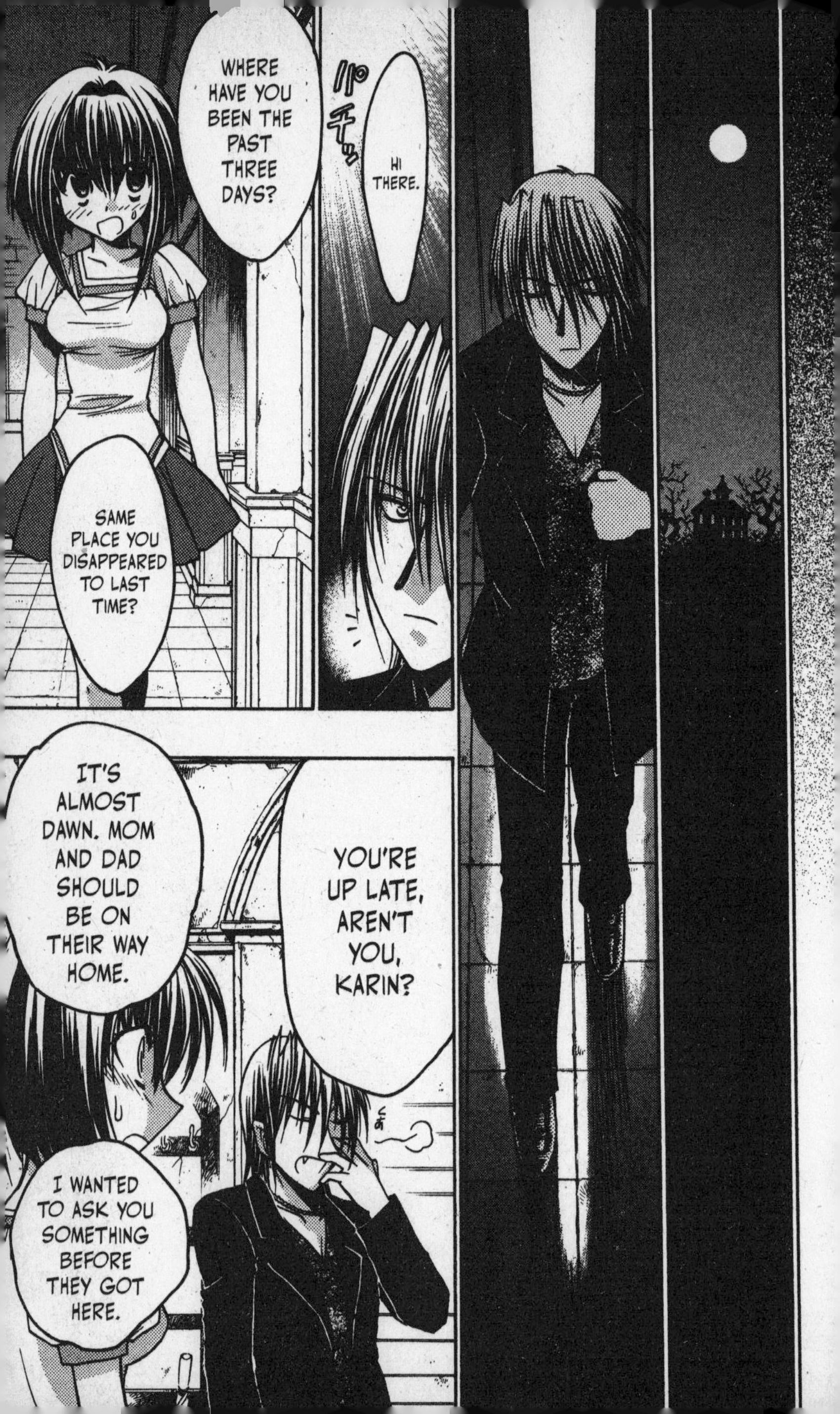
パチッ
HI THERE.
WHERE HAVE YOU BEEN THE PAST THREE DAYS?
SAME PLACE YOU DISAPPEARED TO LAST TIME?
YOU'RE UP LATE, AREN'T YOU, KARIN?
IT'S ALMOST DAWN. MOM AND DAD SHOULD BE ON THEIR WAY HOME.
I WANTED TO ASK YOU SOMETHING BEFORE THEY GOT HERE.

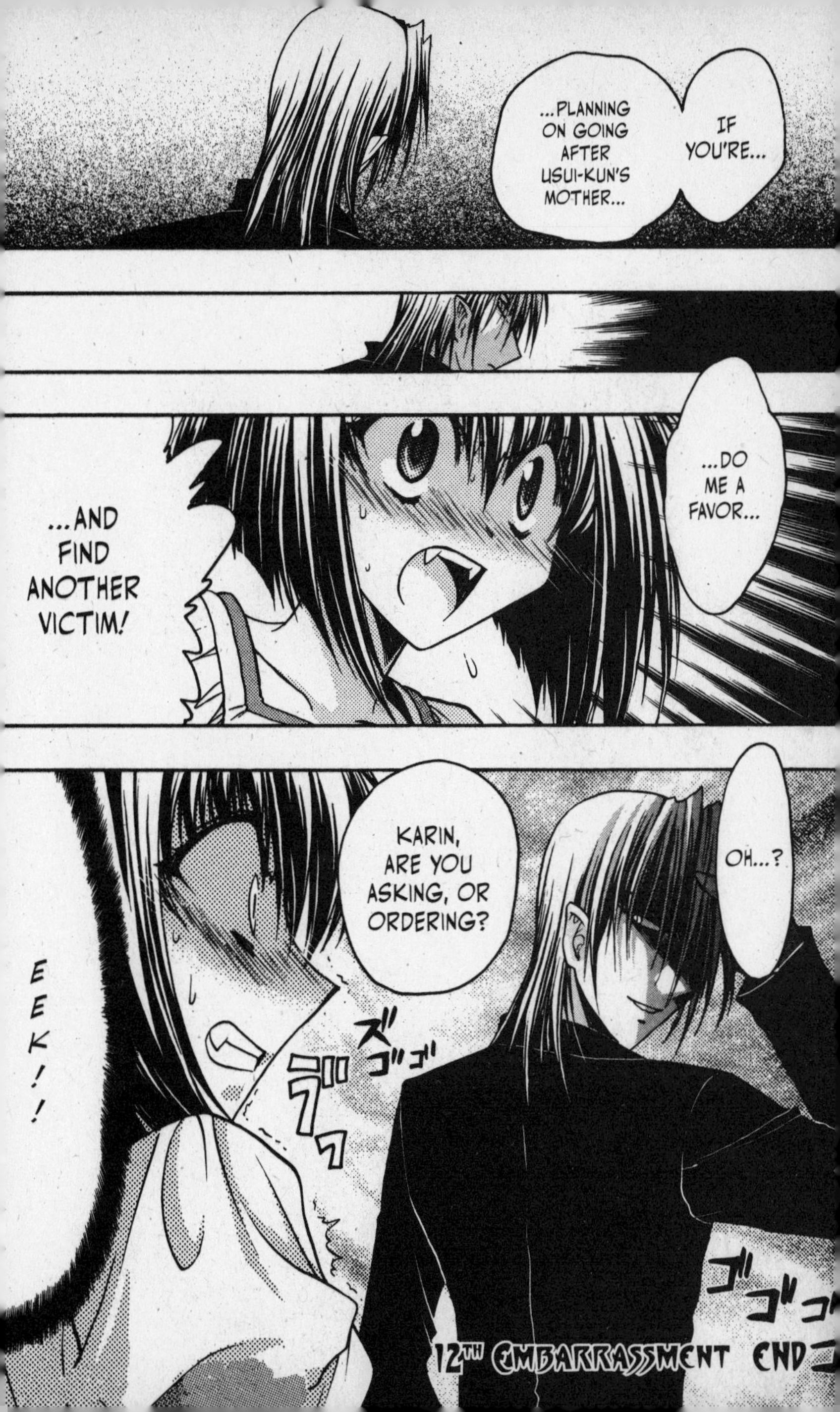
IF YOU'RE...
...PLANNING ON GOING AFTER USUI-KUN'S MOTHER...
...DO ME A FAVOR...
...AND FIND ANOTHER VICTIM!
OH...?
KARIN, ARE YOU ASKING, OR ORDERING?
ズゴゴ
EEK!!
ゴゴゴ
12TH EMBARRASSMENT END

13TH EMBARRASSMENT) FUMIO'S CHOICE AND HARUMI'S RESOLUTION
~RESOLUTION~

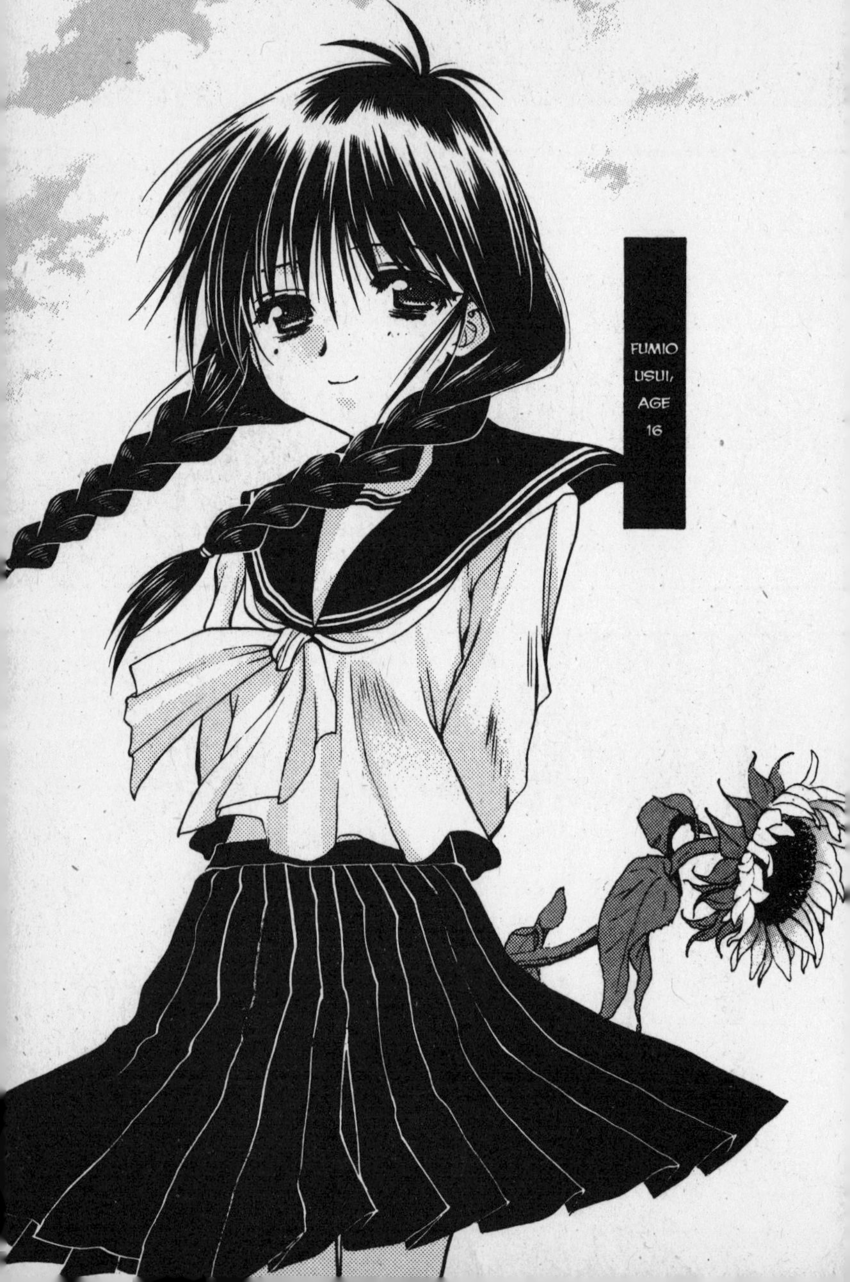
FUMIO USUI, AGE 16

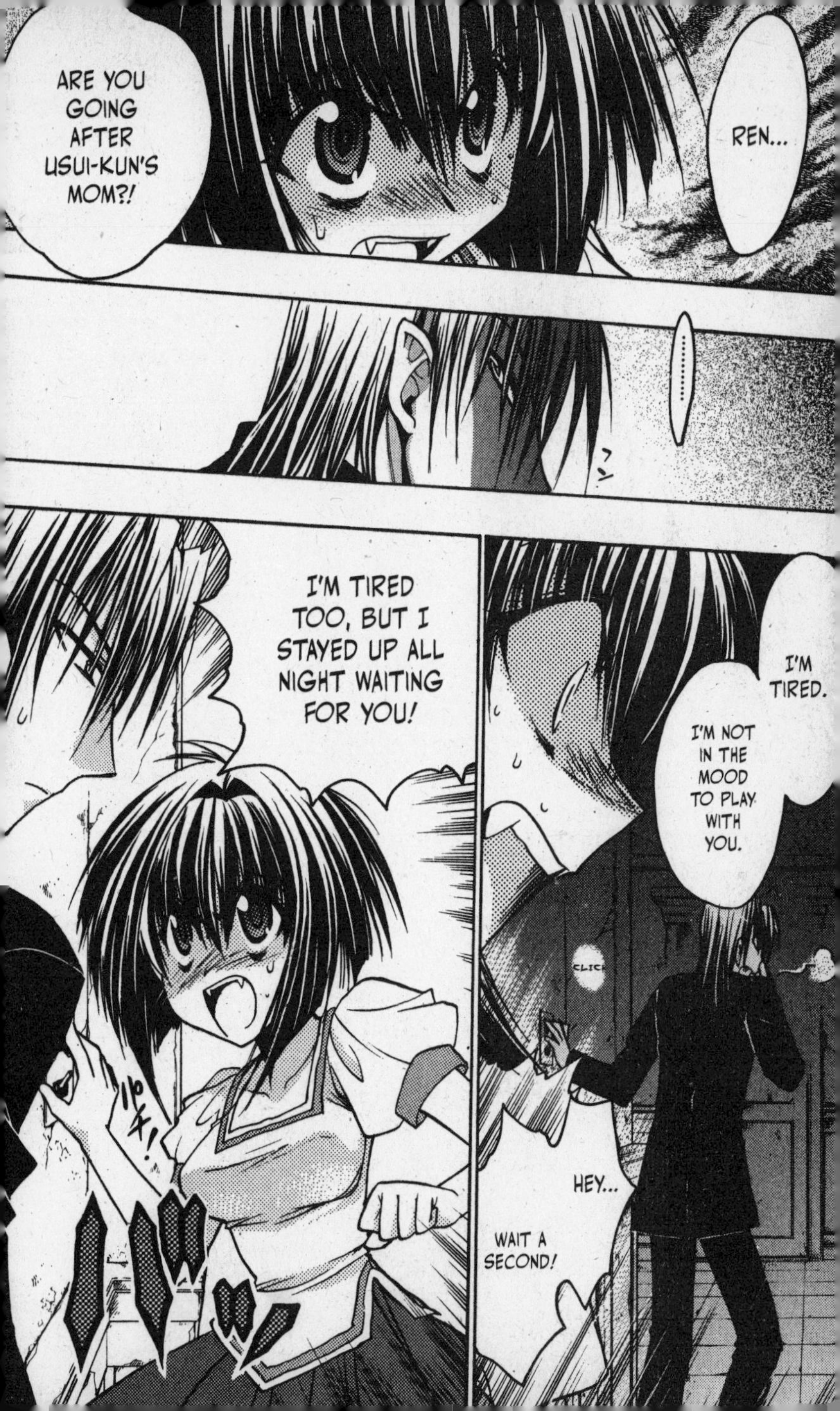
REN...
ARE YOU GOING AFTER USUI-KUN'S MOM?!
......
I'M TIRED.
I'M NOT IN THE MOOD TO PLAY WITH YOU.
CLICK
HEY...
WAIT A SECOND!
I'M TIRED TOO, BUT I STAYED UP ALL NIGHT WAITING FOR YOU!

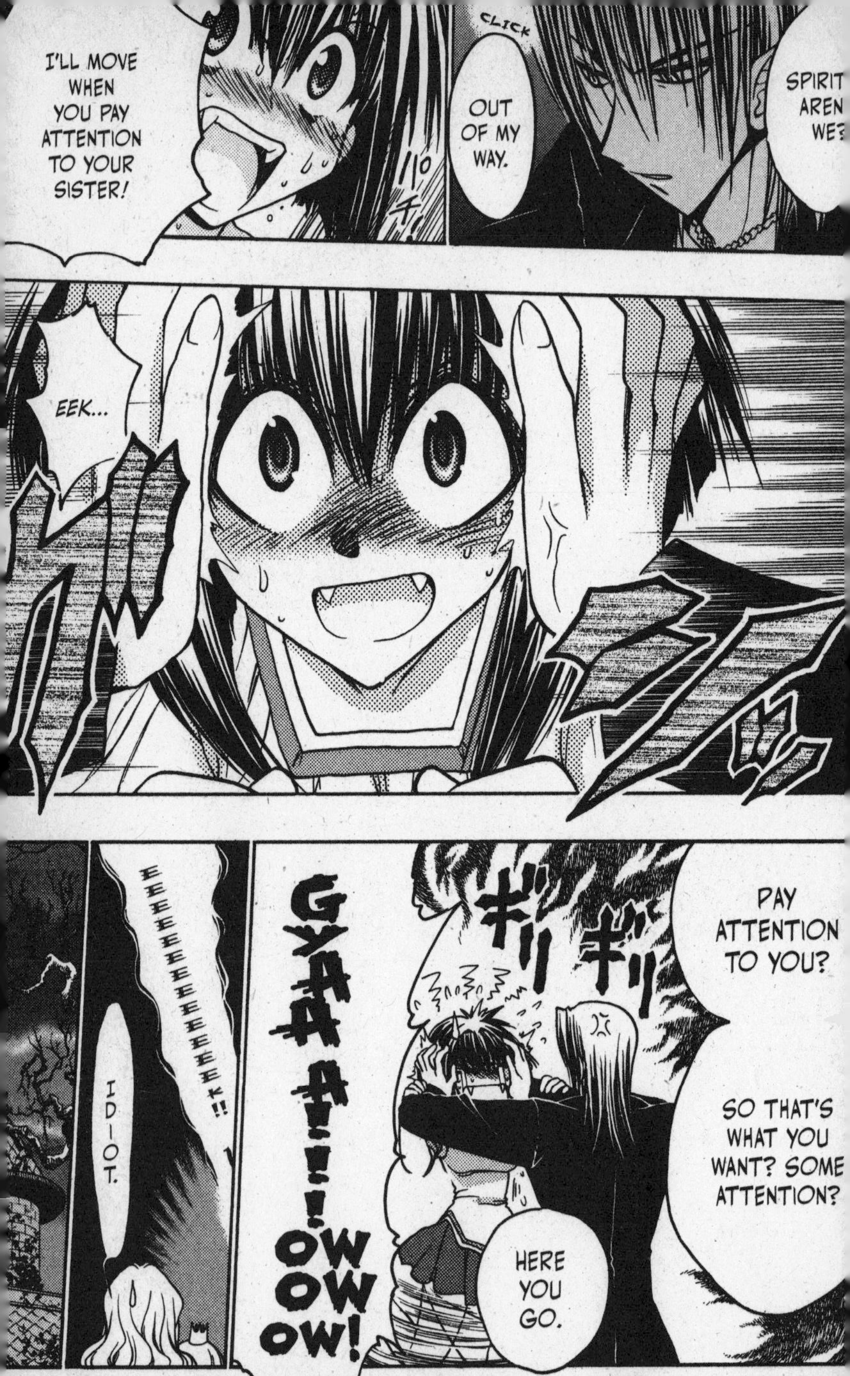

SPIRIT AREN WE?
CLICK
OUT OF MY WAY.
I'LL MOVE WHEN YOU PAY ATTENTION TO YOUR SISTER!
EEK...
PAY ATTENTION TO YOU?
SO THAT'S WHAT YOU WANT? SOME ATTENTION?
HERE YOU GO.
GYAAA!!! OW OW OW!
EEEEEEEEEEEEEEK!!
IDIOT.

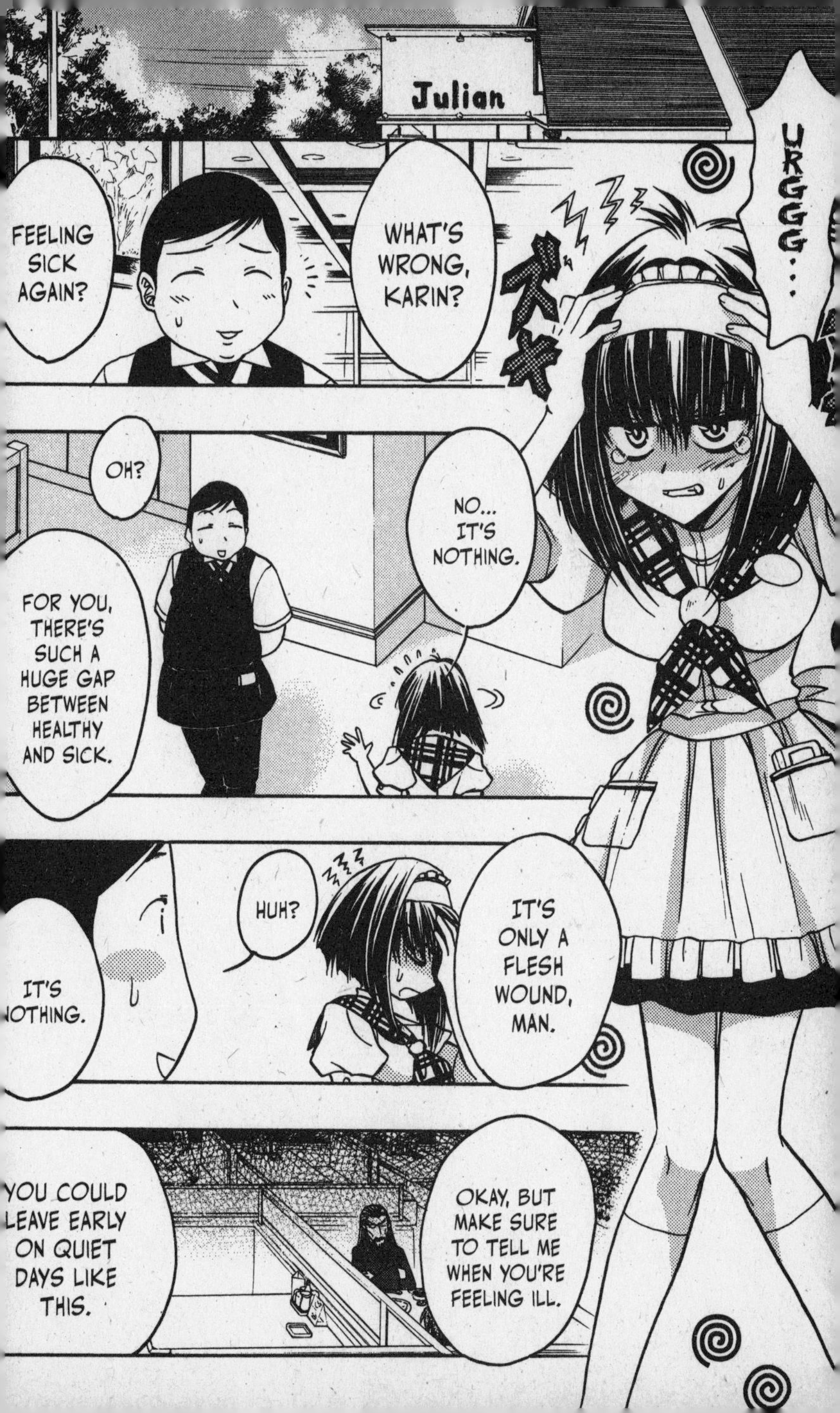

Julian
URGGG...
WHAT'S WRONG, KARIN?
FEELING SICK AGAIN?
NO... IT'S NOTHING.
OH?
FOR YOU, THERE'S SUCH A HUGE GAP BETWEEN HEALTHY AND SICK.
IT'S ONLY A FLESH WOUND, MAN.
HUH?
IT'S NOTHING.
OKAY, BUT MAKE SURE TO TELL ME WHEN YOU'RE FEELING ILL.
YOU COULD LEAVE EARLY ON QUIET DAYS LIKE THIS.

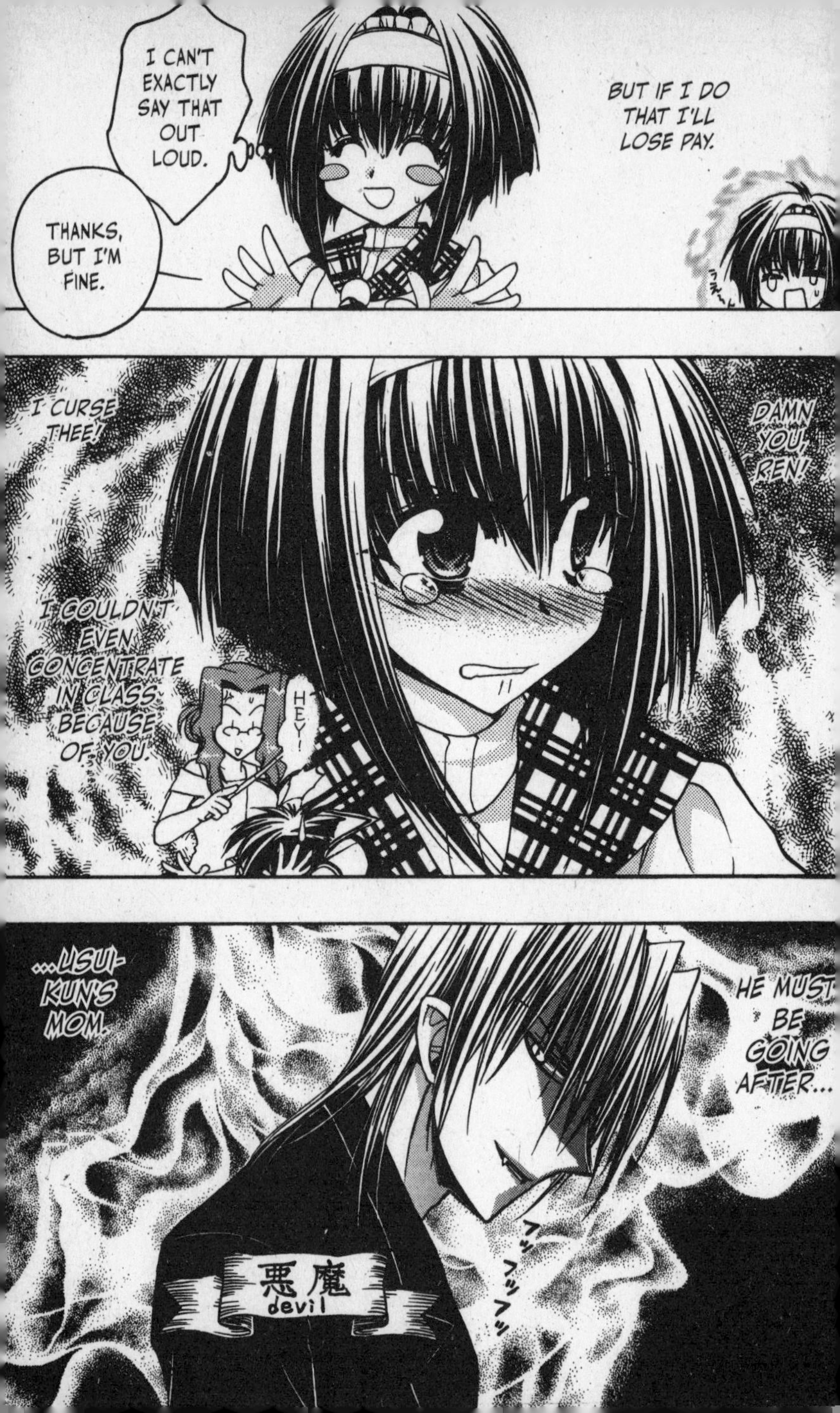

BUT IF I DO THAT I'LL LOSE PAY.
I CAN'T EXACTLY SAY THAT OUT LOUD.
THANKS, BUT I'M FINE.
DAMN YOU, REN!
I CURSE THEE!
HEY!
I COULDN'T EVEN CONCENTRATE IN CLASS BECAUSE OF YOU.
HE MUST BE GOING AFTER...
...USUI-KUN'S MOM.
悪魔
devil

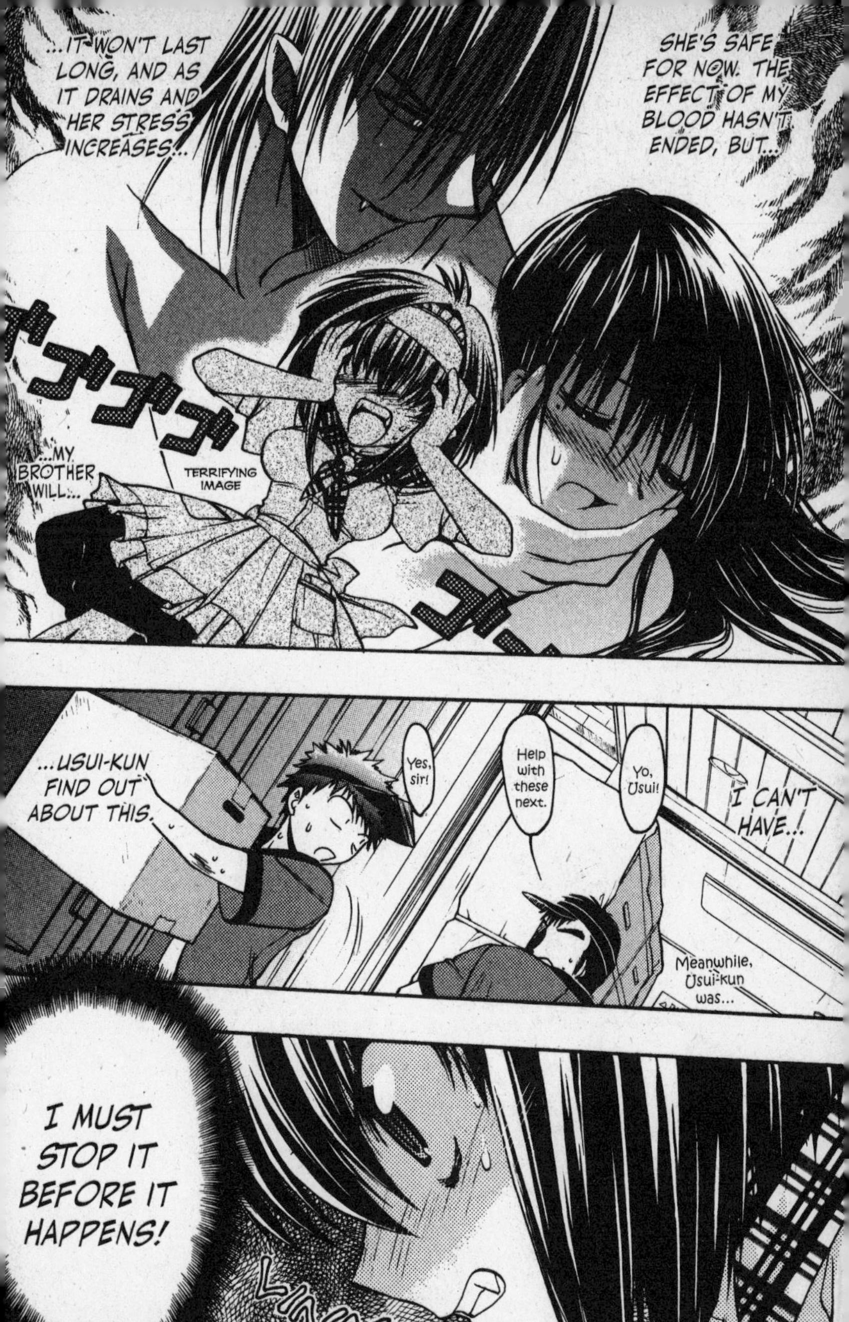
SHE'S SAFE FOR NOW. THE EFFECT OF MY BLOOD HASN'T ENDED, BUT...
...IT WON'T LAST LONG, AND AS IT DRAINS AND HER STRESS INCREASES...
...MY BROTHER WILL...
TERRIFYING IMAGE
I CAN'T HAVE...
Yo, Usui!
Help with these next.
Yes, sir!
Meanwhile, Usui-kun was...
...USUI-KUN FIND OUT ABOUT THIS.
I MUST STOP IT BEFORE IT HAPPENS!

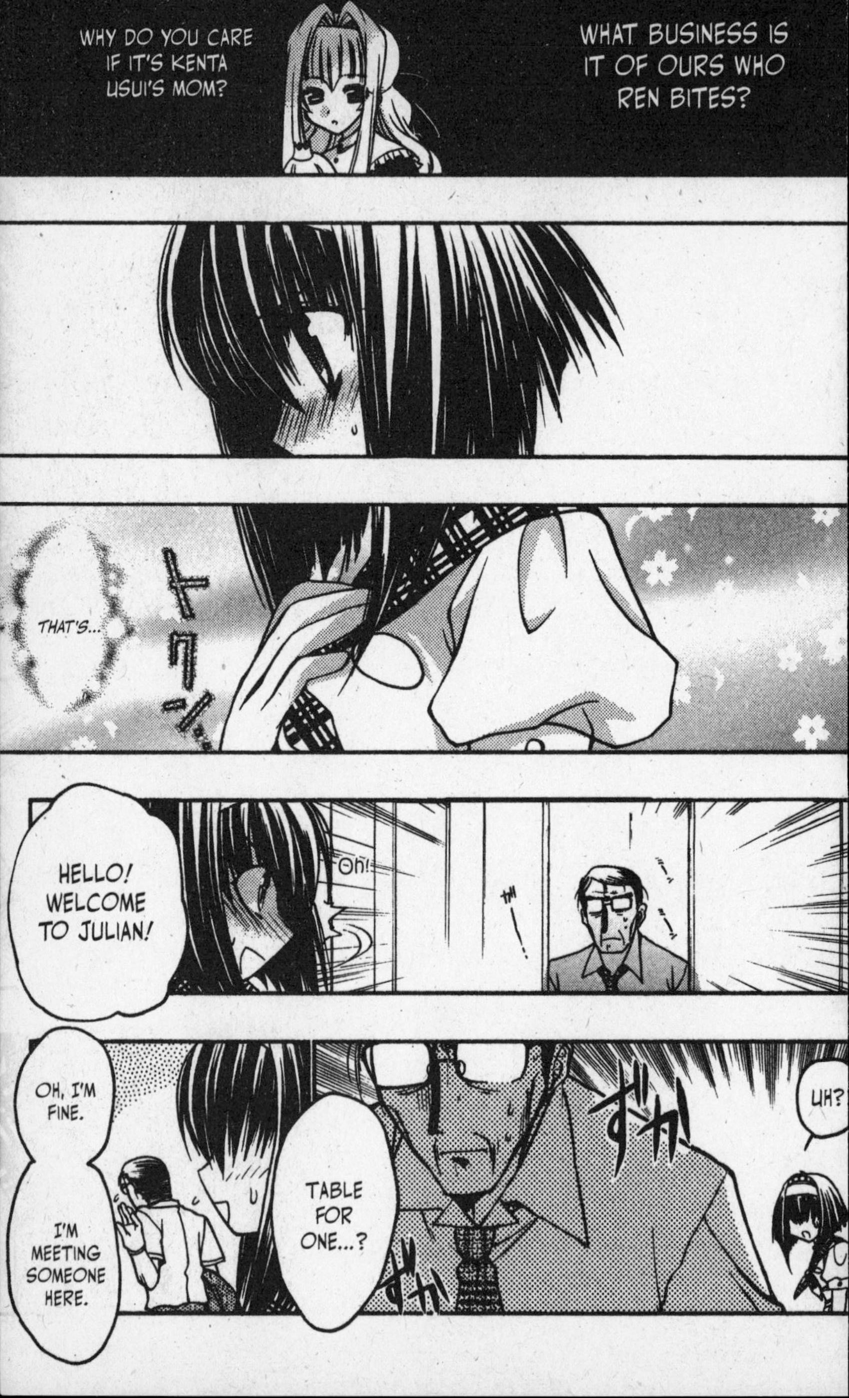
WHAT BUSINESS IS IT OF OURS WHO REN BITES?
WHY DO YOU CARE IF IT'S KENTA USUI'S MOM?
THAT'S...
Oh!
HELLO! WELCOME TO JULIAN!
UH?
TABLE FOR ONE...?
OH, I'M FINE.
I'M MEETING SOMEONE HERE.

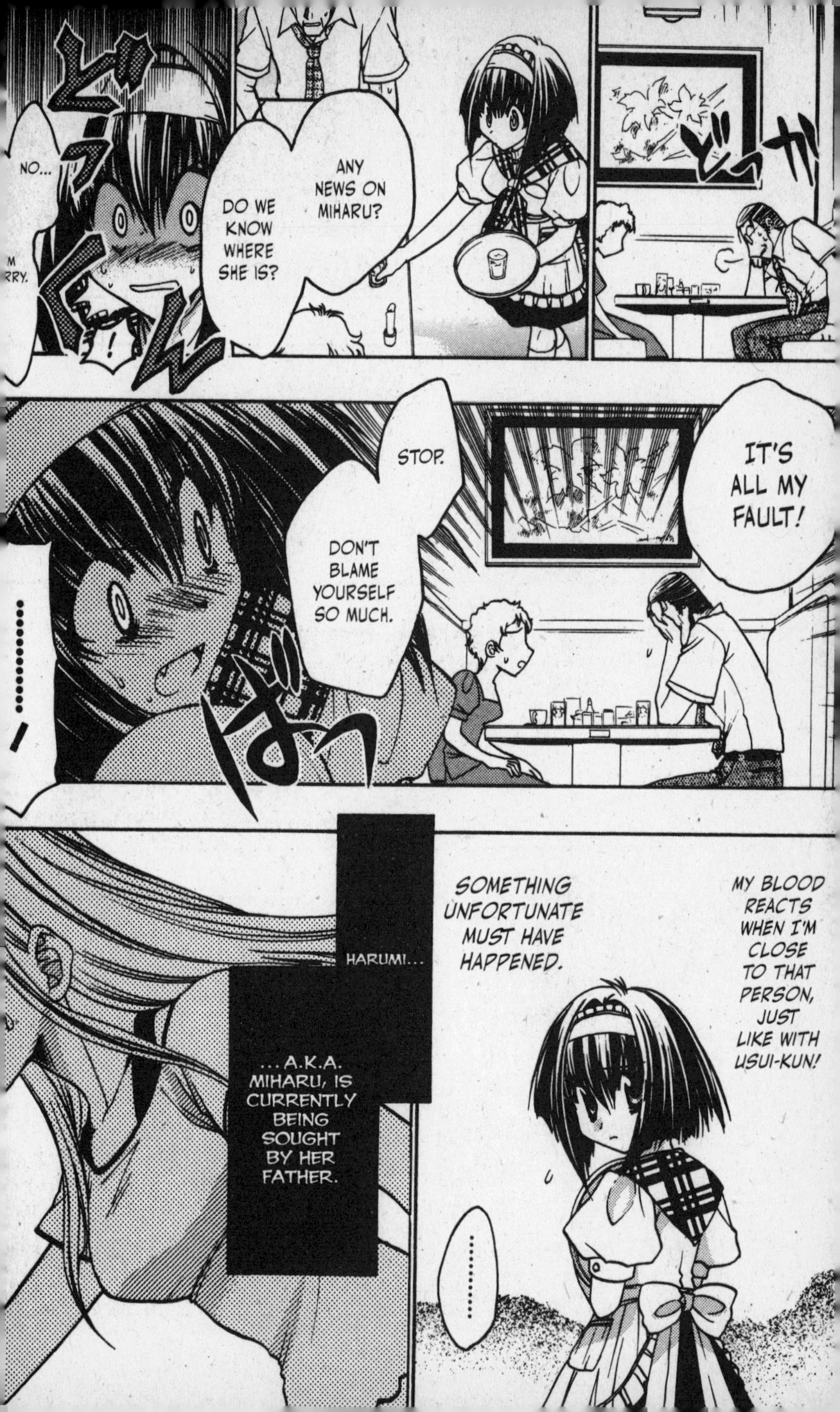
ANY NEWS ON MIHARU?
DO WE KNOW WHERE SHE IS?
NO...
IT'S ALL MY FAULT!
STOP.
DON'T BLAME YOURSELF SO MUCH.
..........!
MY BLOOD REACTS WHEN I'M CLOSE TO THAT PERSON, JUST LIKE WITH USUI-KUN!
SOMETHING UNFORTUNATE MUST HAVE HAPPENED.
......
HARUMI...
...A.K.A. MIHARU, IS CURRENTLY BEING SOUGHT BY HER FATHER.

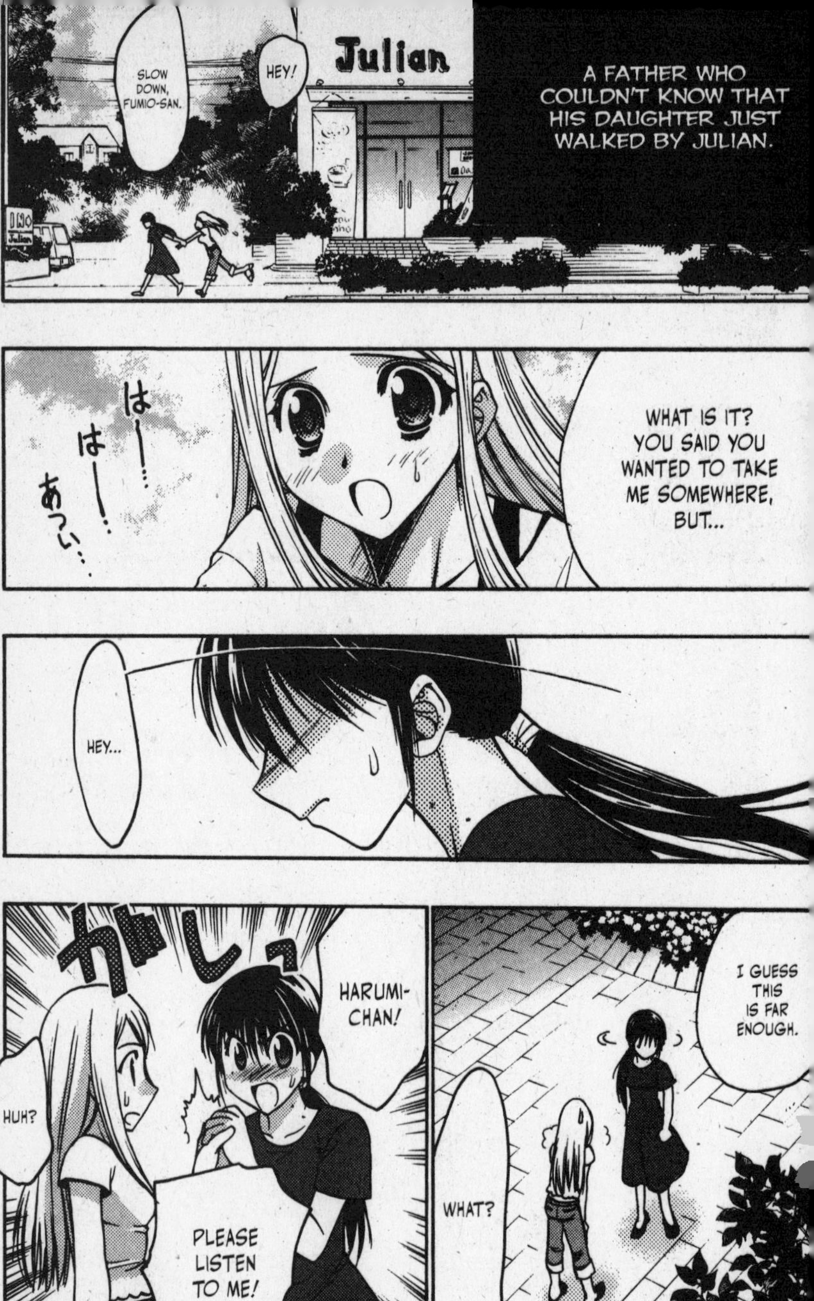
A FATHER WHO COULDN'T KNOW THAT HIS DAUGHTER JUST WALKED BY JULIAN.
Julian
HEY!
SLOW DOWN, FUMIO-SAN.
WHAT IS IT? YOU SAID YOU WANTED TO TAKE ME SOMEWHERE, BUT...
はー…はー…あつい…
HEY...
I GUESS THIS IS FAR ENOUGH.
WHAT?
HARUMI-CHAN!
がしっ
HUH?
PLEASE LISTEN TO ME!

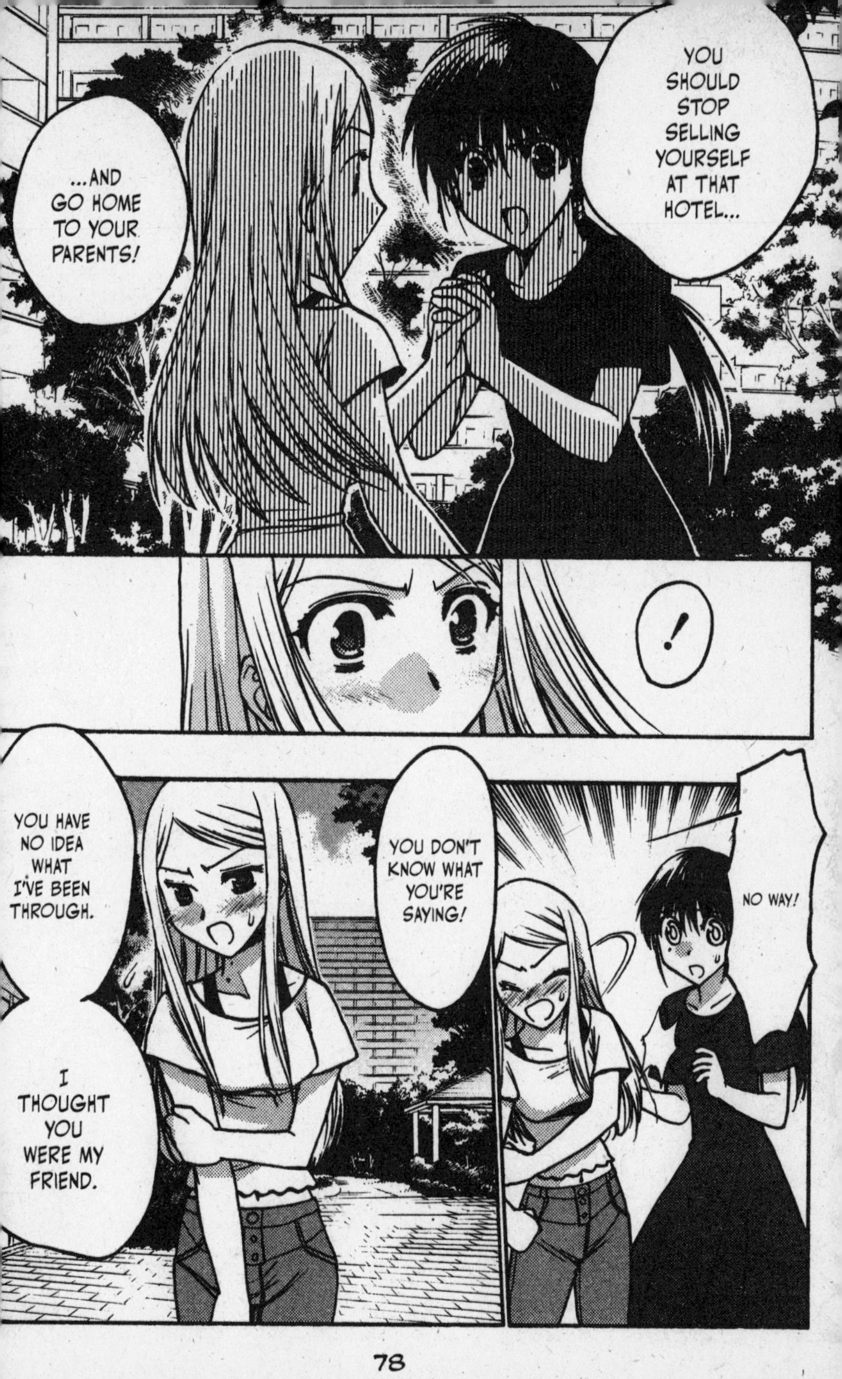
YOU SHOULD STOP SELLING YOURSELF AT THAT HOTEL...
...AND GO HOME TO YOUR PARENTS!
!
NO WAY!
YOU DON'T KNOW WHAT YOU'RE SAYING!
YOU HAVE NO IDEA WHAT I'VE BEEN THROUGH.
I THOUGHT YOU WERE MY FRIEND.

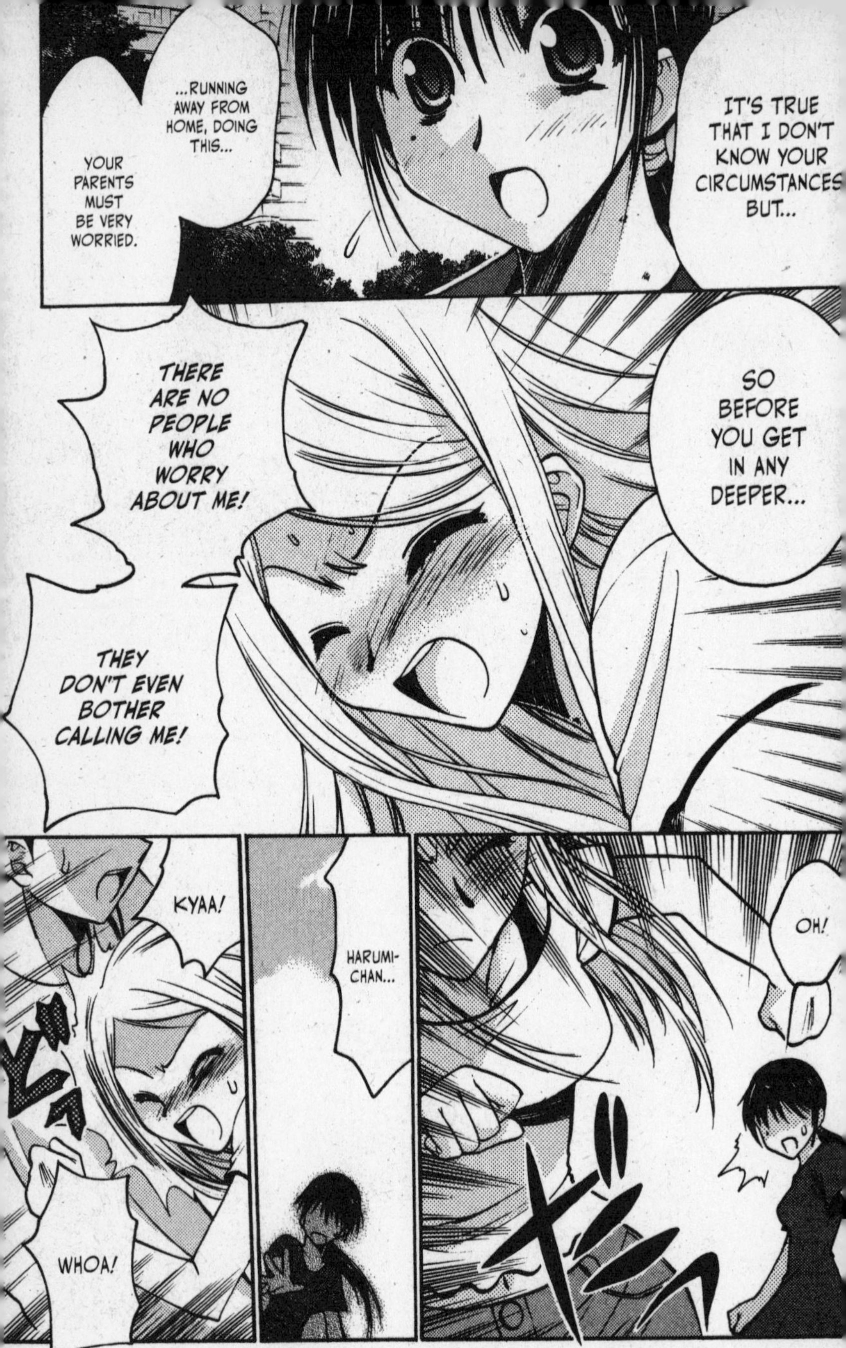
IT'S TRUE THAT I DON'T KNOW YOUR CIRCUMSTANCES BUT...
...RUNNING AWAY FROM HOME, DOING THIS...
YOUR PARENTS MUST BE VERY WORRIED.
SO BEFORE YOU GET IN ANY DEEPER...
THERE ARE NO PEOPLE WHO WORRY ABOUT ME!
THEY DON'T EVEN BOTHER CALLING ME!
OH!
HARUMI-CHAN...
KYAA!
WHOA!

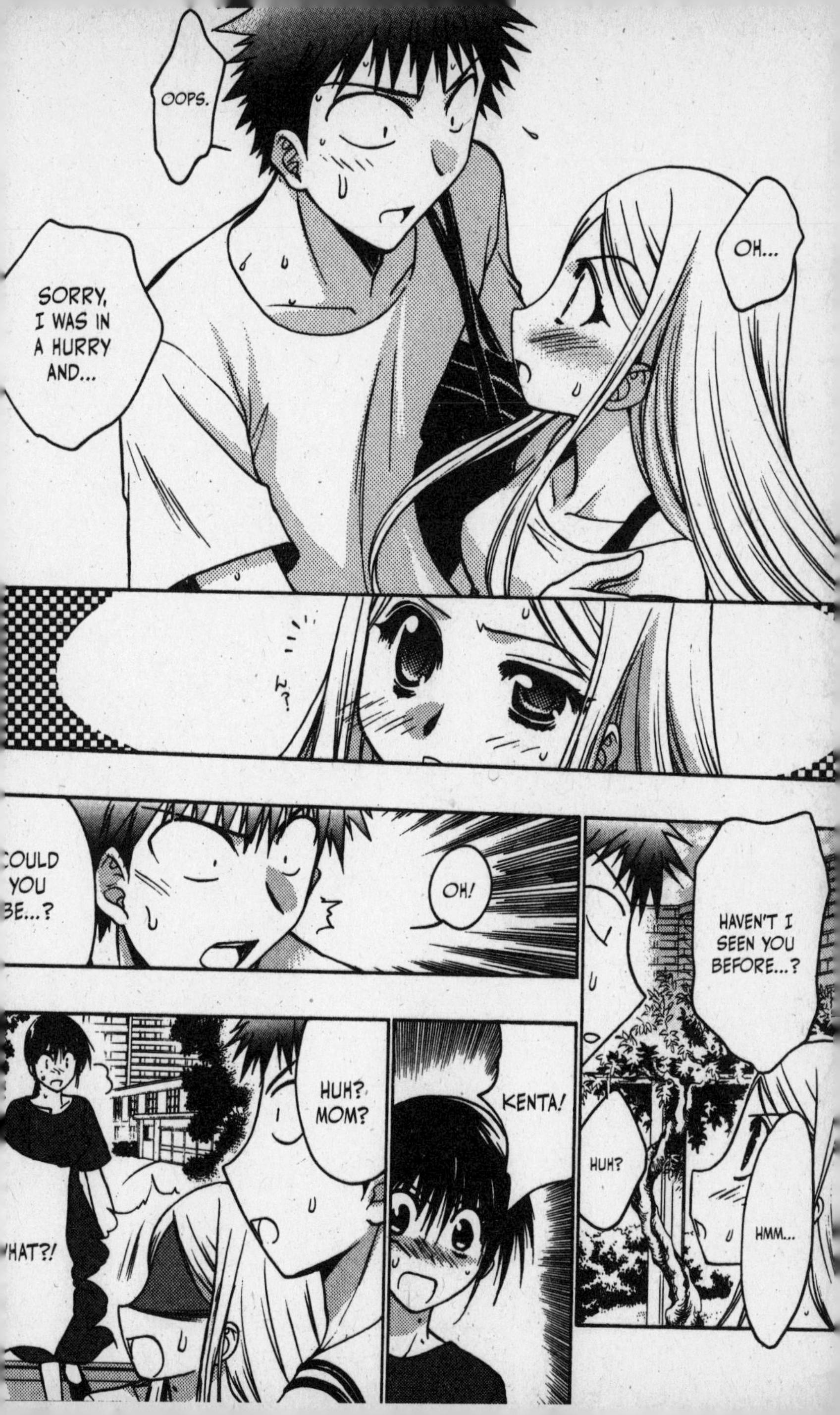
OOPS.
OH...
SORRY, I WAS IN A HURRY AND...
HAVEN'T I SEEN YOU BEFORE...?
HMM...
HUH?
OH!
COULD YOU BE...?
KENTA!
HUH? MOM?
WHAT?!

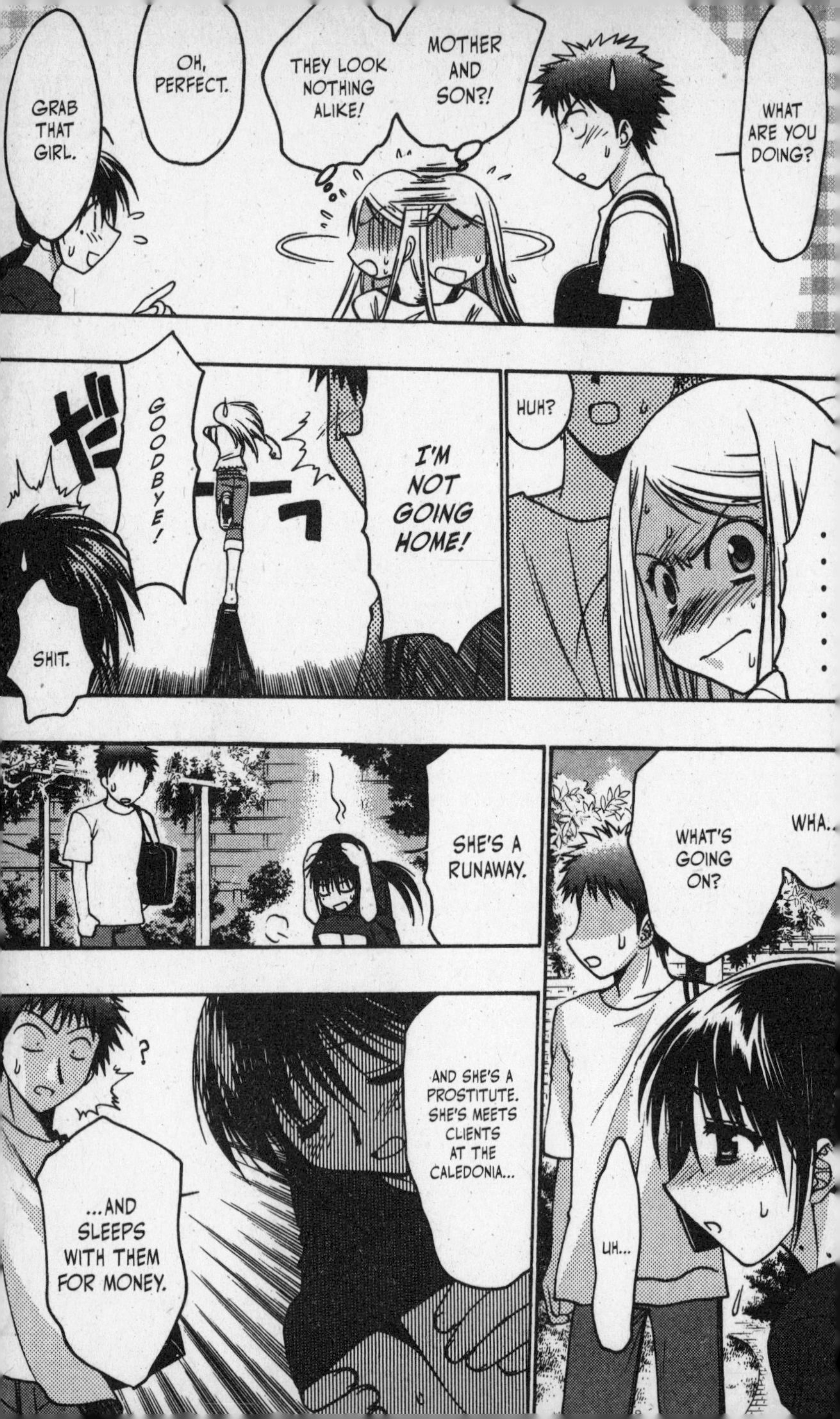
WHAT ARE YOU DOING?
MOTHER AND SON?!
THEY LOOK NOTHING ALIKE!
OH, PERFECT.
GRAB THAT GIRL.
......
HUH?
I'M NOT GOING HOME!
GOODBYE!
SHIT.
WHA..
WHAT'S GOING ON?
UH...
SHE'S A RUNAWAY.
AND SHE'S A PROSTITUTE. SHE'S MEETS CLIENTS AT THE CALEDONIA...
...AND SLEEPS WITH THEM FOR MONEY.

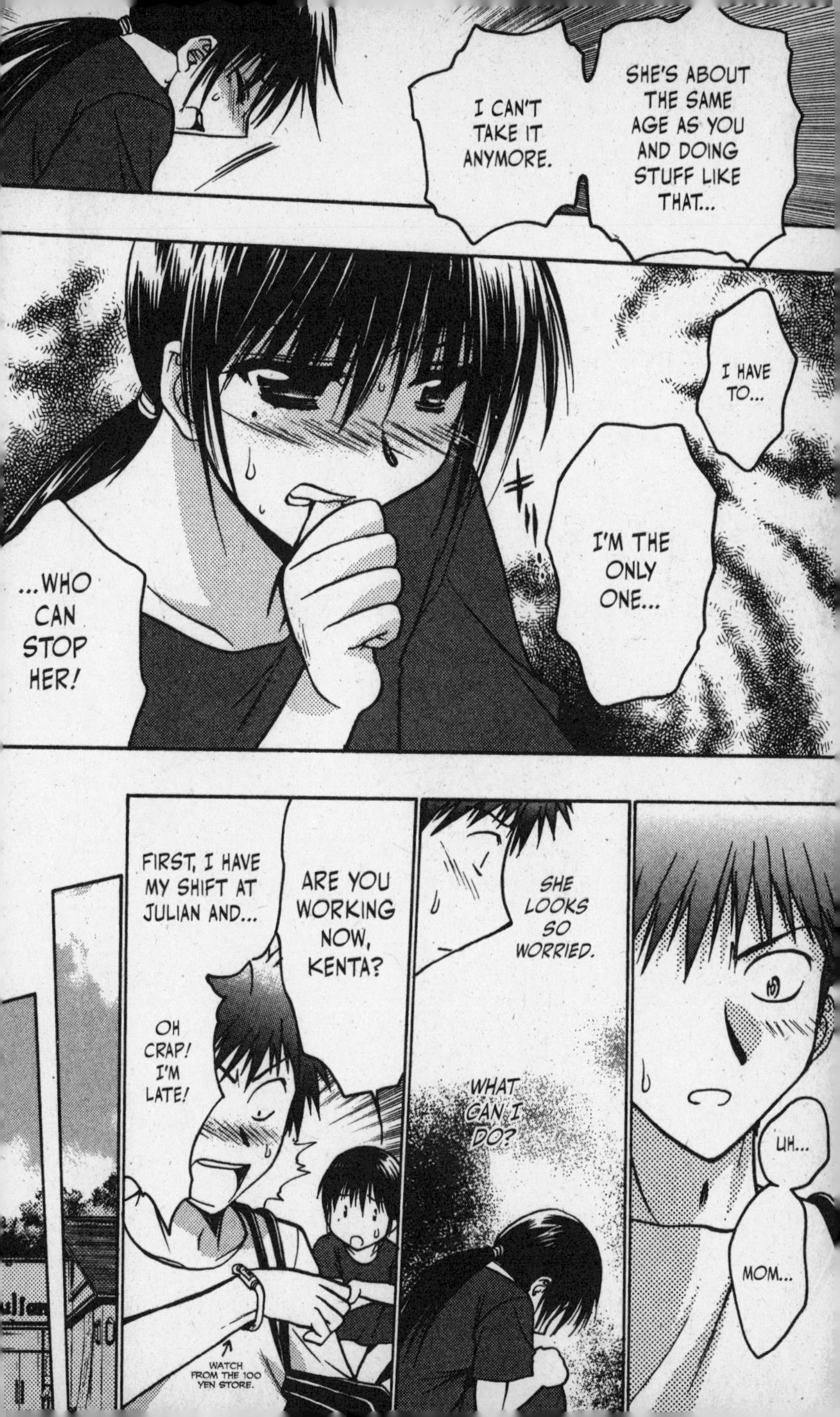
SHE'S ABOUT THE SAME AGE AS YOU AND DOING STUFF LIKE THAT...
I CAN'T TAKE IT ANYMORE.
I HAVE TO...
I'M THE ONLY ONE...
...WHO CAN STOP HER!
UH...
MOM...
SHE LOOKS SO WORRIED.
WHAT CAN I DO?
ARE YOU WORKING NOW, KENTA?
FIRST, I HAVE MY SHIFT AT JULIAN AND...
OH CRAP! I'M LATE!
WATCH FROM THE 100 YEN STORE.

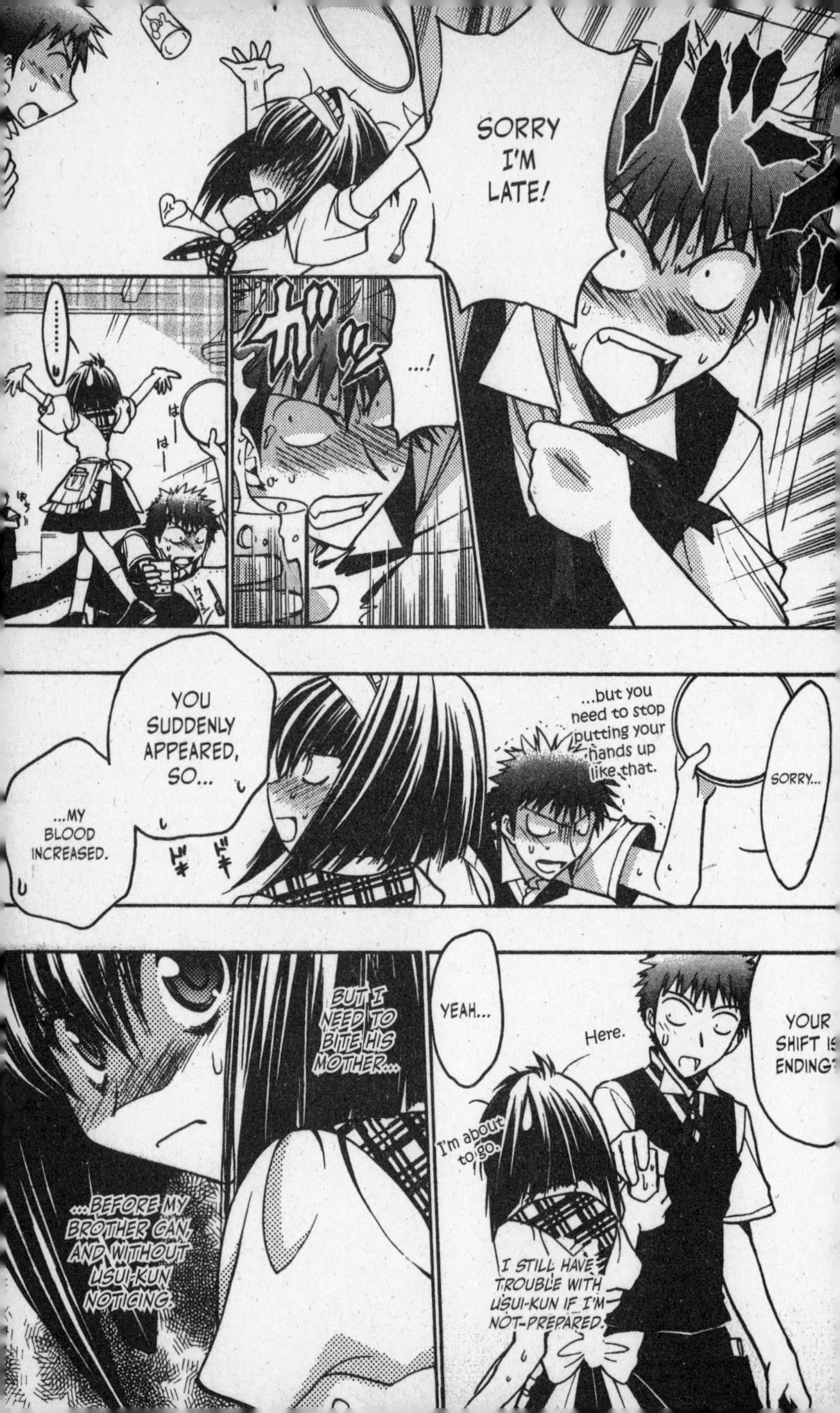
SORRY I'M LATE!
...!
......
SORRY...
...but you need to stop putting your hands up like that.
YOU SUDDENLY APPEARED, SO...
...MY BLOOD INCREASED.
YOUR SHIFT IS ENDING?
Here.
YEAH...
I'm about to go.
I STILL HAVE TROUBLE WITH USUI-KUN IF I'M NOT-PREPARED.
BUT I NEED TO BITE HIS MOTHER...
...BEFORE MY BROTHER CAN, AND WITHOUT USUI-KUN NOTICING.

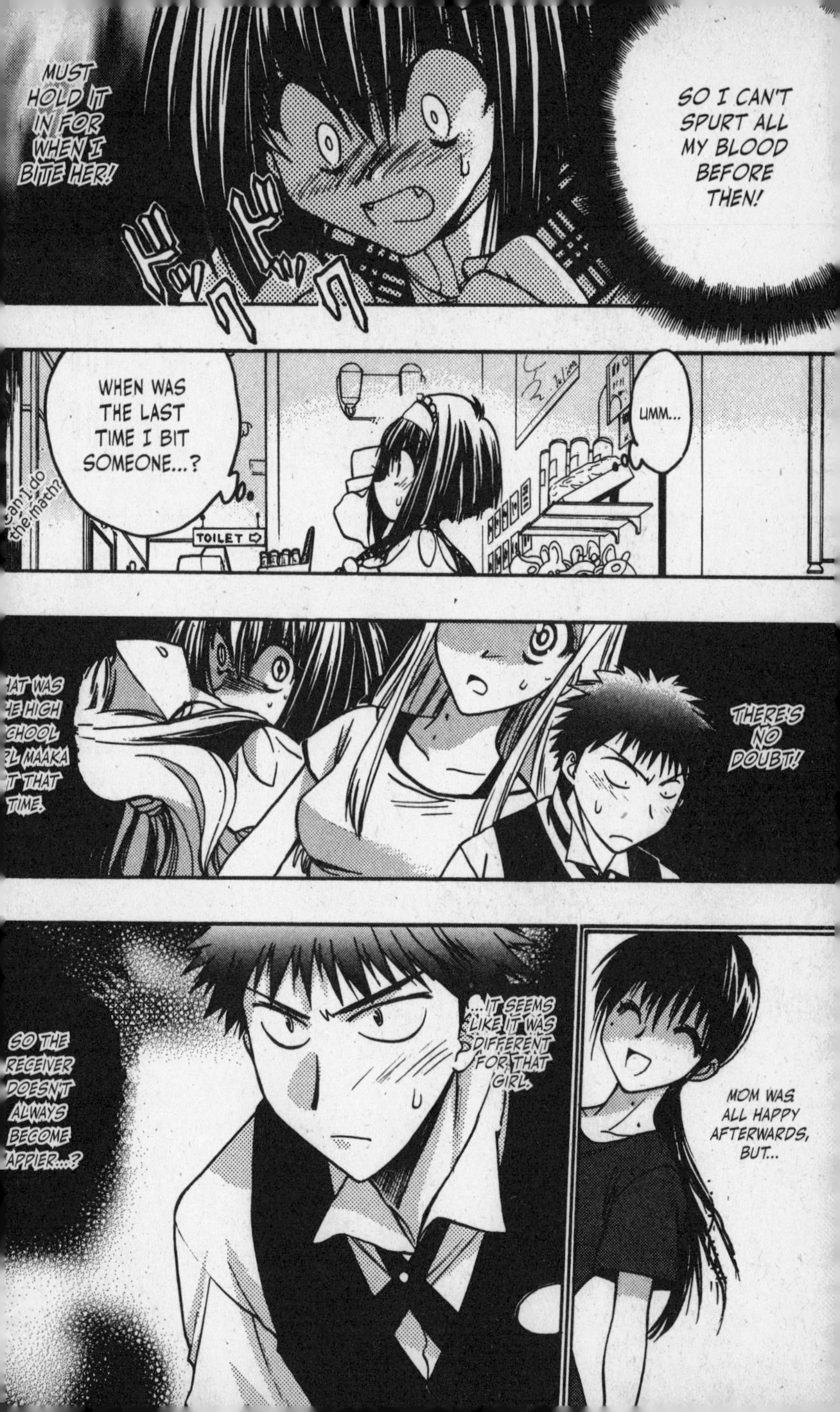
SO I CAN'T SPURT ALL MY BLOOD BEFORE THEN!
MUST HOLD IT IN FOR WHEN I BITE HER!
UMM...
WHEN WAS THE LAST TIME I BIT SOMEONE...?
Can't I do the math?
TOILET
THERE'S NO DOUBT!
AT WAS
HE HIGH
CHOOL
RL MAAKA
T THAT
TIME.
MOM WAS ALL HAPPY AFTERWARDS, BUT...
...IT SEEMS LIKE IT WAS DIFFERENT FOR THAT GIRL.
SO THE RECEIVER DOESN'T ALWAYS BECOME
APPIER...?

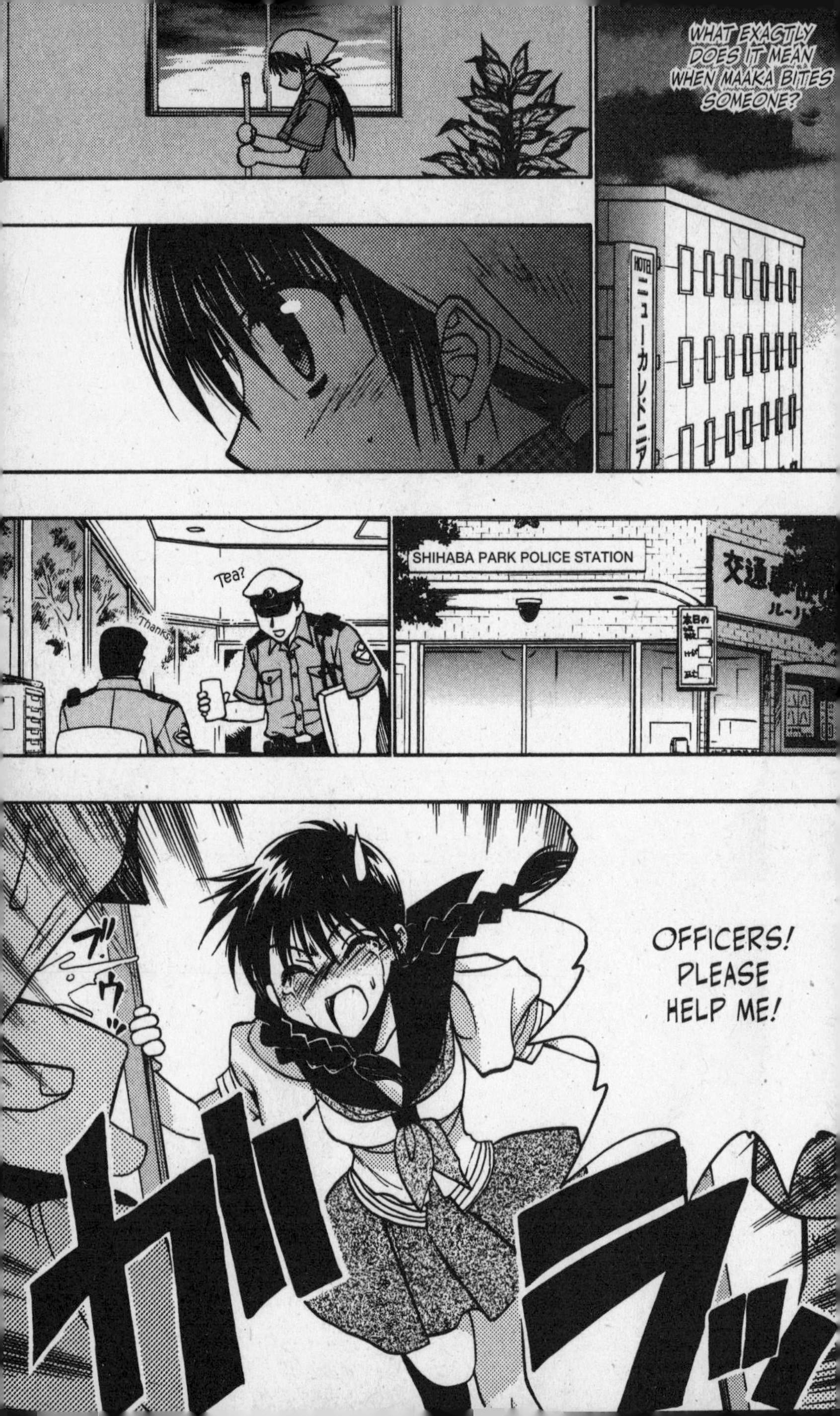
WHAT EXACTLY DOES IT MEAN WHEN MAAKA BITES SOMEONE?
HOTEL
ニューカレドニア
SHIHABA PARK POLICE STATION
Tea?
Thanks.
OFFICERS! PLEASE HELP ME!

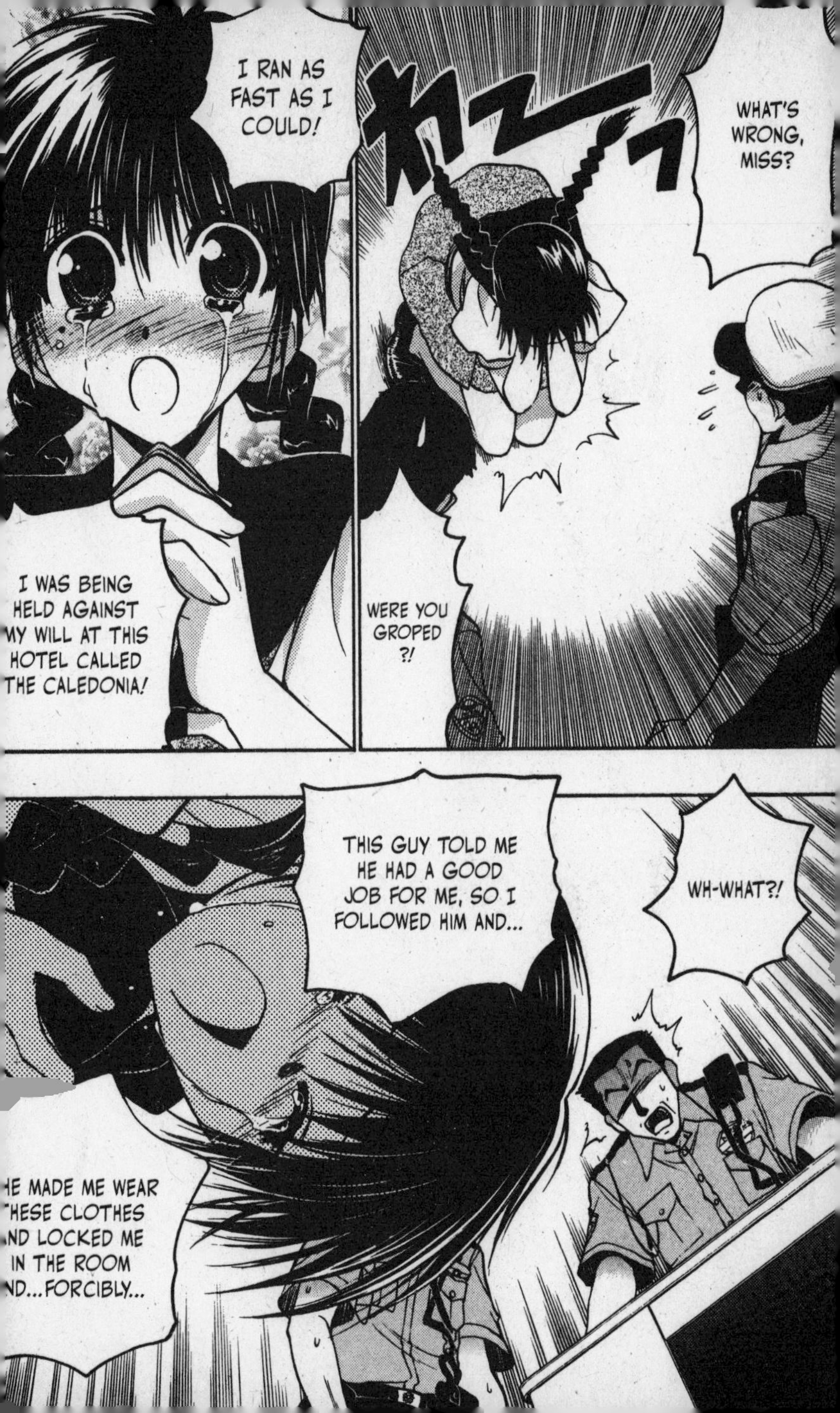
WHAT'S WRONG, MISS?
WERE YOU GROPED?!
I RAN AS FAST AS I COULD!
I WAS BEING HELD AGAINST MY WILL AT THIS HOTEL CALLED THE CALEDONIA!
THIS GUY TOLD ME HE HAD A GOOD JOB FOR ME, SO I FOLLOWED HIM AND...
HE MADE ME WEAR THESE CLOTHES AND LOCKED ME IN THE ROOM AND...FORCIBLY...
WH-WHAT?!

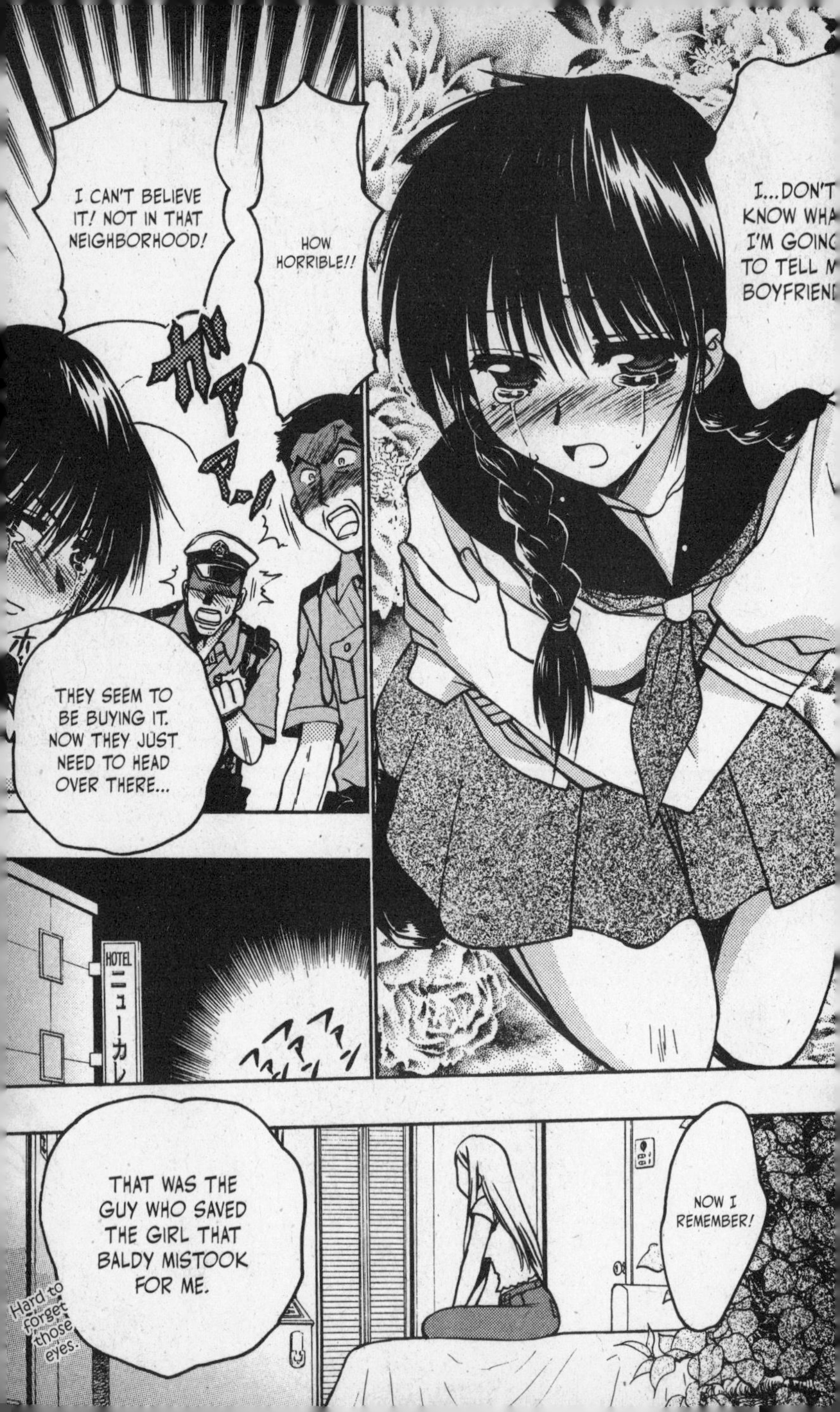
I...DON'T KNOW WHA I'M GOING TO TELL M BOYFRIEND
HOW HORRIBLE!!
I CAN'T BELIEVE IT! NOT IN THAT NEIGHBORHOOD!
ガァァー!
THEY SEEM TO BE BUYING IT. NOW THEY JUST NEED TO HEAD OVER THERE...
HOTEL
ニューカレ
NOW I REMEMBER!
THAT WAS THE GUY WHO SAVED THE GIRL THAT BALDY MISTOOK FOR ME.
Hard to forget those eyes.

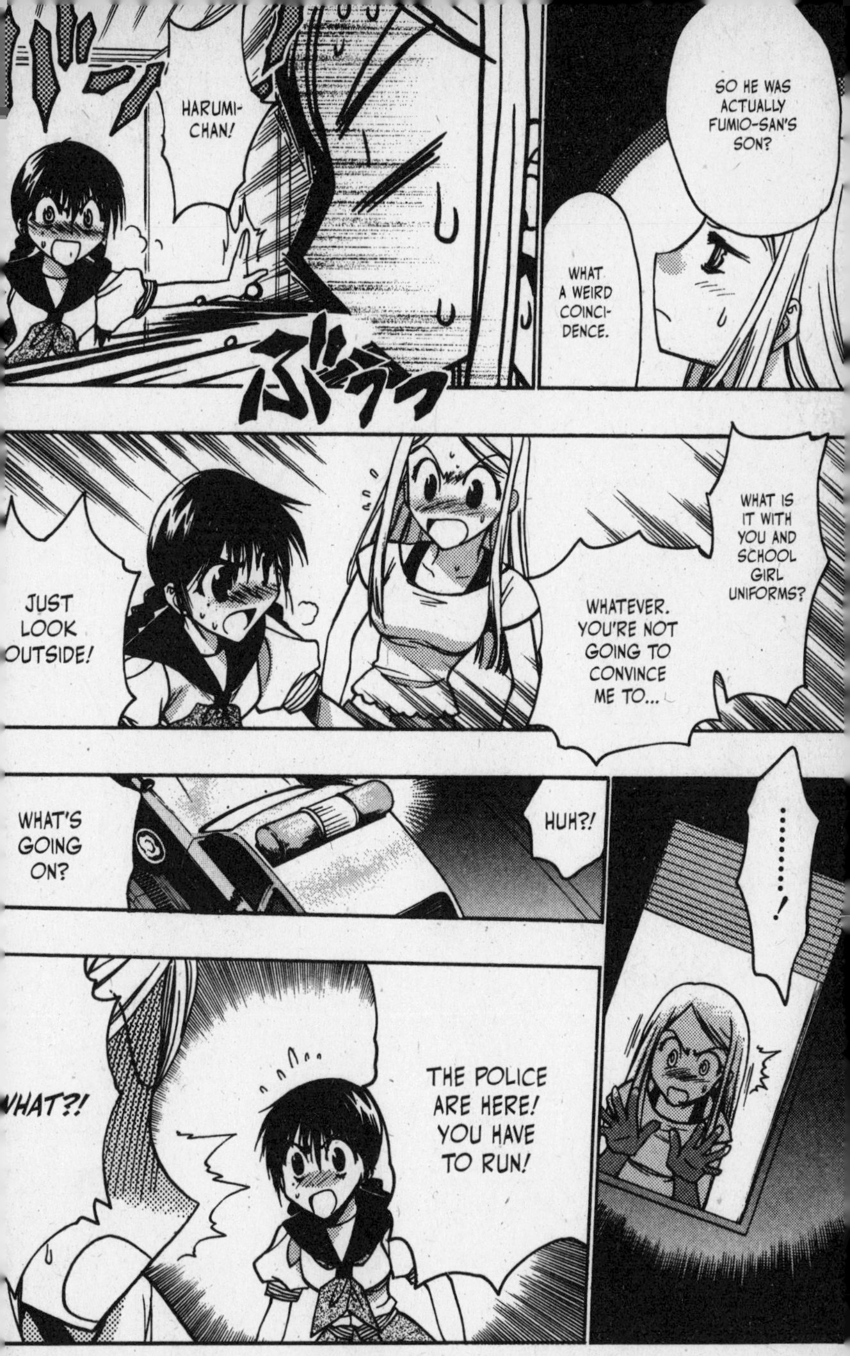
SO HE WAS ACTUALLY FUMIO-SAN'S SON?
WHAT A WEIRD COINCI-DENCE.
HARUMI-CHAN!
WHAT IS IT WITH YOU AND SCHOOL GIRL UNIFORMS?
WHATEVER. YOU'RE NOT GOING TO CONVINCE ME TO...
JUST LOOK OUTSIDE!
......!
HUH?!
WHAT'S GOING ON?
THE POLICE ARE HERE! YOU HAVE TO RUN!
WHAT?!

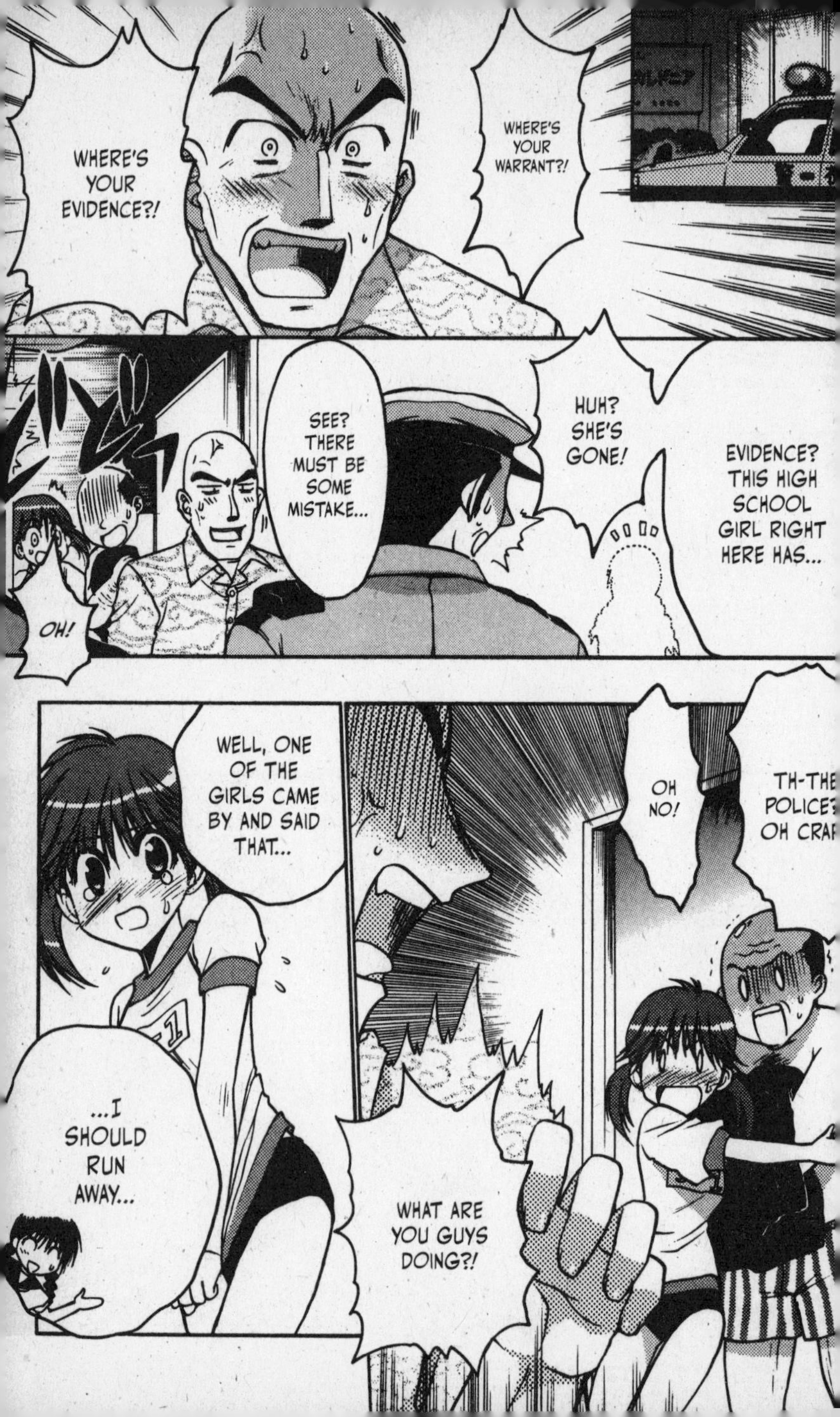
WHERE'S YOUR WARRANT?!
WHERE'S YOUR EVIDENCE?!
EVIDENCE? THIS HIGH SCHOOL GIRL RIGHT HERE HAS...
HUH? SHE'S GONE!
SEE? THERE MUST BE SOME MISTAKE...
OH!
TH-THE POLICE? OH CRA
OH NO!
WHAT ARE YOU GUYS DOING?!
WELL, ONE OF THE GIRLS CAME BY AND SAID THAT...
...I SHOULD RUN AWAY...

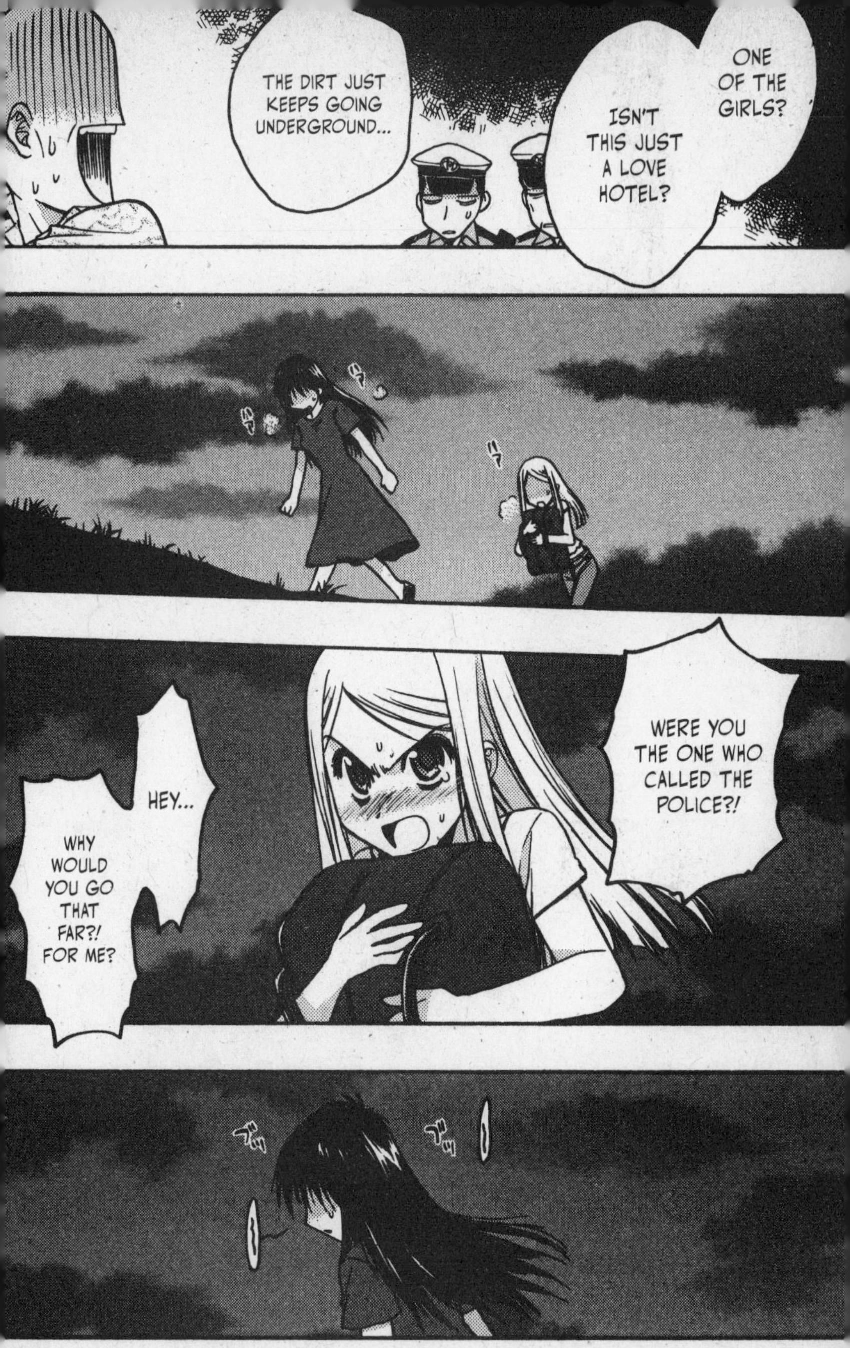
ONE OF THE GIRLS?
ISN'T THIS JUST A LOVE HOTEL?
THE DIRT JUST KEEPS GOING UNDERGROUND...
WERE YOU THE ONE WHO CALLED THE POLICE?!
HEY...
WHY WOULD YOU GO THAT FAR?! FOR ME?

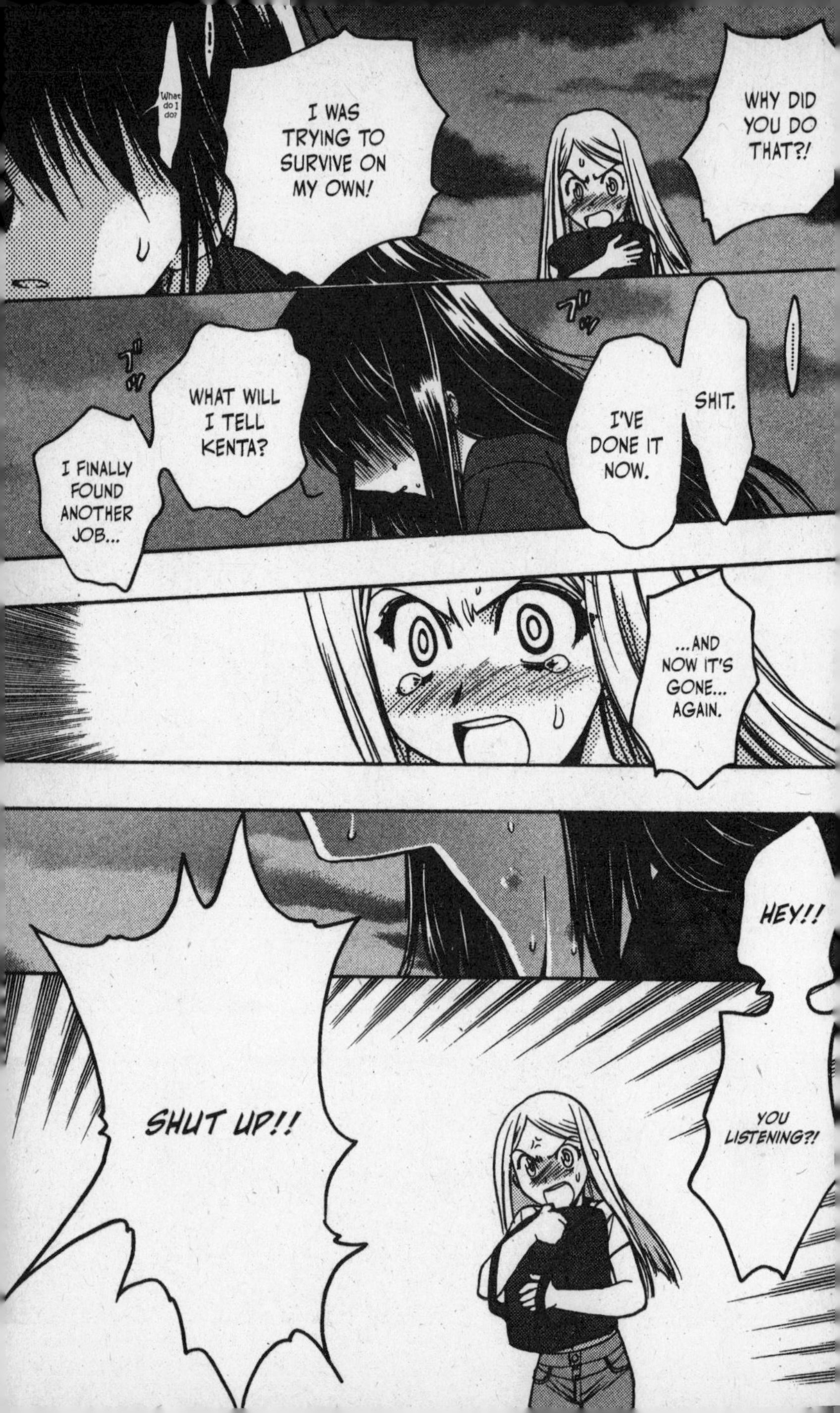
WHY DID YOU DO THAT?!
I WAS TRYING TO SURVIVE ON MY OWN!
What do I do?
SHIT.
I'VE DONE IT NOW.
WHAT WILL I TELL KENTA?
I FINALLY FOUND ANOTHER JOB...
...AND NOW IT'S GONE... AGAIN.
HEY!!
YOU LISTENING?!
SHUT UP!!

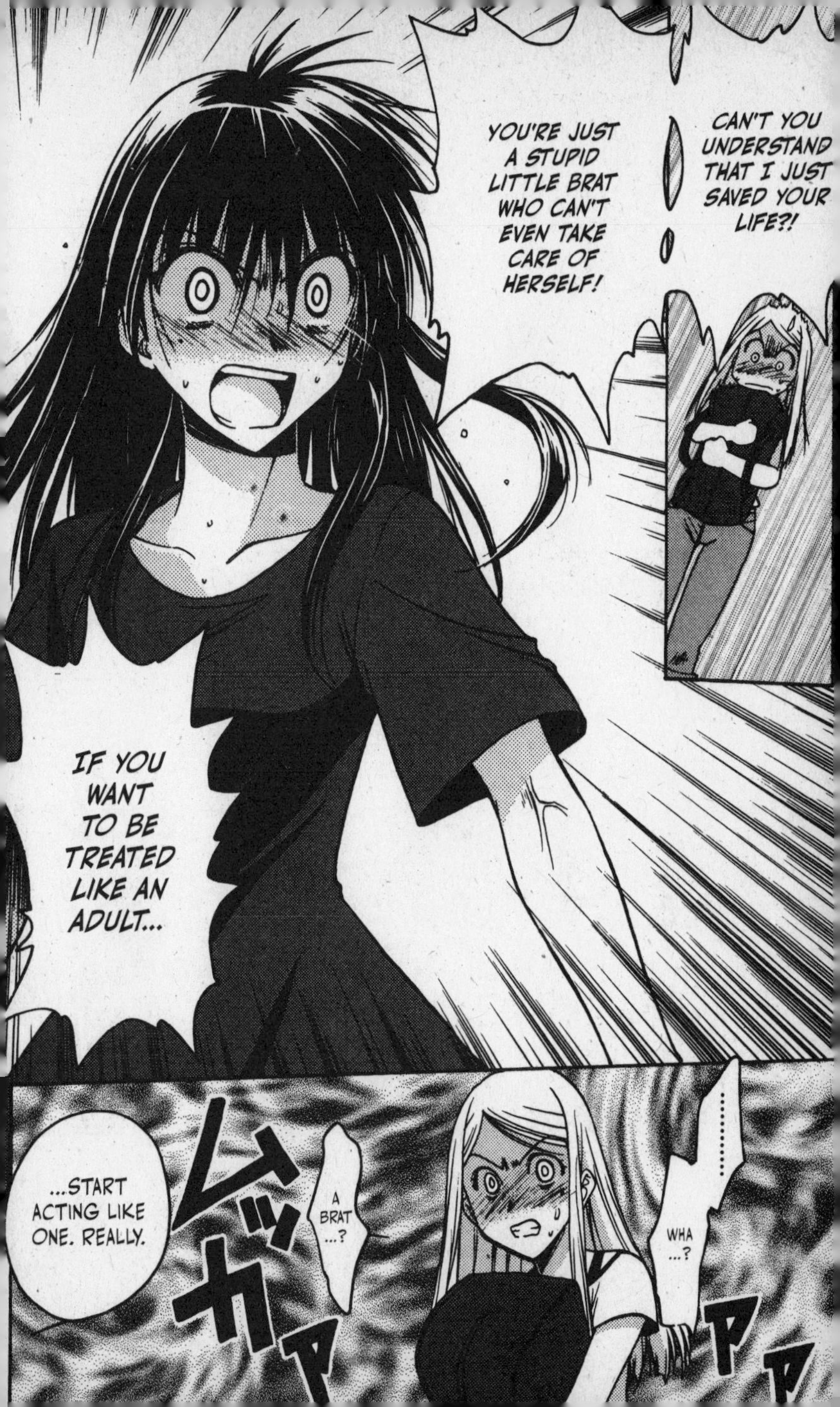
CAN'T YOU UNDERSTAND THAT I JUST SAVED YOUR LIFE?!
YOU'RE JUST A STUPID LITTLE BRAT WHO CAN'T EVEN TAKE CARE OF HERSELF!
IF YOU WANT TO BE TREATED LIKE AN ADULT...
......
WHA ...?
A BRAT ...?
...START ACTING LIKE ONE. REALLY.

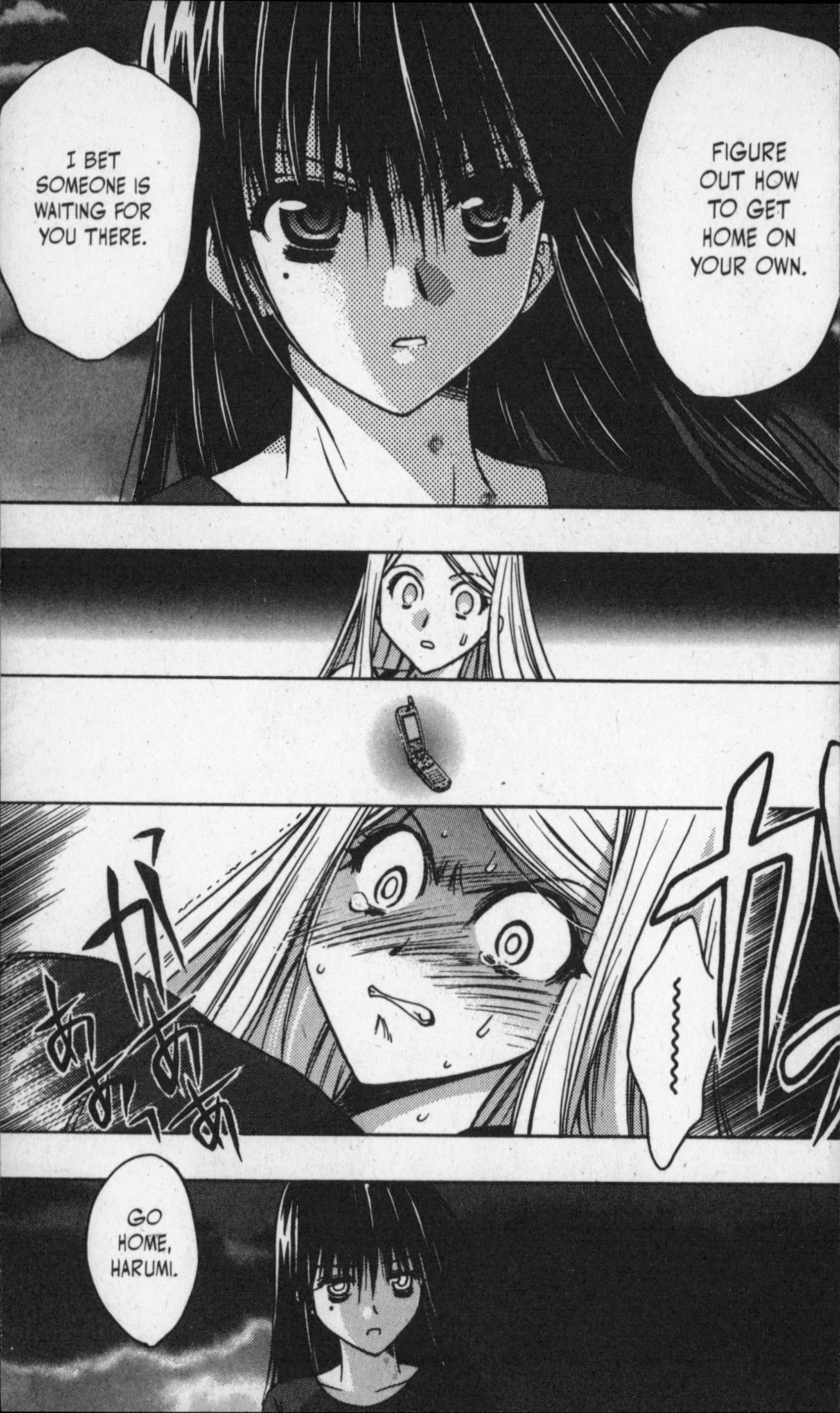
FIGURE OUT HOW TO GET HOME ON YOUR OWN.
I BET SOMEONE IS WAITING FOR YOU THERE.
GO HOME, HARUMI.

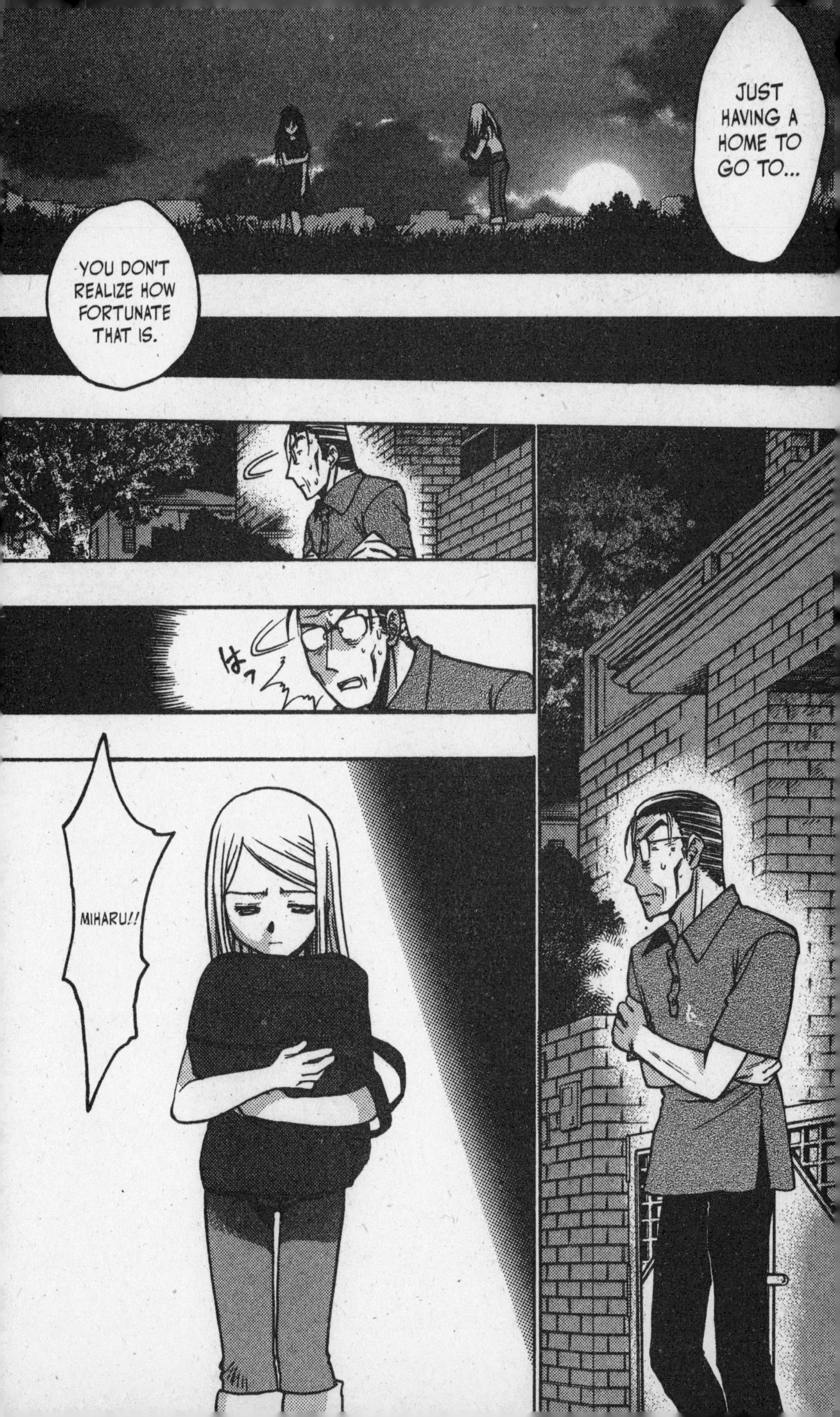
JUST HAVING A HOME TO GO TO...
YOU DON'T REALIZE HOW FORTUNATE THAT IS.
はっ
MIHARU!!

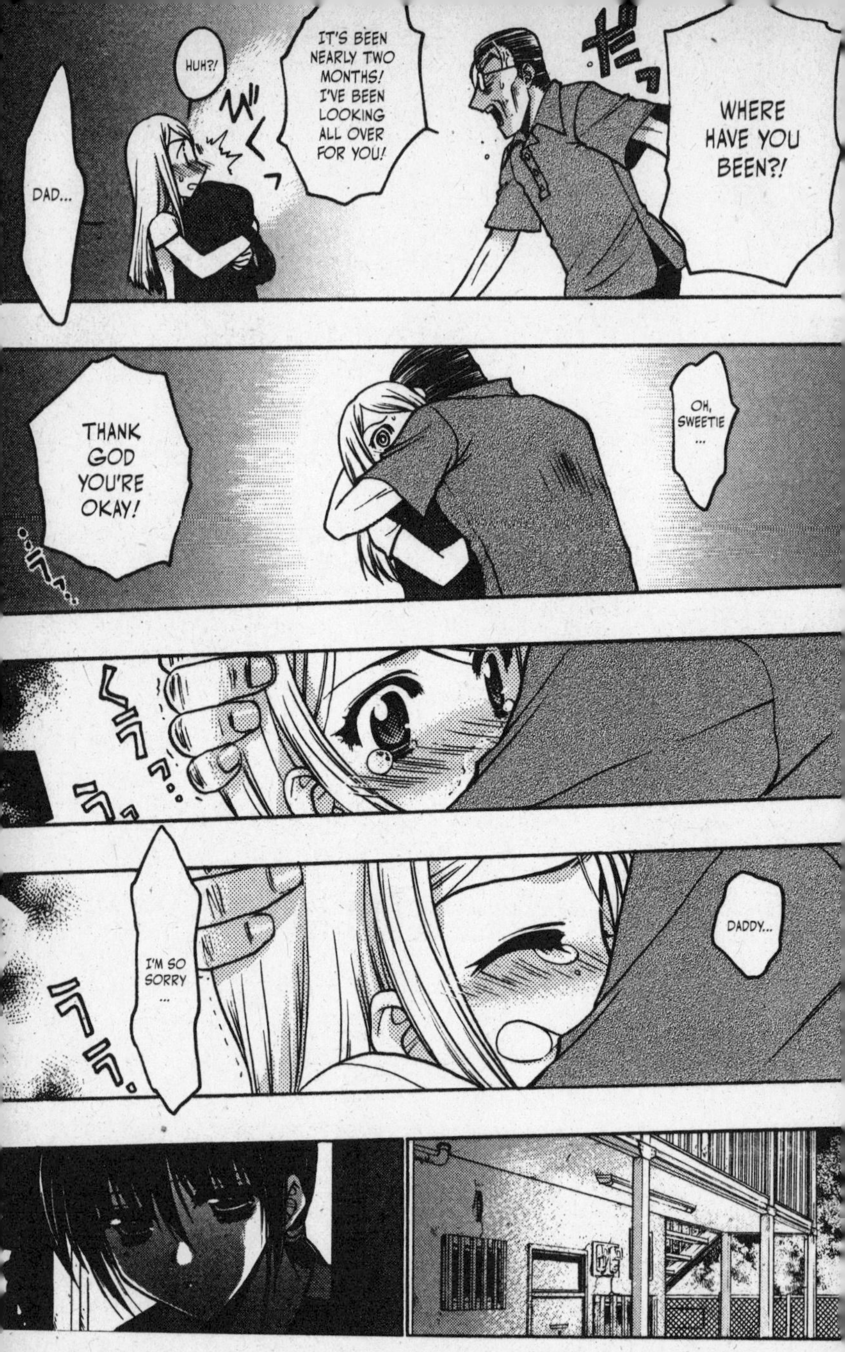
WHERE HAVE YOU BEEN?!
IT'S BEEN NEARLY TWO MONTHS! I'VE BEEN LOOKING ALL OVER FOR YOU!
HUH?!
DAD...
OH, SWEETIE ...
THANK GOD YOU'RE OKAY!
DADDY...
I'M SO SORRY ...

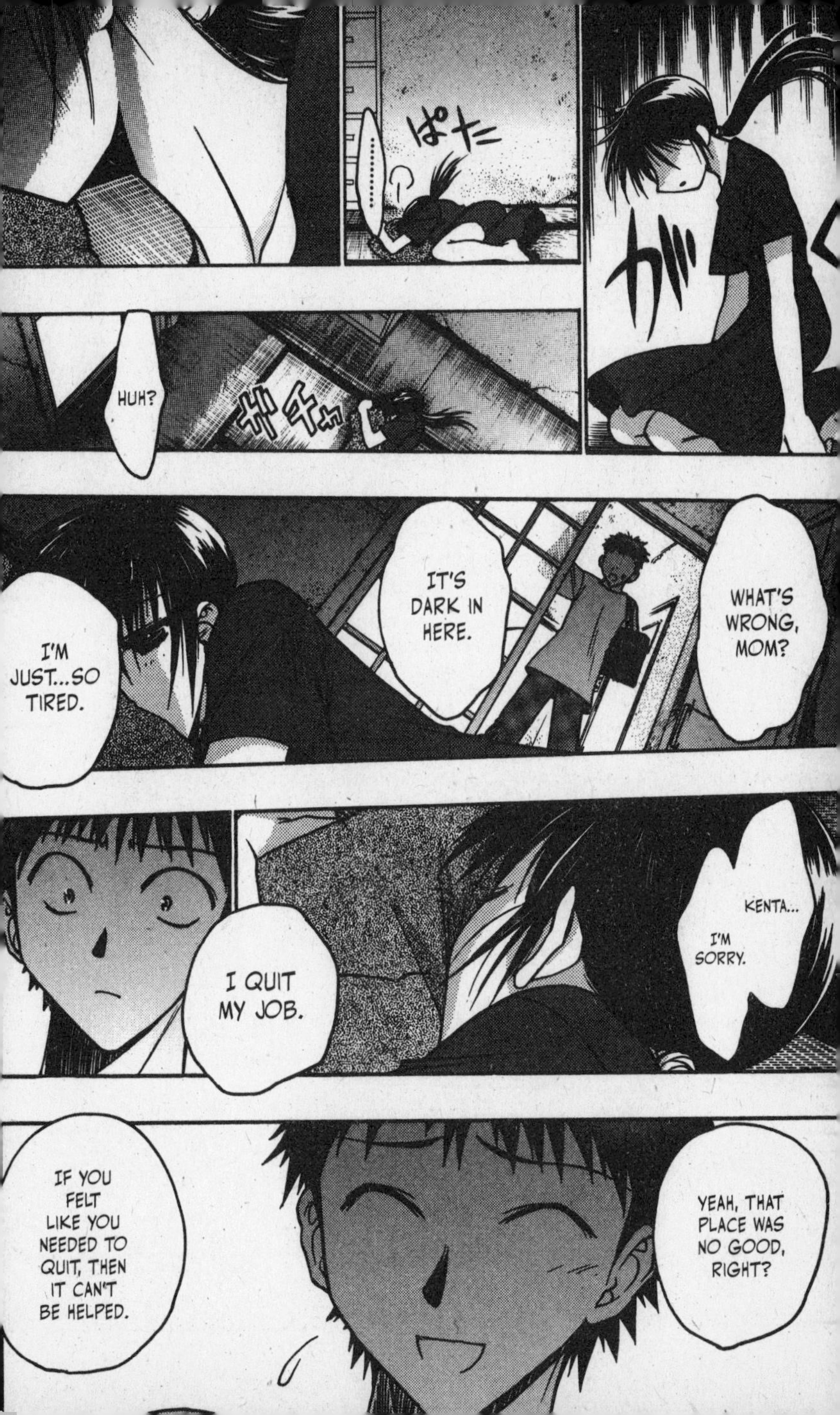

ぱた
......
HUH?
WHAT'S WRONG, MOM?
IT'S DARK IN HERE.
I'M JUST...SO TIRED.
KENTA...
I'M SORRY.
I QUIT MY JOB.
YEAH, THAT PLACE WAS NO GOOD, RIGHT?
IF YOU FELT LIKE YOU NEEDED TO QUIT, THEN IT CAN'T BE HELPED.

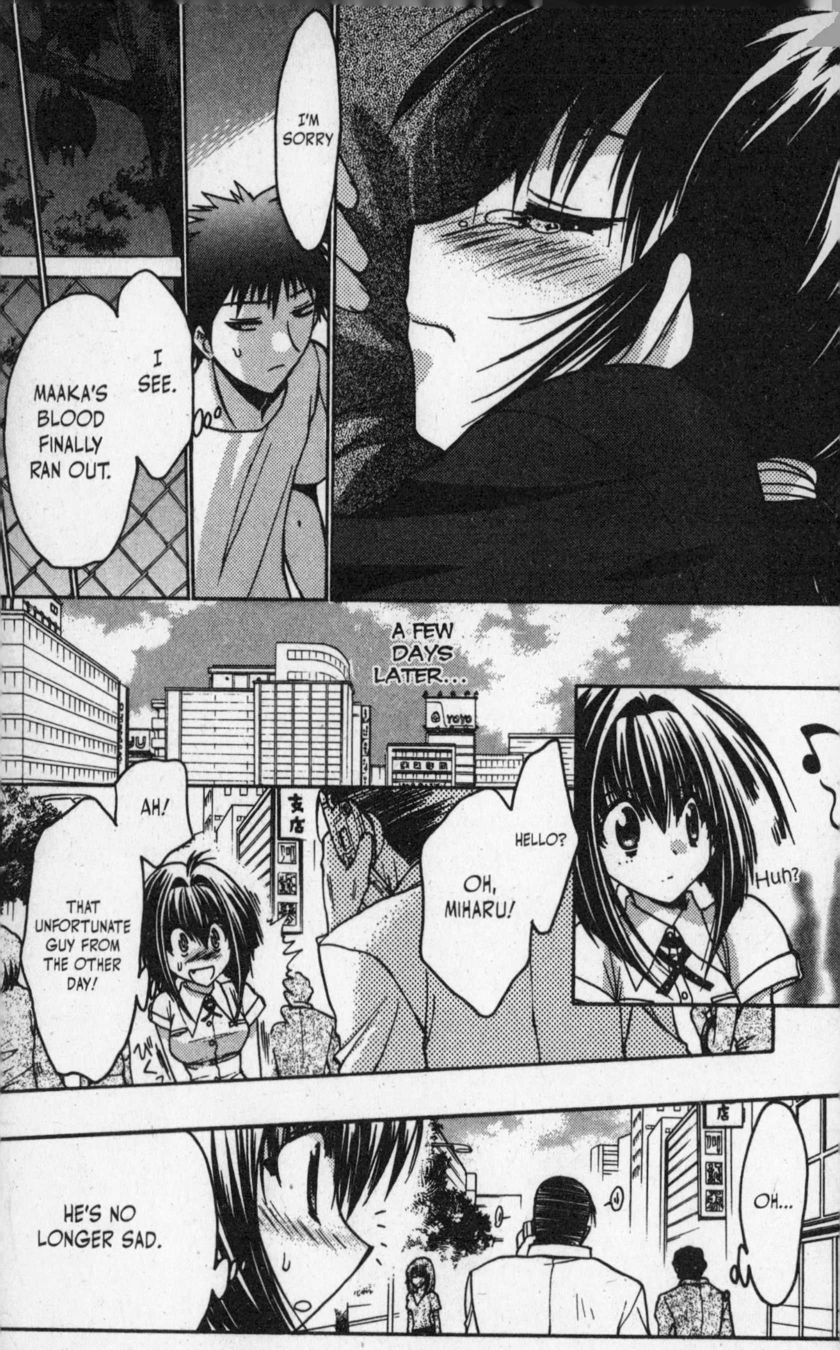
I'M SORRY
I SEE.
MAAKA'S BLOOD FINALLY RAN OUT.
A FEW DAYS LATER...
Huh?
HELLO?
OH, MIHARU!
AH!
THAT UNFORTUNATE GUY FROM THE OTHER DAY!
OH...
HE'S NO LONGER SAD.

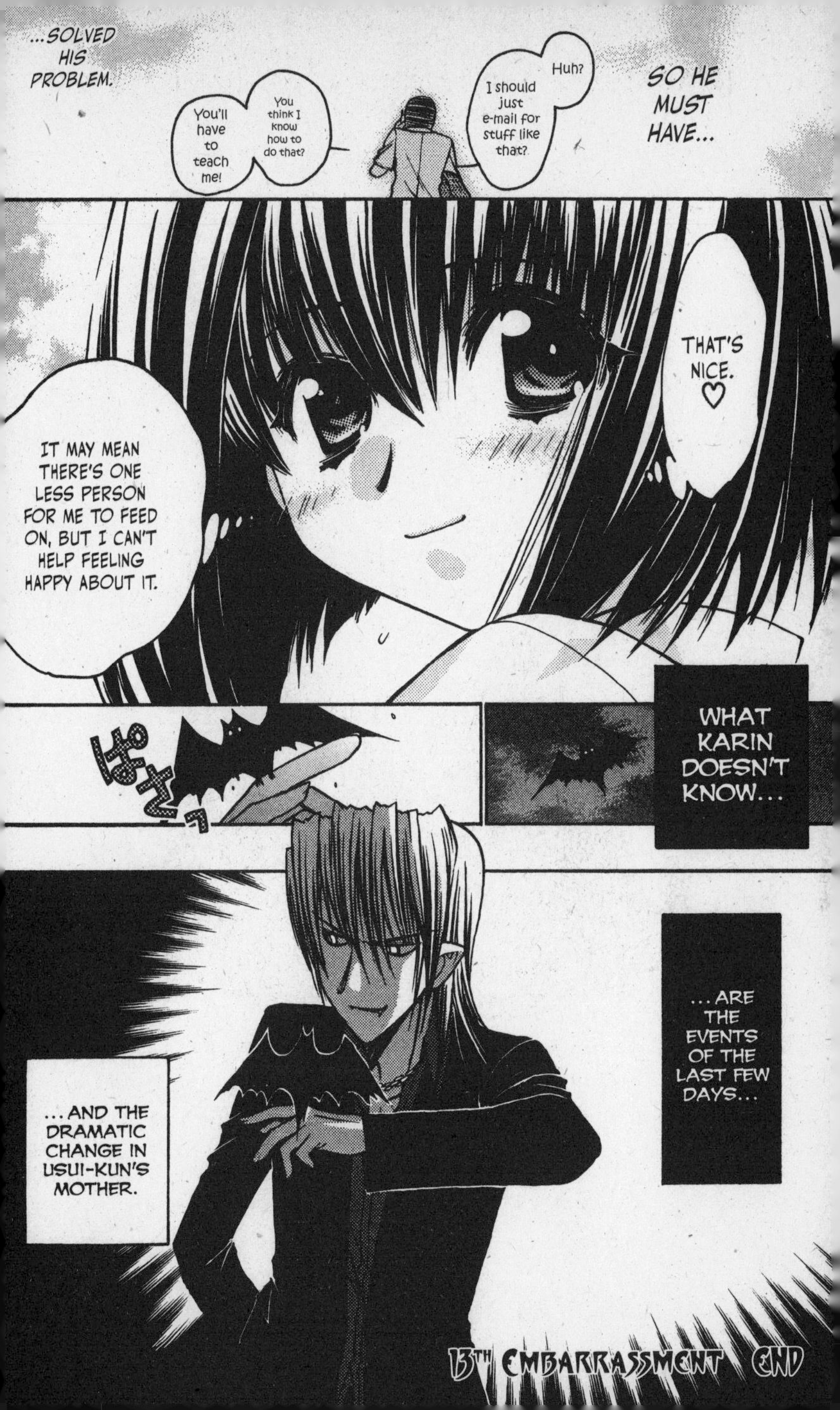
SO HE MUST HAVE...
...SOLVED HIS PROBLEM.
Huh? I should just e-mail for stuff like that?
You think I know how to do that?
You'll have to teach me!
THAT'S NICE. ♡
IT MAY MEAN THERE'S ONE LESS PERSON FOR ME TO FEED ON, BUT I CAN'T HELP FEELING HAPPY ABOUT IT.
WHAT KARIN DOESN'T KNOW...
...ARE THE EVENTS OF THE LAST FEW DAYS...
...AND THE DRAMATIC CHANGE IN USUI-KUN'S MOTHER.
13TH EMBARRASSMENT END

Bonus Story #1) Anju's School and Boogie-kun's Return

~Anju Special~

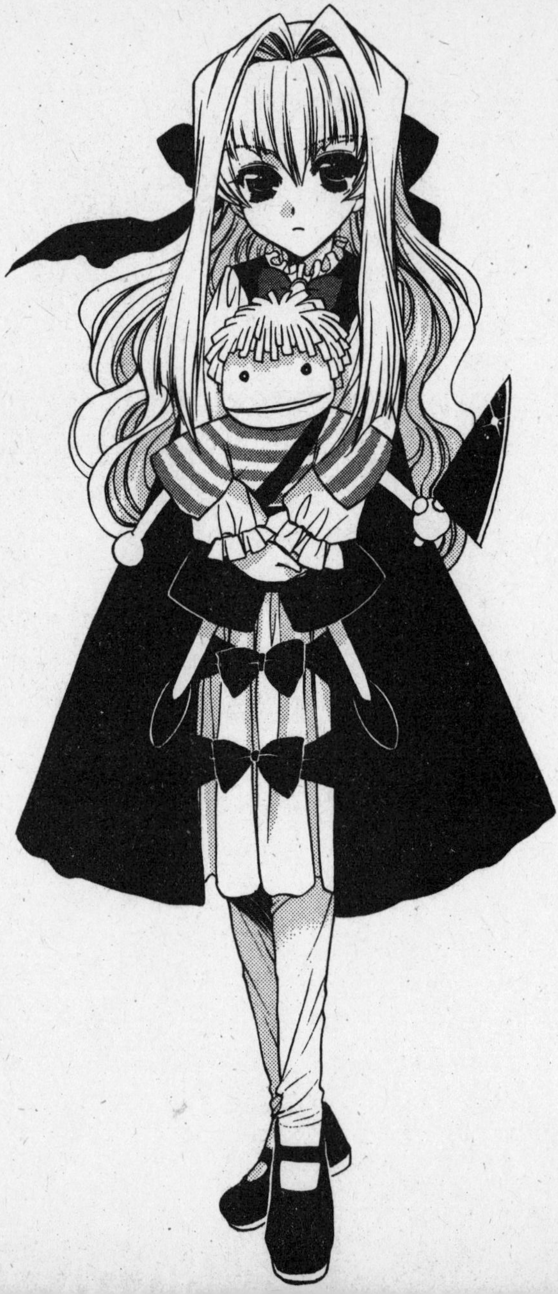

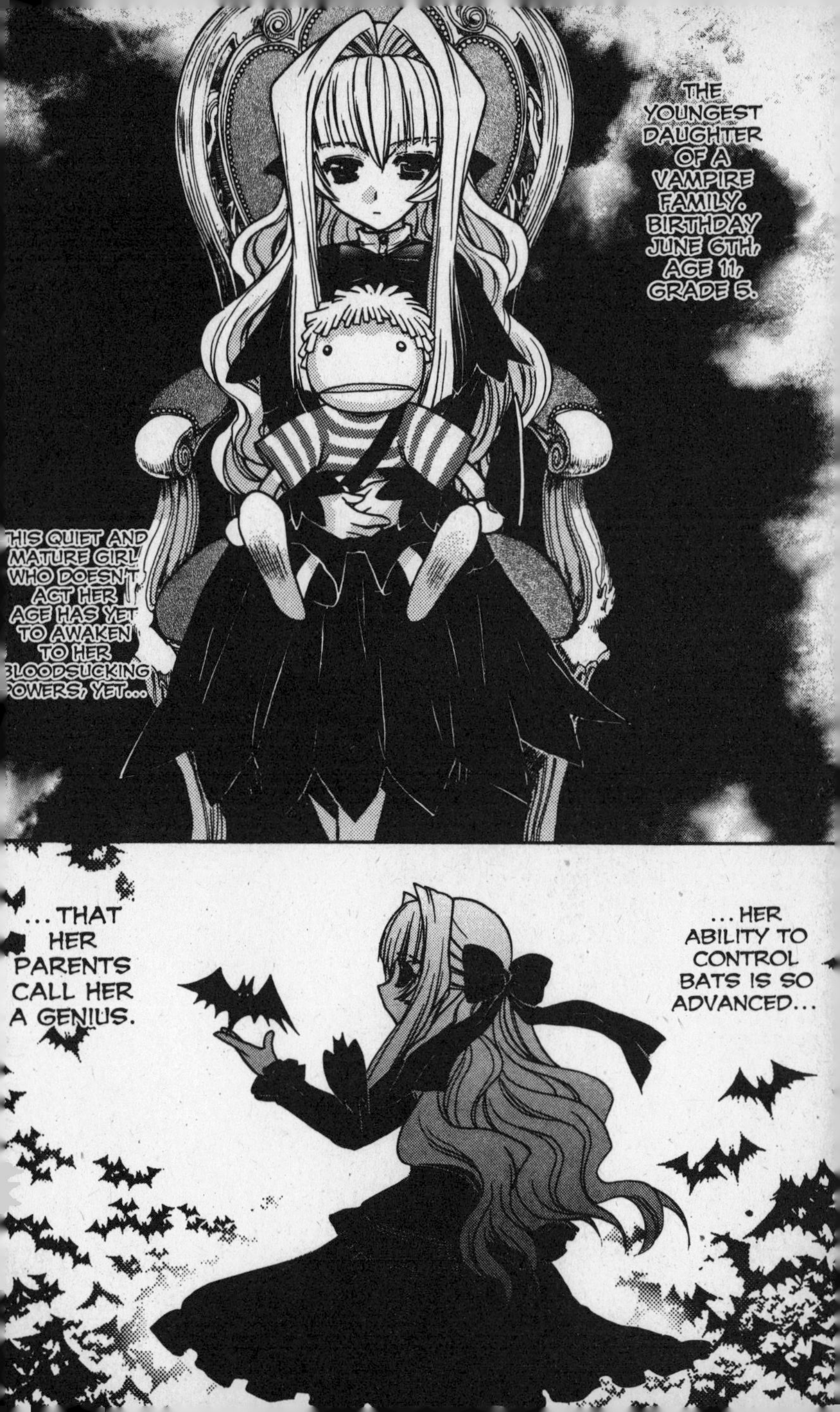
THE YOUNGEST DAUGHTER OF A VAMPIRE FAMILY. BIRTHDAY JUNE 6TH, AGE 11, GRADE 5.
THIS QUIET AND MATURE GIRL WHO DOESN'T ACT HER AGE HAS YET TO AWAKEN TO HER BLOODSUCKING POWERS, YET...
...HER ABILITY TO CONTROL BATS IS SO ADVANCED...
...THAT HER PARENTS CALL HER A GENIUS.

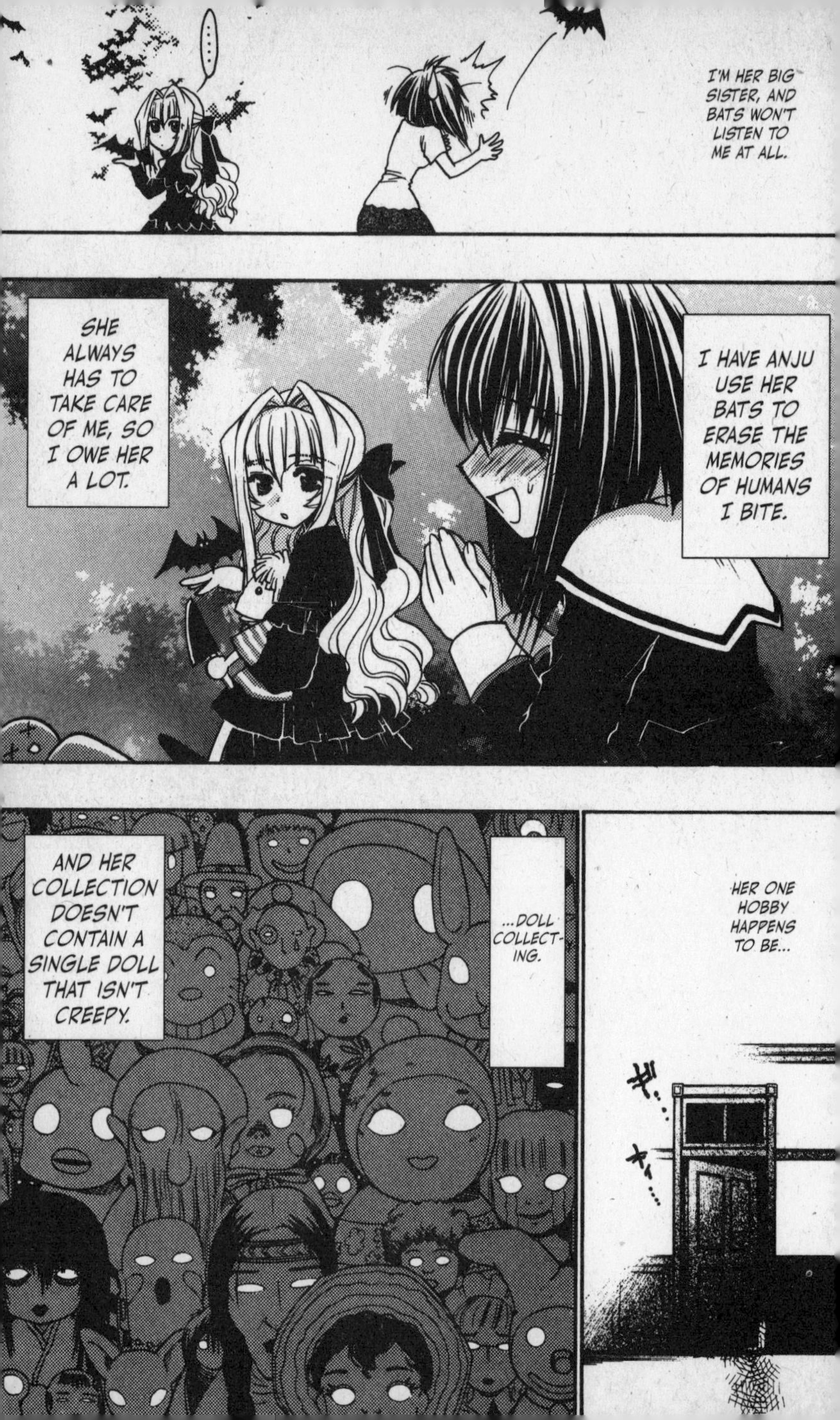
I'M HER BIG SISTER, AND BATS WON'T LISTEN TO ME AT ALL.
...
I HAVE ANJU USE HER BATS TO ERASE THE MEMORIES OF HUMANS I BITE.
SHE ALWAYS HAS TO TAKE CARE OF ME, SO I OWE HER A LOT.
HER ONE HOBBY HAPPENS TO BE...
ギ...
ャイ...
...DOLL COLLECT-ING.
AND HER COLLECTION DOESN'T CONTAIN A SINGLE DOLL THAT ISN'T CREEPY.

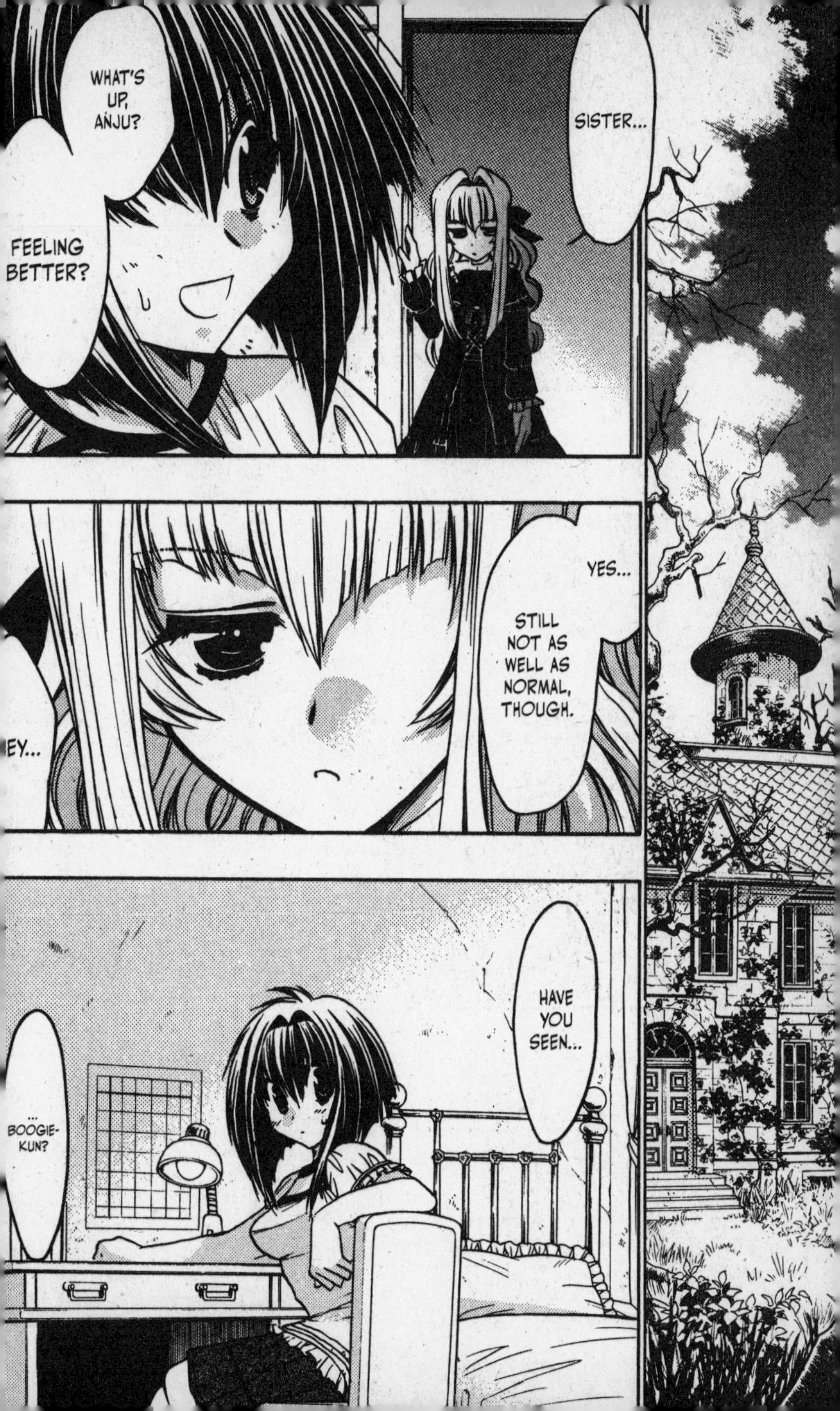
SISTER...
WHAT'S UP, ANJU?
FEELING BETTER?
YES...
STILL NOT AS WELL AS NORMAL, THOUGH.
HAVE YOU SEEN...
... BOOGIE-KUN?

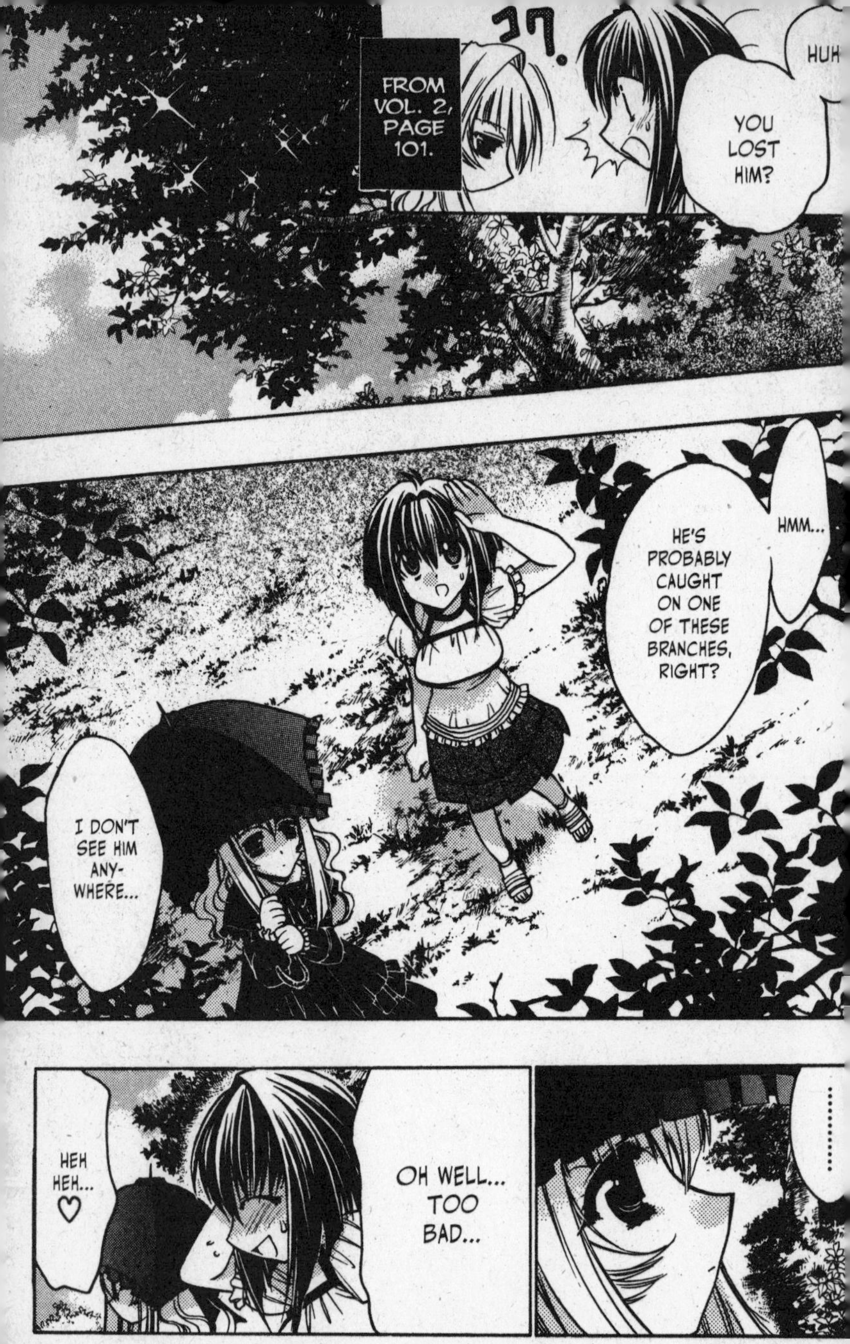

HUH
YOU LOST HIM?
コク.
FROM VOL. 2, PAGE 101.
HMM...
HE'S PROBABLY CAUGHT ON ONE OF THESE BRANCHES, RIGHT?
I DON'T SEE HIM ANYWHERE...
......
OH WELL... TOO BAD...
HEH HEH... ♡

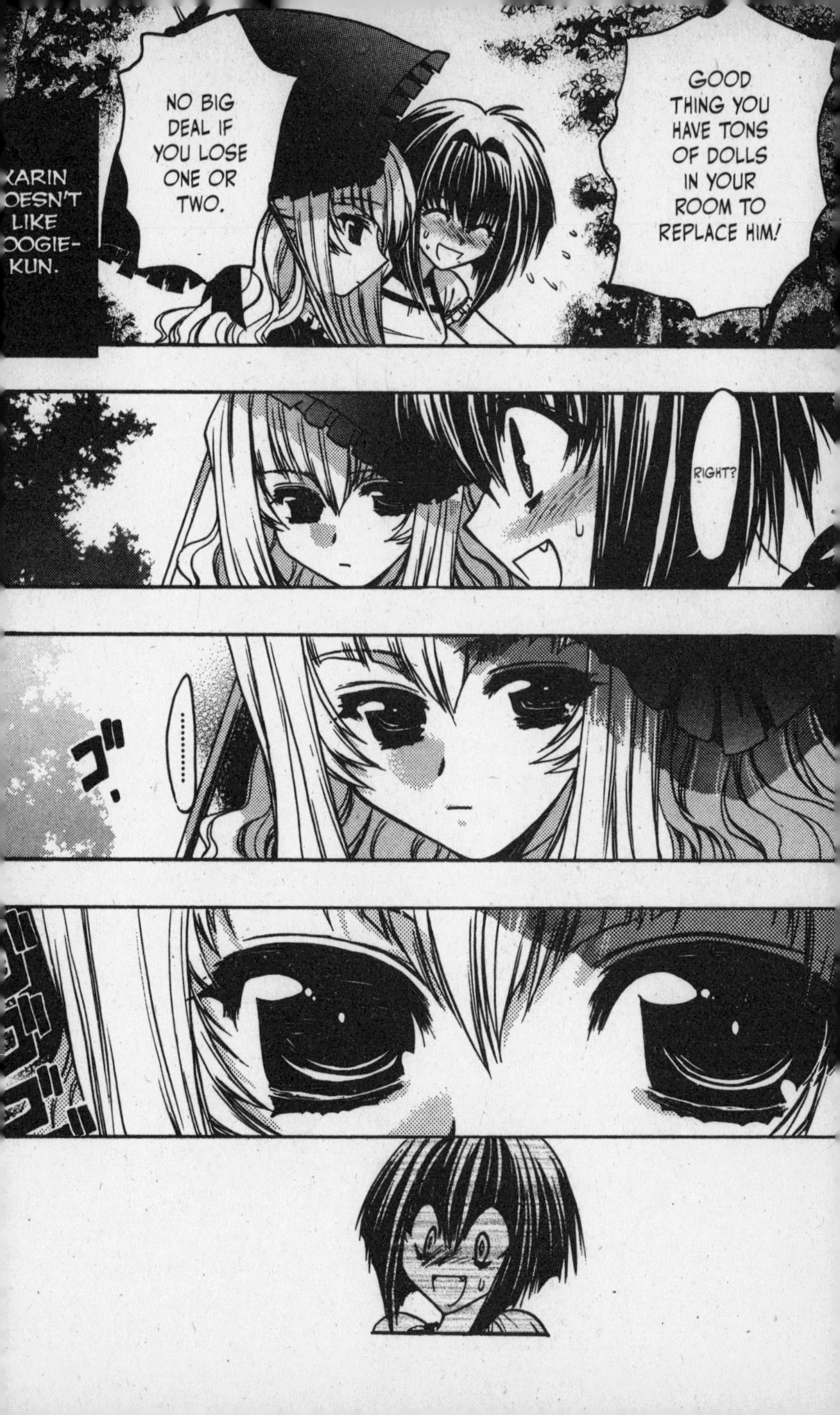
GOOD THING YOU HAVE TONS OF DOLLS IN YOUR ROOM TO REPLACE HIM!
NO BIG DEAL IF YOU LOSE ONE OR TWO.
ARIN OESN'T LIKE OOGIE-KUN.
RIGHT?
....
ゴ

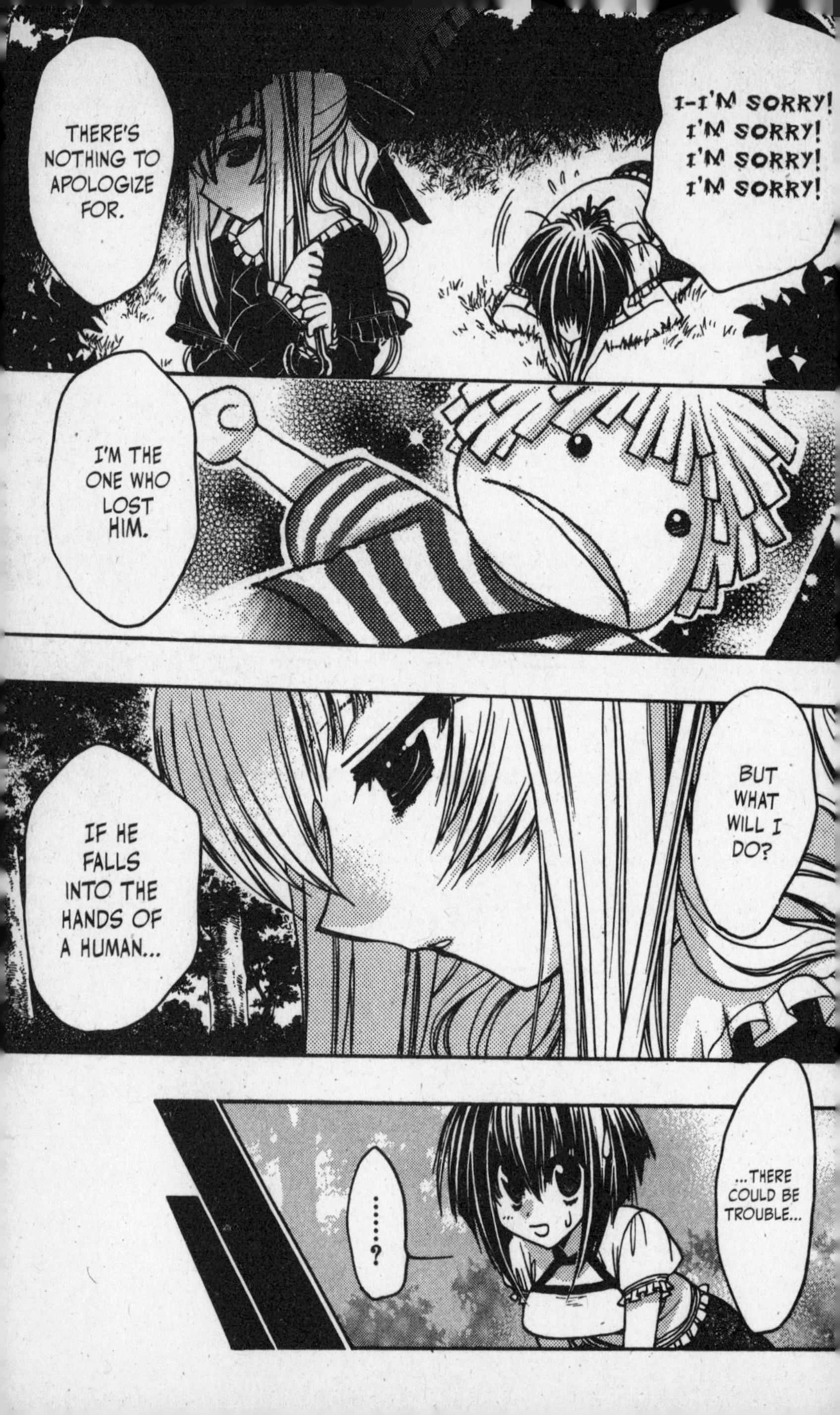
I-I'M SORRY! I'M SORRY! I'M SORRY! I'M SORRY!
THERE'S NOTHING TO APOLOGIZE FOR.
I'M THE ONE WHO LOST HIM.
BUT WHAT WILL I DO?
IF HE FALLS INTO THE HANDS OF A HUMAN...
...THERE COULD BE TROUBLE...
.....?

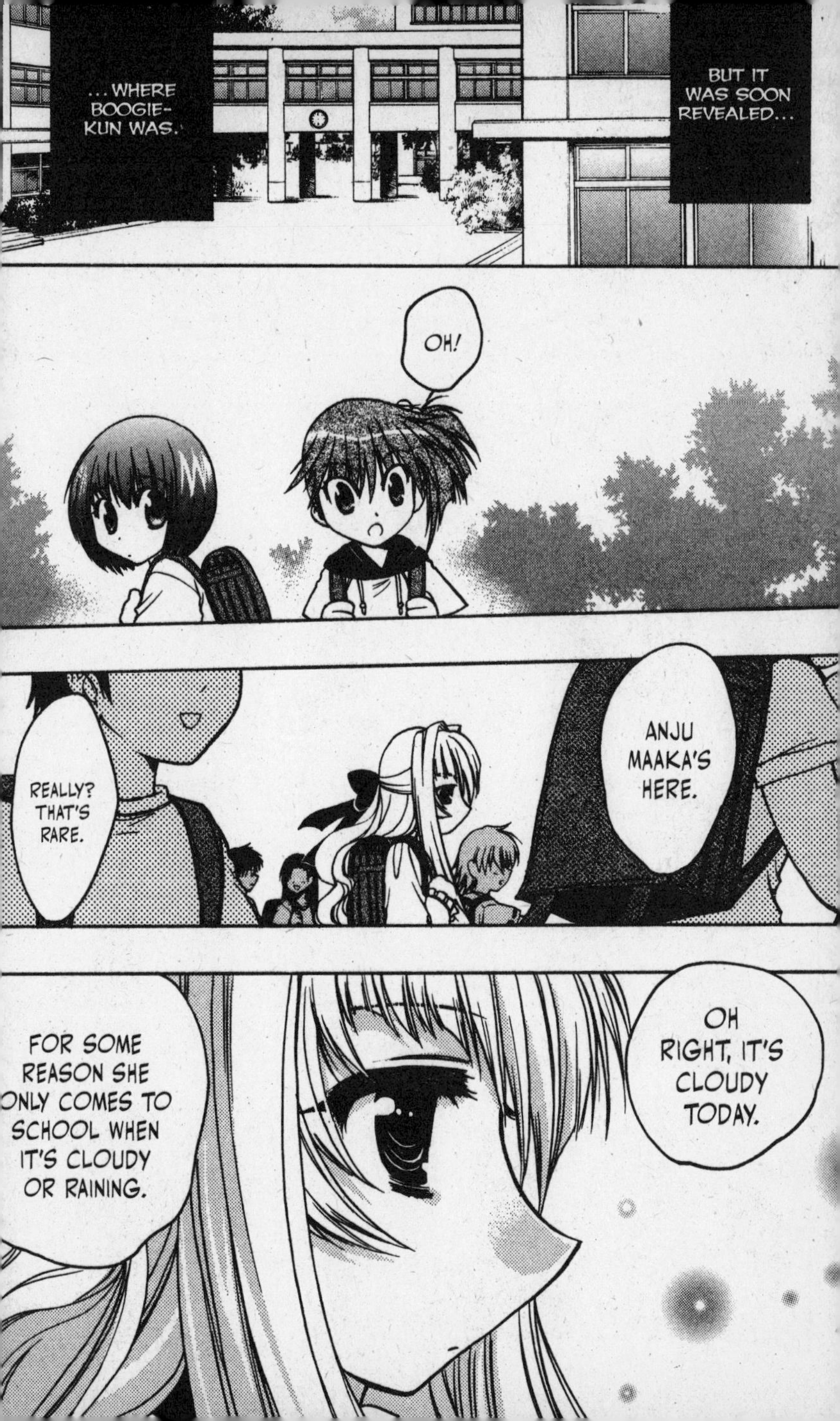
BUT IT WAS SOON REVEALED...
...WHERE BOOGIE-KUN WAS.
OH!
ANJU MAAKA'S HERE.
REALLY? THAT'S RARE.
OH RIGHT, IT'S CLOUDY TODAY.
FOR SOME REASON SHE ONLY COMES TO SCHOOL WHEN IT'S CLOUDY OR RAINING.

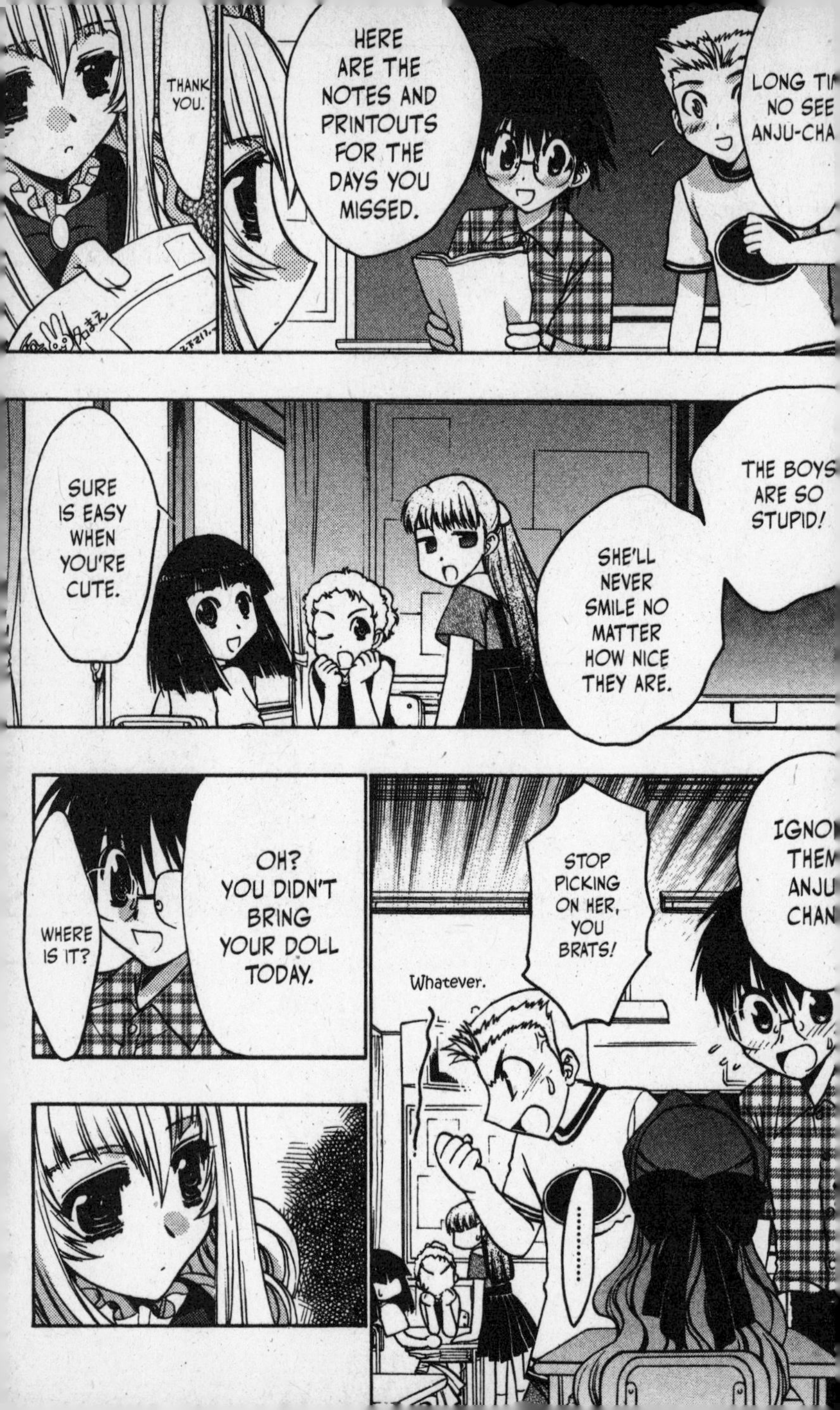
LONG TI NO SEE ANJU-CHA
HERE ARE THE NOTES AND PRINTOUTS FOR THE DAYS YOU MISSED.
THANK YOU.
THE BOYS ARE SO STUPID!
SHE'LL NEVER SMILE NO MATTER HOW NICE THEY ARE.
SURE IS EASY WHEN YOU'RE CUTE.
IGNO THEM ANJU CHAN
STOP PICKING ON HER, YOU BRATS!
Whatever.
......
OH? YOU DIDN'T BRING YOUR DOLL TODAY.
WHERE IS IT?

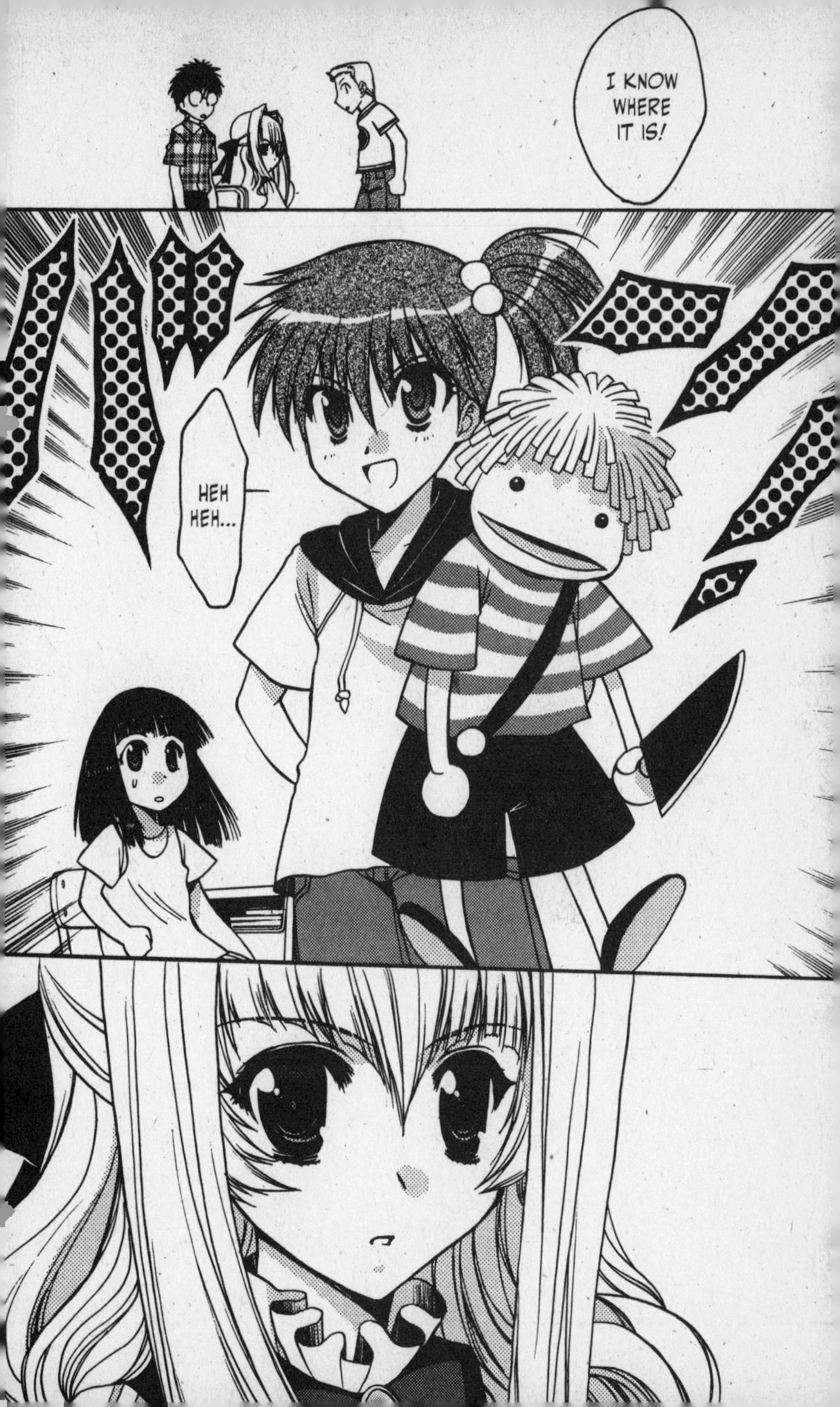
I KNOW WHERE IT IS!
HEH HEH...

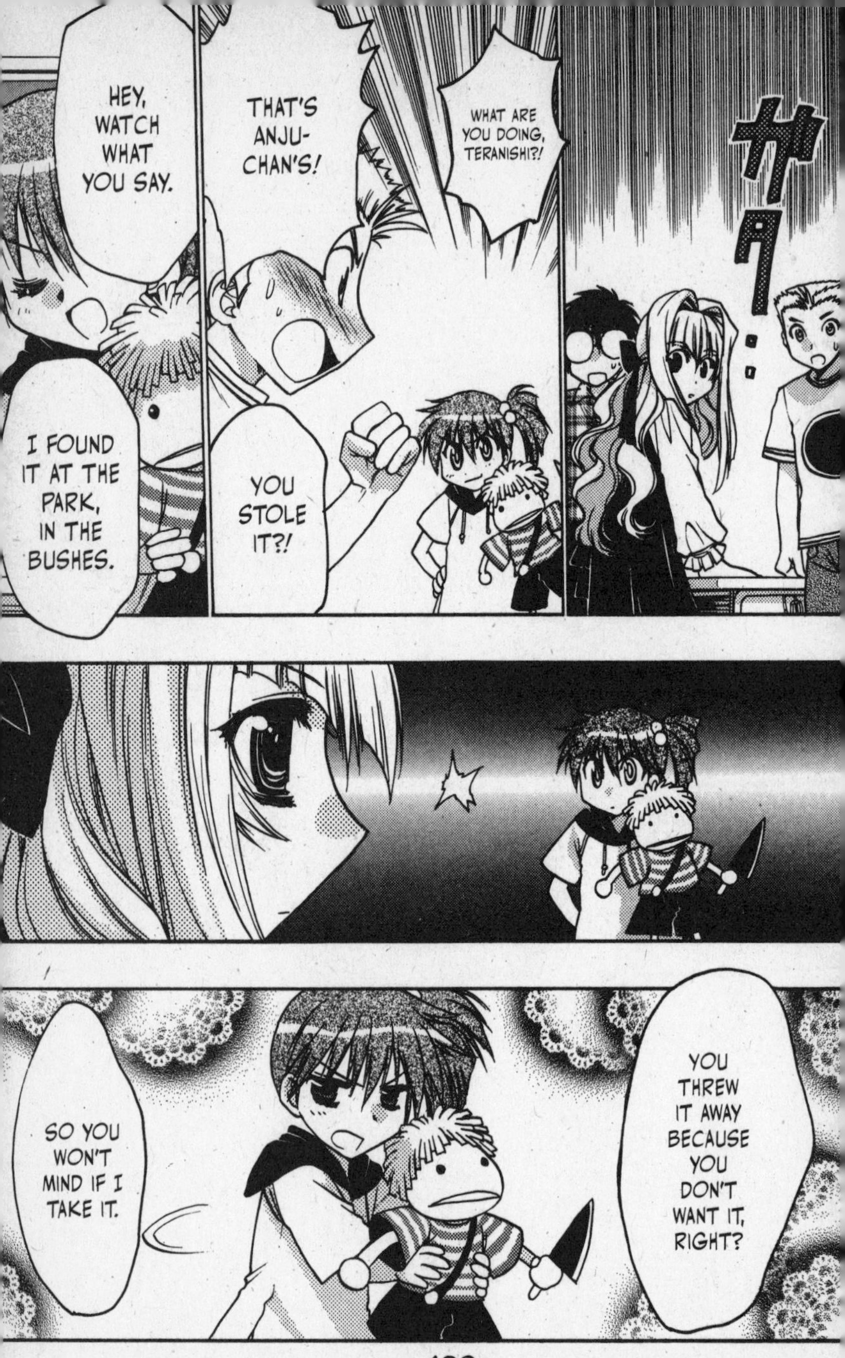
カタ
WHAT ARE YOU DOING, TERANISHI?!
THAT'S ANJU-CHAN'S!
YOU STOLE IT?!
HEY, WATCH WHAT YOU SAY.
I FOUND IT AT THE PARK, IN THE BUSHES.
YOU THREW IT AWAY BECAUSE YOU DON'T WANT IT, RIGHT?
SO YOU WON'T MIND IF I TAKE IT.

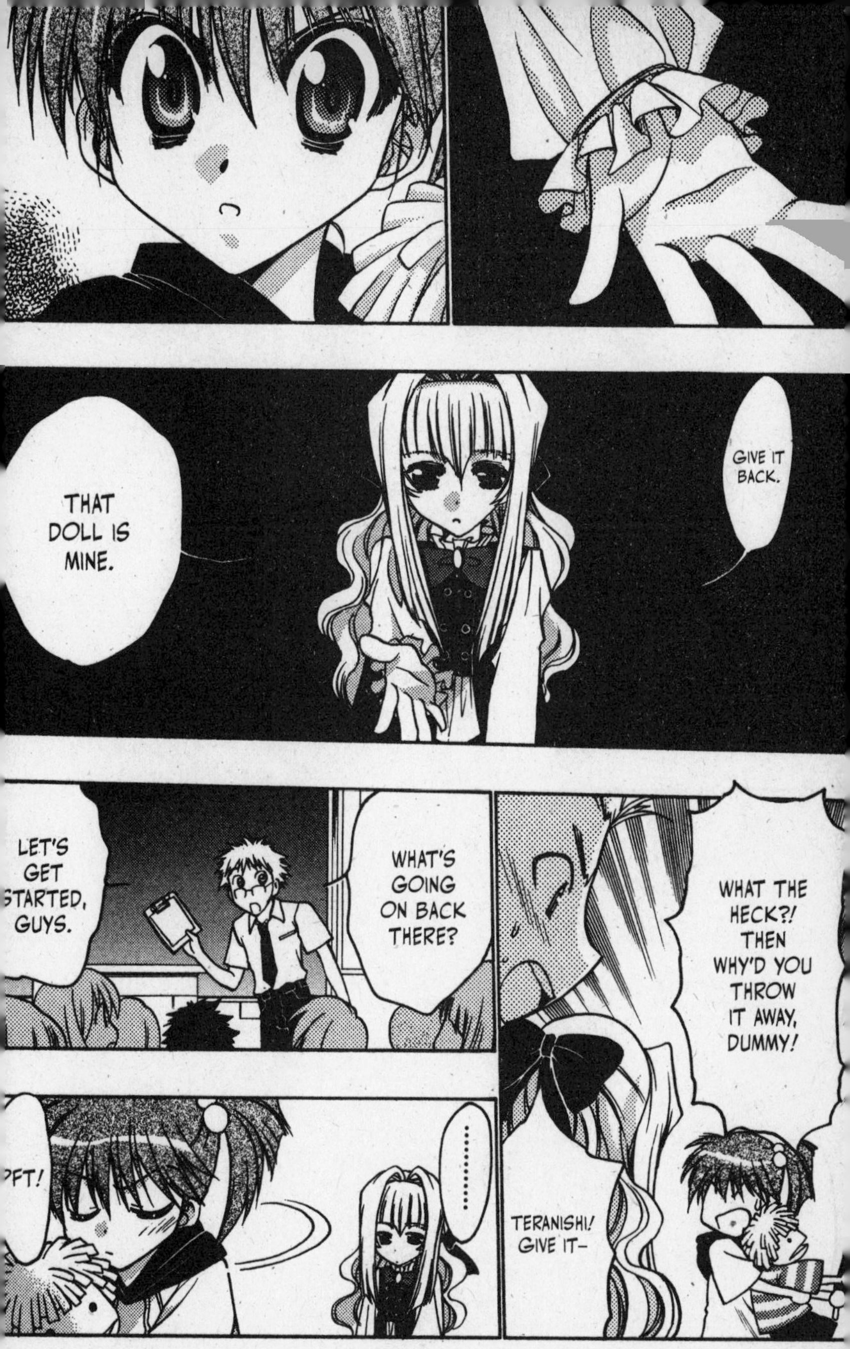
GIVE IT BACK.
THAT DOLL IS MINE.
WHAT THE HECK?! THEN WHY'D YOU THROW IT AWAY, DUMMY!
TERANISHI! GIVE IT–
WHAT'S GOING ON BACK THERE?
LET'S GET STARTED, GUYS.
....
PFT!

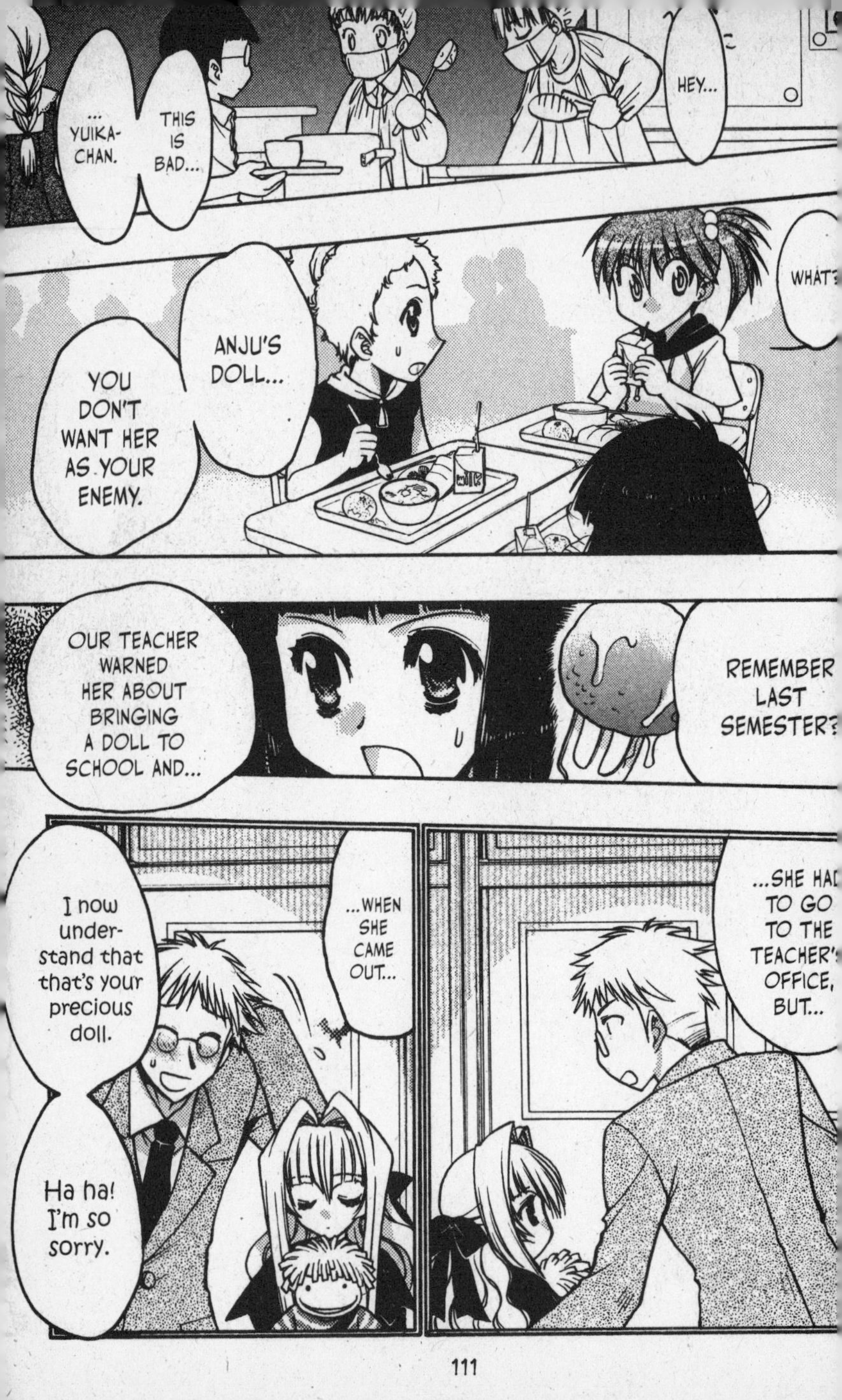
HEY...
THIS IS BAD...
...YUIKA-CHAN.
WHAT?
ANJU'S DOLL...
YOU DON'T WANT HER AS YOUR ENEMY.
REMEMBER LAST SEMESTER?
OUR TEACHER WARNED HER ABOUT BRINGING A DOLL TO SCHOOL AND...
...SHE HAD TO GO TO THE TEACHER'S OFFICE, BUT...
...WHEN SHE CAME OUT...
I now understand that that's your precious doll.
Ha ha! I'm so sorry.

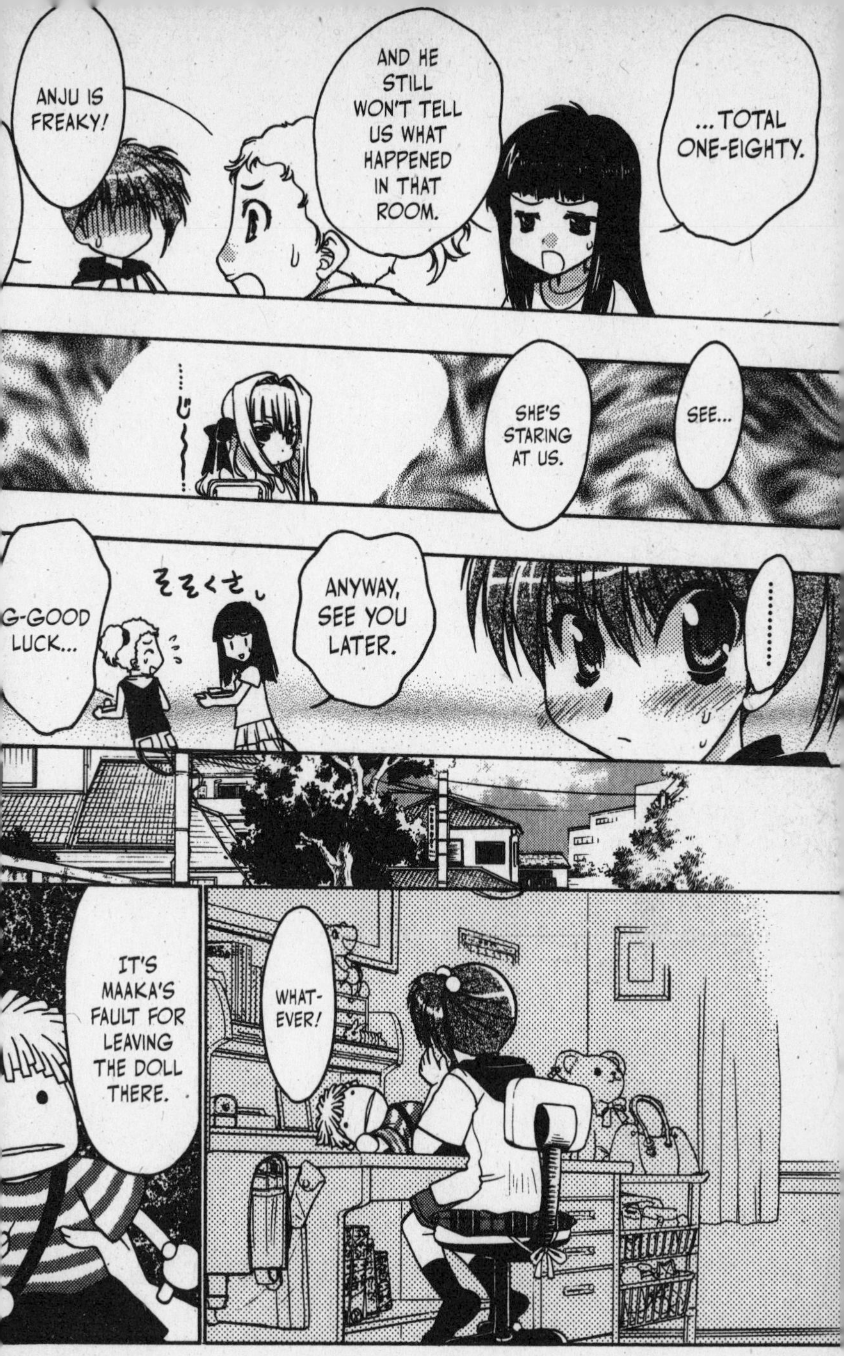
...TOTAL ONE-EIGHTY.
AND HE STILL WON'T TELL US WHAT HAPPENED IN THAT ROOM.
ANJU IS FREAKY!
SEE...
SHE'S STARING AT US.
.....じ〜〜〜
......
ANYWAY, SEE YOU LATER.
そそくさ
G-GOOD LUCK...
WHAT-EVER!
IT'S MAAKA'S FAULT FOR LEAVING THE DOLL THERE.

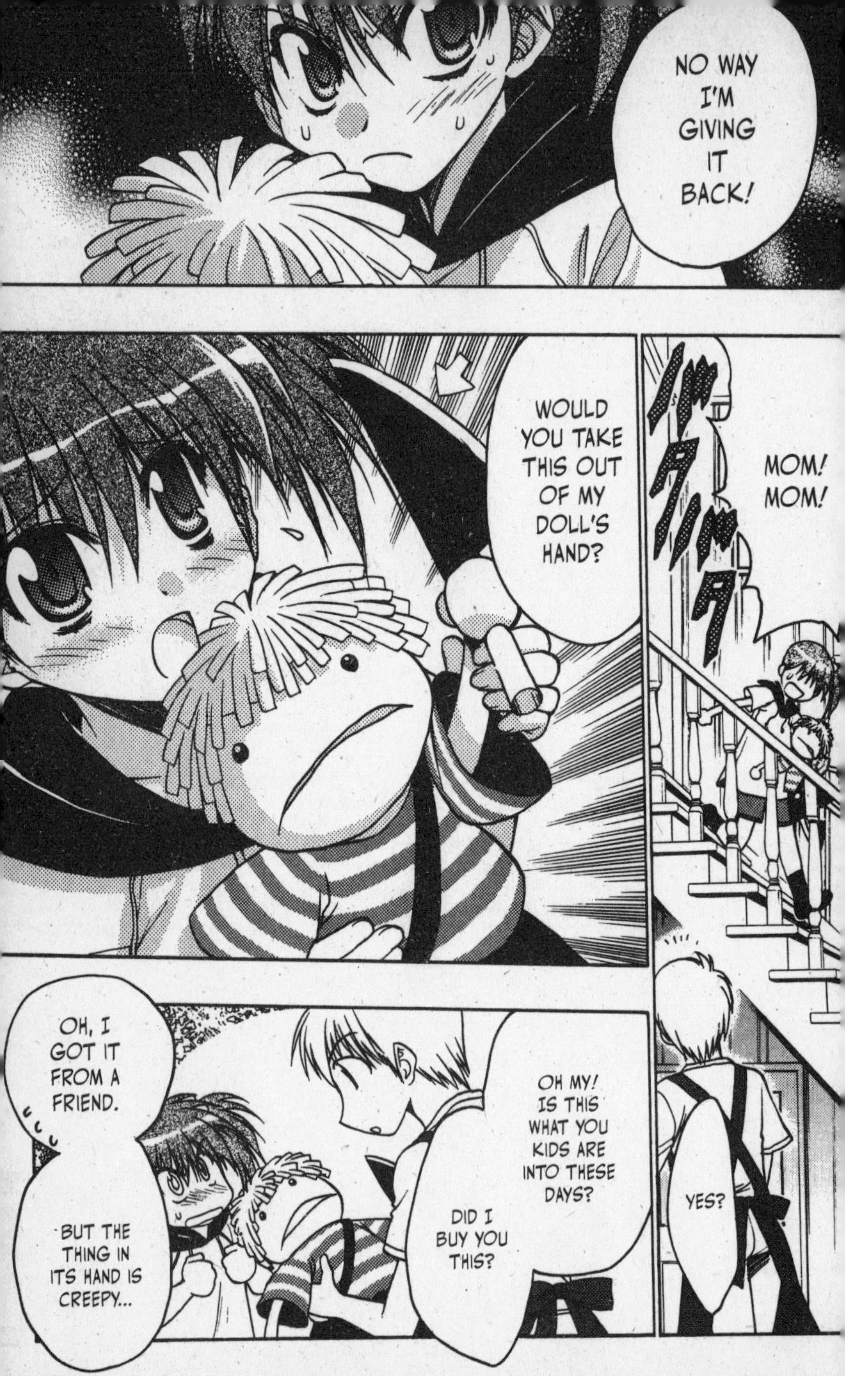
NO WAY I'M GIVING IT BACK!
MOM! MOM!
WOULD YOU TAKE THIS OUT OF MY DOLL'S HAND?
YES?
OH MY! IS THIS WHAT YOU KIDS ARE INTO THESE DAYS?
DID I BUY YOU THIS?
OH, I GOT IT FROM A FRIEND.
BUT THE THING IN ITS HAND IS CREEPY...

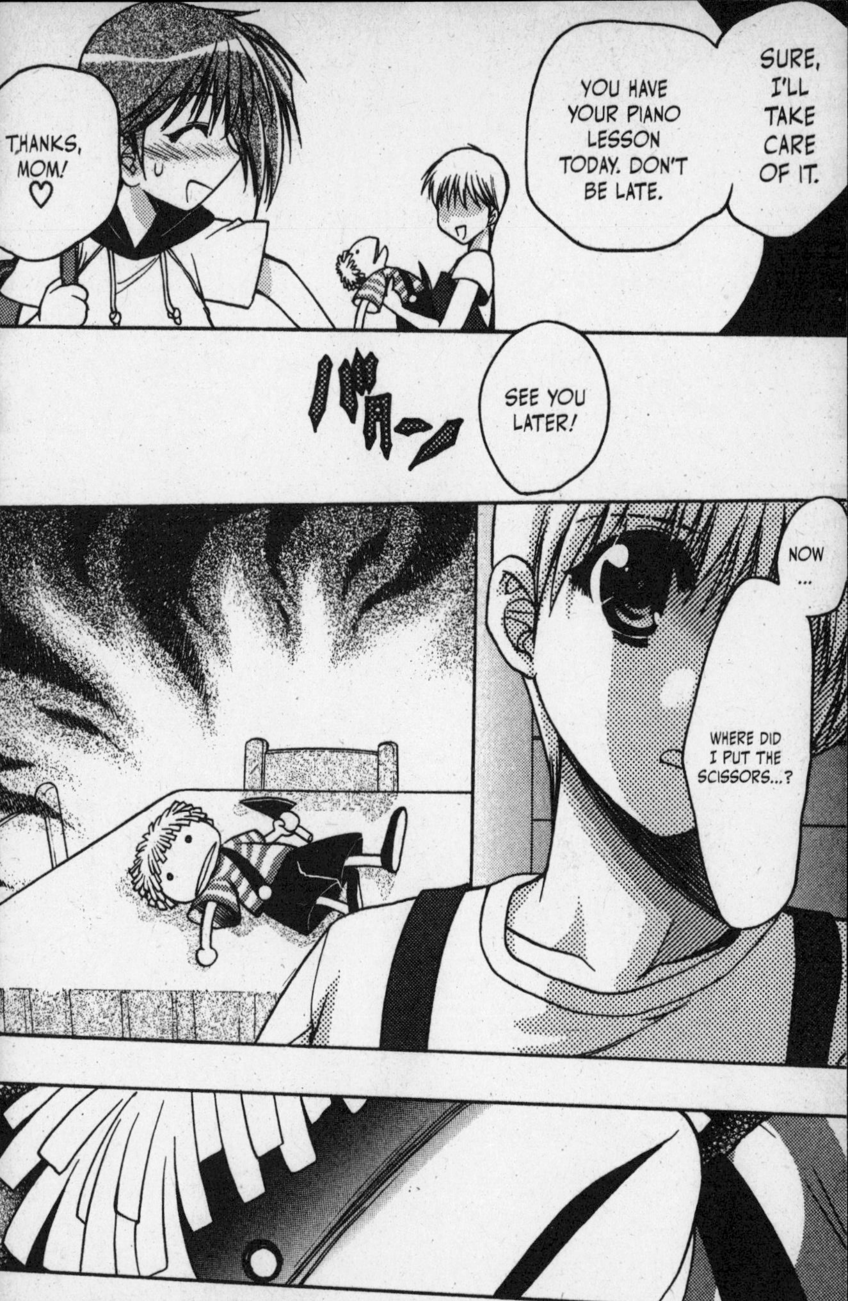
SURE, I'LL TAKE CARE OF IT.
YOU HAVE YOUR PIANO LESSON TODAY. DON'T BE LATE.
THANKS, MOM! ♡
SEE YOU LATER!
バターン
NOW ...
WHERE DID I PUT THE SCISSORS...?

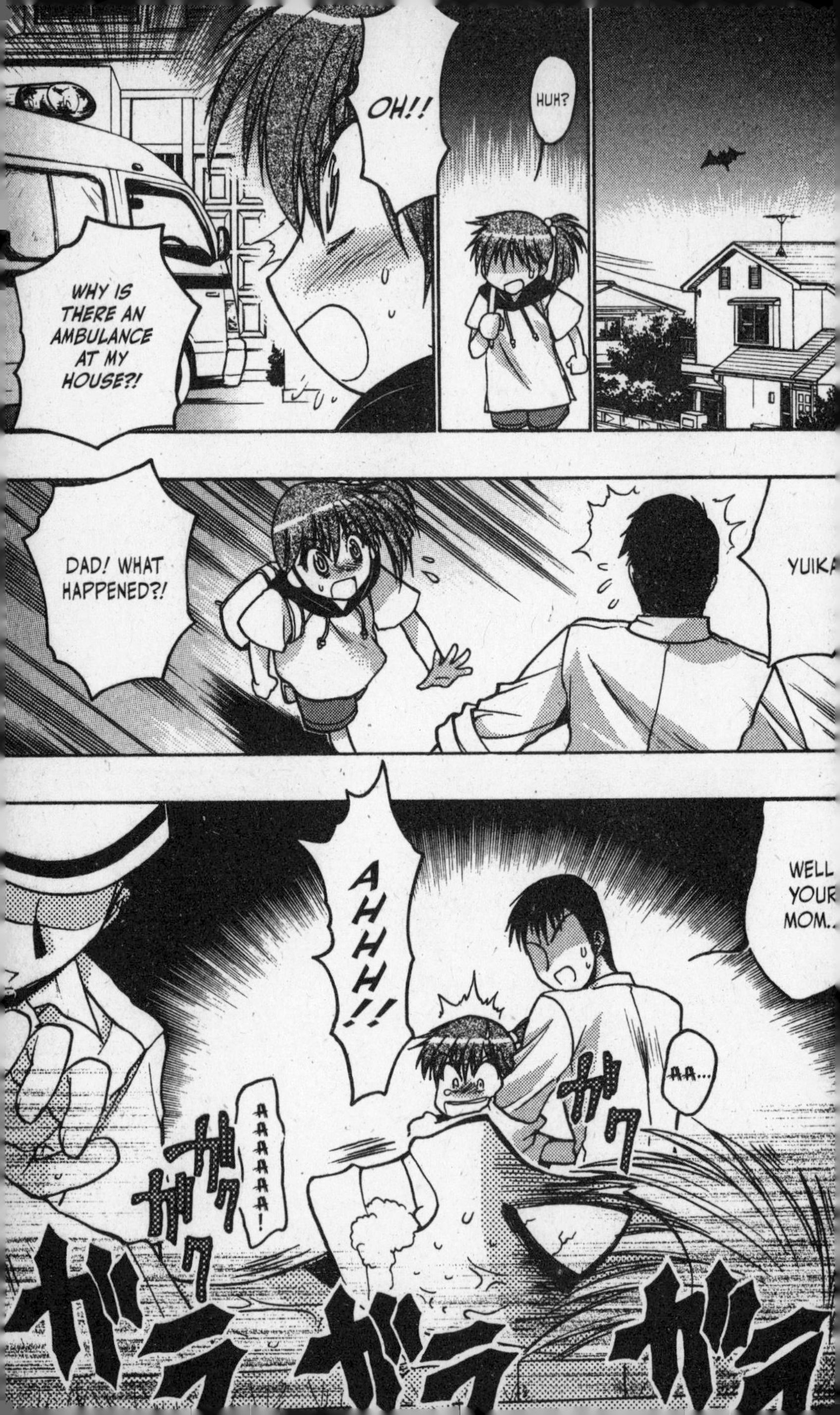
HUH?
OH!!
WHY IS THERE AN AMBULANCE AT MY HOUSE?!
YUIKA
DAD! WHAT HAPPENED?!
WELL YOUR MOM...
AHHHH!!
AA...
ガク
AAAAAAAA!
ガク ガク

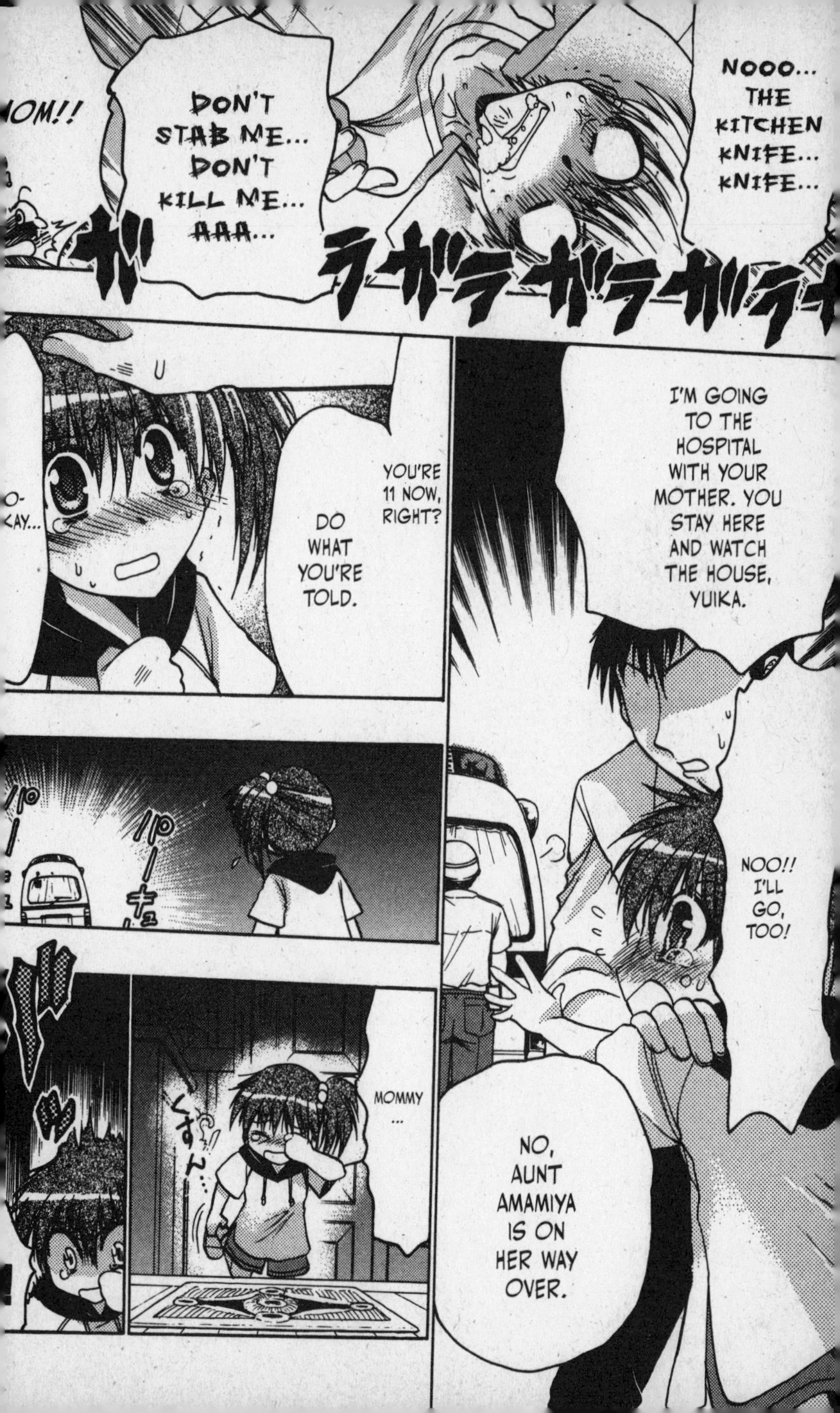
NOOO... THE KITCHEN KNIFE... KNIFE...
DON'T STAB ME... DON'T KILL ME... AAA...
OM!!
I'M GOING TO THE HOSPITAL WITH YOUR MOTHER. YOU STAY HERE AND WATCH THE HOUSE, YUIKA.
NOO!! I'LL GO, TOO!
NO, AUNT AMAMIYA IS ON HER WAY OVER.
YOU'RE 11 NOW, RIGHT?
DO WHAT YOU'RE TOLD.
O-KAY...
MOMMY ...

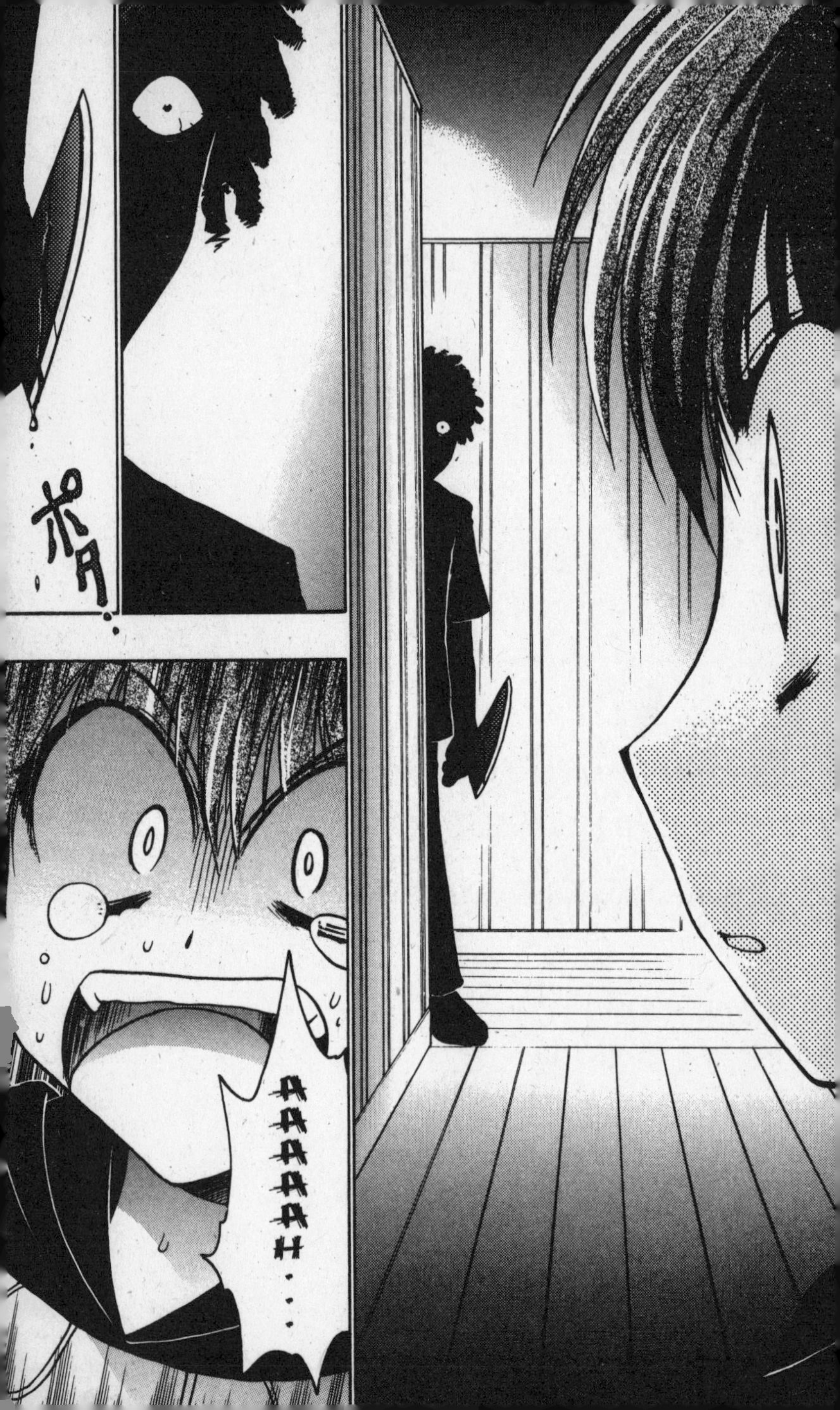
ポタ
AAAAAAH...

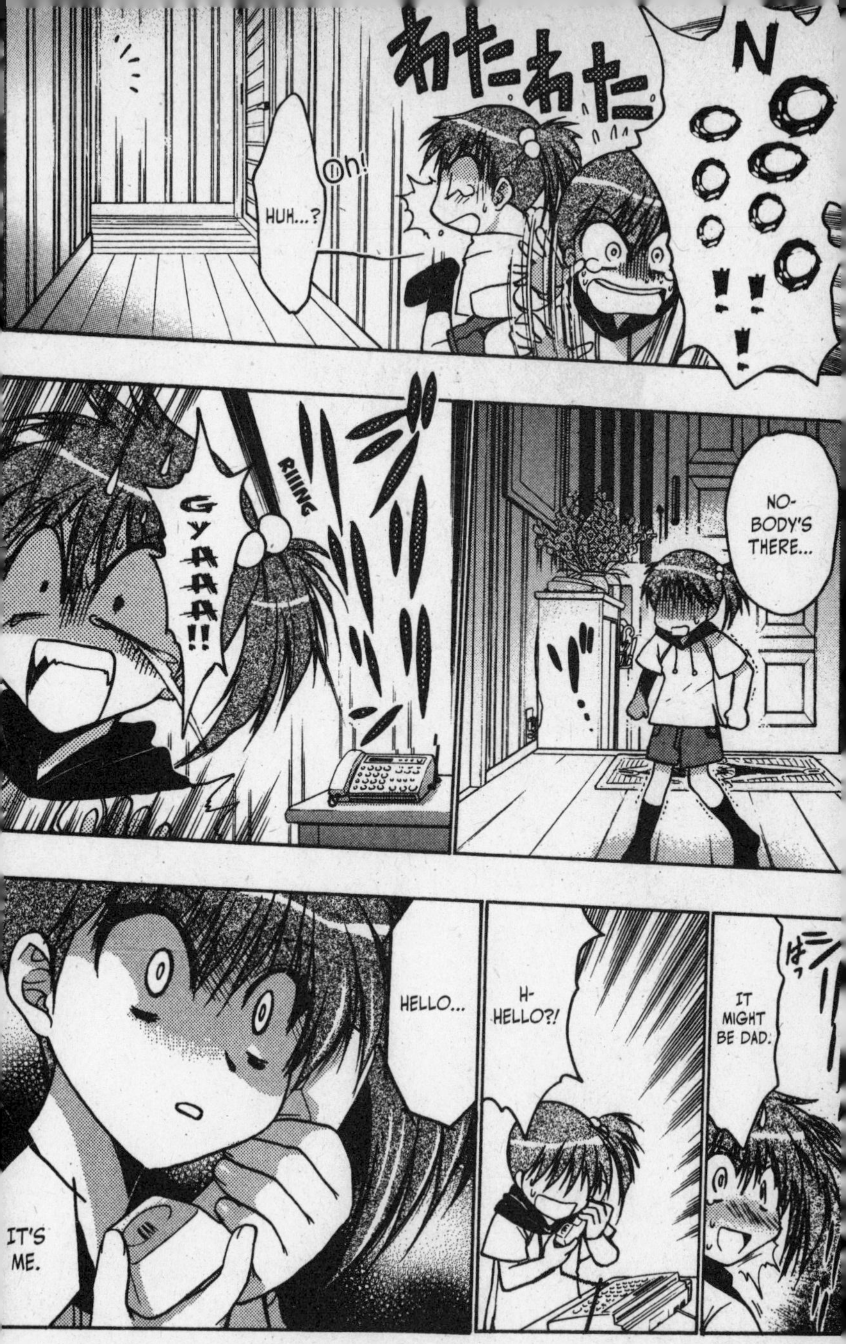
NOOOOOOOOO!!!
わたわた
Oh!
HUH...?
NO-BODY'S THERE...
RIIING
GYAAAA!!
はっ
IT MIGHT BE DAD.
H-HELLO?!
HELLO...
IT'S ME.

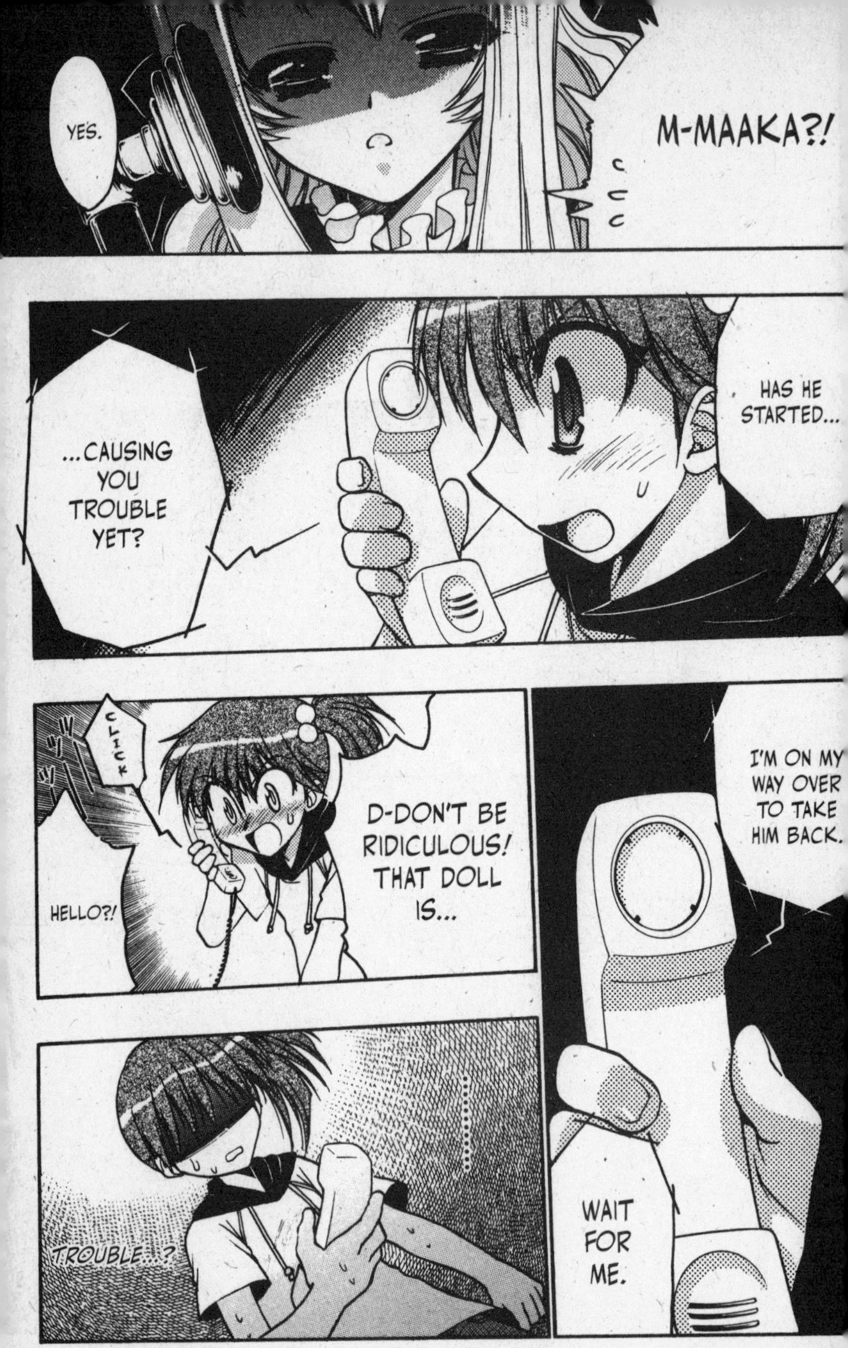
M-MAAKA?!
YES.
HAS HE STARTED...
...CAUSING YOU TROUBLE YET?
I'M ON MY WAY OVER TO TAKE HIM BACK.
WAIT FOR ME.
D-DON'T BE RIDICULOUS! THAT DOLL IS...
CLICK
HELLO?!
TROUBLE...?

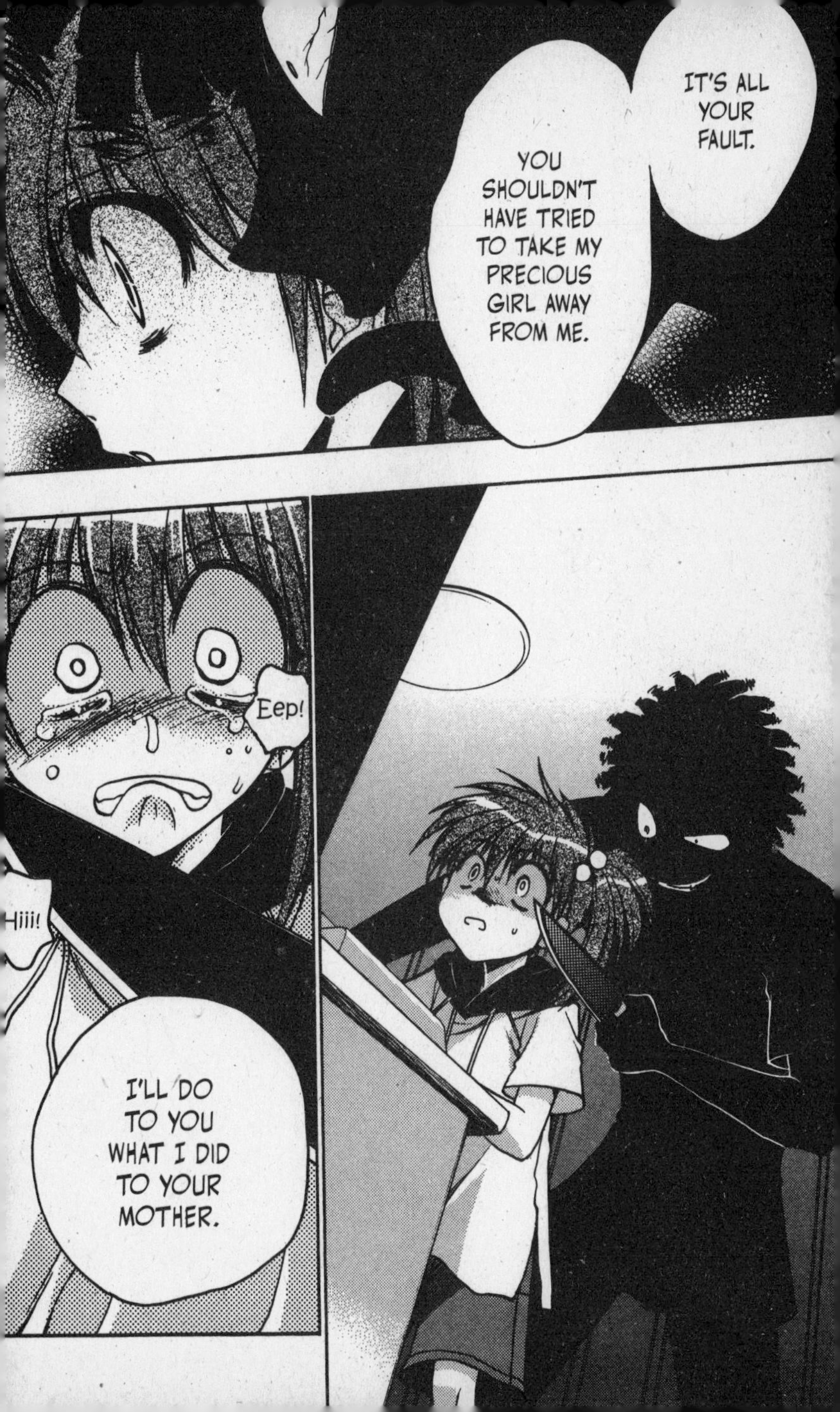
IT'S ALL YOUR FAULT.
YOU SHOULDN'T HAVE TRIED TO TAKE MY PRECIOUS GIRL AWAY FROM ME.
Eep!
Hiiii!
I'LL DO TO YOU WHAT I DID TO YOUR MOTHER.

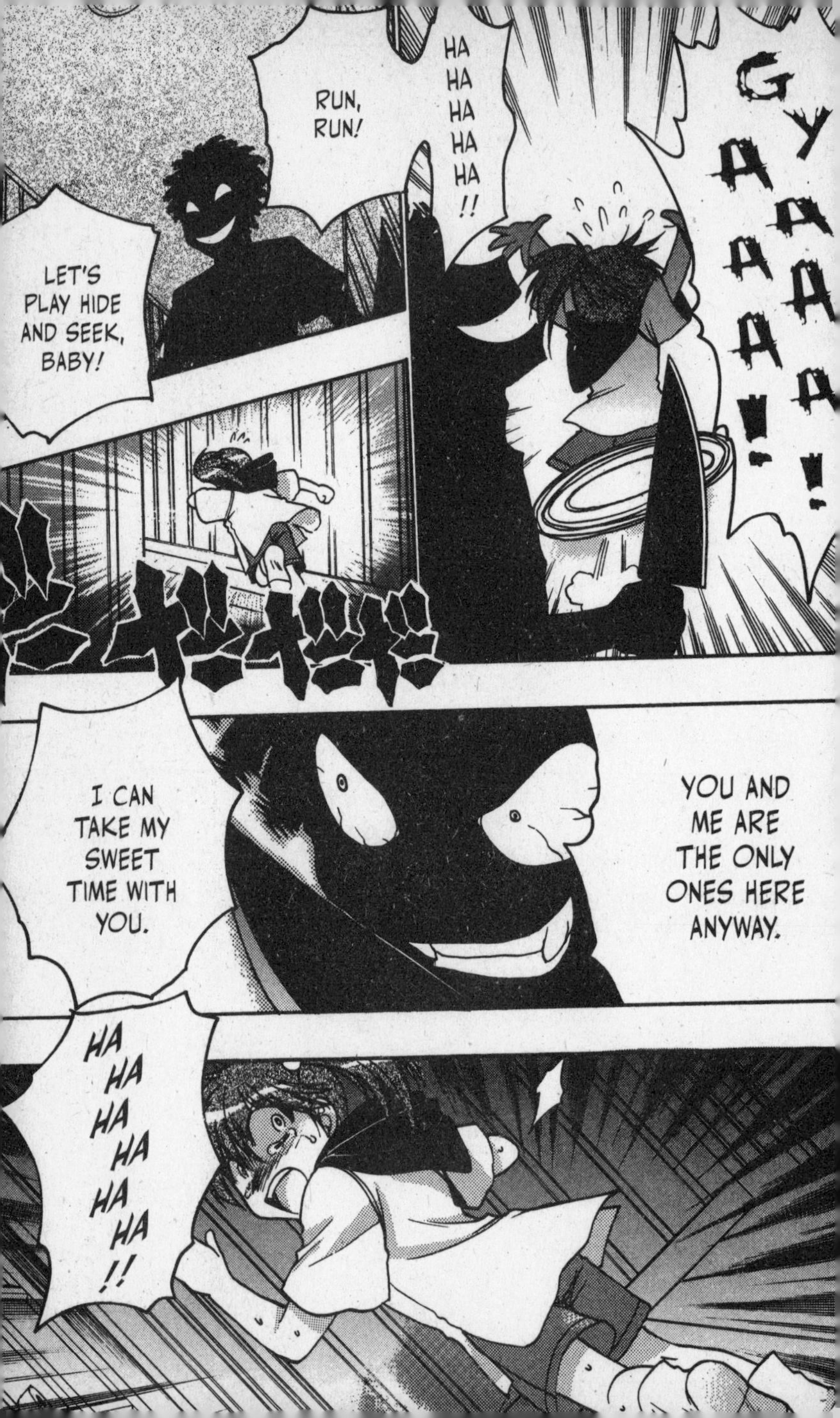
HA HA HA HA HA!!
GYAAAAAAA!!
RUN, RUN!
LET'S PLAY HIDE AND SEEK, BABY!
YOU AND ME ARE THE ONLY ONES HERE ANYWAY.
I CAN TAKE MY SWEET TIME WITH YOU.
HA HA HA HA HA HA!!

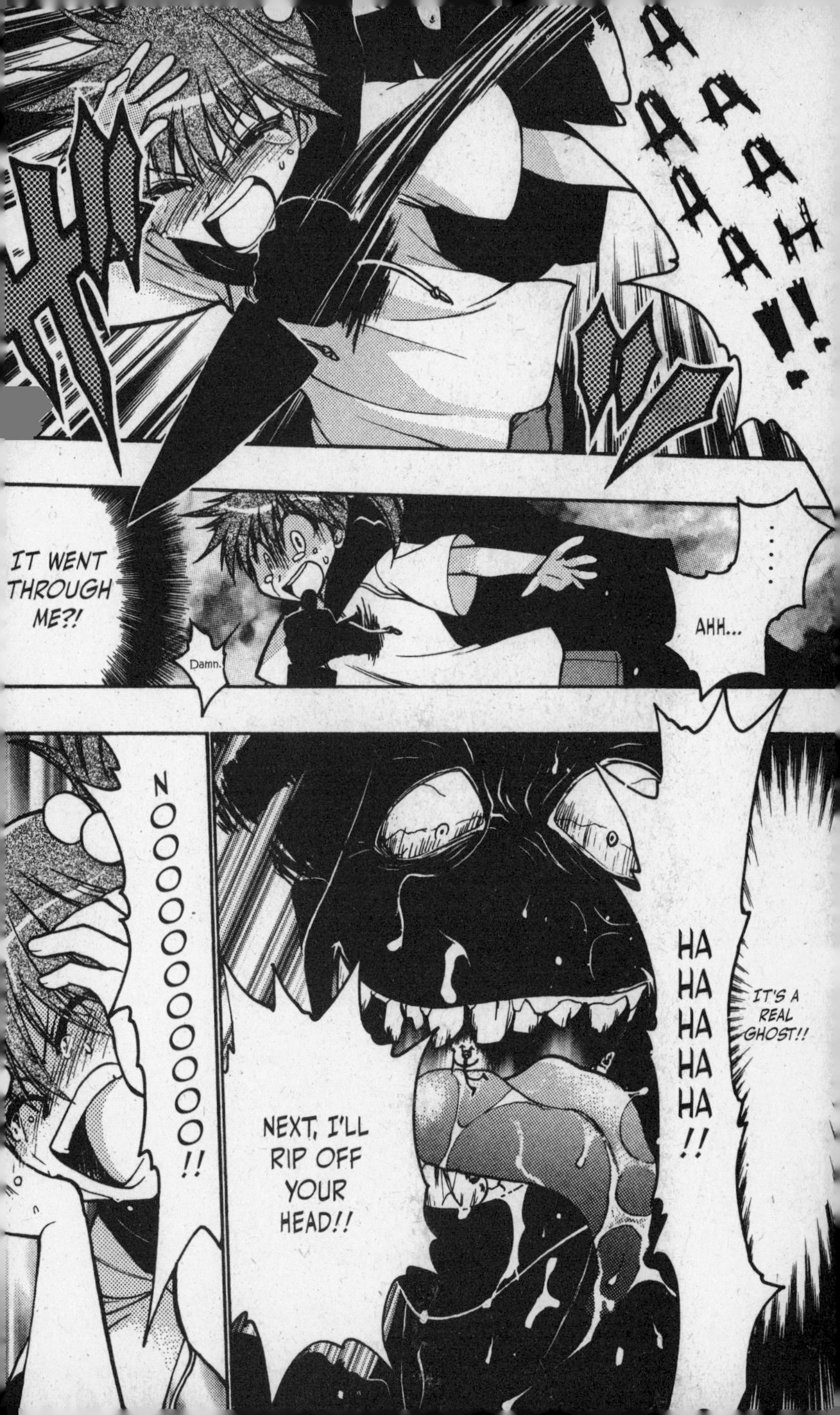
AAAAAAAAH!!
......
AHH...
IT WENT THROUGH ME?!
Damn.
IT'S A REAL GHOST!!
HAHAHAHAHAHA!!
NEXT, I'LL RIP OFF YOUR HEAD!!
NOOOOOOOOOOOOO!!

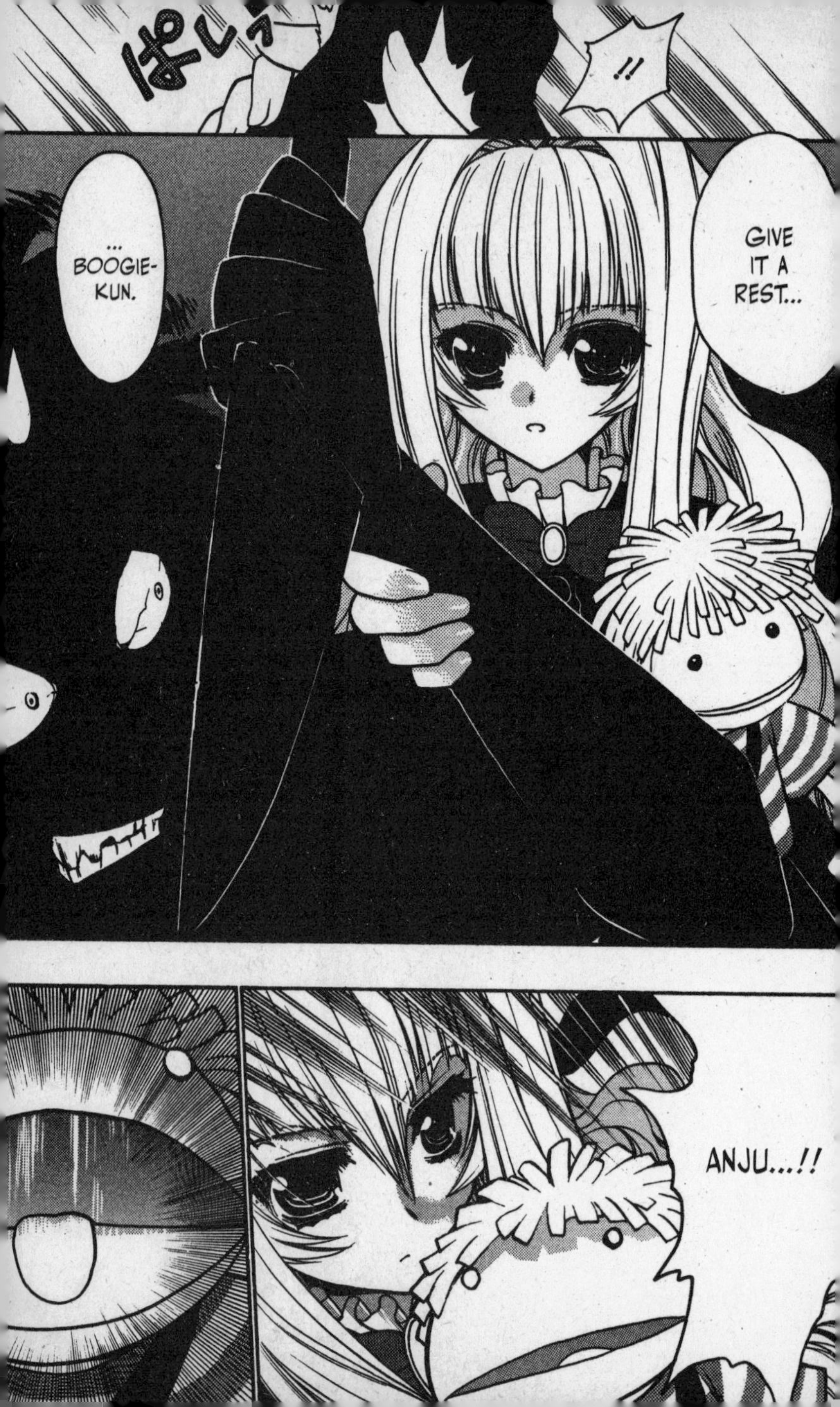
!!
ぱしっ
GIVE IT A REST...
...BOOGIE-KUN.
ANJU...!!

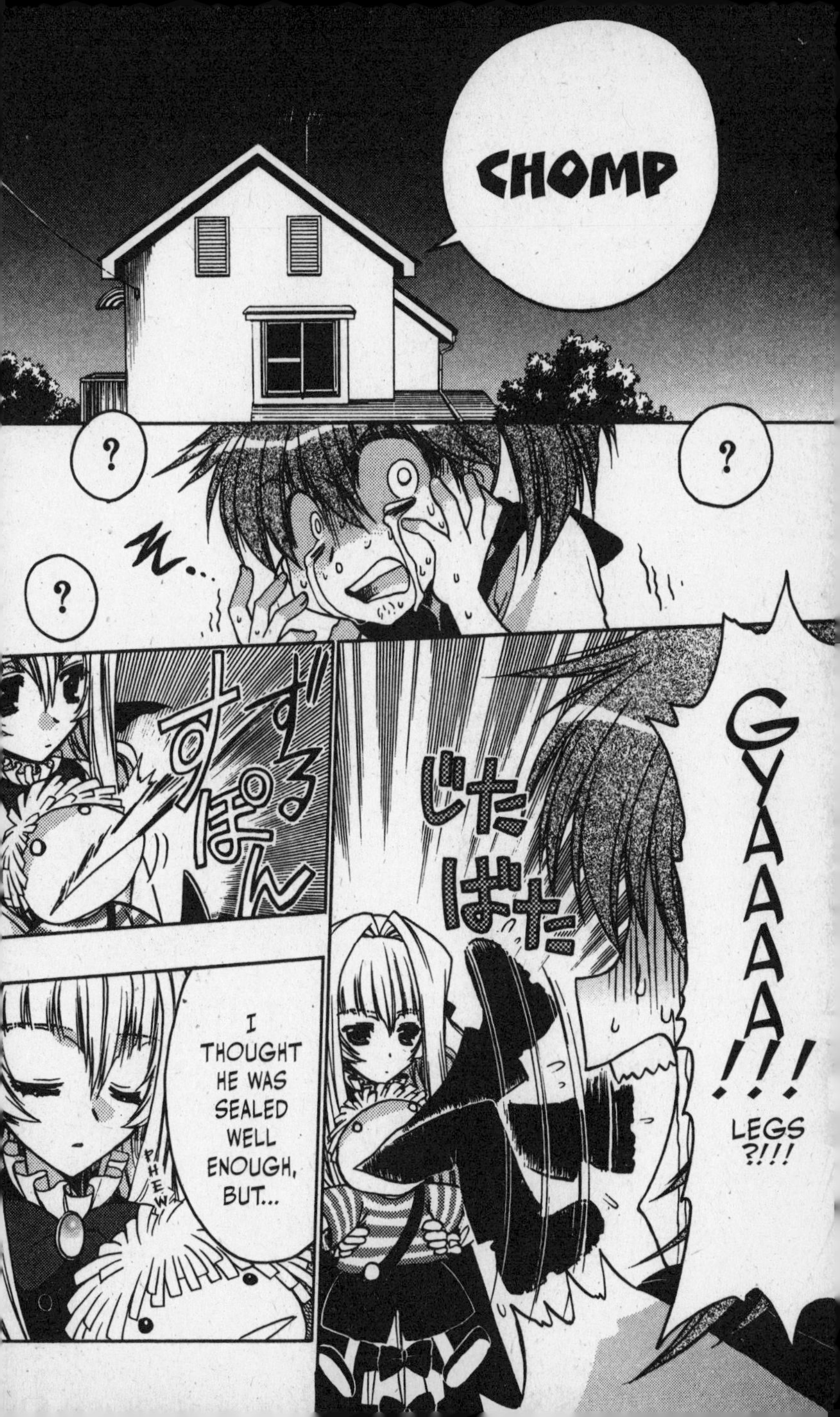

CHOMP
?
?
?
ん…
GYAAAA!!!
じたばた
LEGS?!!!
するぽん
I THOUGHT HE WAS SEALED WELL ENOUGH, BUT...
PHEW

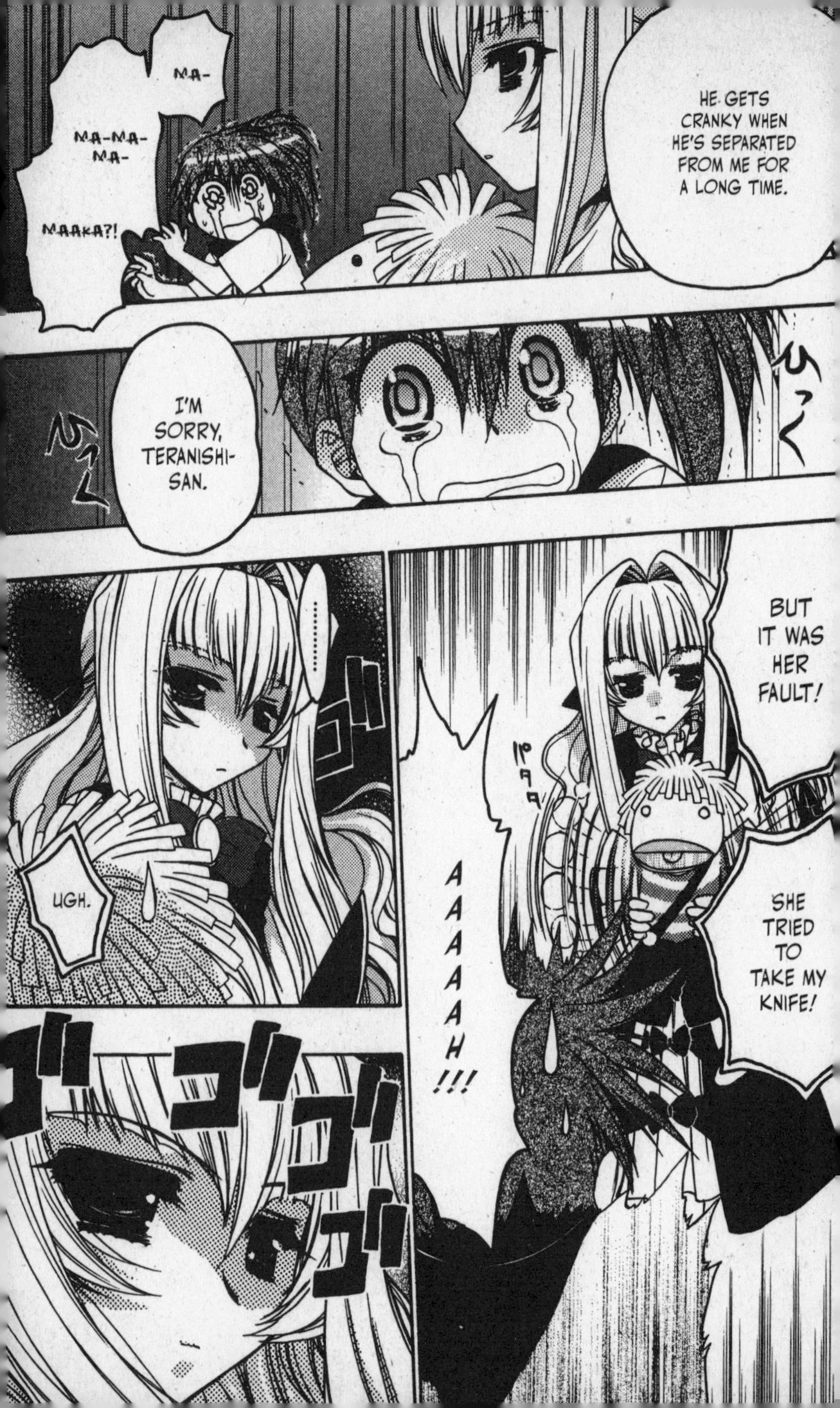
HE GETS CRANKY WHEN HE'S SEPARATED FROM ME FOR A LONG TIME.
MA-
MA-MA-MA-
MAAKA?!
I'M SORRY, TERANISHI-SAN.
BUT IT WAS HER FAULT!
SHE TRIED TO TAKE MY KNIFE!
AAAAAAH!!!
...
UGH.

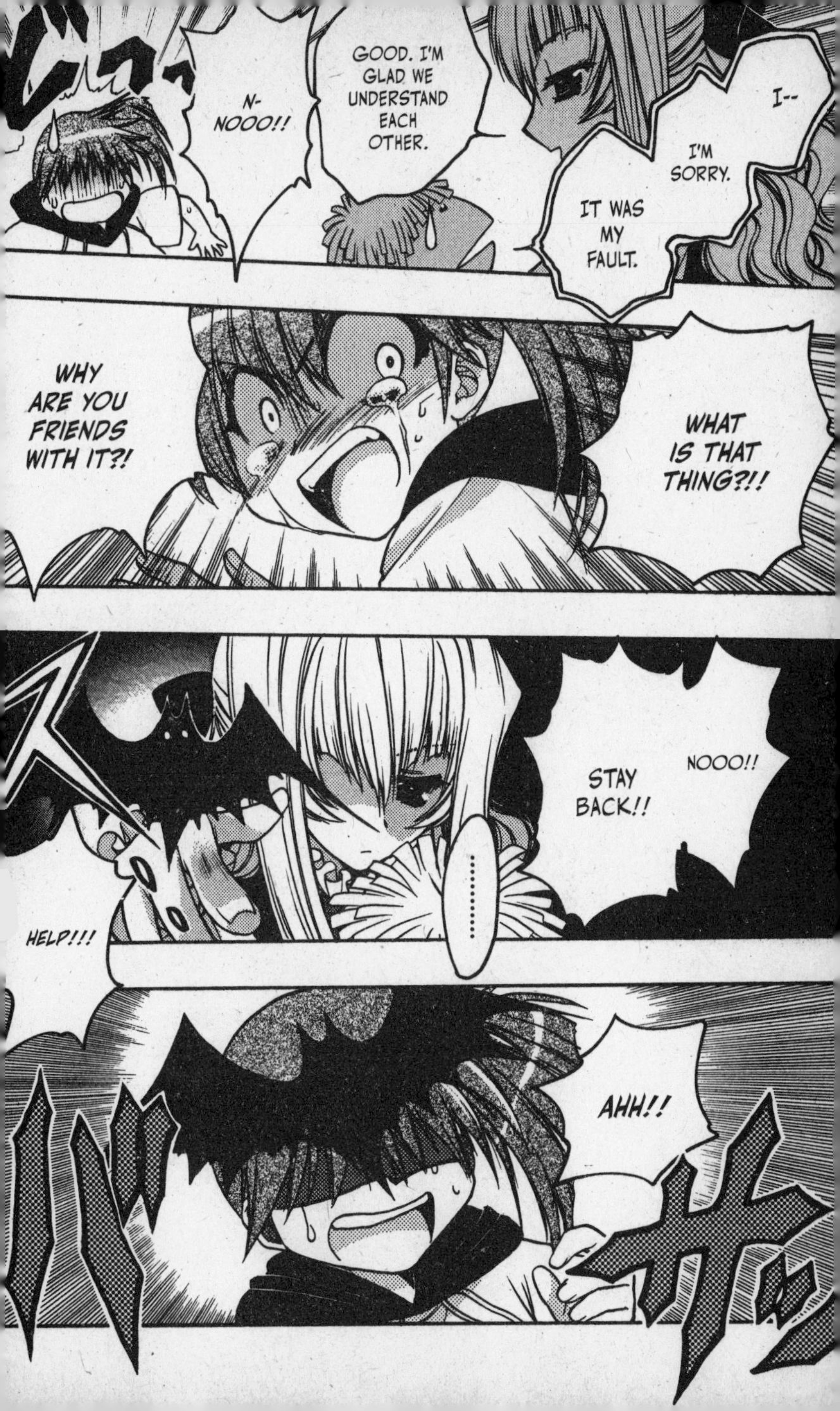
I--
I'M SORRY.
IT WAS MY FAULT.
GOOD. I'M GLAD WE UNDERSTAND EACH OTHER.
N- NOOO!!
WHAT IS THAT THING?!!
WHY ARE YOU FRIENDS WITH IT?!
NOOO!!
STAY BACK!!
......
HELP!!!
AHH!!

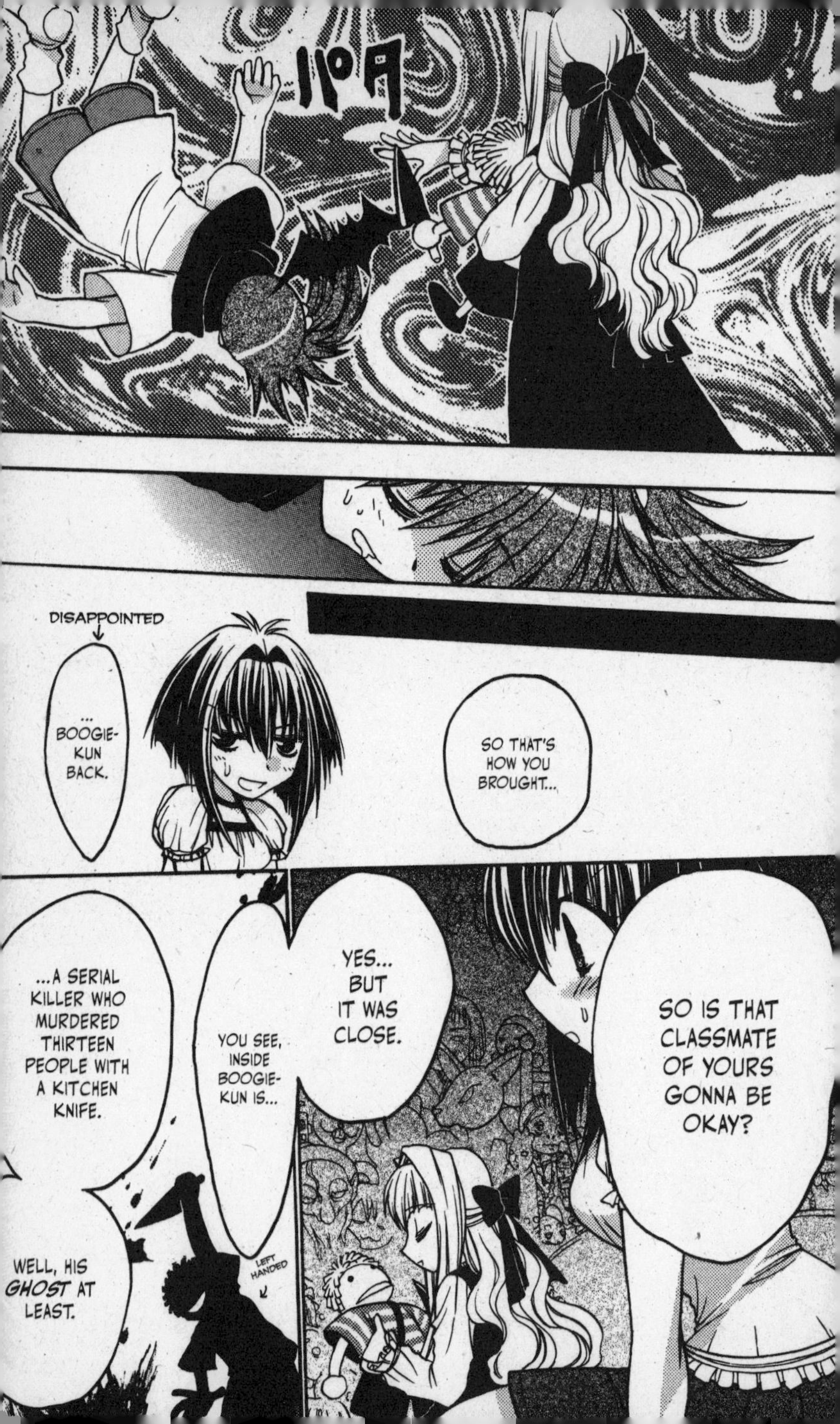
SO THAT'S HOW YOU BROUGHT...
DISAPPOINTED
...BOOGIE-KUN BACK.
SO IS THAT CLASSMATE OF YOURS GONNA BE OKAY?
YES... BUT IT WAS CLOSE.
YOU SEE, INSIDE BOOGIE-KUN IS...
LEFT HANDED
...A SERIAL KILLER WHO MURDERED THIRTEEN PEOPLE WITH A KITCHEN KNIFE.
WELL, HIS *GHOST* AT LEAST.

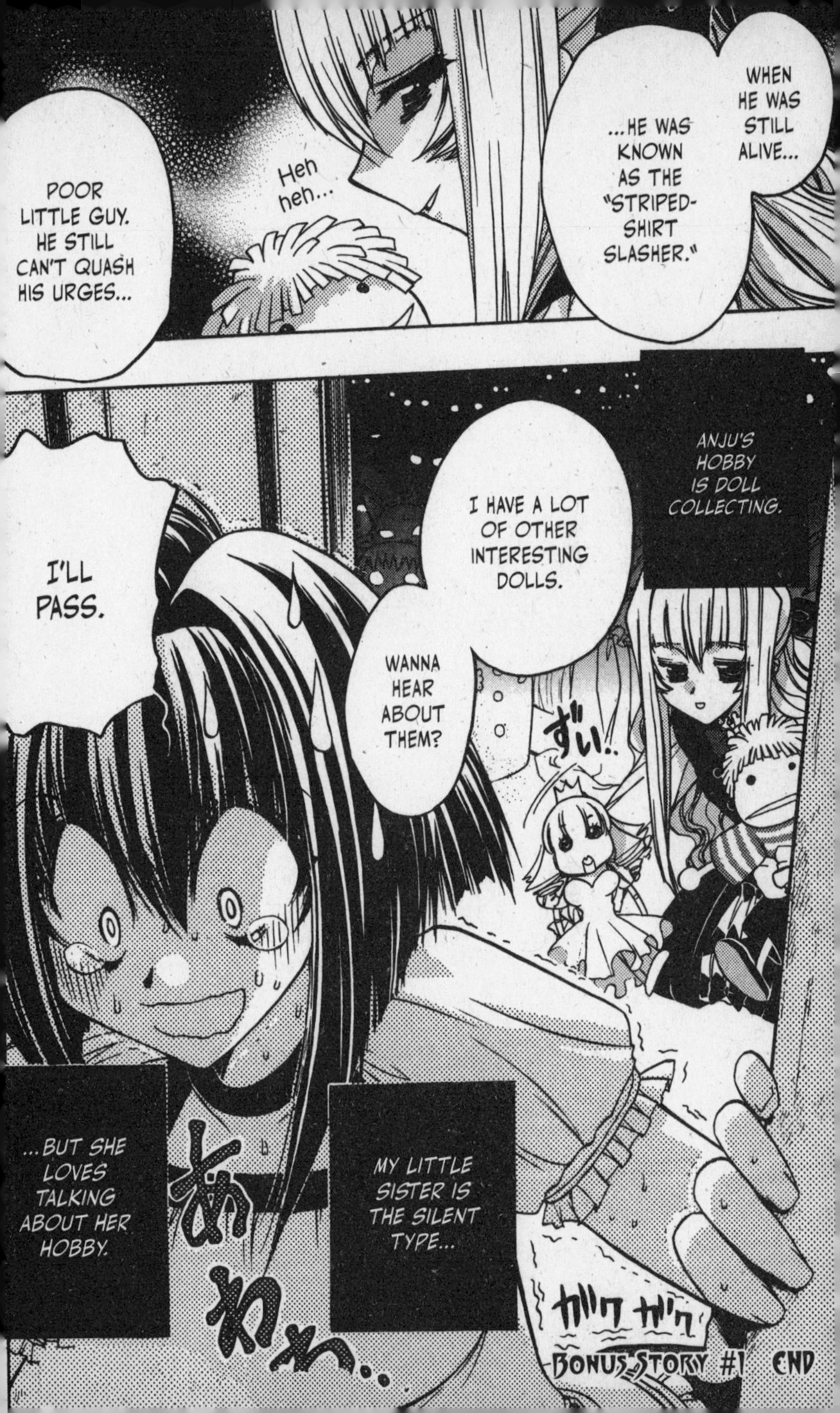
WHEN HE WAS STILL ALIVE...
...HE WAS KNOWN AS THE "STRIPED-SHIRT SLASHER."
Heh heh...
POOR LITTLE GUY. HE STILL CAN'T QUASH HIS URGES...
ANJU'S HOBBY IS DOLL COLLECTING.
I HAVE A LOT OF OTHER INTERESTING DOLLS.
WANNA HEAR ABOUT THEM?
ずい...
I'LL PASS.
MY LITTLE SISTER IS THE SILENT TYPE...
...BUT SHE LOVES TALKING ABOUT HER HOBBY.
ガクガク ガクガク
あわわ...
BONUS STORY #1 END

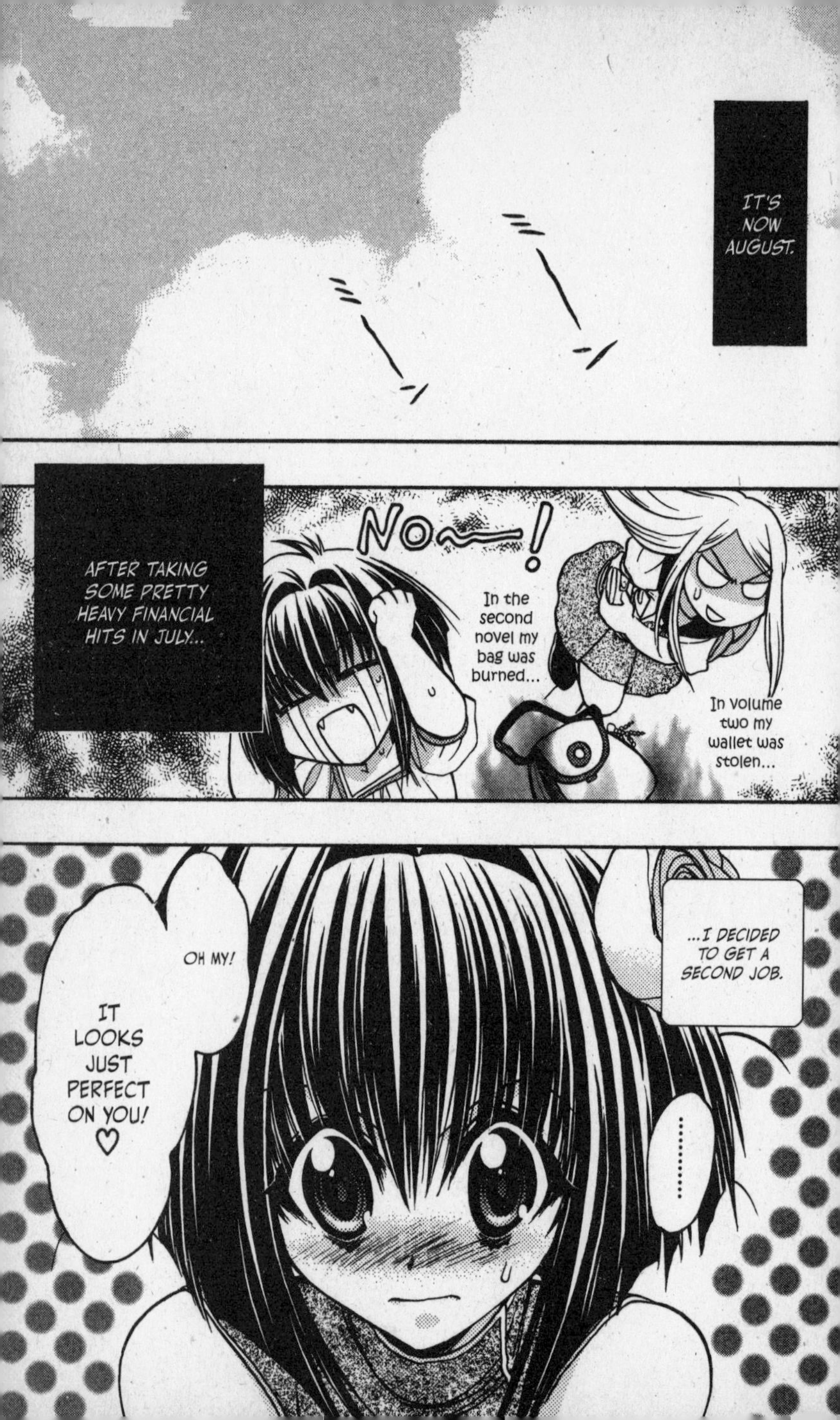
IT'S NOW AUGUST.
AFTER TAKING SOME PRETTY HEAVY FINANCIAL HITS IN JULY...
NO~~!
In volume two my wallet was stolen...
In the second novel my bag was burned...
...I DECIDED TO GET A SECOND JOB.
......
OH MY!
IT LOOKS JUST PERFECT ON YOU! ♡

4th Embarrassment) The Family Secret and Karin the Outcast
~Secret~

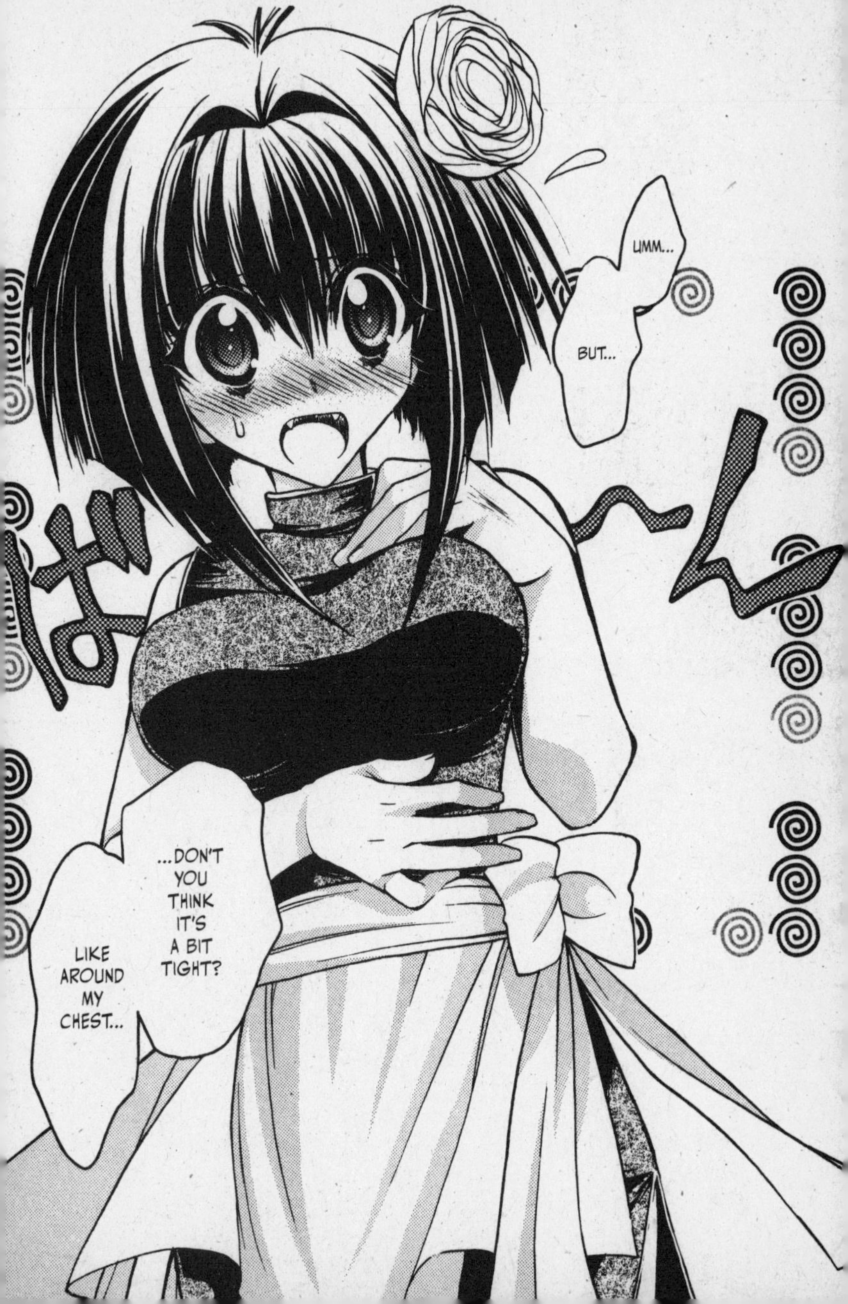
UMM...
BUT...
ば〜ん
...DON'T YOU THINK IT'S A BIT TIGHT?
LIKE AROUND MY CHEST...

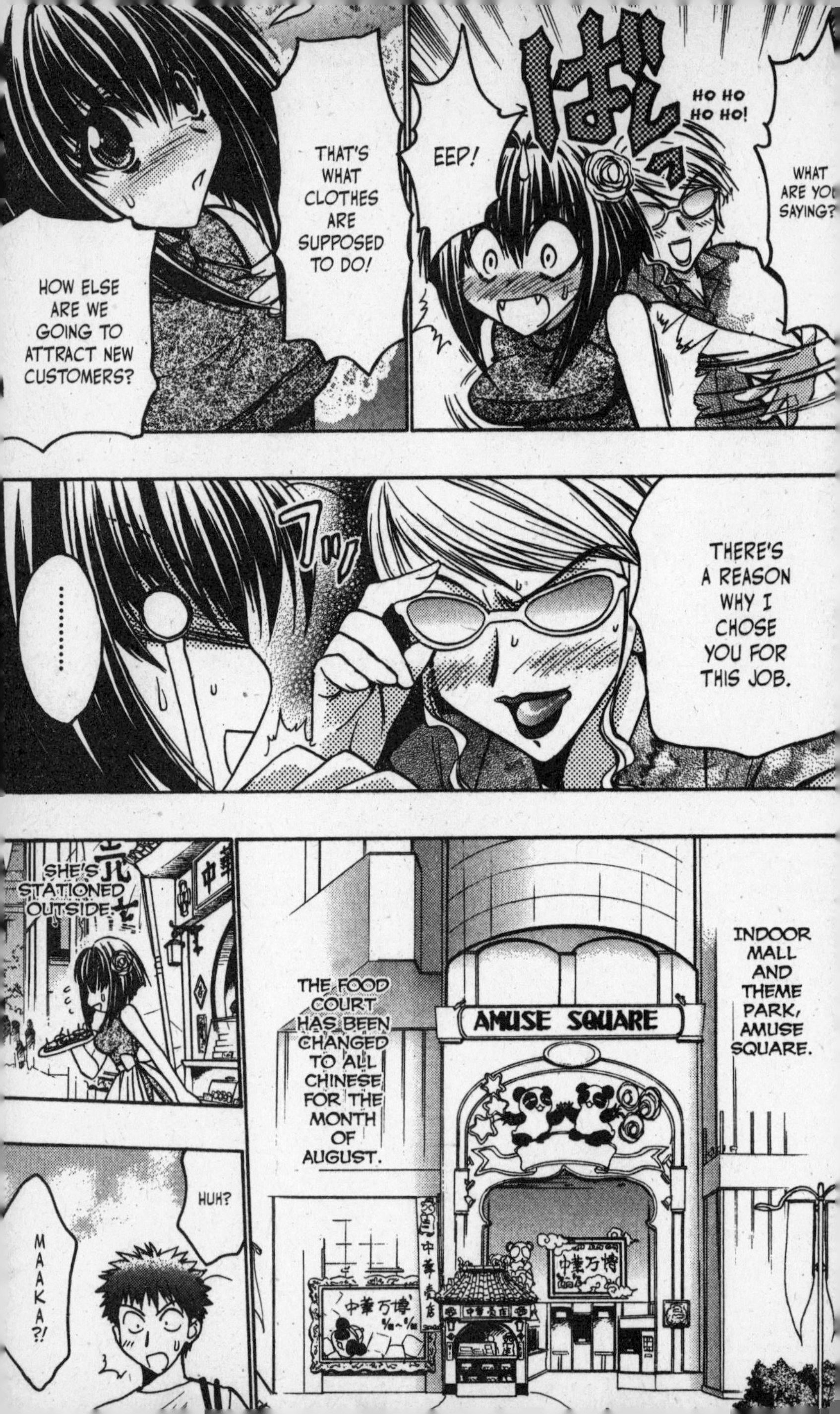
WHAT ARE YOU SAYING?
HO HO HO HO!
EEP!
THAT'S WHAT CLOTHES ARE SUPPOSED TO DO!
HOW ELSE ARE WE GOING TO ATTRACT NEW CUSTOMERS?
THERE'S A REASON WHY I CHOSE YOU FOR THIS JOB.
....
INDOOR MALL AND THEME PARK, AMUSE SQUARE.
AMUSE SQUARE
中華万博
THE FOOD COURT HAS BEEN CHANGED TO ALL CHINESE FOR THE MONTH OF AUGUST.
SHE'S STATIONED OUTSIDE.
HUH?
MAAKA?!

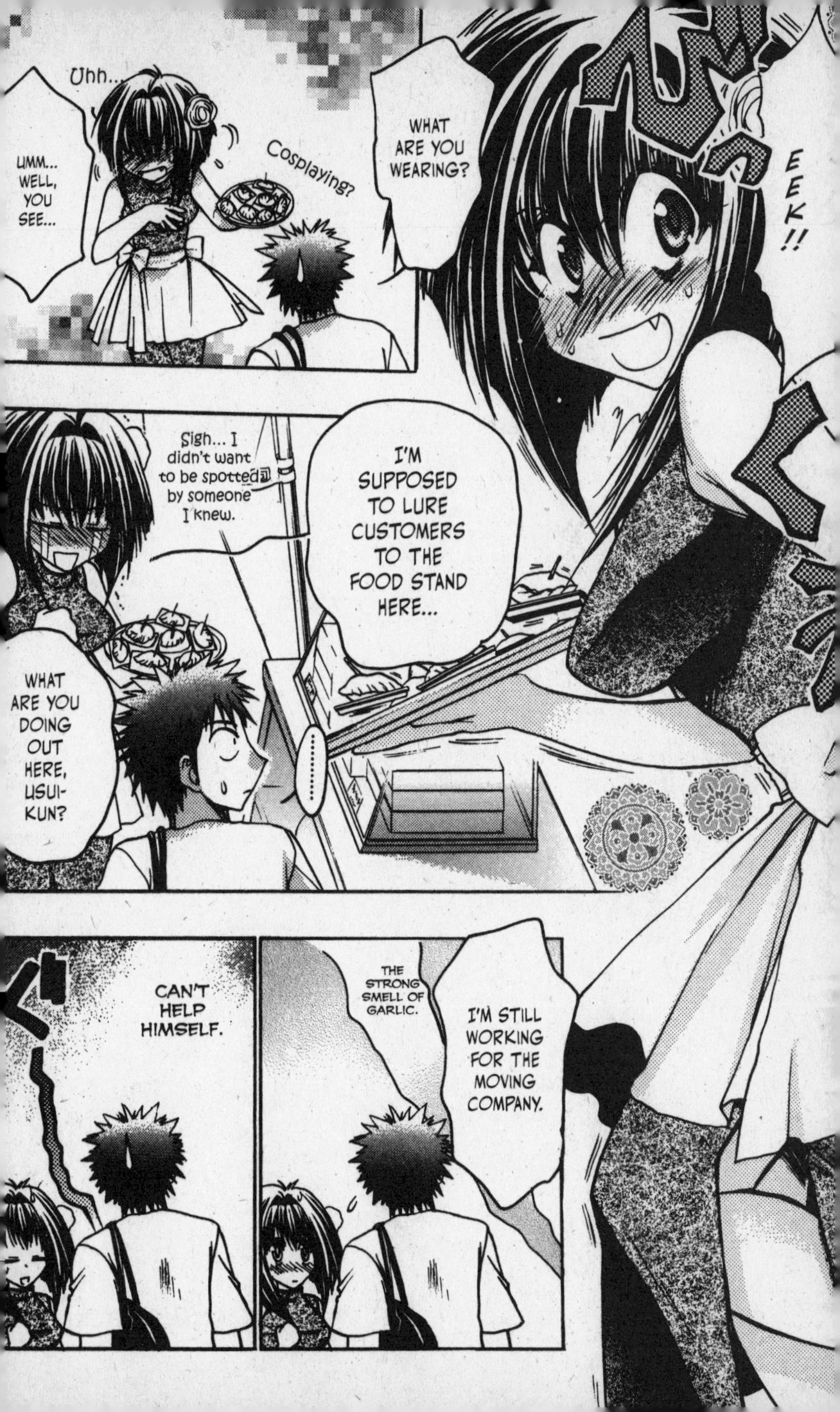
EEK!!
WHAT ARE YOU WEARING?
Cosplaying?
Uhh...
UMM... WELL, YOU SEE...
I'M SUPPOSED TO LURE CUSTOMERS TO THE FOOD STAND HERE...
Sigh... I didn't want to be spotted by someone I knew.
......
WHAT ARE YOU DOING OUT HERE, USUI-KUN?
I'M STILL WORKING FOR THE MOVING COMPANY.
THE STRONG SMELL OF GARLIC.
CAN'T HELP HIMSELF.

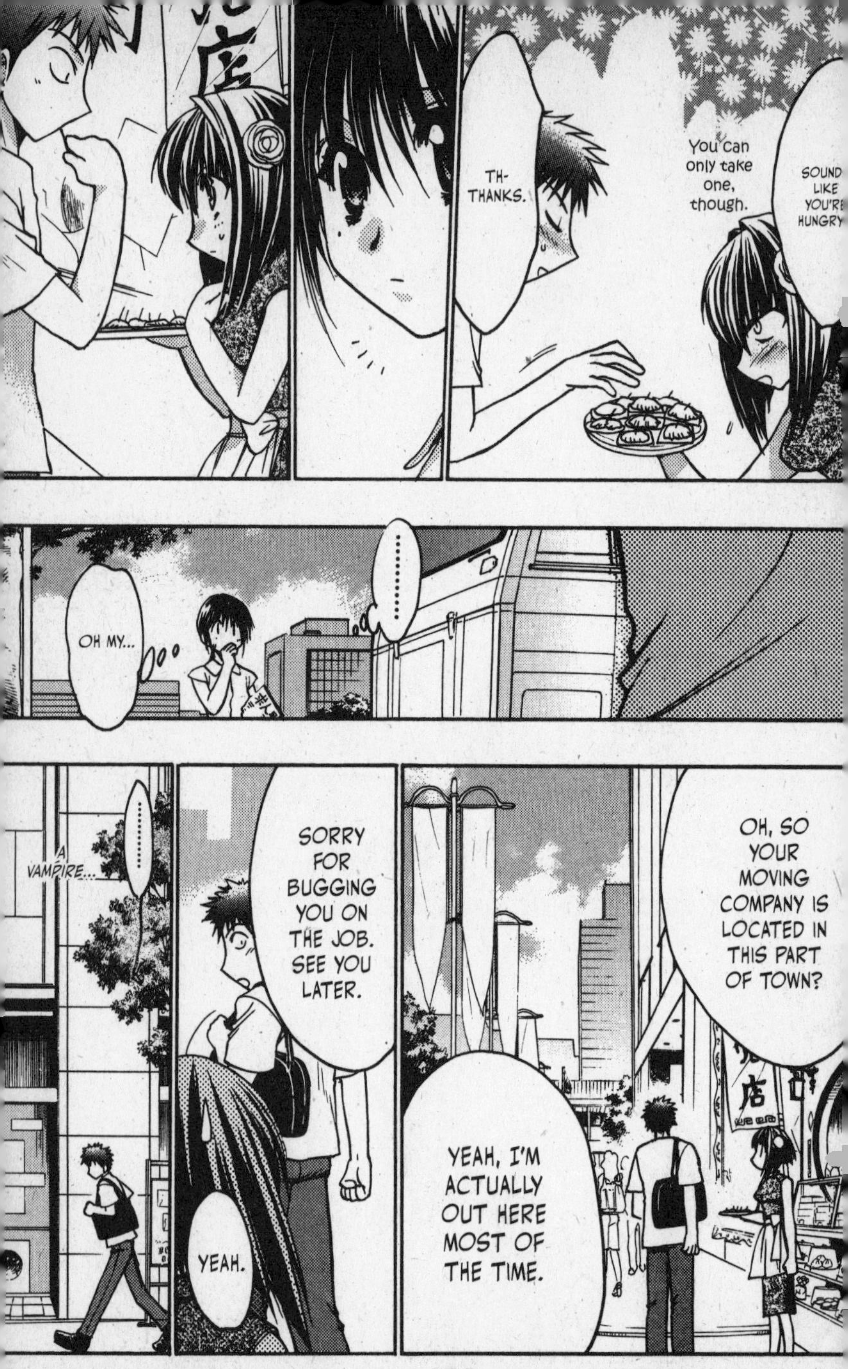
SOUND LIKE YOU'RE HUNGRY
You can only take one, though.
TH- THANKS.
......
OH MY...
OH, SO YOUR MOVING COMPANY IS LOCATED IN THIS PART OF TOWN?
YEAH, I'M ACTUALLY OUT HERE MOST OF THE TIME.
SORRY FOR BUGGING YOU ON THE JOB. SEE YOU LATER.
YEAH.
......
A VAMPIRE...

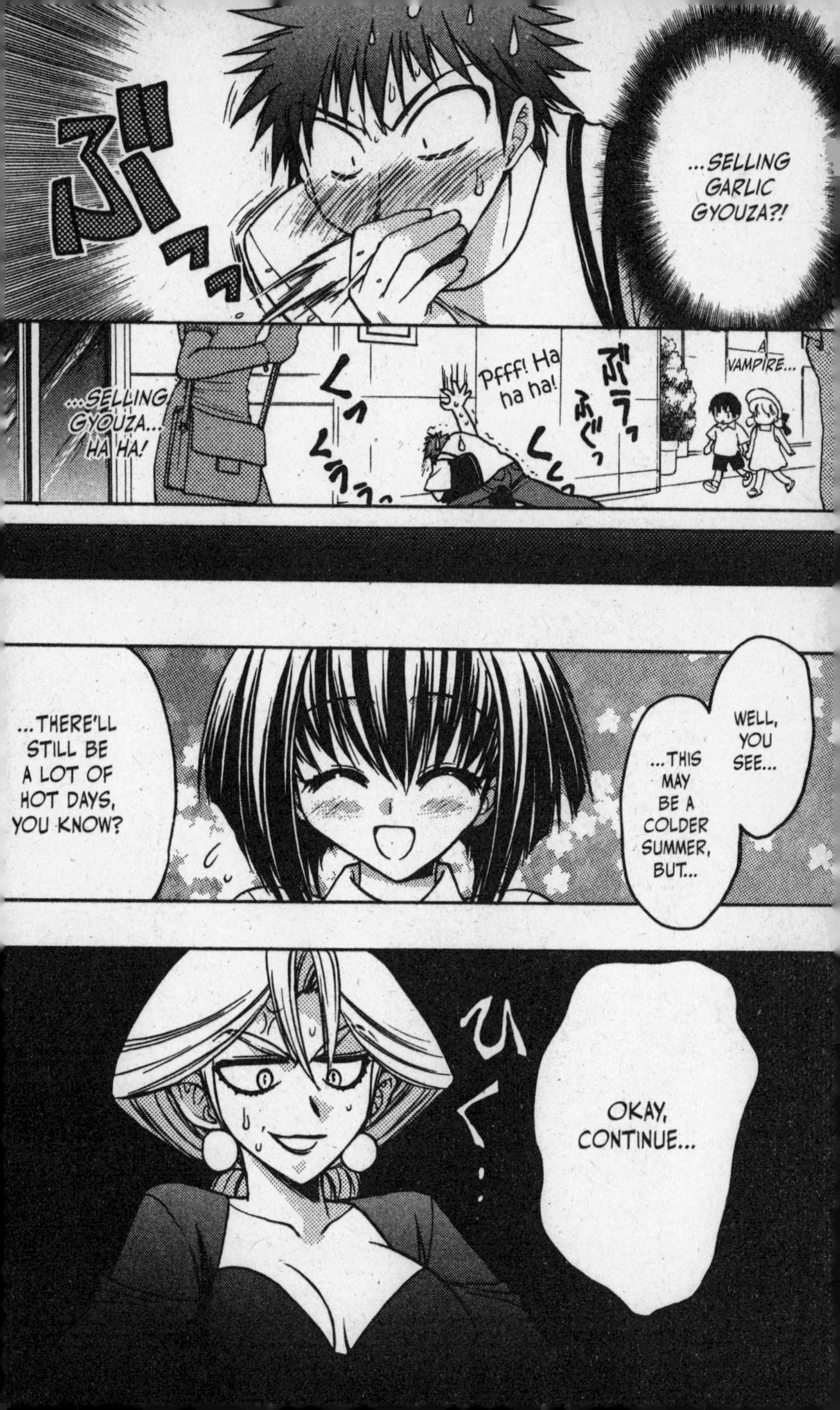
ぶっ
...SELLING GARLIC GYOUZA?!
A VAMPIRE...
Pffff! Ha ha ha!
...SELLING GYOUZA... HA HA!
WELL, YOU SEE...
...THIS MAY BE A COLDER SUMMER, BUT...
...THERE'LL STILL BE A LOT OF HOT DAYS, YOU KNOW?
OKAY, CONTINUE...

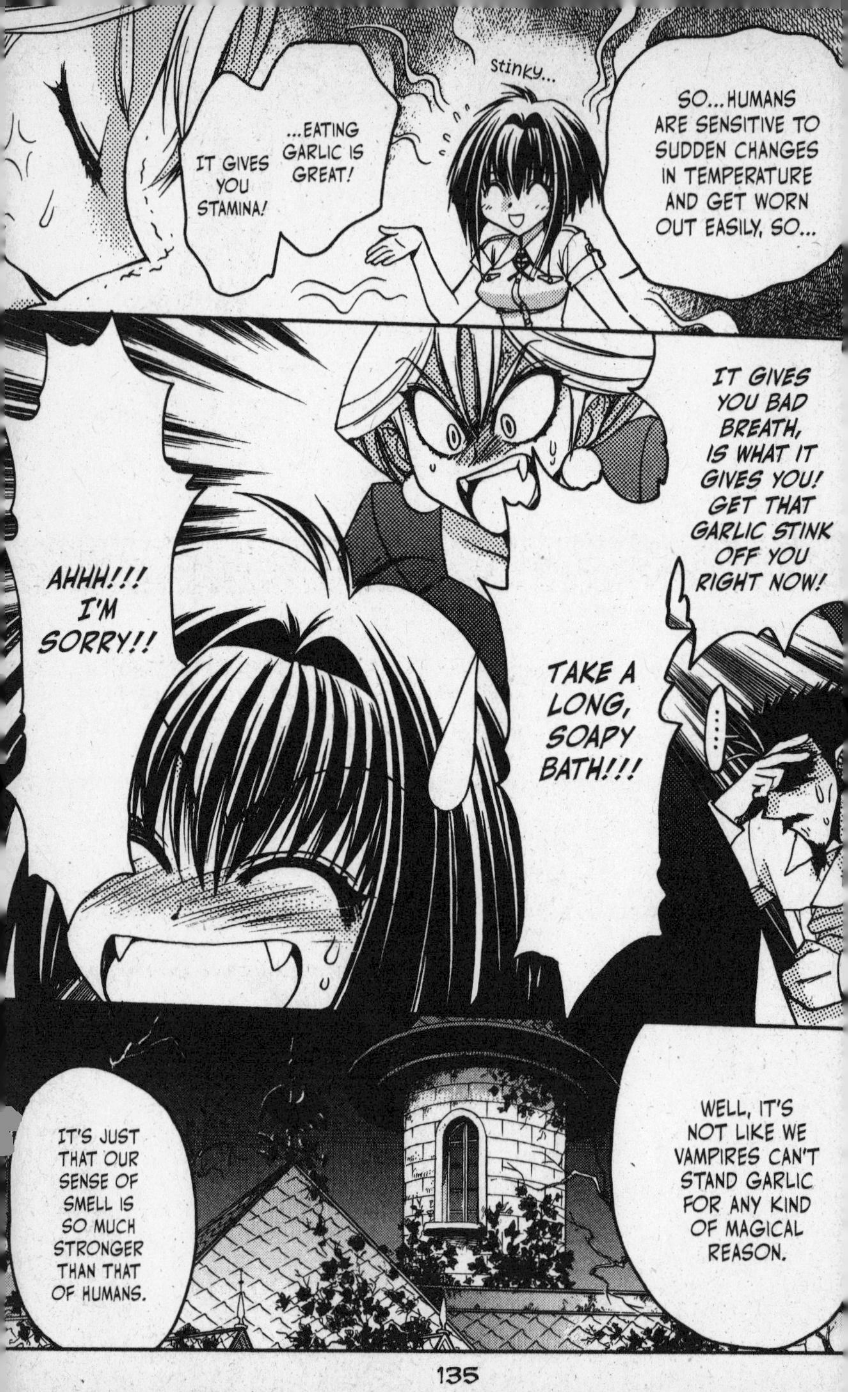
SO...HUMANS ARE SENSITIVE TO SUDDEN CHANGES IN TEMPERATURE AND GET WORN OUT EASILY, SO...
Stinky...
...EATING GARLIC IS GREAT!
IT GIVES YOU STAMINA!
IT GIVES YOU BAD BREATH, IS WHAT IT GIVES YOU! GET THAT GARLIC STINK OFF YOU RIGHT NOW!
....
TAKE A LONG, SOAPY BATH!!!
AHHH!!! I'M SORRY!!
WELL, IT'S NOT LIKE WE VAMPIRES CAN'T STAND GARLIC FOR ANY KIND OF MAGICAL REASON.
IT'S JUST THAT OUR SENSE OF SMELL IS SO MUCH STRONGER THAN THAT OF HUMANS.

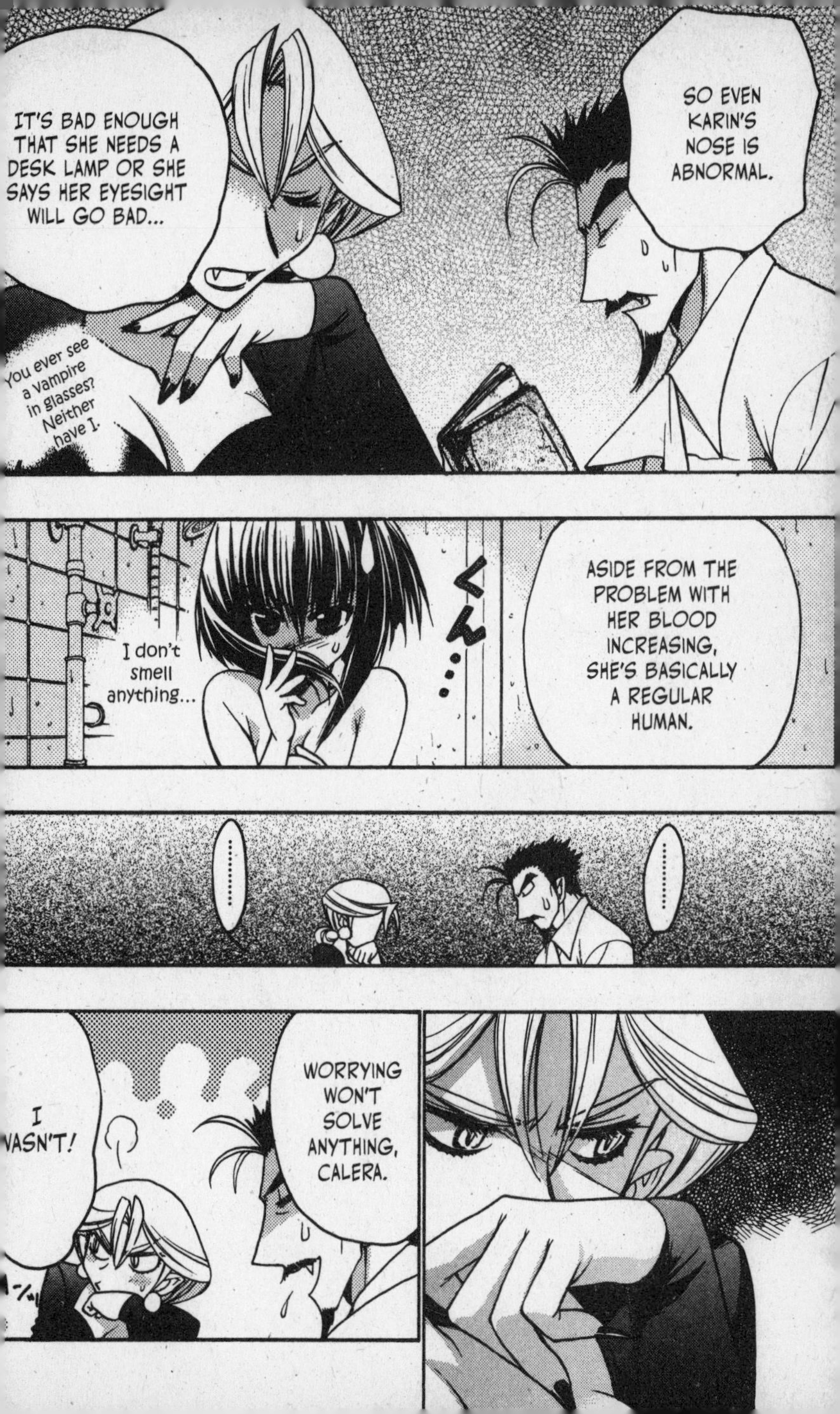
SO EVEN KARIN'S NOSE IS ABNORMAL.
IT'S BAD ENOUGH THAT SHE NEEDS A DESK LAMP OR SHE SAYS HER EYESIGHT WILL GO BAD...
You ever see a vampire in glasses? Neither have I.
ASIDE FROM THE PROBLEM WITH HER BLOOD INCREASING, SHE'S BASICALLY A REGULAR HUMAN.
くん…
I don't smell anything...
....
....
WORRYING WON'T SOLVE ANYTHING, CALERA.
I WASN'T!

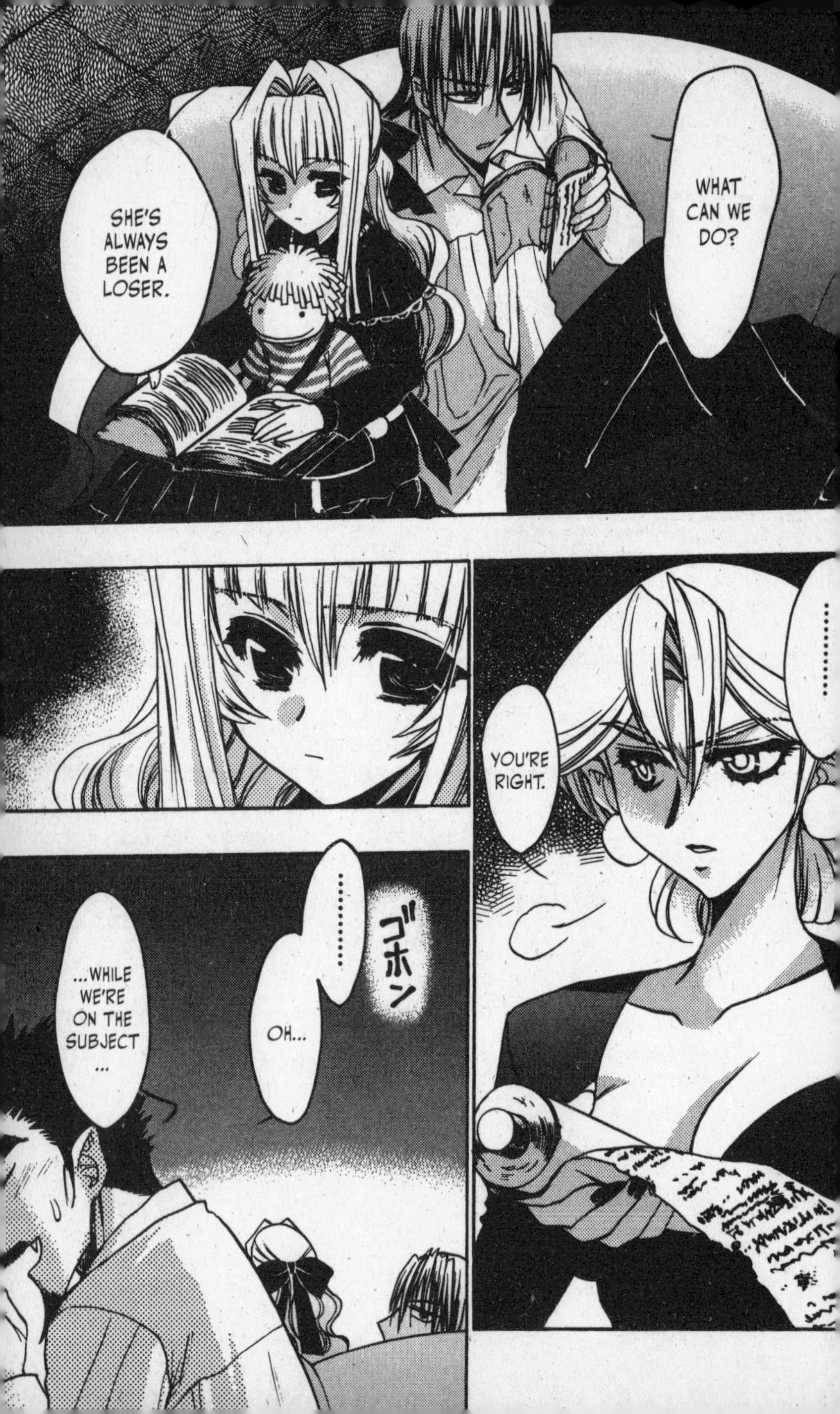
WHAT CAN WE DO?
SHE'S ALWAYS BEEN A LOSER.
YOU'RE RIGHT.
......
ゴホン
OH...
...WHILE WE'RE ON THE SUBJECT ...

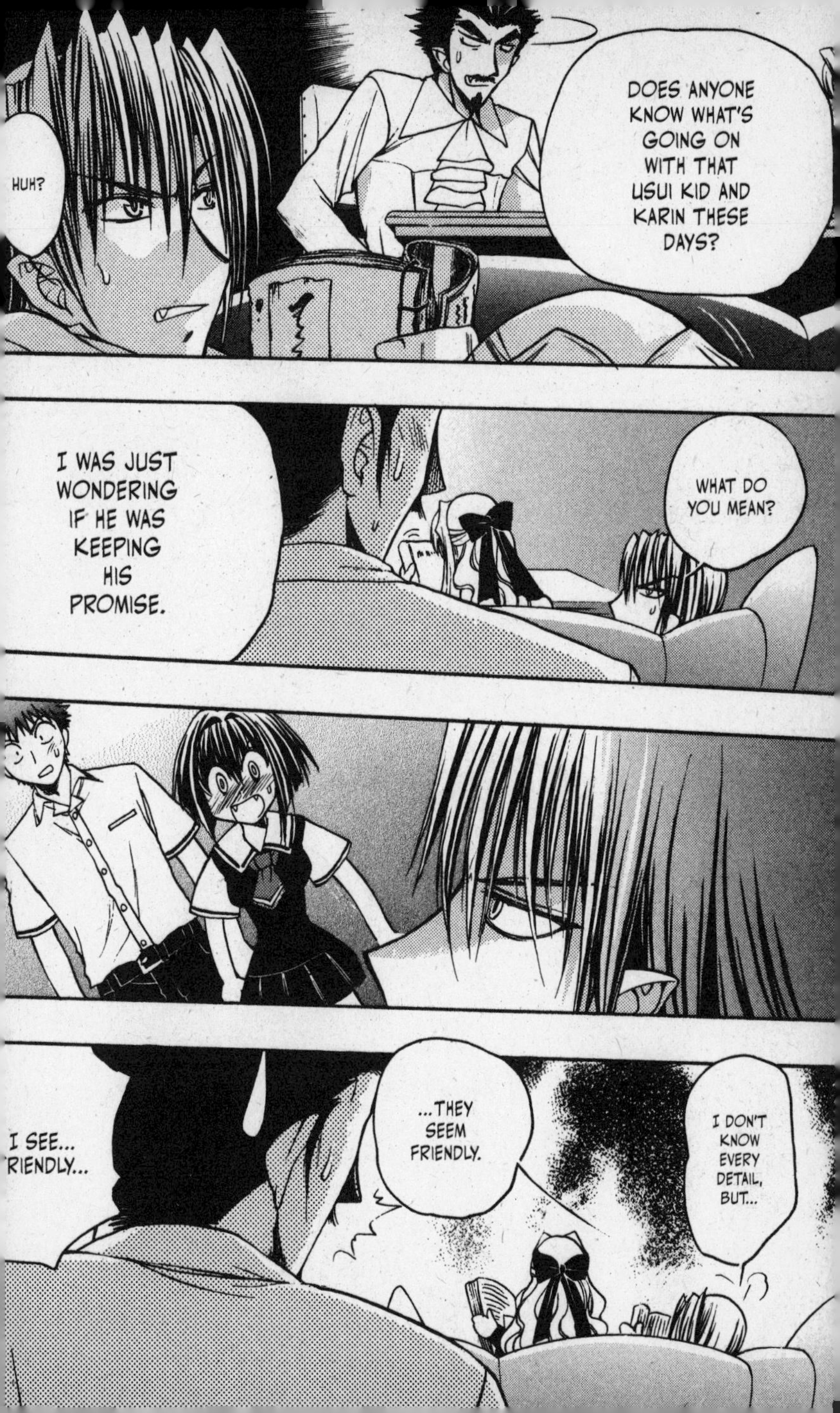
DOES ANYONE KNOW WHAT'S GOING ON WITH THAT USUI KID AND KARIN THESE DAYS?
HUH?
WHAT DO YOU MEAN?
I WAS JUST WONDERING IF HE WAS KEEPING HIS PROMISE.
I DON'T KNOW EVERY DETAIL, BUT...
...THEY SEEM FRIENDLY.
I SEE... RIENDLY...

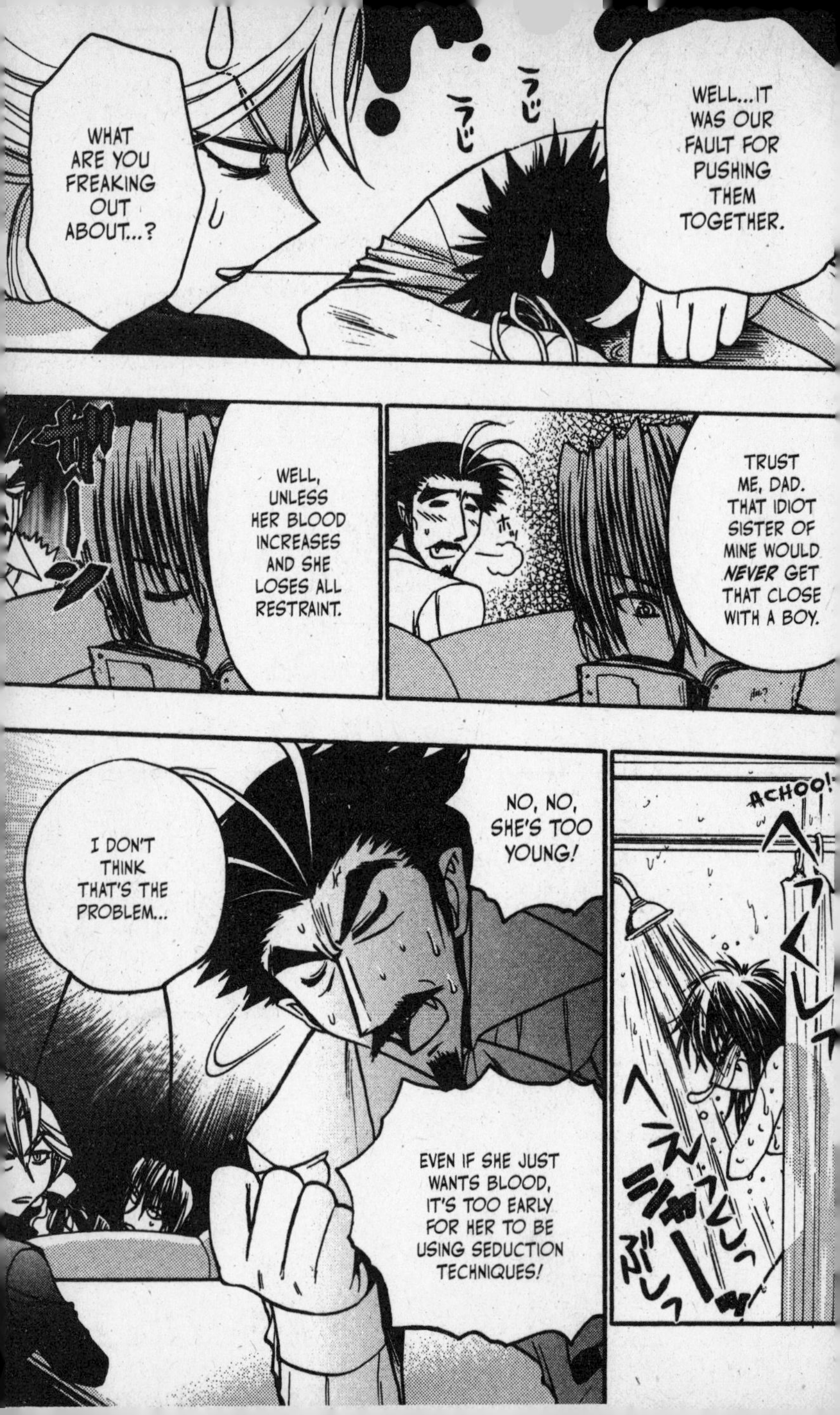
WELL...IT WAS OUR FAULT FOR PUSHING THEM TOGETHER.
WHAT ARE YOU FREAKING OUT ABOUT...?
TRUST ME, DAD. THAT IDIOT SISTER OF MINE WOULD *NEVER* GET THAT CLOSE WITH A BOY.
WELL, UNLESS HER BLOOD INCREASES AND SHE LOSES ALL RESTRAINT.
ACHOO!
NO, NO, SHE'S TOO YOUNG!
EVEN IF SHE JUST WANTS BLOOD, IT'S TOO EARLY FOR HER TO BE USING SEDUCTION TECHNIQUES!
I DON'T THINK THAT'S THE PROBLEM...

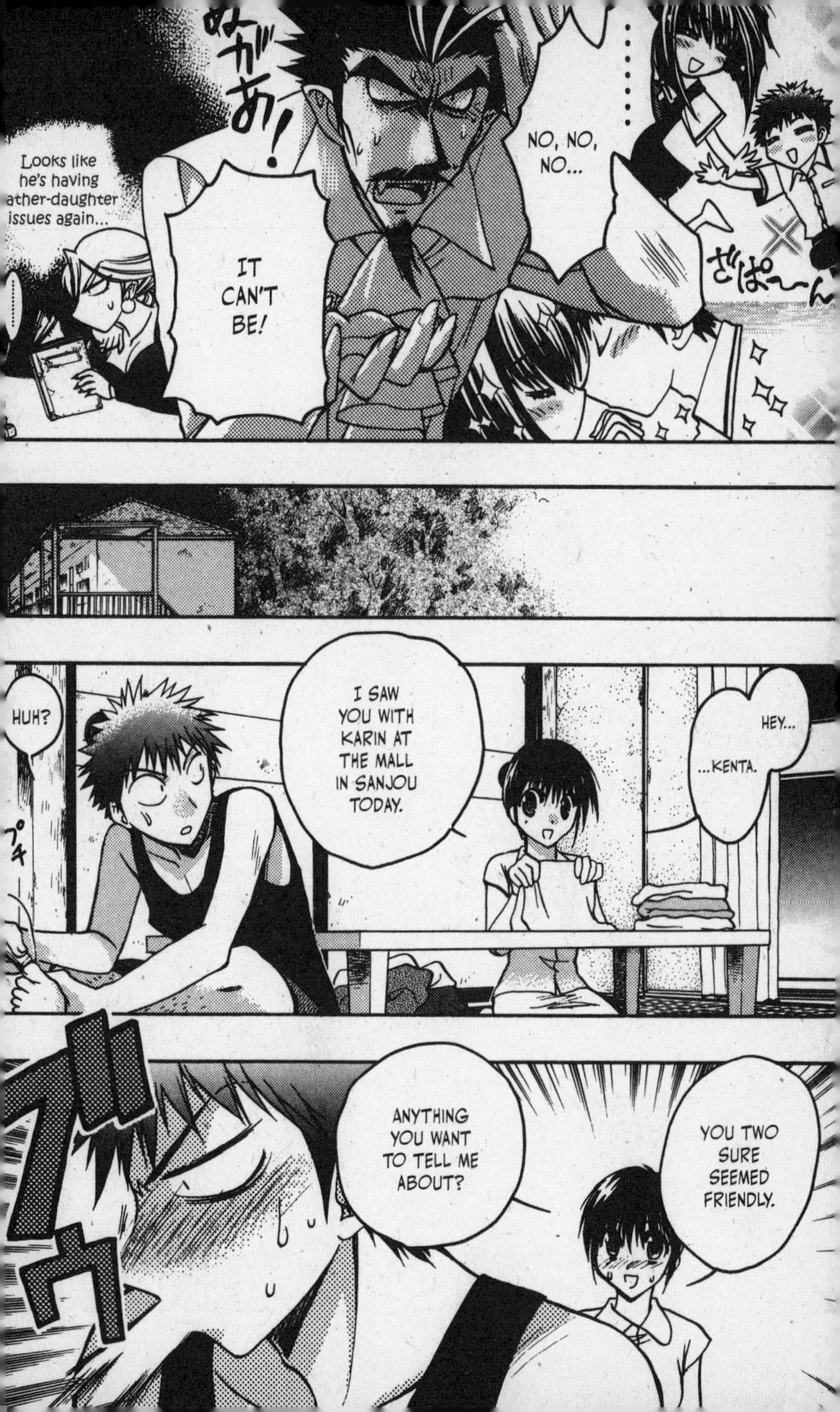
......
NO, NO, NO...
ざぱ〜〜ん
ぬがぁ！
IT CAN'T BE!
Looks like he's having ather-daughter issues again...
......
HEY... ...KENTA.
I SAW YOU WITH KARIN AT THE MALL IN SANJOU TODAY.
HUH?
プチ
YOU TWO SURE SEEMED FRIENDLY.
ANYTHING YOU WANT TO TELL ME ABOUT?

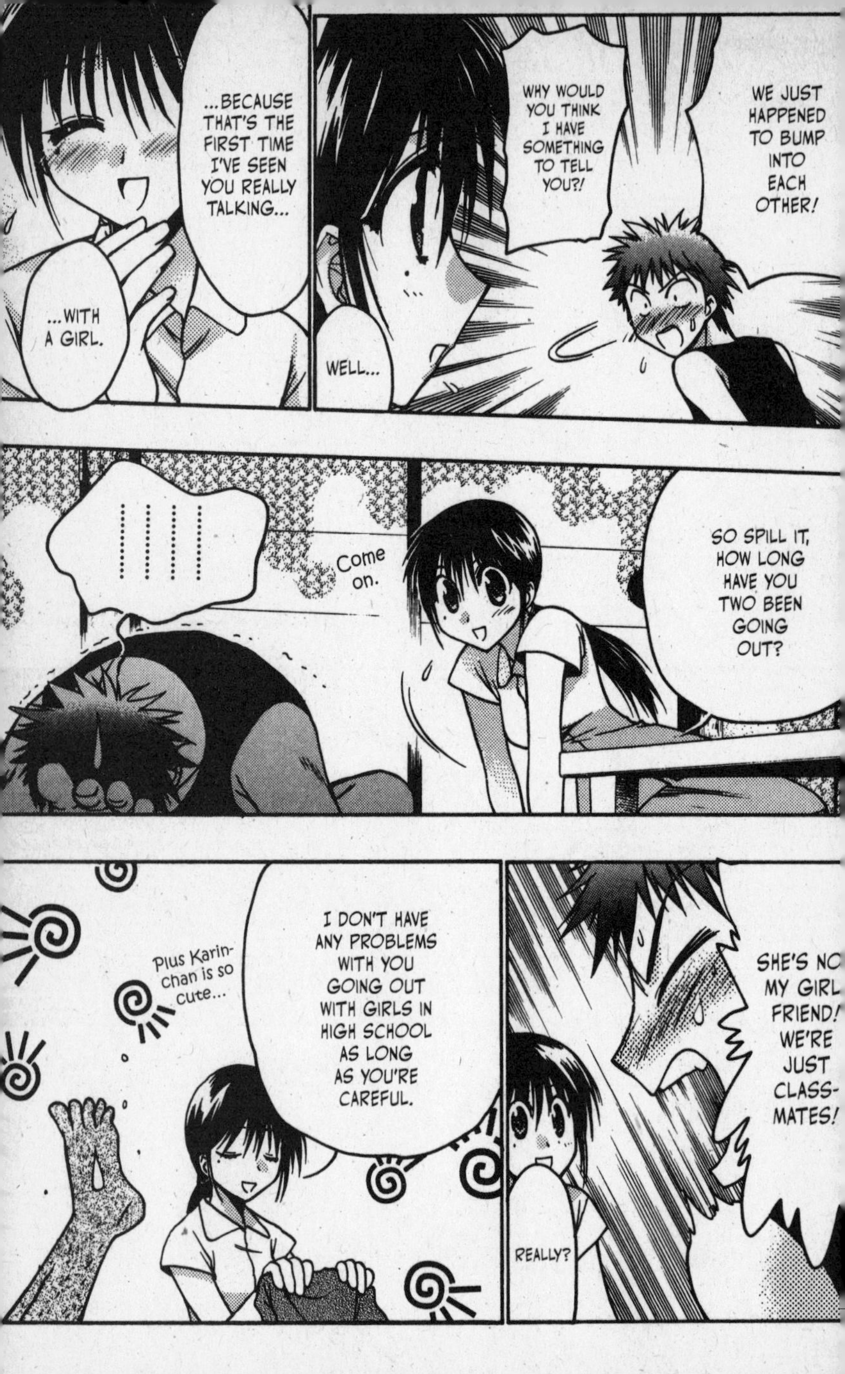
WE JUST HAPPENED TO BUMP INTO EACH OTHER!
WHY WOULD YOU THINK I HAVE SOMETHING TO TELL YOU?!
WELL...
...BECAUSE THAT'S THE FIRST TIME I'VE SEEN YOU REALLY TALKING...
...WITH A GIRL.
SO SPILL IT, HOW LONG HAVE YOU TWO BEEN GOING OUT?
Come on.
SHE'S NO MY GIRL FRIEND! WE'RE JUST CLASS-MATES!
REALLY?
I DON'T HAVE ANY PROBLEMS WITH YOU GOING OUT WITH GIRLS IN HIGH SCHOOL AS LONG AS YOU'RE CAREFUL.
Plus Karin-chan is so cute...

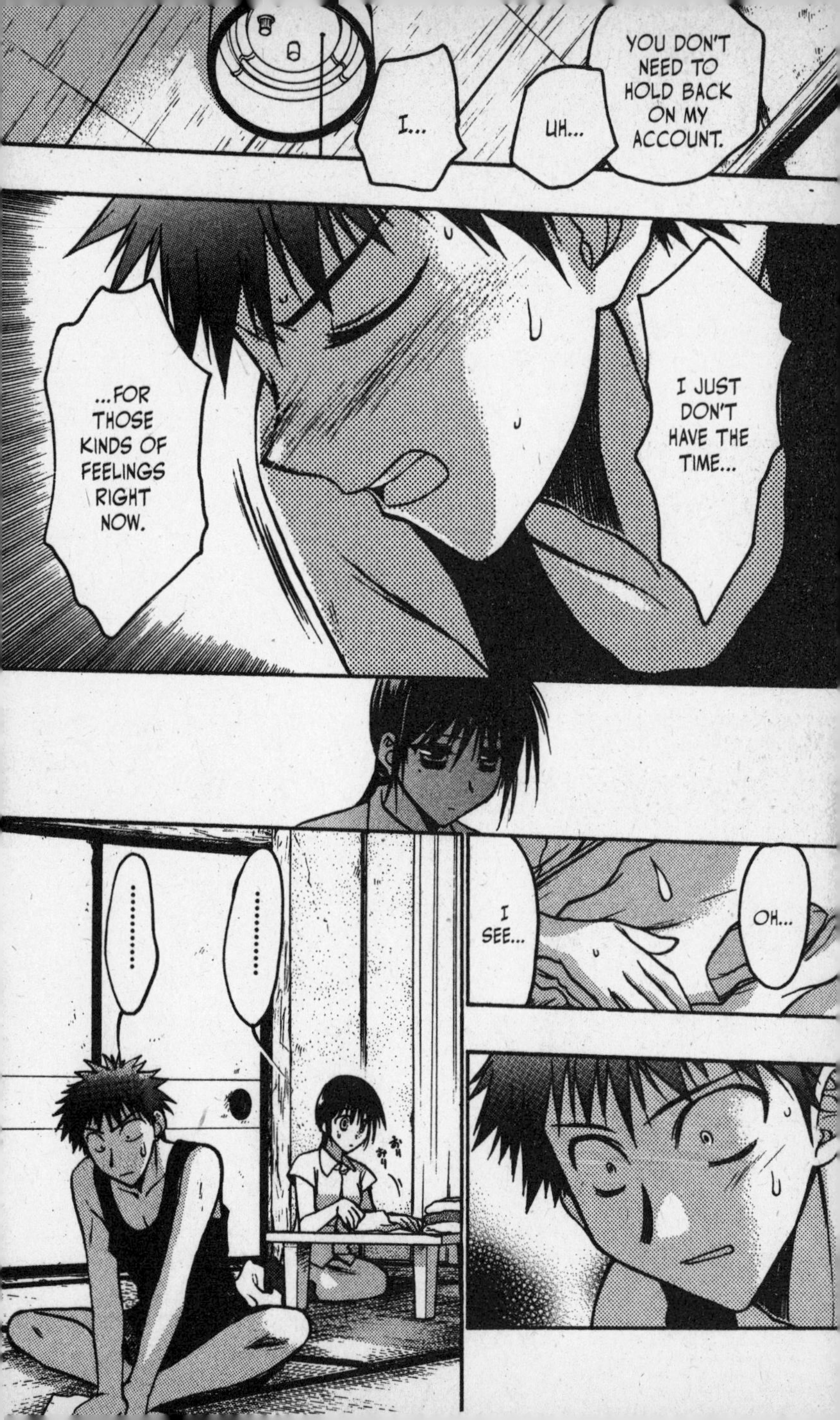
YOU DON'T NEED TO HOLD BACK ON MY ACCOUNT.
UH...
I...
I JUST DON'T HAVE THE TIME...
...FOR THOSE KINDS OF FEELINGS RIGHT NOW.
OH...
I SEE...
....
....

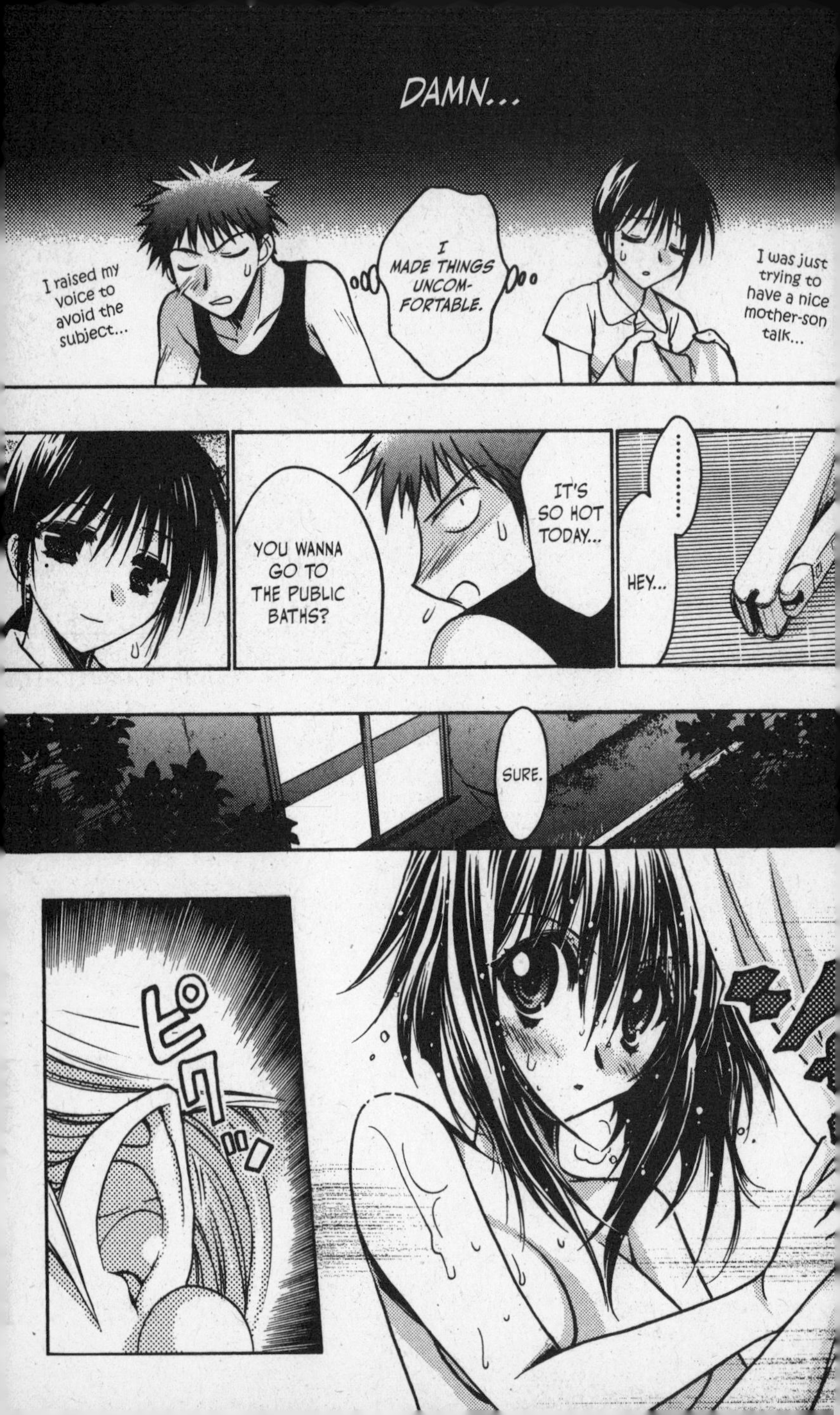
DAMN...
I was just trying to have a nice mother-son talk...
I MADE THINGS UNCOMFORTABLE.
I raised my voice to avoid the subject...
......
HEY...
IT'S SO HOT TODAY...
YOU WANNA GO TO THE PUBLIC BATHS?
......
SURE.

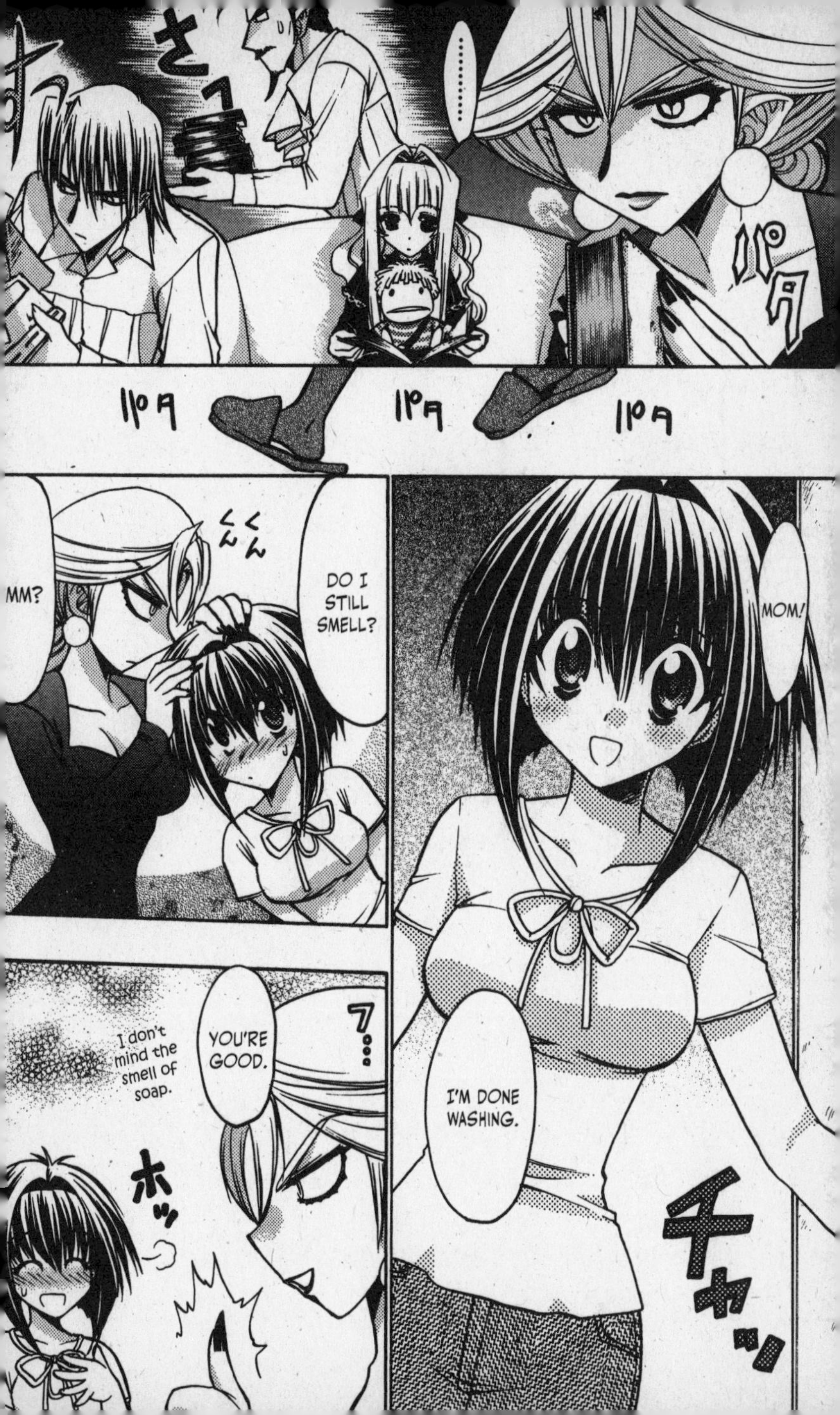
......
パタ
さっ
すっ
パタ
パタ
パタ
MOM!
I'M DONE WASHING.
チャッ
DO I STILL SMELL?
くんくん
MM?
YOU'RE GOOD.
フ...
I don't mind the smell of soap.
ホッ

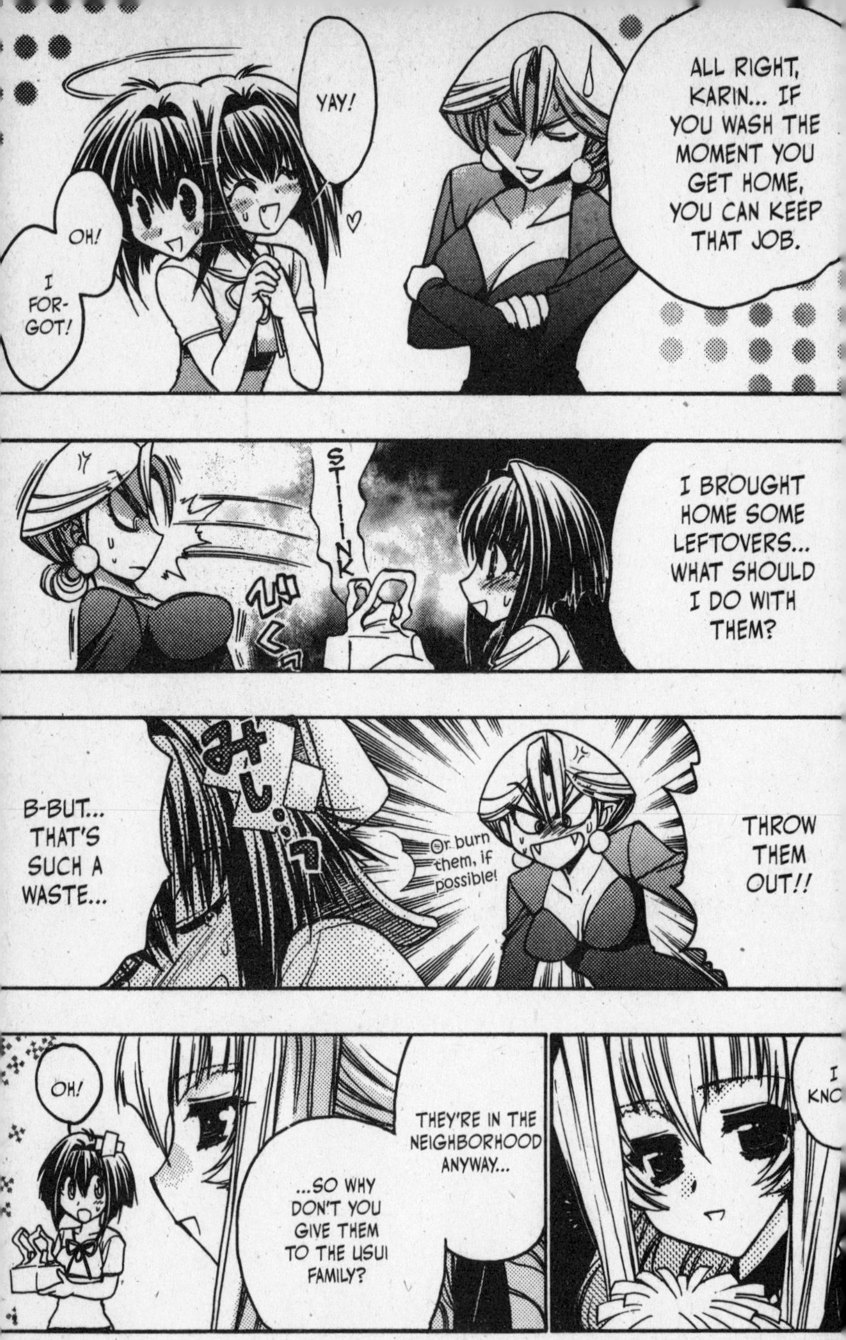
ALL RIGHT, KARIN... IF YOU WASH THE MOMENT YOU GET HOME, YOU CAN KEEP THAT JOB.
YAY!
OH! I FOR-GOT!
I BROUGHT HOME SOME LEFTOVERS... WHAT SHOULD I DO WITH THEM?
STIIINK
THROW THEM OUT!!
Or burn them, if possible!
B-BUT... THAT'S SUCH A WASTE...
I KNO
THEY'RE IN THE NEIGHBORHOOD ANYWAY...
...SO WHY DON'T YOU GIVE THEM TO THE USUI FAMILY?
OH!

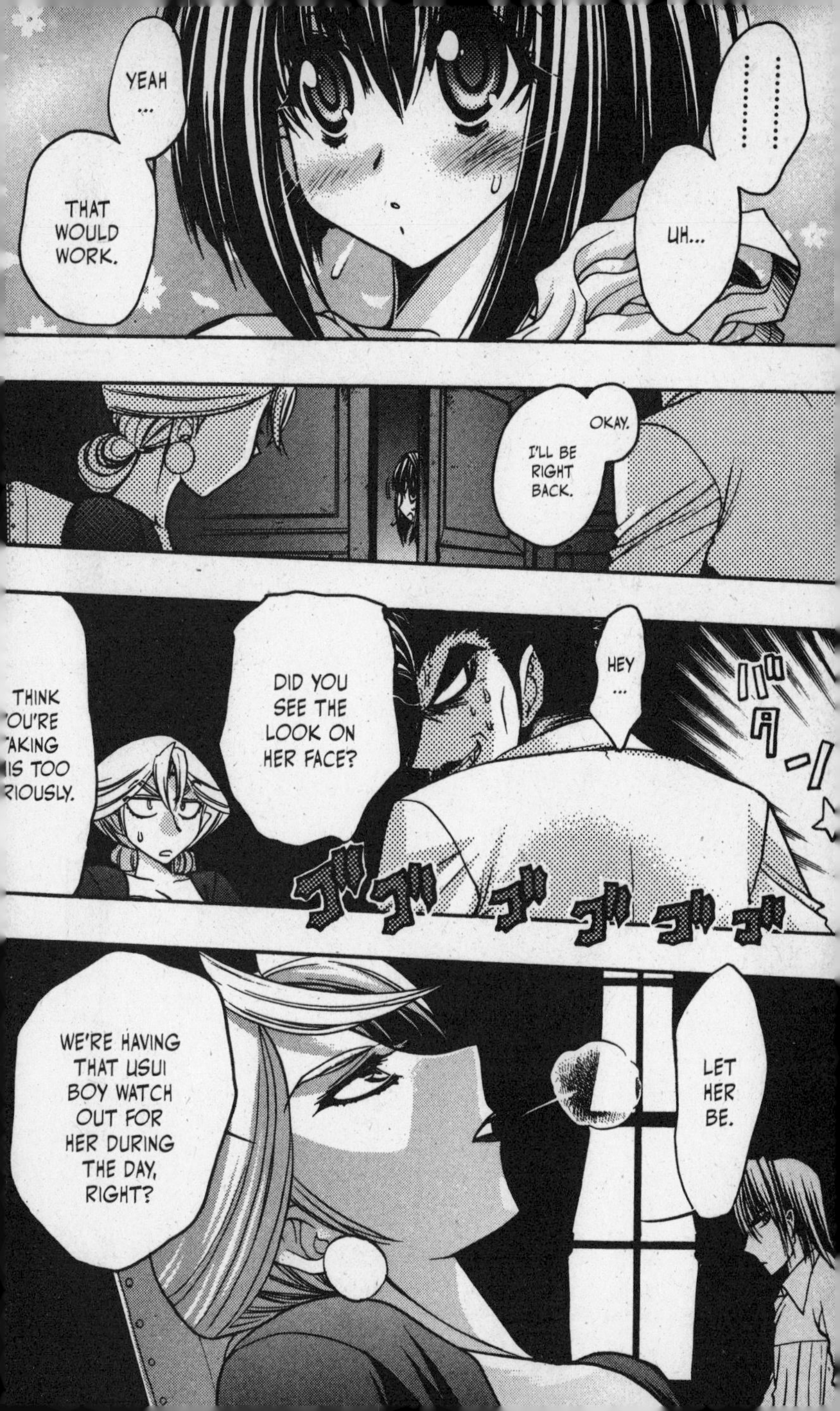
......
UH...
YEAH ...
THAT WOULD WORK.
OKAY.
I'LL BE RIGHT BACK.
HEY ...
DID YOU SEE THE LOOK ON HER FACE?
THINK
OU'RE
AKING
IS TOO
RIOUSLY.
LET HER BE.
WE'RE HAVING THAT USUI BOY WATCH OUT FOR HER DURING THE DAY, RIGHT?

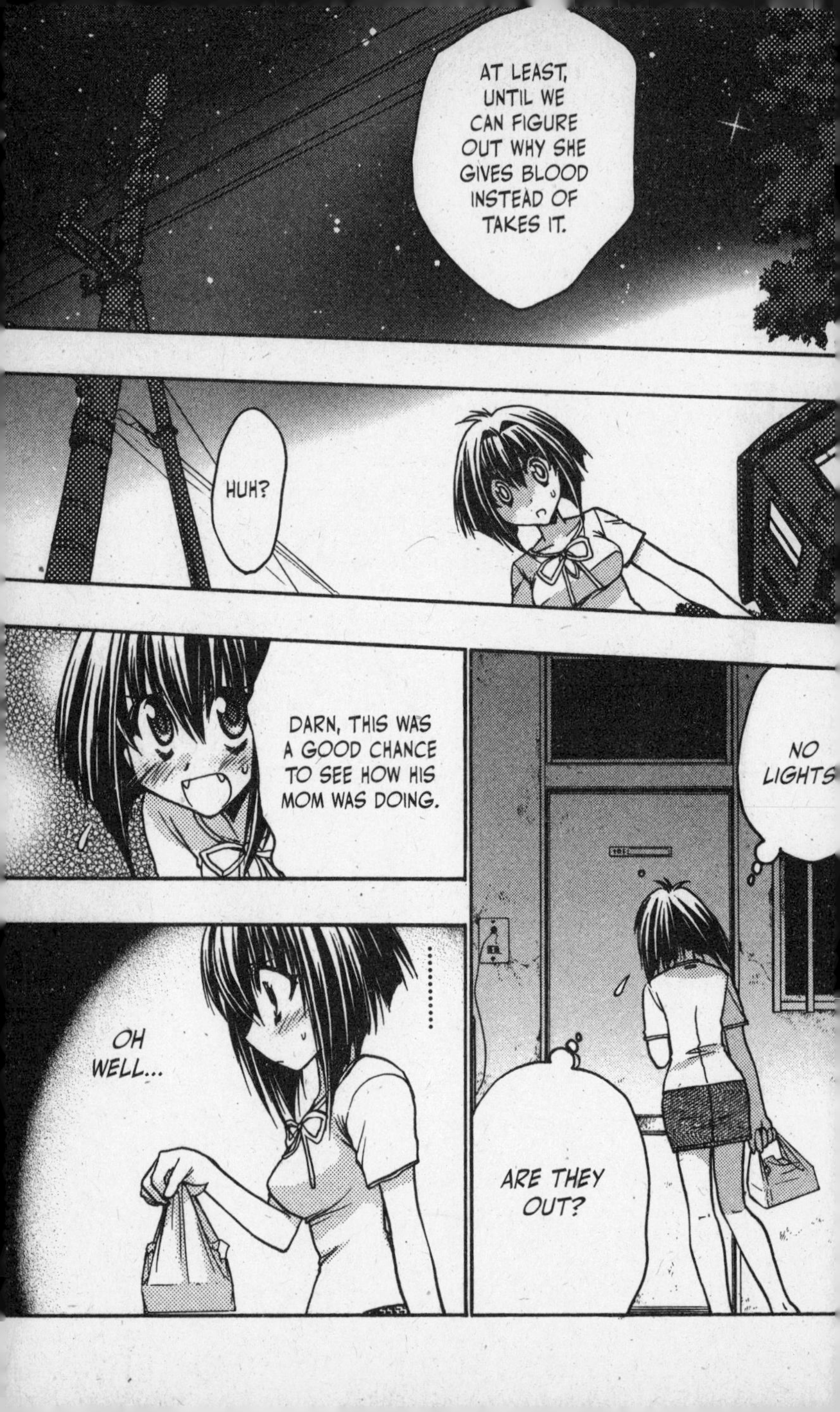
AT LEAST, UNTIL WE CAN FIGURE OUT WHY SHE GIVES BLOOD INSTEAD OF TAKES IT.
HUH?
NO LIGHTS
ARE THEY OUT?
DARN, THIS WAS A GOOD CHANCE TO SEE HOW HIS MOM WAS DOING.
OH WELL...

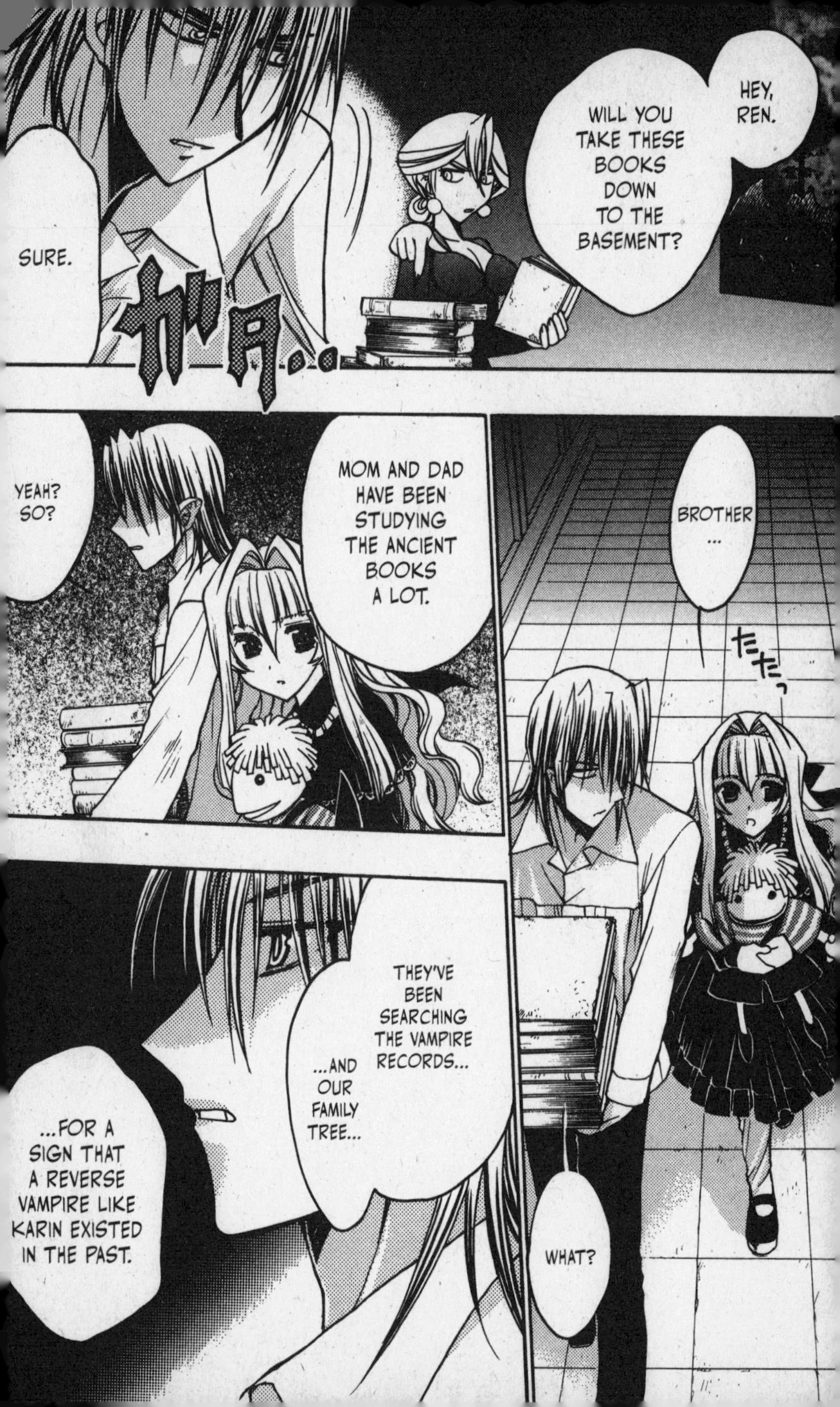
HEY, REN.
WILL YOU TAKE THESE BOOKS DOWN TO THE BASEMENT?
SURE.
BROTHER ...
たたっ
WHAT?
MOM AND DAD HAVE BEEN STUDYING THE ANCIENT BOOKS A LOT.
YEAH? SO?
THEY'VE BEEN SEARCHING THE VAMPIRE RECORDS...
...AND OUR FAMILY TREE...
...FOR A SIGN THAT A REVERSE VAMPIRE LIKE KARIN EXISTED IN THE PAST.

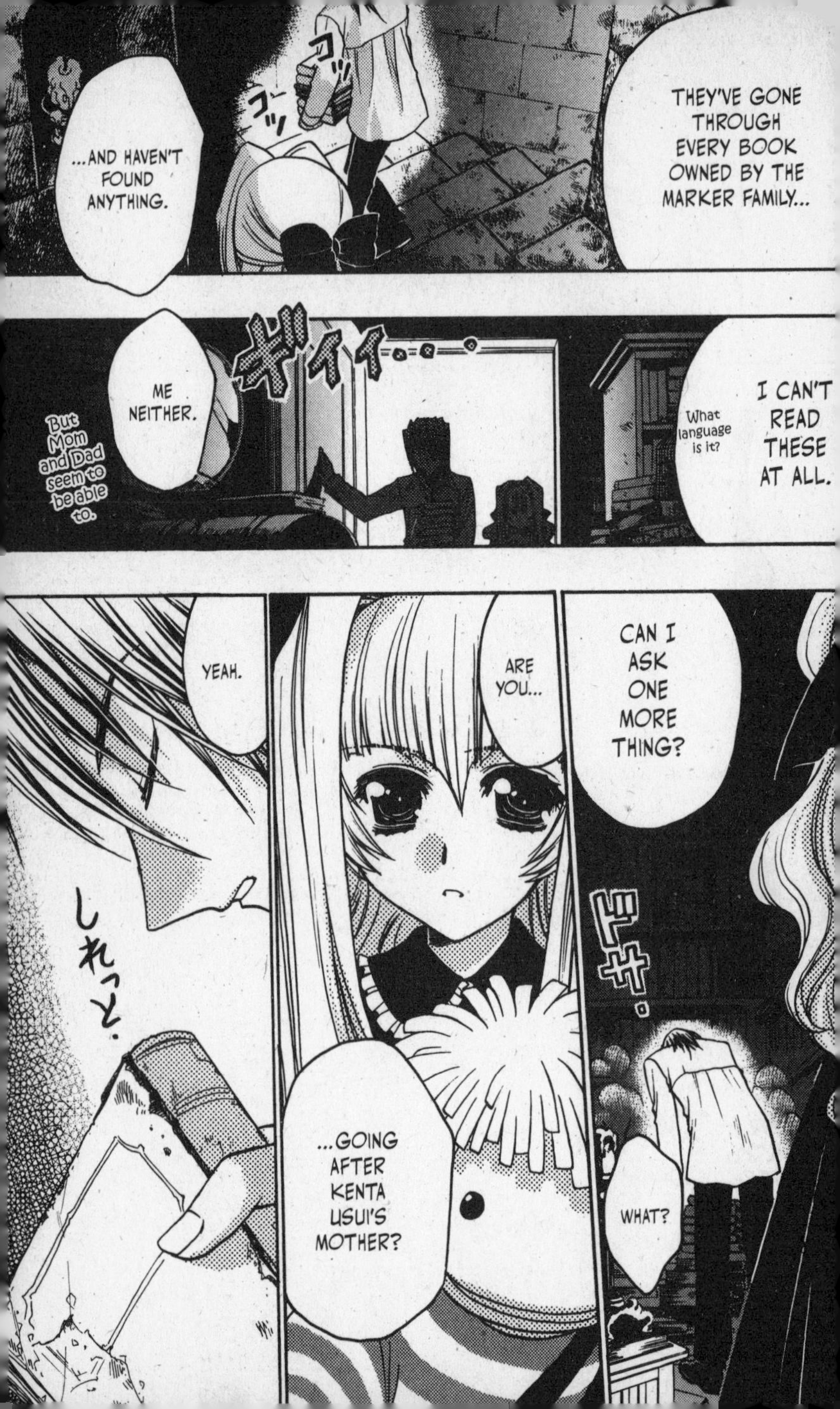
THEY'VE GONE THROUGH EVERY BOOK OWNED BY THE MARKER FAMILY...
...AND HAVEN'T FOUND ANYTHING.
I CAN'T READ THESE AT ALL.
What language is it?
ギイイ…
ME NEITHER.
But Mom and Dad seem to be able to.
CAN I ASK ONE MORE THING?
ドサッ。
WHAT?
ARE YOU...
...GOING AFTER KENTA USUI'S MOTHER?
YEAH.
しれっと。

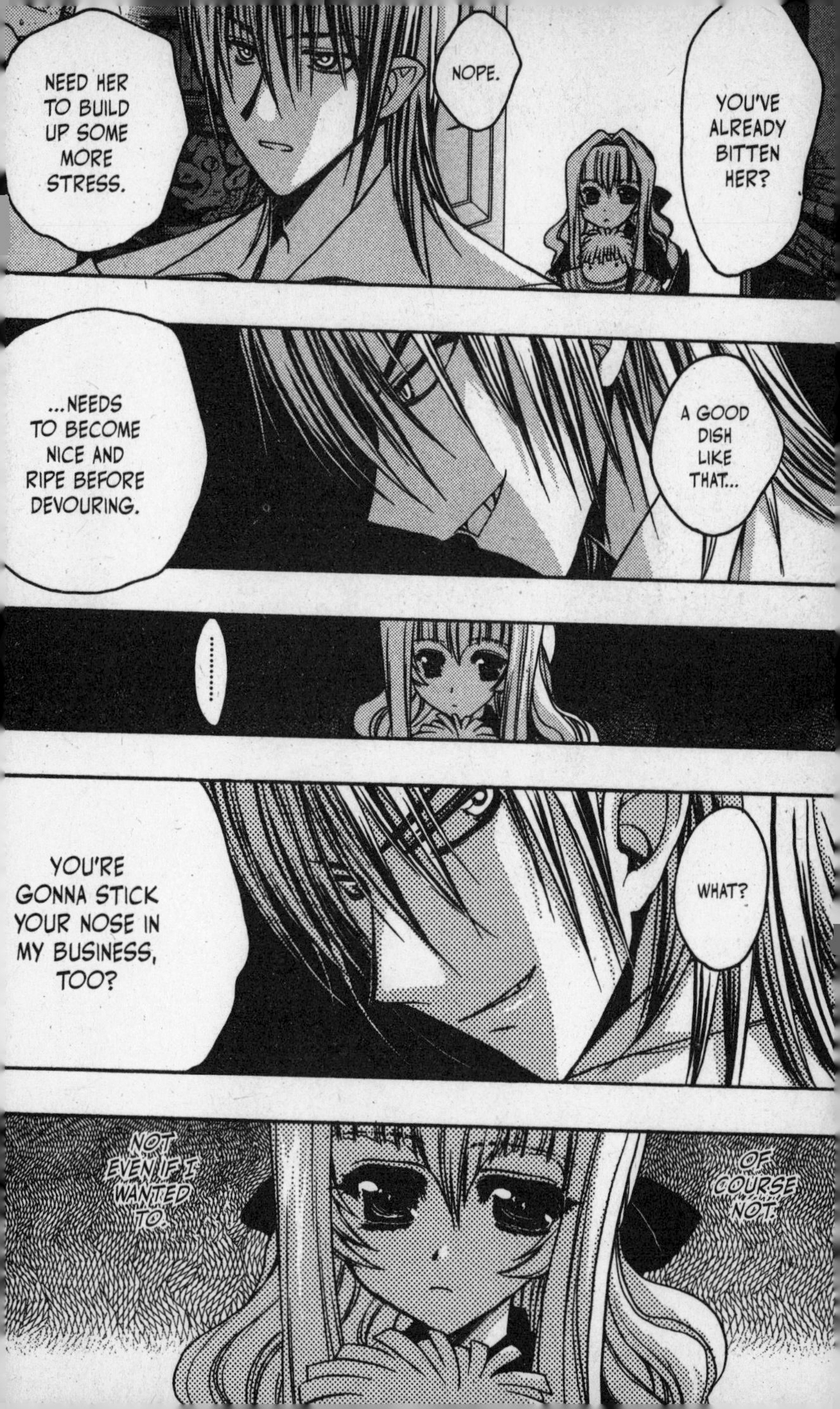
YOU'VE ALREADY BITTEN HER?
NOPE.
NEED HER TO BUILD UP SOME MORE STRESS.
A GOOD DISH LIKE THAT...
...NEEDS TO BECOME NICE AND RIPE BEFORE DEVOURING.
......
WHAT?
YOU'RE GONNA STICK YOUR NOSE IN MY BUSINESS, TOO?
OF COURSE NOT.
NOT EVEN IF I WANTED TO.

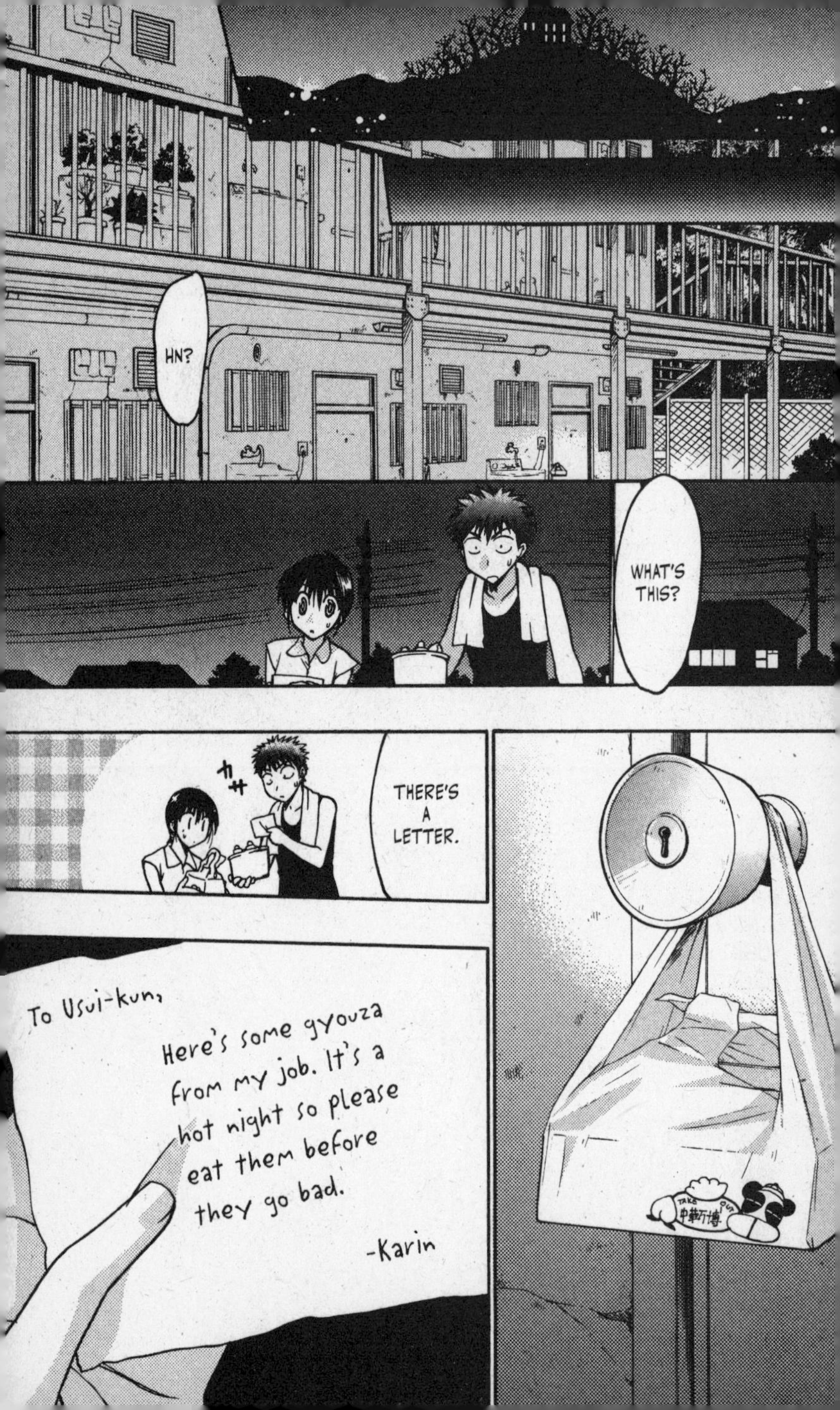
HN?
WHAT'S THIS?
THERE'S A LETTER.
To Usui-kun,
Here's some gyouza from my job. It's a hot night so please eat them before they go bad.
-Karin

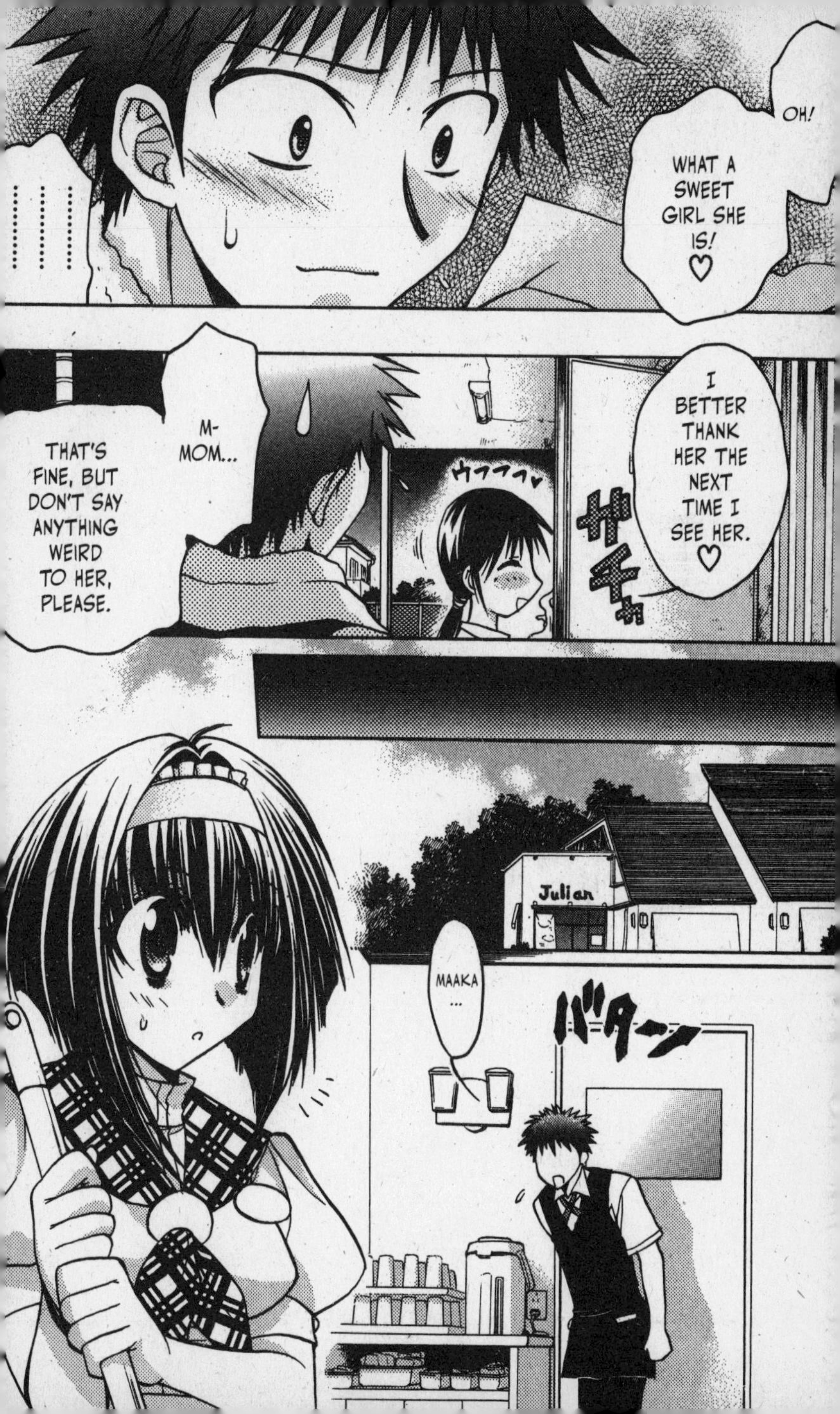

OH!
WHAT A SWEET GIRL SHE IS! ♥
......
I BETTER THANK HER THE NEXT TIME I SEE HER. ♥
M- MOM...
THAT'S FINE, BUT DON'T SAY ANYTHING WEIRD TO HER, PLEASE.
Julian
MAAKA ...

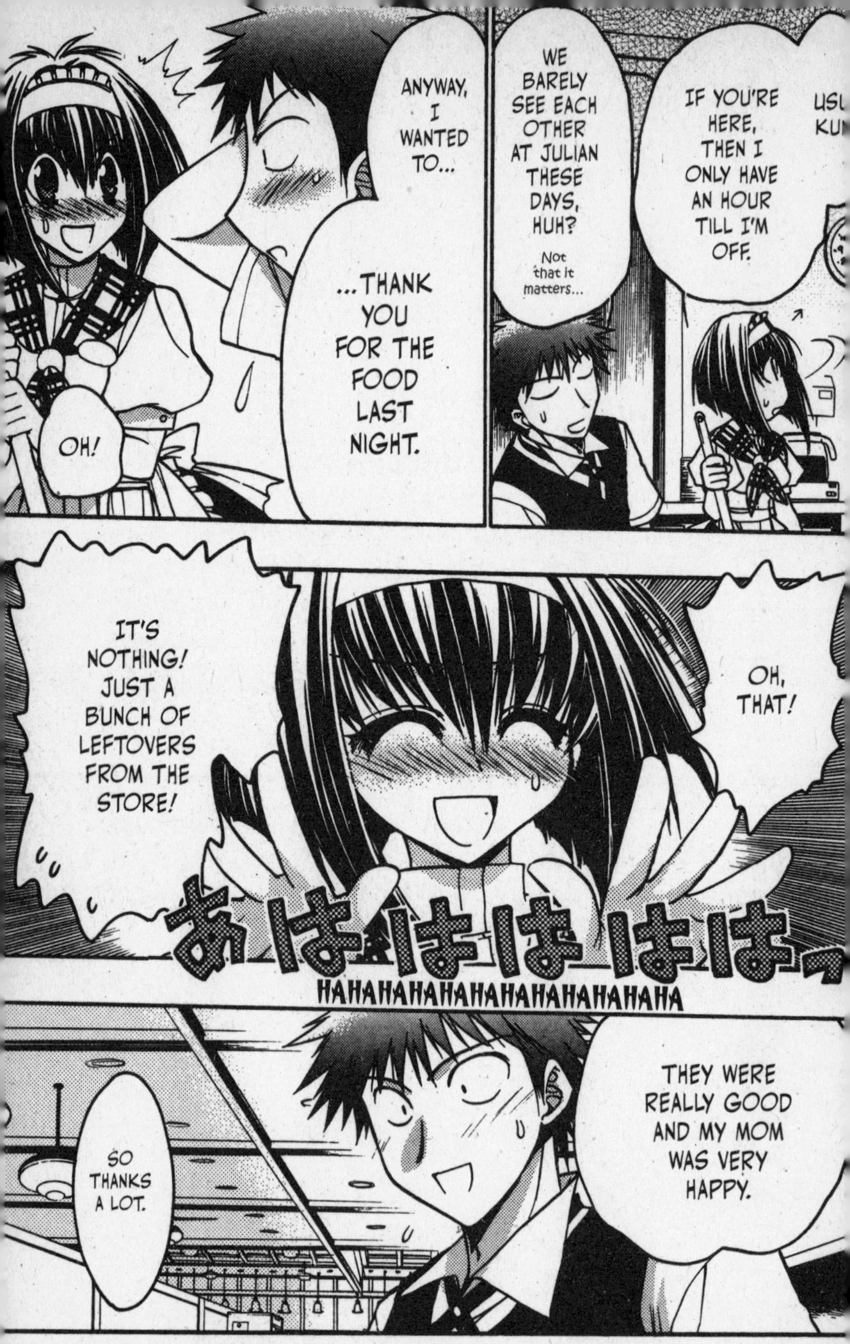
IF YOU'RE HERE, THEN I ONLY HAVE AN HOUR TILL I'M OFF.
WE BARELY SEE EACH OTHER AT JULIAN THESE DAYS, HUH?
Not that it matters...
ANYWAY, I WANTED TO...
...THANK YOU FOR THE FOOD LAST NIGHT.
OH!
OH, THAT!
IT'S NOTHING! JUST A BUNCH OF LEFTOVERS FROM THE STORE!
あはははははっ
HAHAHAHAHAHAHAHAHAHAHAHA
THEY WERE REALLY GOOD AND MY MOM WAS VERY HAPPY.
SO THANKS A LOT.

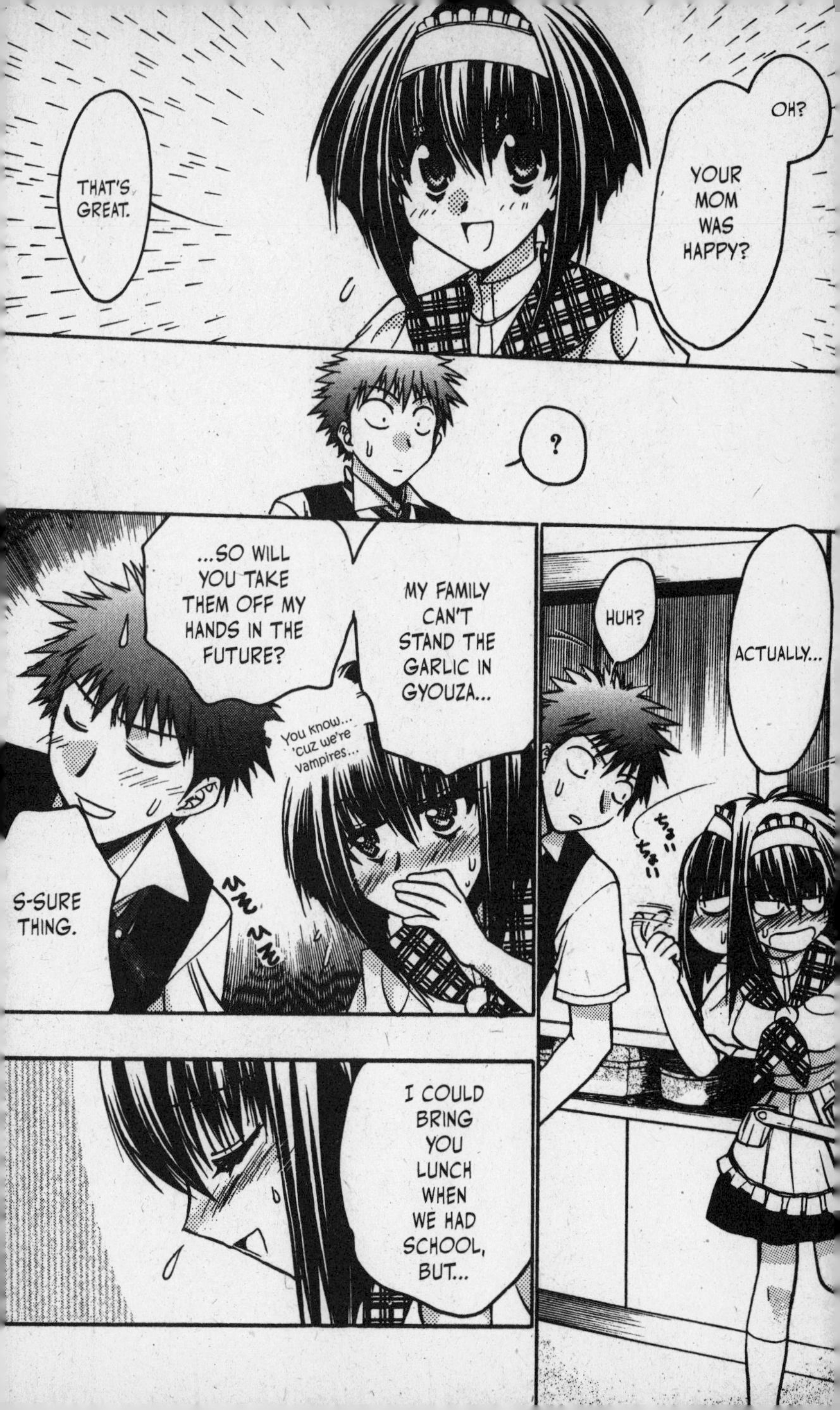
OH?
YOUR MOM WAS HAPPY?
THAT'S GREAT.
?
ACTUALLY...
HUH?
ちょい ちょい
MY FAMILY CAN'T STAND THE GARLIC IN GYOUZA...
...SO WILL YOU TAKE THEM OFF MY HANDS IN THE FUTURE?
You know... 'cuz we're vampires...
S-SURE THING.
I COULD BRING YOU LUNCH WHEN WE HAD SCHOOL, BUT...

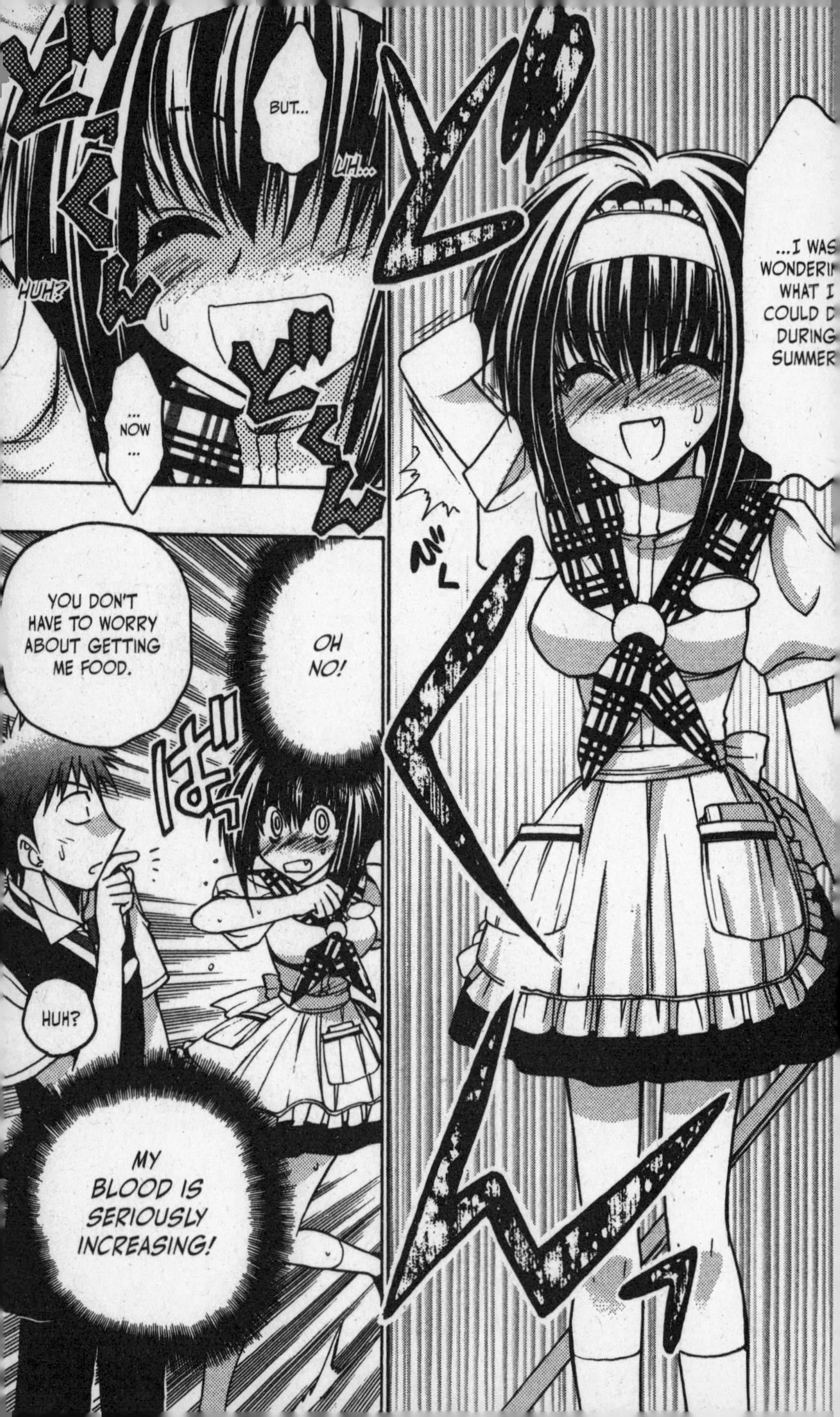
...I WAS WONDERI WHAT I COULD D DURING SUMMER
BUT...
UH...
HUH?
...NOW...
YOU DON'T HAVE TO WORRY ABOUT GETTING ME FOOD.
OH NO!
HUH?
MY BLOOD IS SERIOUSLY INCREASING!

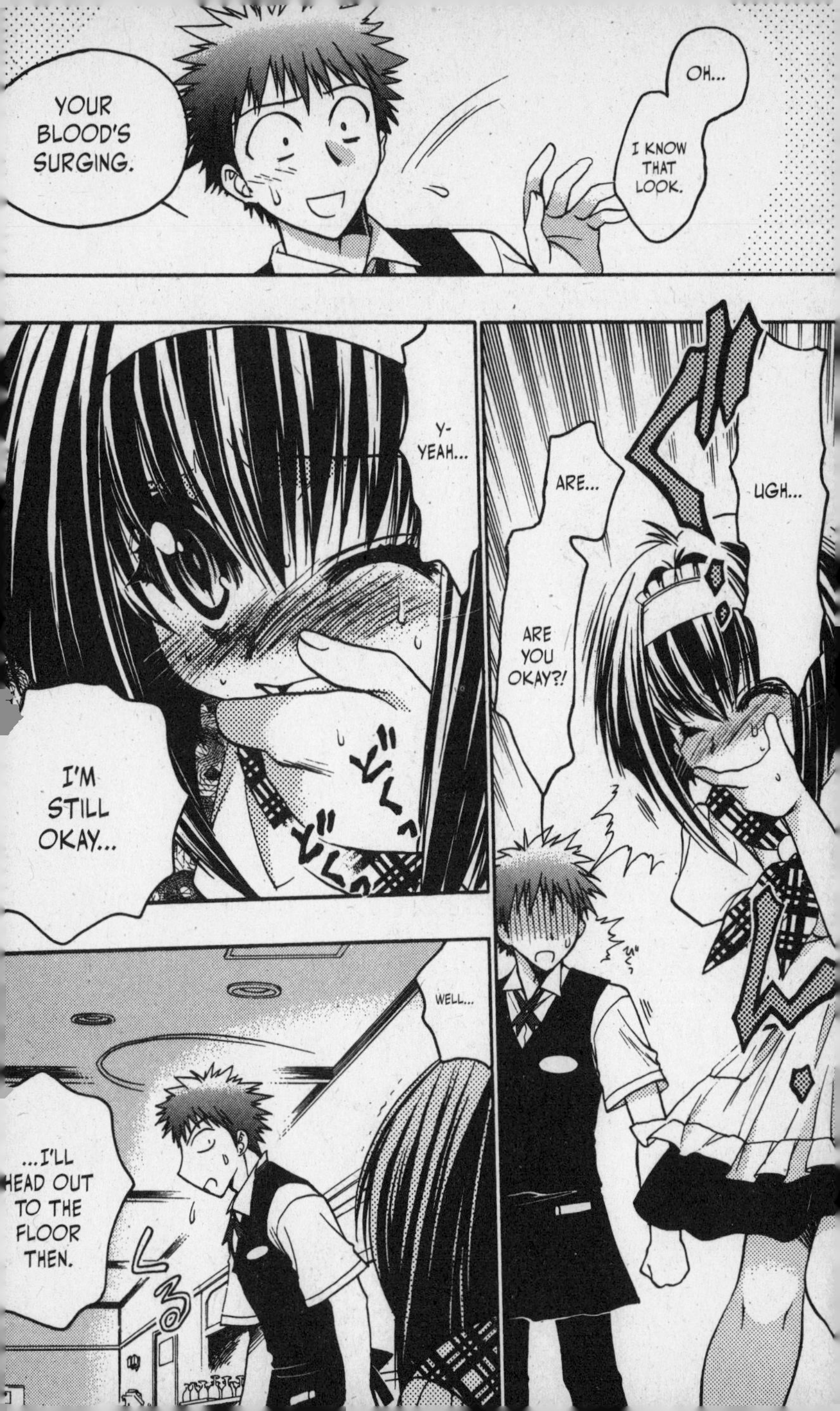
OH...
I KNOW THAT LOOK.
YOUR BLOOD'S SURGING.
UGH...
ARE...
ARE YOU OKAY?!
Y-YEAH...
I'M STILL OKAY...
WELL...
...I'LL HEAD OUT TO THE FLOOR THEN.

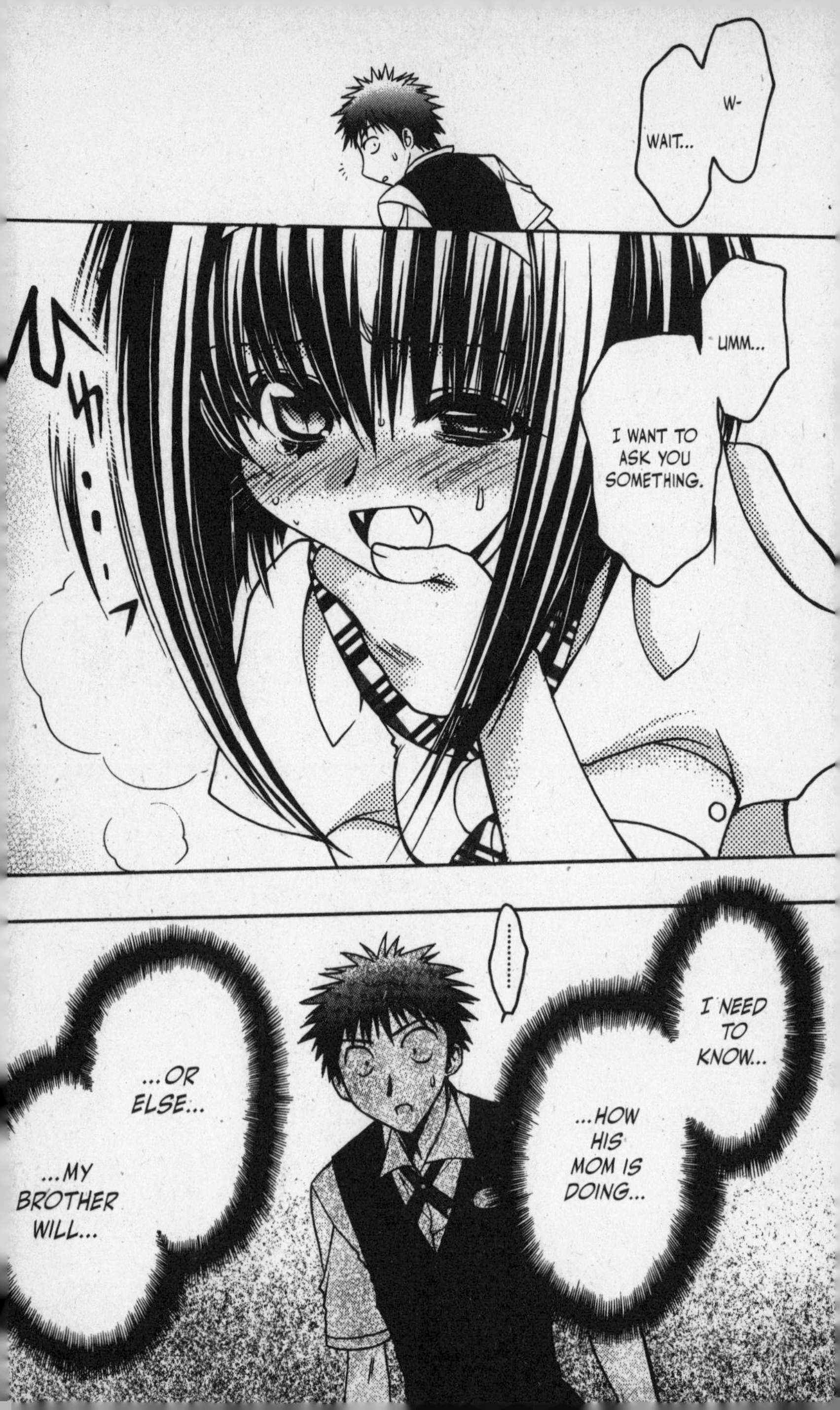
W- WAIT...
UMM... I WANT TO ASK YOU SOMETHING.
......
I NEED TO KNOW...
...HOW HIS MOM IS DOING...
...OR ELSE...
...MY BROTHER WILL...

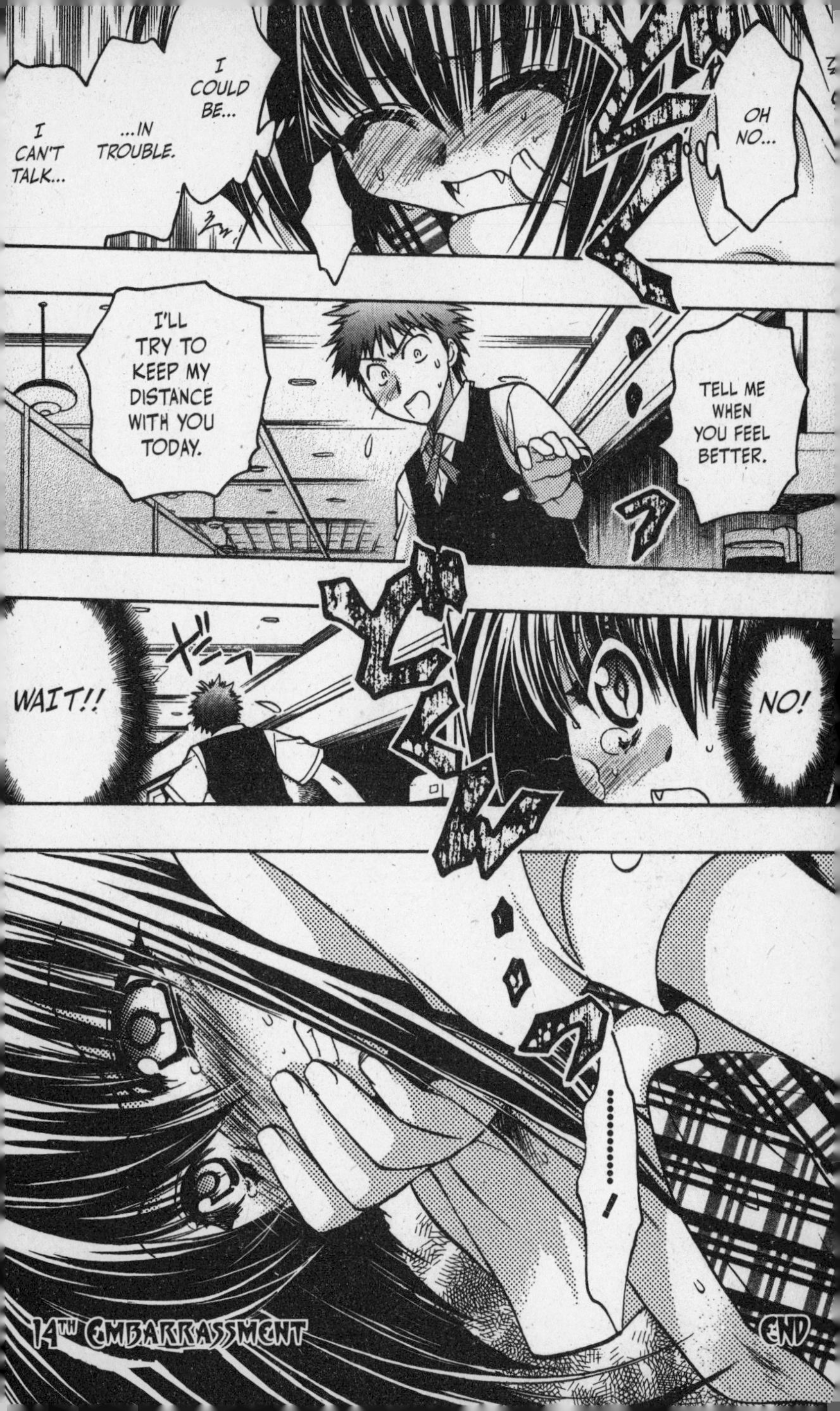
OH NO...
I COULD BE...
...IN TROUBLE.
I CAN'T TALK...
TELL ME WHEN YOU FEEL BETTER.
I'LL TRY TO KEEP MY DISTANCE WITH YOU TODAY.
NO!
WAIT!!
......!
14TH EMBARRASSMENT
END

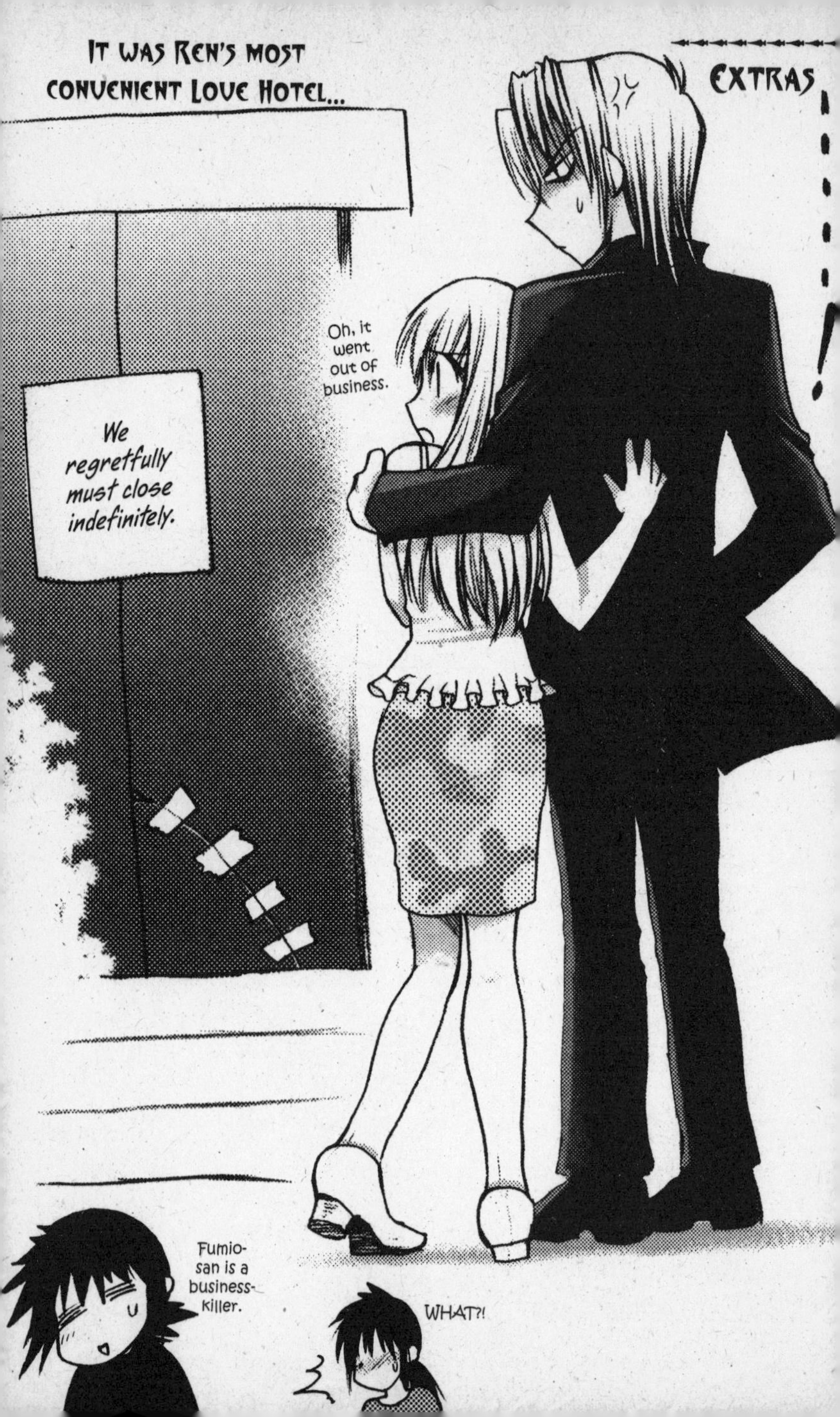
EXTRAS!
It was Ren's most convenient love hotel...
Oh, it went out of business.
We regretfully must close indefinitely.
Fumio-san is a business-killer.
WHAT?!

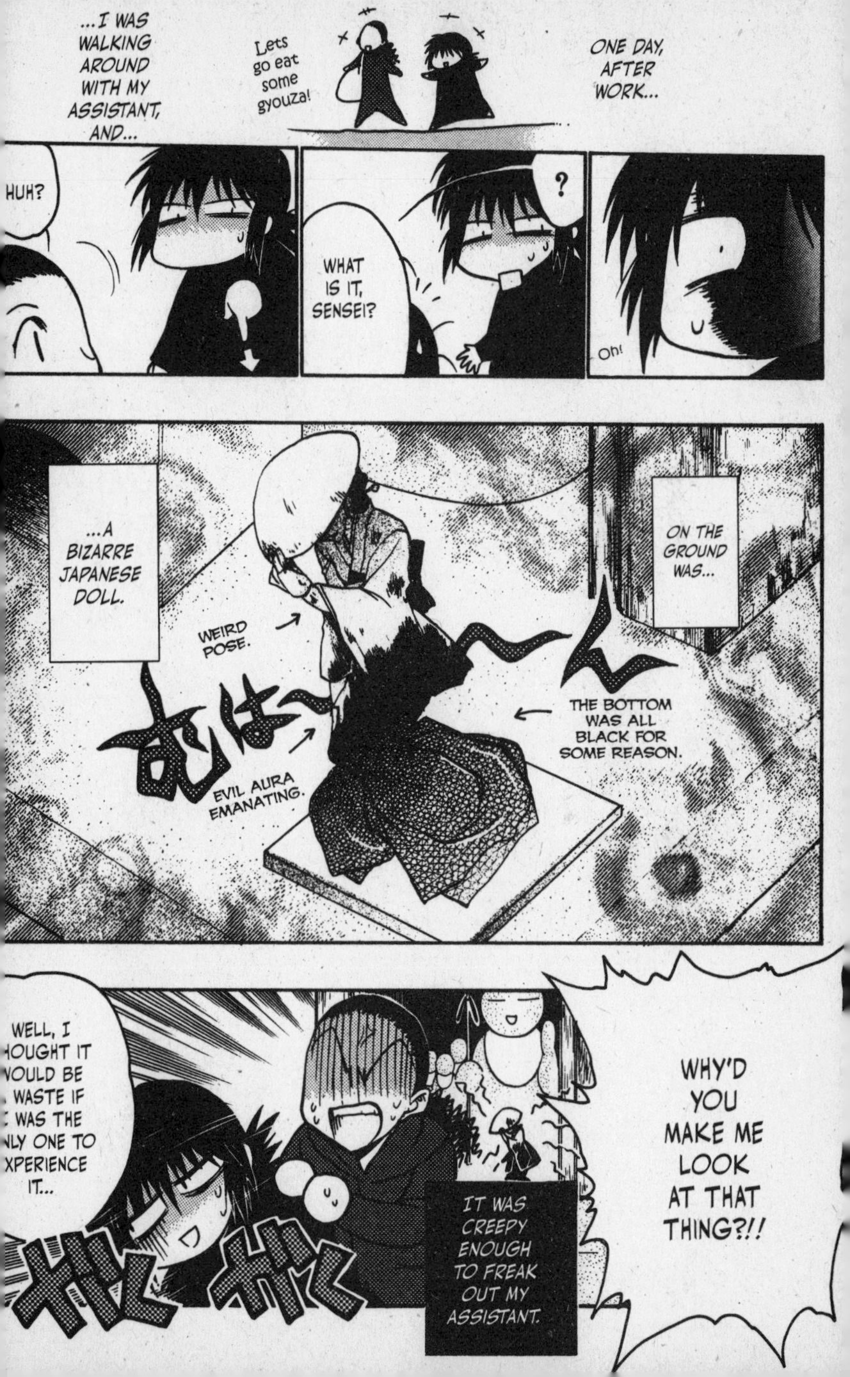

ONE DAY, AFTER WORK...
Lets go eat some gyouza!
...I WAS WALKING AROUND WITH MY ASSISTANT, AND...
Oh!
?
WHAT IS IT, SENSEI?
HUH?
ON THE GROUND WAS...
THE BOTTOM WAS ALL BLACK FOR SOME REASON.
...A BIZARRE JAPANESE DOLL.
WEIRD POSE.
EVIL AURA EMANATING.
WHY'D YOU MAKE ME LOOK AT THAT THING?!!
IT WAS CREEPY ENOUGH TO FREAK OUT MY ASSISTANT.
WELL, I HOUGHT IT VOULD BE WASTE IF WAS THE NLY ONE TO XPERIENCE IT...

Passing By

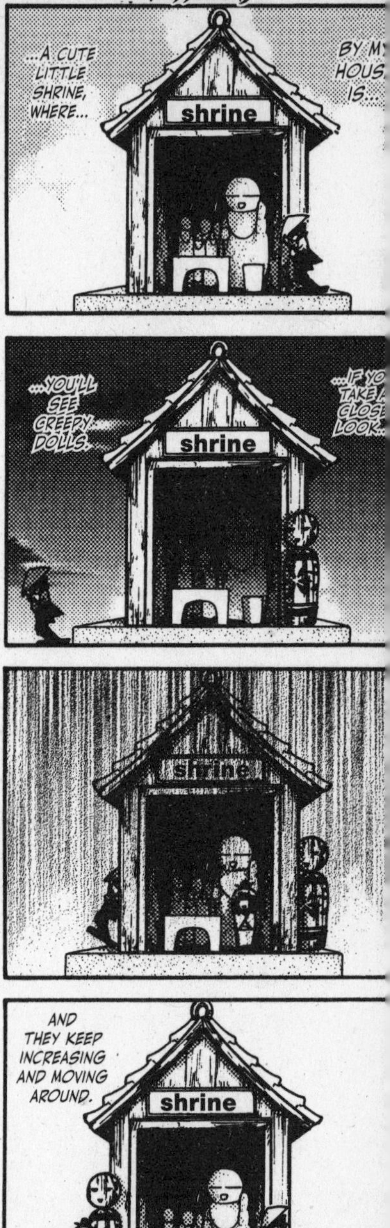
BY MY HOUS IS...
...A CUTE LITTLE SHRINE, WHERE...
shrine
...IF YO TAKE A CLOSE LOOK...
...YOU'LL SEE CREEPY DOLLS.
shrine
shrine
AND THEY KEEP INCREASING AND MOVING AROUND.
shrine

How Anju Adds to her Collection

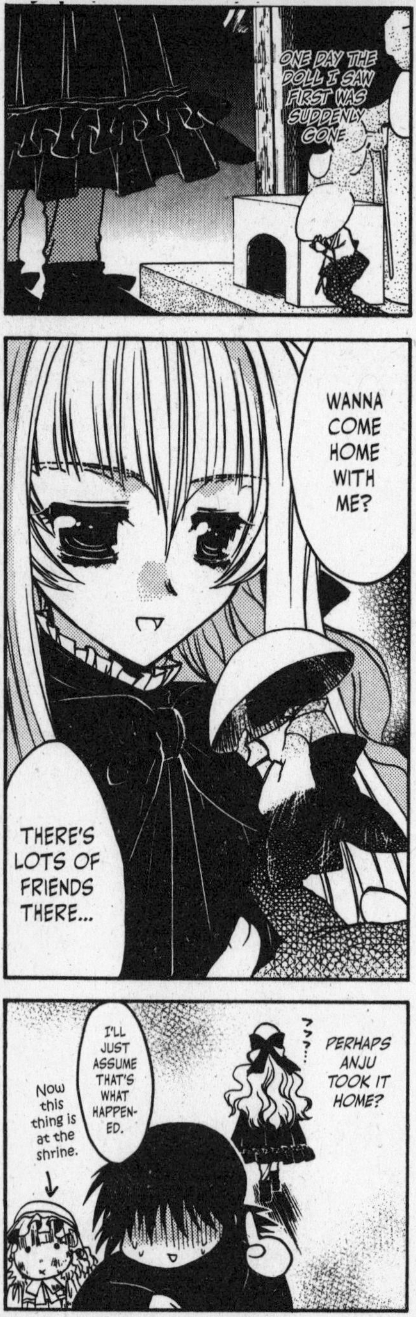
ONE DAY THE DOLL I SAW FIRST WAS SUDDENLY GONE.
WANNA COME HOME WITH ME?
THERE'S LOTS OF FRIENDS THERE...
???
PERHAPS ANJU TOOK IT HOME?
I'LL JUST ASSUME THAT'S WHAT HAPPEN-ED.
Now this thing is at the shrine.

THE MAN WITH HORRIBLE TIMING

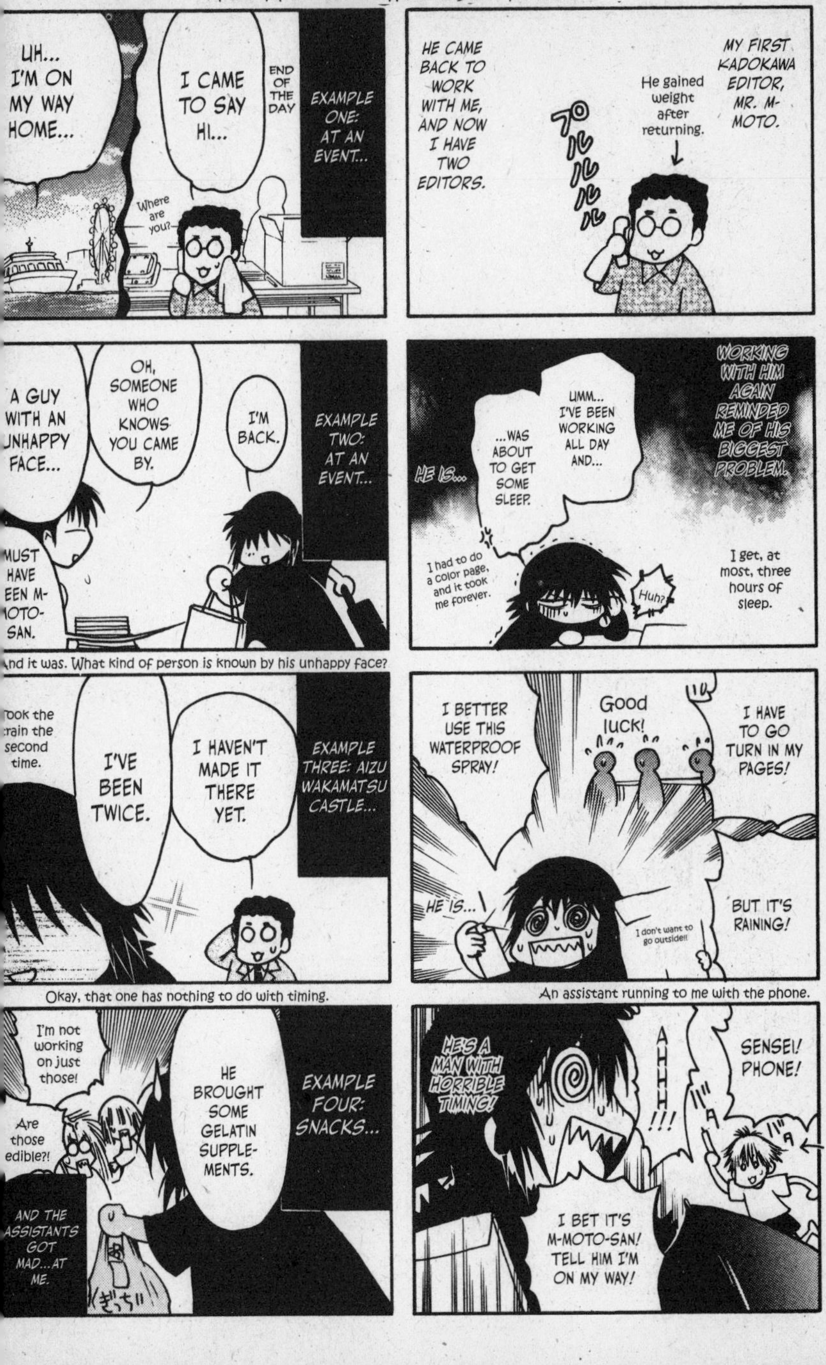

MY FIRST KADOKAWA EDITOR, MR. M-MOTO.
He gained weight after returning.
プルルル
HE CAME BACK TO WORK WITH ME, AND NOW I HAVE TWO EDITORS.
WORKING WITH HIM AGAIN REMINDED ME OF HIS BIGGEST PROBLEM.
I get, at most, three hours of sleep.
UMM... I'VE BEEN WORKING ALL DAY AND...
...WAS ABOUT TO GET SOME SLEEP.
Huh?
HE IS...
I had to do a color page, and it took me forever.
I HAVE TO GO TURN IN MY PAGES!
Good luck!
I BETTER USE THIS WATERPROOF SPRAY!
BUT IT'S RAINING!
I don't want to go outside!!
HE IS...
An assistant running to me with the phone.
SENSEI! PHONE!
AHHH!!!
HE'S A MAN WITH HORRIBLE TIMING!
I BET IT'S M-MOTO-SAN! TELL HIM I'M ON MY WAY!
EXAMPLE ONE: AT AN EVENT...
END OF THE DAY
I CAME TO SAY HI...
UH... I'M ON MY WAY HOME...
Where are you?
EXAMPLE TWO: AT AN EVENT...
I'M BACK.
OH, SOMEONE WHO KNOWS YOU CAME BY.
A GUY WITH AN UNHAPPY FACE...
MUST HAVE EEN M-IOTO-SAN.
nd it was. What kind of person is known by his unhappy face?
EXAMPLE THREE: AIZU WAKAMATSU CASTLE...
I HAVEN'T MADE IT THERE YET.
I'VE BEEN TWICE.
ook the rain the second time.
Okay, that one has nothing to do with timing.
EXAMPLE FOUR: SNACKS...
HE BROUGHT SOME GELATIN SUPPLEMENTS.
I'm not working on just those!
Are those edible?!
AND THE ASSISTANTS GOT MAD...AT ME.

KAGESAKI GETS INCREDIBLE LEG CRAMPS

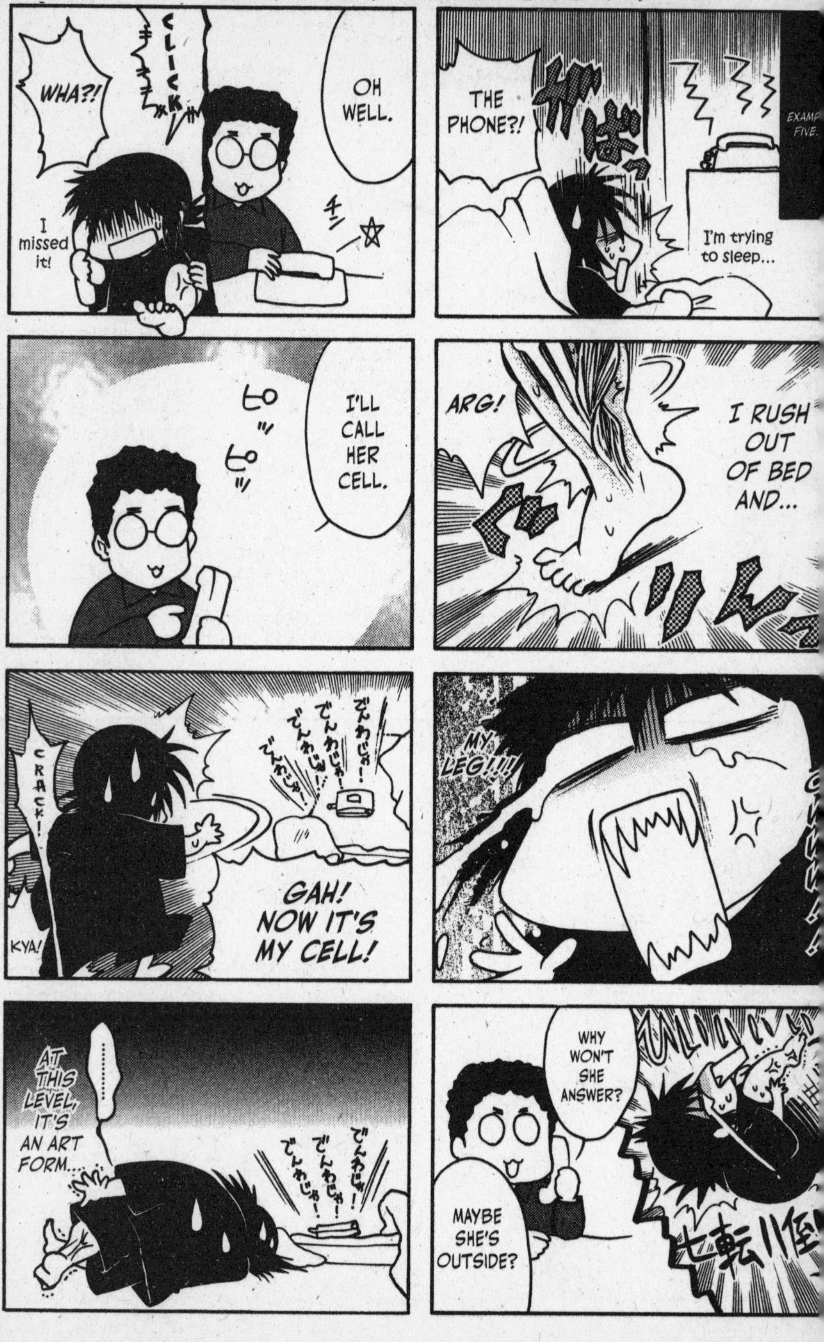
EXAMP
FIVE.
THE PHONE?!
I'm trying to sleep...
I RUSH OUT OF BED AND...
ARG!
MY LEG!!!
WHY WON'T SHE ANSWER?
MAYBE SHE'S OUTSIDE?
OH WELL.
CLICK
WHA?!
I missed it!
I'LL CALL HER CELL.
GAH! NOW IT'S MY CELL!
CRACK!
KYA!
AT THIS LEVEL, IT'S AN ART FORM...

WHILE DRAWING CHAPTER 15...

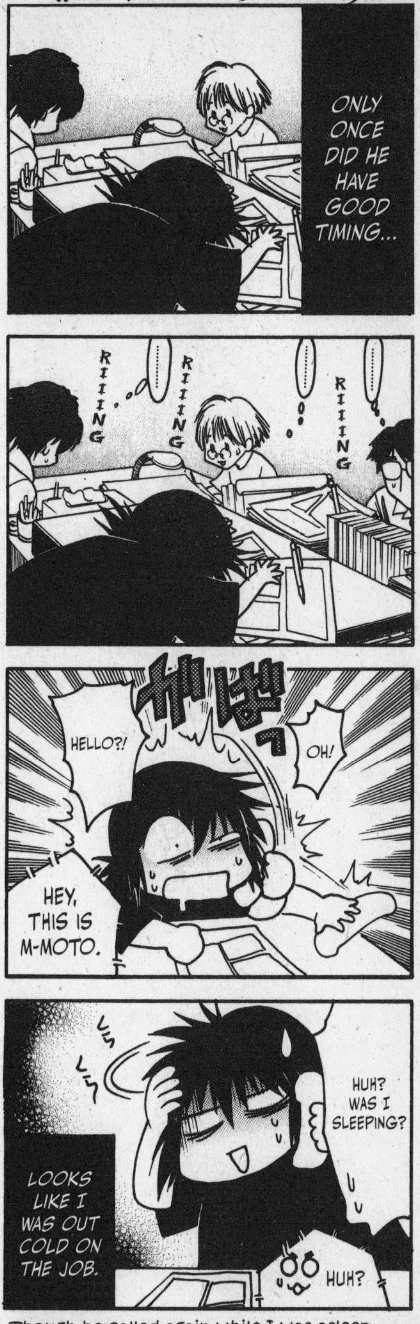

ONLY ONCE DID HE HAVE GOOD TIMING...
RIIING
RIIING
RIIING
がばっ
OH!
HELLO?!
HEY, THIS IS M-MOTO.
HUH? WAS I SLEEPING?
LOOKS LIKE I WAS OUT COLD ON THE JOB.
HUH?

Though he called again while I was asleep...

MORE FROM CHAPTER 14

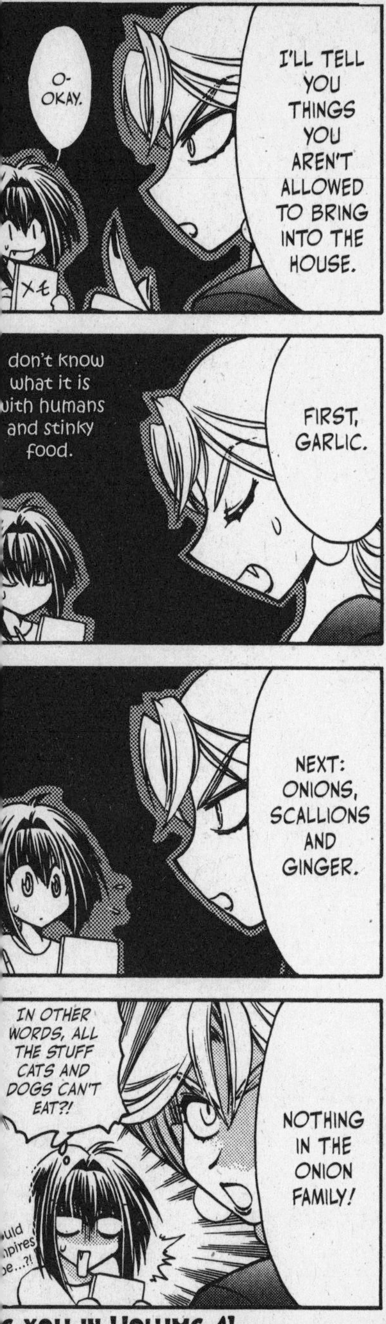

I'LL TELL YOU THINGS YOU AREN'T ALLOWED TO BRING INTO THE HOUSE.
O-OKAY.
メモ
FIRST, GARLIC.
don't know what it is with humans and stinky food.
NEXT: ONIONS, SCALLIONS AND GINGER.
NOTHING IN THE ONION FAMILY!
IN OTHER WORDS, ALL THE STUFF CATS AND DOGS CAN'T EAT?!

E YOU IN VOLUME 4!

IN OUR NEXT VOLUME...

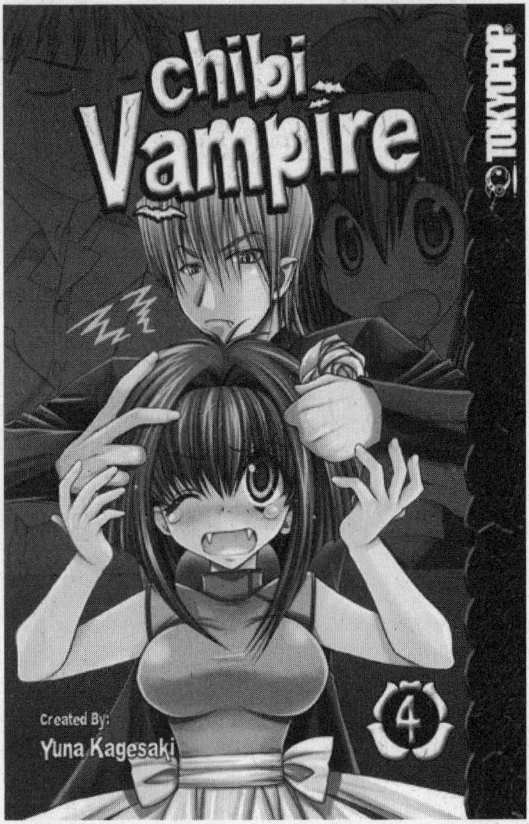
chibi Vampire
TOKYOPOP
Created By:
Yuna Kagesaki
4

AH, LOVE (OR A VAGUE APPROXIMATION OF IT) AND THE SMELL OF GARLIC IS IN THE AIR IN OUR NEXT VOLUME OF CHIBI VAMPIRE. HER BLOOD EVER SWELLING, KARIN IS FINDING IT MORE AND MORE DIFFICULT TO AVOID BITING THE HANDSOME, IF MISFORTUNATE, KENTA. YET, SOMETHING STOPS HER EVERY TIME. COULD IT BE SOMETHING OTHER THAN BLOOD LOSS THAT MAKES KARIN LIGHTHEADED EVERY TIME KENTA'S NEARBY? ALSO IN OUR NEXT VOLUME, WE DELVE A BIT INTO REN'S SORDID PAST IN THE SIDE STORY, "REN'S GRADUATION."

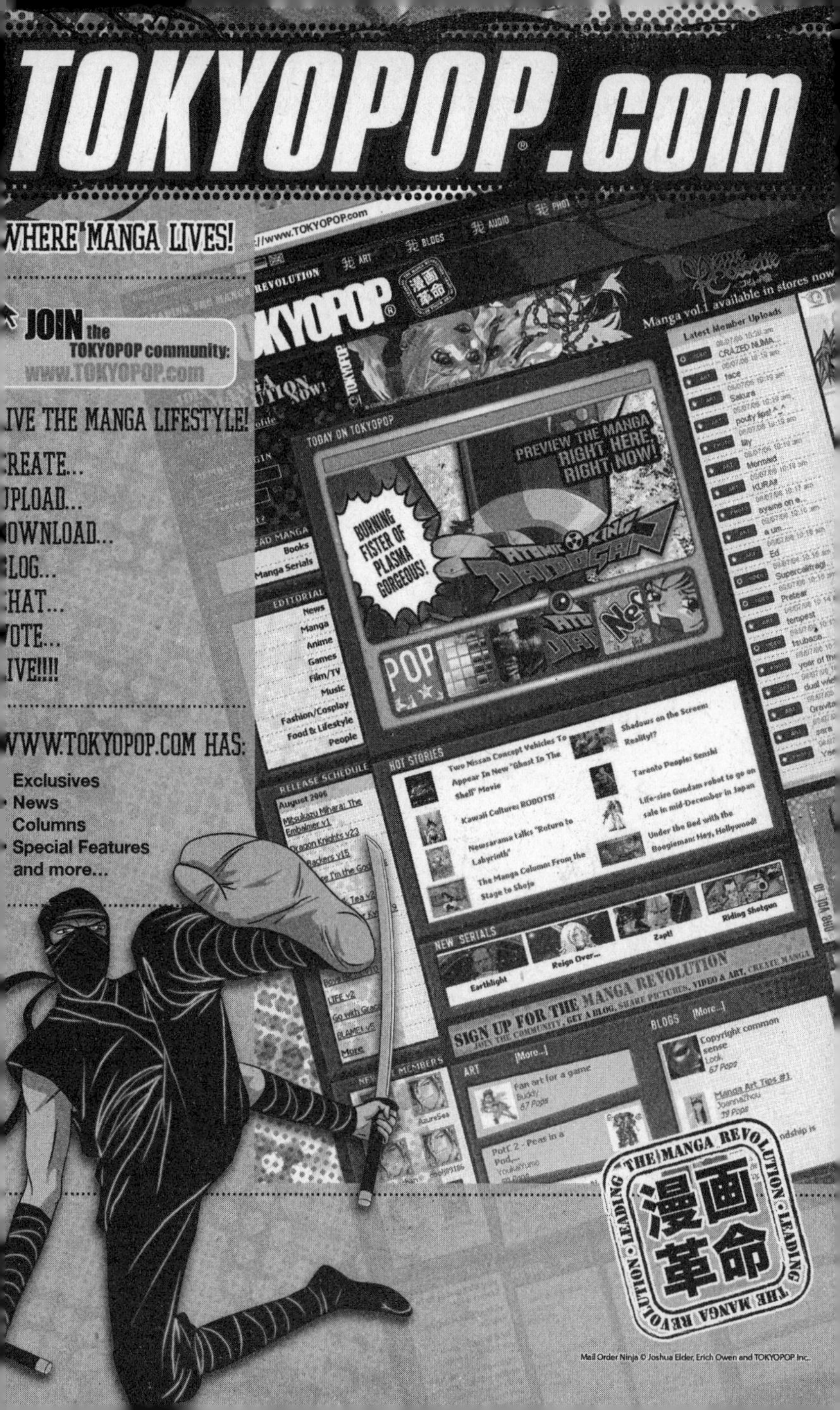
TOKYOPOP®.com
WHERE MANGA LIVES!
JOIN the TOKYOPOP community:
www.TOKYOPOP.com
LIVE THE MANGA LIFESTYLE!
CREATE...
UPLOAD...
DOWNLOAD...
BLOG...
CHAT...
VOTE...
LIVE!!!!
WWW.TOKYOPOP.COM HAS:
• Exclusives
• News
• Columns
• Special Features
and more...
PREVIEW THE MANGA RIGHT HERE, RIGHT NOW!
BURNING FISTER OF PLASMA GORGEOUS!
SIGN UP FOR THE MANGA REVOLUTION
THE MANGA REVOLUTION • LEADING • THE MANGA REVOLUTION • LEADING
漫画革命
Mail Order Ninja © Joshua Elder, Erich Owen and TOKYOPOP Inc.

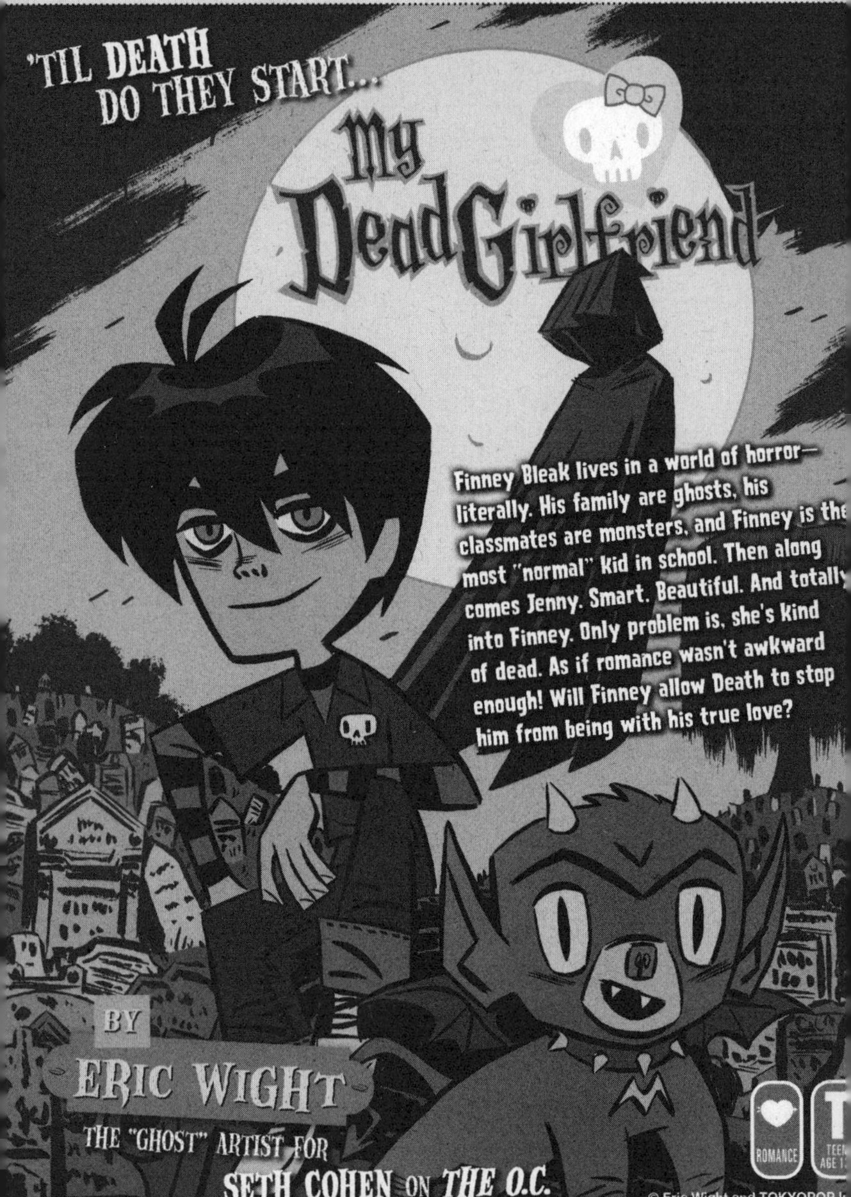

'TIL DEATH
DO THEY START...
My Dead Girlfriend
Finney Bleak lives in a world of horror—literally. His family are ghosts, his classmates are monsters, and Finney is the most "normal" kid in school. Then along comes Jenny. Smart. Beautiful. And totally into Finney. Only problem is, she's kind of dead. As if romance wasn't awkward enough! Will Finney allow Death to stop him from being with his true love?
BY
ERIC WIGHT
THE "GHOST" ARTIST FOR
SETH COHEN ON THE O.C.
ROMANCE
© Eric Wight and TOKYOPOP In

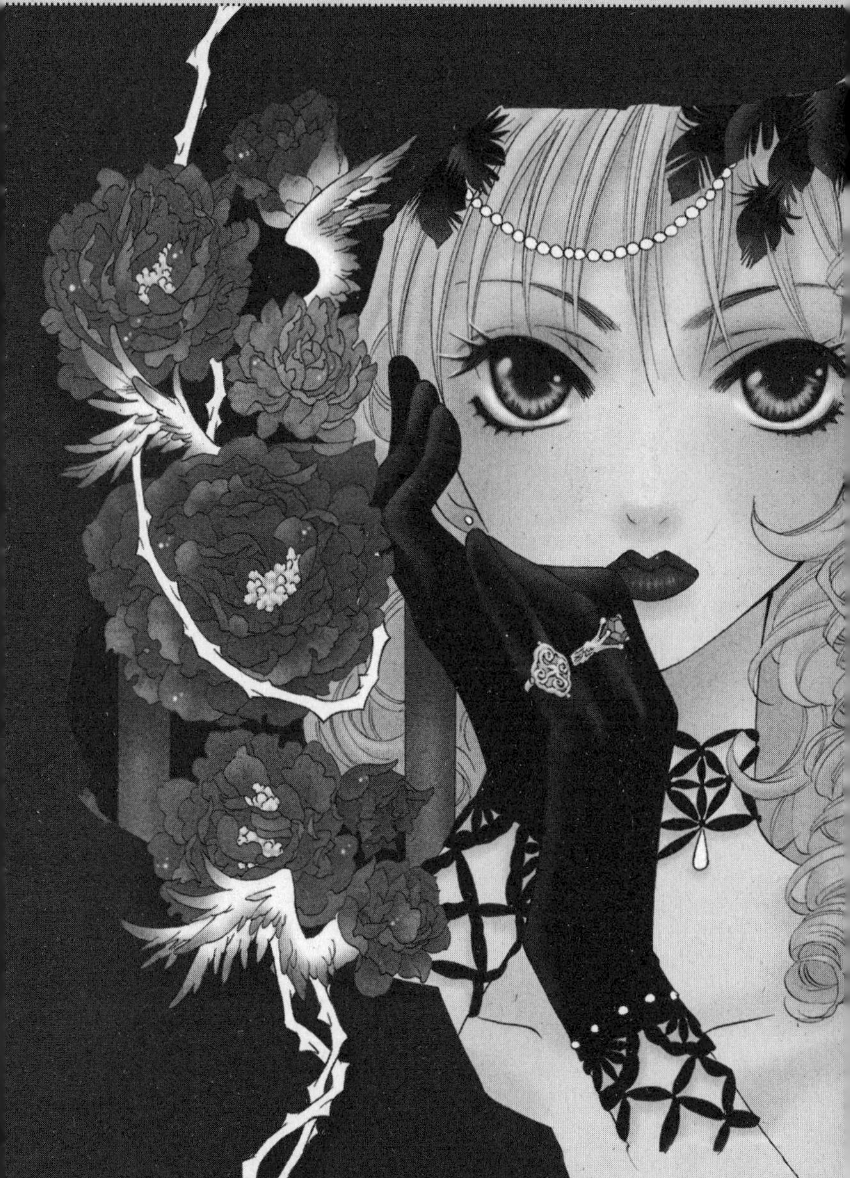

WWW.TOKYOPOP.COM

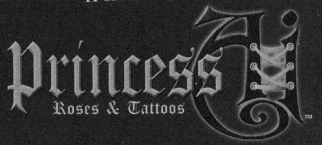
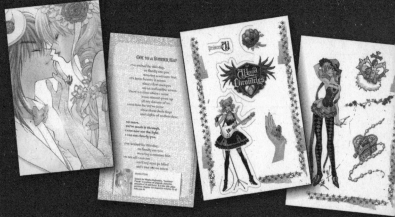

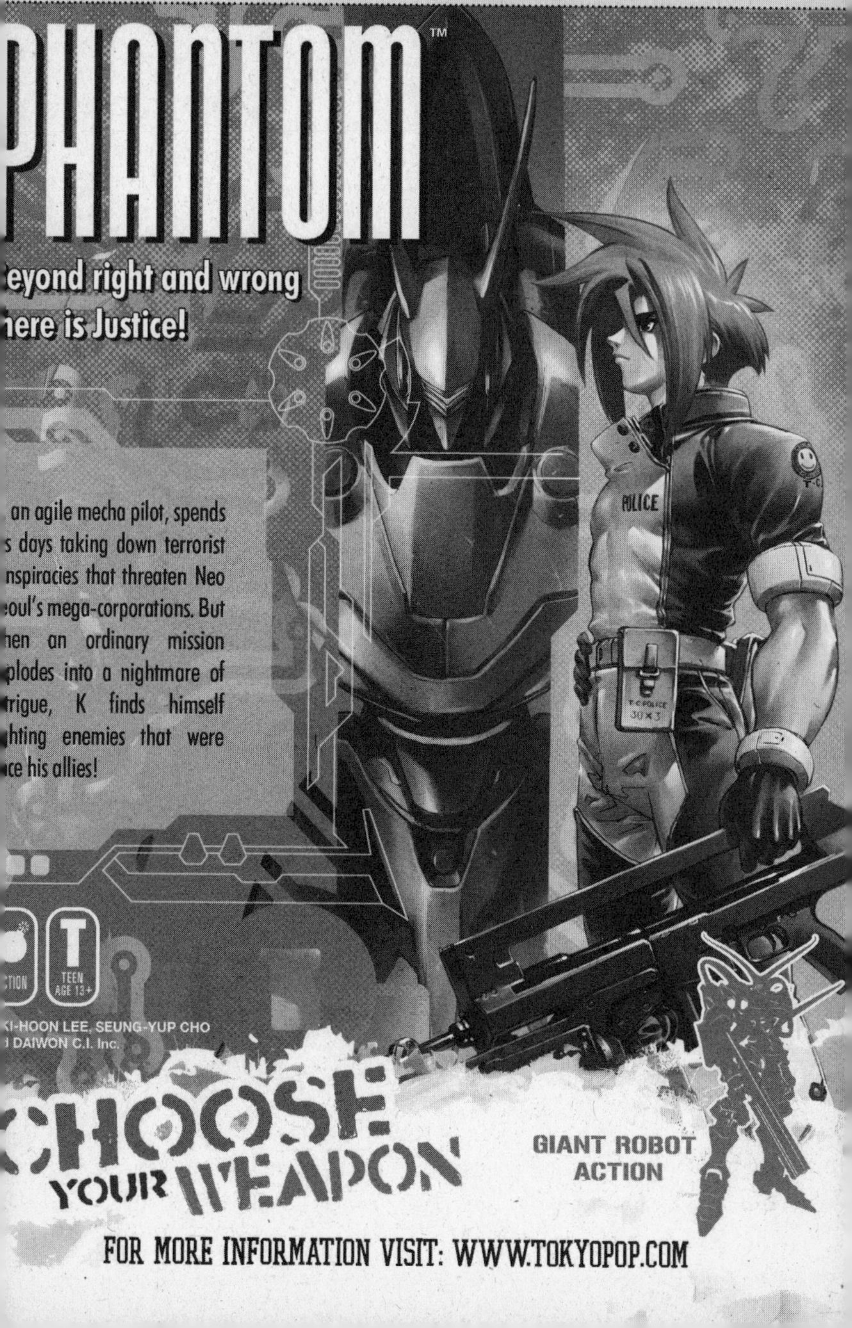
PHANTOM™
eyond right and wrong
here is Justice!
an agile mecha pilot, spends
s days taking down terrorist
nspiracies that threaten Neo
oul's mega-corporations. But
hen an ordinary mission
plodes into a nightmare of
rigue, K finds himself
hting enemies that were
ce his allies!
POLICE
TION
T
TEEN AGE 13+
I-HOON LEE, SEUNG-YUP CHO
DAIWON C.I. Inc.
CHOOSE YOUR WEAPON
GIANT ROBOT ACTION
FOR MORE INFORMATION VISIT: WWW.TOKYOPOP.COM

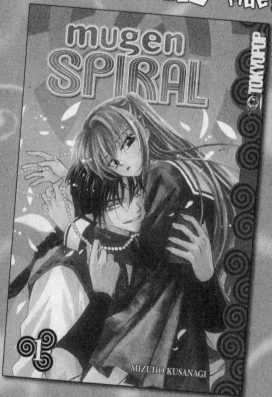

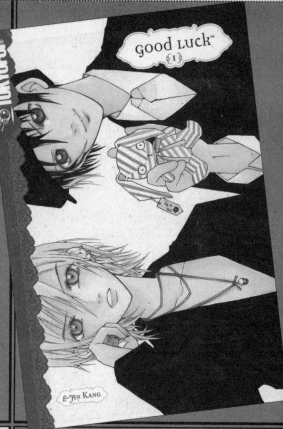
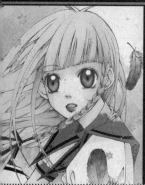

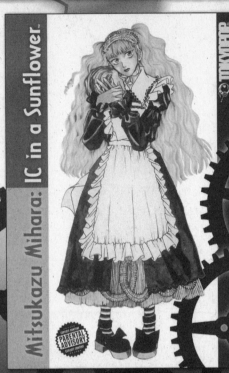

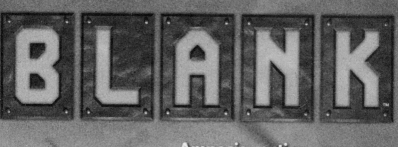

LAUNCHING TOKYOPOP MUSIC
THE NEW SOUND FROM TOKYOPOP!

THE HIGHLY ANTICIPATED LAUNCH OF THE TOKYOPOP MUSIC LABEL IS HERE!

THE MANGA REVOLUTION INFILTRATES MUSIC WITH AN AMAZING ASSORTMENT OF MANGA SOUNDTRACKS AND SONGS FROM PRINCESS AI, INITIAL D, RAVE MASTER, AND MUCH MORE.

HERE IS MUSIC THAT WILL MAKE YOU WANT TO GROOVE, TO RIDE, TO DRIFT, AND TO DREAM...

TOKYOPOP PRESENTS
ANIME TRAX
Music by D.J. Milky and b_nCHANt_d

CHECK OUT THE DEBUT ALBUMS NOW

BEATZ 4 RIDERZ
PRODUCED BY D.J. Milky AND b_nCHANt_d
TOKYOPOP PRESENTS

THIS FALL LOOK OUT FOR MORE NEW RELEASES!

TOKYOPOP PRESENTS
DRIFT 2 DIE
PRODUCED BY D.J. Milky AND b_nCHANt_d

AVAILABLE ON ITUNES AND WHEREVER DOWNLOADABLE MUSIC IS SOLD

keyword: TOKYOPOP
Music available online only

FOR MORE INFORMATION VISIT: WWW.TOKYOPOP.COM

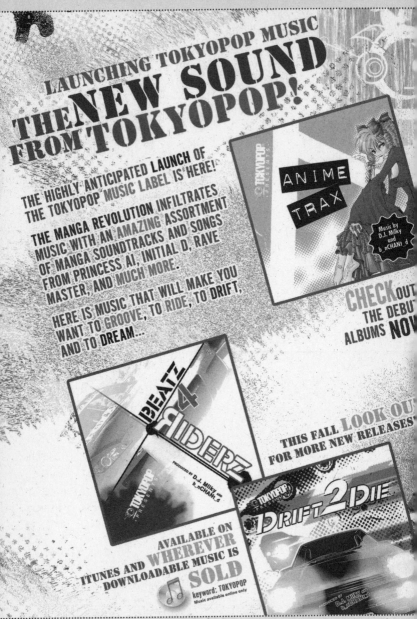

STOP!

This is the back of the book.
You wouldn't want to spoil a great ending!

This book is printed "manga-style," in the authentic Japanese right-to-left format. Since none of the artwork has been flipped or altered, readers get to experience the story just as the creator intended. You've been asking for it, so TOKYOPOP® delivered: authentic, hot-off-the-press, and far more fun!

DIRECTIONS

If this is your first time reading manga-style, here's a quick guide to help you understand how it works.

It's easy... just start in the top right panel and follow the numbers. Have fun, and look for more 100% authentic manga from TOKYOPOP®!

1
2
3
4
5
6
7
8
9
10

THE MANGA REVOLUTION · LEADING · 漫画革命 · LEADING THE MANGA REVOLUTION